Titus

Apostolic Leadership

CLINTON'S
BIBLICAL LEADERSHIP
COMMENTARY SERIES

J. Robert Clinton, D. Miss., Ph.D.

BARNABAS
PUBLISHERS

Roy May

Barnabas Publishers
P.O. Box 6006
Altadena, CA 91003-6006

Printed in the United States of America

Fuller Seminary Press / Fuller Copy Services
R&D Design Services

Series & Title Cover Design: D. M. Battermann, R&D Design Services
Book Design & Layout: D.M. & R.D. Battermann, R&D Design Services

Table of Contents

List of Tables

List of Figures

Abbreviations

Bible Books

Genesis	Ge	Nahum	Na
Exodus	Ex	Habakkuk	Hab
Leviticus	Lev	Zephaniah	Zep
Numbers	Nu	Haggai	Hag
Deuteronomy	Dt	Zechariah	Zec
Joshua	Jos	Malachi	Mal
Judges	Jdg	Matthew	Mt
Ruth	Ru	Mark	Mk
1 Samuel	1Sa	Luke	Lk
2 Samuel	2Sa	John	Jn
1 Kings	1Ki	Acts	Ac
2 Kings	2Ki	Romans	Ro
1 Chronicles	1Ch	1 Corinthians	1Co
2 Chronicles	2Ch	2 Corinthians	2Co
Ezra	Ezr	Galatians	Gal
Nehemiah	Ne	Ephesians	Eph
Esther	Est	Philippians	Php
Job	Job	Colossians	Col
Psalms	Ps	1 Thessalonians	1Th
Proverbs	Pr	2 Thessalonians	2Th
Ecclesiastes	Ecc	1 Timothy	1Ti
Song of Songs	SS	2 Timothy	2Ti
Isaiah	Isa	Titus	Tit
Jeremiah	Jer	Philemon	Phm
Lamentations	La	Hebrews	Heb
Ezekiel	Eze	James	Jas
Daniel	Da	1 Peter	1Pe
Hosea	Hos	2 Peter	2Pe
Joel	Joel	1 John	1Jn
Amos	Am	2 John	2Jn
Obadiah	Ob	3 John	3Jn
Jonah	Jnh	Jude	Jude
Micah	Mic	Revelation	Rev

Other

fn	footnote(s)
KJV	King James Version of the Bible
NEB	New English Bible
NLT	New Living Translation
N.T.	New Testament
O.T.	Old Testament
Phillips	The New Testament in Modern English, J.B. Phillips
SRN	Strong's Reference Number
TEV	Today's English Version (also called Good News Bible)
Vs	verse(s)

What this Commentary is and How to Use it

This leadership commentary on Titus is part of a series, *Clinton's Leadership Commentary Series.* For the past 11 years I have been researching leadership concepts in the Bible. As a result of that I have identified the 25 most helpful Bible books that contribute to an understanding of leadership. I have done nine of these commentaries to date and am continuing on the rest. I originally published eight of those leadership commentaries in a draft manuscript for use in classes. But it became clear that I would need to break that large work (735 pages) into smaller works. The commentary series does that. Titus is the first of the series that is being done as an individual work.

This is a leadership commentary, not an exegetical commentary. That means I have worked with the text to see what implications of leadership are suggested by it. A given commentary in the series is made up of an *Overview Section*, which seeks to analyze the book as a whole for historical background, plan, theme, and fit into the Bible as a whole. In addition, I identify, up front, the basic leadership topics that are dealt with in the book. Then I educe leadership observations, guidelines, principles, and values for each of these leadership topics. This *Overview Section* primes the reader to look with leadership eyes. Then I have the *Commentary Proper*. I use my own translation of the text. I give commentary on various aspects of the text. A given context, paragraph size, will usually have 3 to 4 comments dealing with some suggestion about leadership things.

The *Commentary Proper* suggests *Leadership Concepts* and connects you to leadership articles that further explain these leadership concepts. The emphasis on the comments is not exegetical though I do make those kind of comments when they are helpful for my leadership purpose.

The *Leadership Articles*, in Titus there are 49 totaling more than 200 pages, carry much of what I have learned about leadership in my 36 years of ministry. In one sense, these articles and others in the series are my legacy. I plan to publish all of the articles of the total series in a separate work, *Clinton's Encyclopedia of Biblical Leadership Insights,* which will be updated periodically as the series expands. I think a leader at almost any level of leadership can be helped greatly by getting leadership perspectives from these articles.

I also include a *Glossary* which lists all the leadership concepts labeled in the comments.

Other books in the series, to be released over the next two years, include:

1,2 Timothy — Apostolic Leadership Picking Up the Mantle
1,2 Corinthians — Problematic Apostolic Leadership
Daniel — A Model Leader in Tough times
Philemon — A Study in Leadership Style
Philippians — A Study in Modeling
John — Jesus' Incarnational Leadership (John)

Other books anticipated in the Series over the next five years, will deal with:

Deuteronomy — A Study in Moses' Inspirational Leadership (Deuteronomy)
Numbers — Moses, Spiritual Authority, and Maintenance Leadership (Numbers)
Haggai — A Study in Task Oriented Inspirational Leadership (Haggai)
Mark — Jesus' Power Ministry (Mark)
Luke-Acts — Apostolic Leadership Illustrated (Luke, Acts)
Habbakuk — A Leadership Faith Crisis (Habbakuk)
Jonah — A Study of A Leadership Paradigm Shift (Jonah)
Joshua — Courageous Leadership (Joshua)
Malachi — Renewal Leadership Lessons (Malachi)
Nehemiah — Focused Leadership (Nehemiah)
Mathew — A Study in Leadership Selection and Development (Matthew)
1,2 Samuel — 3 Leaders Compared and Contrasted (1,2 Samuel)

I have already done a study of each book in the Bible from a leadership standpoint and have identified and written up a number of leadership topics for each book. This analysis is captured in my book, *The Bible and Leadership Values*.

In an age of relativity, I believe the Bible speaks loudly concerning leadership concepts offering suggestions, guidelines, and even absolutes. We, as Christian leaders, desperately need this leadership help as we seek to influence our followers toward God's purposes for them.

J. Robert Clinton,

November 2000

Where Titus Fits

Every Scripture inspired of God is profitable for leadership insights (doctrine), pointing out of leadership errors (reproof), suggesting what to do about leadership errors (correction), for highlighting how to model a righteous life (instruction in righteousness) in order that God's leader (Timothy) may be well equipped to lead God's people (the special good work given in the book Timothy to the young leader Timothy) .

(2 Timothy 3:16,17—Clinton paraphrase–slanted toward Timothy's leadership situation)

The Bible — a Major Source of Leadership Values and Principles

No more wonderful source of leadership values and principles exists than the Bible. It is filled with influential people and the results of their influence — both good and bad. Yet it remains so little used to expose leadership values and principles. What is needed to break this *leadership barrier*? Three things:

1. a conviction that the Bible is authoritative and can give leadership insights;

2. leadership perspectives to stimulate our findings in the Bible — we are blind in general to leadership ideas and hence do not see them in the Bible;

3. a willful decision to study and use the Bible as a source of leadership insights.

These three assumptions underlie the writing of my leadership commentary series. **Titus** is one of a series of books intended to help leaders cross the *leadership barrier*.

Leadership Framework

Perhaps it might be helpful to put the notion of leadership insights from Titus in the bigger picture of leadership in the Bible. Three major leadership elements give us our most general framework (cross-culturally applicable as well) for categorizing leadership insights. The study of leadership involves:

1. **THE LEADERSHIP BASAL ELEMENTS** (The *What* of Leadership)
   a. leaders
   b. followers
   c. situations

2. **LEADERSHIP INFLUENCE MEANS** (The *How* of Leadership)
   a. individual means
   b. corporate means

3. **LEADERSHIP VALUE BASES** (The *Why* of Leadership)
   a. cultural
   b. theological

It is these elements that enable us to analyze leadership throughout the whole Bible. Using these major notions we recognize that leadership at different times in the Bible operates sufficiently different so as to suggest leadership eras — that is, time periods within which leadership follows more closely certain commonalties than in the time preceding it and following it. This allows us to identify six such eras in the Bible.

Six Bible Leadership Eras

The six leadership eras include,

1. **Patriarchal Era**

2. **Pre-Kingdom Era**
   A.   Desert Years
   B.   The War Years
   C.   The Tribal Years

3. **Kingdom Era**
   A. United Kingdom
   B. Divided Kingdom
   C. Southern Kingdom

4. **Post-Kingdom Era**
   A. Exilic
   B. A Foothold Back in the Land

5. **Pre-Church Era**

6. **Church Era**

For each of these major eras we are dealing with some fundamental leadership questions. We ask ourselves these major questions about every leadership era.[1] Usually the answers are sufficiently diverse as to justify identification of a unique leadership era.

---

[1]   The six questions we use to help us differentiate between leadership eras includes: 1. What is the major leadership focus? 2. What are the influence means used? 3.What are the basic leadership functions? 4. What are the characteristics of the followers? 5. What was the existing cultural forms of leadership? 6. Other? I comment on each of these in the *Clinton's Encyclopedia of Biblical Leadership Insights*.

Where does Titus fit?

The book of Titus obviously fits in the sixth leadership era, *The Church Era*. This is a tremendous time involving foundational leadership issues. The church, a new form, for taking God's work into all cultures is being developed. Its leadership evolves. Its nature is defined. Its purposes become established. It is in the latter stages of the pioneer development with the church that Titus is written. Paul is in the final years of his life. He has established a number of church plants in a number of diverse cultural settings. He has personally trained a number of leaders. He is the leading church expert. Titus is one of those close friends of Paul, a mentoree who has developed well and has been launched into *Apostolic Ministry*. The issues faced in Crete are not unique. They have been faced by missionaries, church planters, and pioneer organizational leaders throughout the history of the Christian endeavor. Titus has something to say to us — leaders in these kinds of ventures today.

This present leadership commentary seeks to address a major apostolic ministry task, *setting the church in order*, which involves the appointing of leadership, modeling and teaching of truth so as to impact followers, and applying truth cross-culturally to a young church.

What does Titus say?

Before we can look at leadership insights from Titus we need to be sure that we understand why Titus is in the Scriptures and what it is saying in general. Having done our homework, hermeneutically speaking, we are free then to go beyond and look for other interpretative insights — such as leadership insights. But we must remember, always, first of all to interpret in light of the historical times, purpose of, theme of, and structure of the book.

Traditionally, Titus has been attributed to the Apostle Paul. Leaders mentioned or involved in the book include Paul the Apostle, Titus the recipient of the letter, Artemas, Tychicus, Zenas, and Apollos. All of these are people to whom Paul related and with whom Paul co-labored in Christian ministry in various ways.

Titus is one of two of Paul's most famous protégés, Timothy being the other. He is mentioned in the New Testament fourteen times in four different books: Galatians, 2 Corinthians, 2 Timothy and the book of Titus. Titus has the difficult task of confronting church problems on the island of Crete. He is a gentile and is one of Paul's co-laborers who has traveled with him extensively and learned ministry via personal mentoring and on-the-job training. Frequently he is sent on ministry assignments which involve confrontation. Notably this was so with the church at Corinth and all its problems. Such is also the case in the church at Crete. Leadership is lacking. Daily life is basically unaffected by Christian teaching. There is little difference between a Christian and any other Cretan as to daily life. Paul sees the problem as one of leadership. Titus is sent to select, develop and establish leadership that can turn the church around. He needs authority to do that — authority that a person like Paul has. Paul seeks to give that authority vicariously through this letter which would be read by the believers in Crete. It would be nice if we had some detailed treatment in the New Testament of Paul's church planting work on Crete. We don't have that. But the very fact that he can write, seeking to impart some authority to Titus in the situation, infers that he was involved in founding the work and was well respected by the Christians there.

As to literature genre Titus is very intentional (one of Paul's shorter epistles). It follows the standard epistolary form, with certain Pauline adaptations.   There are four elements of the epistolary form worth commenting on.

A. **Greeting**—from Paul to Titus. This follows the usually Pauline adaptations, in which along with the greetings he intertwines special phrasing which will hint at thematic content that will come in the body. Paul seems to like to foreshadow and point a thoughtful person to what he will detail later. For example, note the phrases: in the knowledge of the truth that comes from a God-fearing life; in the hope of the everlasting life which God who can not lie; promised before the beginning of time; entrusted to me. Notice the warm description of Titus — my true son in the common faith. Already Paul is establishing where he will go in the body of the epistle and that he thinks well of Titus.

B. **Thankfulness, mention of prayer**. Usually Paul gives some news about his praying for the church or the individual being addressed. Normally he says something by way of special affirmation of the individual or things that are positive in the situation. He does not here — nor does he in Galatians. The significance of this is striking. In both Galatians and Titus, Paul is highly **task oriented**. For the moment relational thinking is out the door. He moves immediately into the body of the letter — hurries on to the thing that has captured his mind about Titus and the church in Crete. He launches himself into the body of the letter very quickly.

C. **Body of letter**—He opens this section with the strong task that he sees for Titus and this church. Those words, "I left you in Crete to set the church in order" are the subject of the book. They permeate all of the instructions which follow.

D. **Salutation, personal greetings, other personal information**. Typically Paul closes with his usual personal items — in this case information to Titus about his desires to meet Titus in Nicopolis. He mentions Tychicus, one of his messengers. He sponsors Zenas the lawyer and Apollos in the eyes of the church in Crete — helping them get financial backing. He also puts a parting shot of exhortation concerning teaching needed at Crete — all our Christian people should learn to work and earn money to meet needs and live an honest productive life. And like many of his letters he imparts a blessing about grace — that enabling force that stimulates a believer to persevere victoriously.

Very simply then, let me summarize some of the historical situation.   Paul sees the church problems in Crete as one of leadership. Titus, a trusted cohort, is sent to select, develop and establish leadership that can turn the church around. He needs **authority to do that** — authority that a person like Paul has. Paul seeks to give that authority vicariously through this letter which would be read by the believers in Crete.

One way of analyzing the structure, that is, the way the author organizes his material to accomplish his purposes would be:

I.   (ch 1:15-16)   Leadership — An Essential Basis for a Well Ordered Church

II. (ch 2:1-14)   Application of Practical Teaching — An Essential Function of a well ordered Church

III. (ch 3:1-11)   Godly Living — An Essential Outward Sign To Society of A Well Ordered Church

The overall thematic intent of this short epistle could be represented by a subject which permeates all of what Paul is hoping to accomplish in Crete — and it sounds a universal need wherever young churches and Christian organizations are emerging. Note that subject and its three major ideas.

Theme   **SETTING THE CHURCH IN ORDER**
  • involves the appointing of qualified leaders,
  • requires leaders who are sound in teaching and who model a Christian life style, and
  • necessitates leaders who exhort others to practical Christian living.

Key words are always helpful in focusing attention on important issues. A number of such key words are repeated in Titus including: sound (5 times 1:9,13 2:1,2,8), works (5 times 2:7, 14 3:8 twice, 3:14), good (11 times, translates 4 different Greek words), doctrine (4 times — 1:9 2:1,2,8). You can already see that these words are reflected in the theme statement given above.

It is always difficult to synthesize statements of purpose when the author does not directly and explicitly say them. But it seems reasonable to imply that the following are some of what Paul had in mind when he penned this important leadership epistle.

  • to give Titus authoritative backing in the eyes of the Cretan church,
  • to give Titus perspective on leadership selection,
  • to give Titus perspective on how leadership can best influence the situation — teaching and modeling,
  • to encourage the Cretan believers to good works,
  • to motivate outward behavior by focusing on the return of Christ.
  • to model several mentoring styles: contemporary model, counselor, teacher, sponsor,
  • to refute the legalistic heresy being propagated in Crete.

With this back ground in mind, we can now proceed to the leadership commentary including its *General Reflection*, *Commentary notes*, *Articles*, and *Glossary*.

General Reflection — Titus

Today, we live in the church leadership era. Titus was a book written to an apostolic leader in that leadership era. It is right on for today's world. I consider it, along with 1, 2 Timothy and the two Corinthian books to be the most important leadership books in the New Testament. Each of these five books deals with important leadership issues, most of which, leaders today face.

Titus is especially insightful for leadership. Consider these several reasons:

(1) it is one of the last books Paul wrote — we have accumulated wisdom dealing with a multiple-church/regional situation; see **Article,** *Regional Churches.*

(2) it is filled with cross-cultural application — the Cretan Island culture was dominated by values which Paul refuted.

(3) it highlights leadership selection (character issues in focus) as a major function for establishing an effective church; see **Articles,** *Leadership Selection; Levels of Leadership.*

(4) it shows the importance of obedience to truth — truth must be lived out in the lives of all church members whether older men, older women, young men or younger women; see **Article,** *Adorning the Gospel — One's Personal Application of Truth; Principles of Truth.*

(5) it highlights Titus' apostolic ministry — we find out more about apostolic ministry as we observe what Titus had to do; See **Articles:** *Apostolic Functions; Titus — An Apostolic Worker.*

(6) it serves to illustrate the development of a leader, Titus — especially showing the mature use of ministry task as a final finishing school for an apostolic worker. See **Article,** *Titus And Ministry Tasks;*

(7) it also illustrates Paul's variety in leadership styles — he varies his leadership style in terms of situation and personality of the leader he is influencing; see **Articles** *Timothy, A Beloved Son in the Faith; Pauline Leadership Styles.*

What does it mean to establish a church — to ground it so it can continue to be effective in its culture? The book of Titus gives strong answers to this question. Along with 1

Timothy it points out just how important it is for churches to develop leaders who know and obey truth and influence their followers to do that too.

Suggested Approach for Studying Titus

Read through the overview to get a general feeling of what Titus is about. Note particularly the *Theme* of the book and its *Plan* for developing that theme, i.e. the outline for developing that theme. Then note the various purposes that I suggest that Paul is trying to accomplish through this book. Then read through each of the leadership findings that I suggest are in the book. This is all preparation for the first reading of the text.

Read the text itself, all three chapters at one sitting, without referring to any of the commentary notes. Just see if you can *see what of the overview information* and the *leadership lessons* are suggested to you as you read the text.

Then reread the text, probably a chapter at a time and note the comments I give.[1] From time-to-time, go back and read a leadership lesson again when it is brought to your mind as you read the text and the commentary. Also feel free to stop and go to the **Glossary** for explanation of leadership terms suggested by the commentary. And do the same thing with the **Articles**. These articles capture what I have learned about leadership over the years as I have observed it, researched it, and taught it. It is these articles that will enlighten your leadership understanding.

I have provided some *note space* at the conclusion of the Titus commentary where you can jot down ideas for future study. Have fun as you work through Titus, and by all means learn something about *SETTING THE CHURCH IN ORDER.*

---

[1]. From time-to-time in the comments, I will use the abbreviation SRN. SRN stands for Strong's Reference Number. Strong, in his exhaustive concordance, labeled each word in the Old Testament (dominantly Hebrew words but also some Aramaic/ Chaldean) and New Testament (Greek Words mostly) with an identifying number. He then constructed an Old Testament and New Testament lexicon (dictionary). If you have a Strong's Exhaustive Concordance with lexicon, you can look up the words I refer to. Many modern day reference works (lexicons and word studies and Bible Dictionaries and encyclopedias) use this Strong's Reference Number.

BOOK — TITUS　　　AUTHOR — PAUL

Characters	People mentioned or involved: Paul, Titus, Artemas, Tychicus, Zenas, Apollos
Who To/For	To Titus, a protégé of Paul, who is confronting church problems on the island of Crete
Literature Type	an authoritative personal letter to Titus containing strong advice, teaching, and exhortation.
Story Line	Titus is a gentile and is one of Paul's mentorees who has traveled with him and learned ministry via on -the-job training. Frequently he is sent on ministry assignments which involve confrontation. Such is the case in the church at Crete. Leadership is lacking. Daily life is basically unaffected by Christian teaching. There is little difference between a Christian and any other Cretan as to daily life. Paul sees the problem as one of leadership. Titus is sent to select, develop and establish leadership that can turn the church around. He needs authority to do that — authority that a person like Paul has. Paul seeks to give that authority vicariously through this letter which would be read by the believers in Crete.
Structure	I.　(ch 1:1-16)　　Leadership — An Essential Basis for a Well Ordered Church
	II.　(ch 2:1-14)　　Application of Practical Teaching — An Essential Function of a well ordered Church
	III. (ch 3:1-11)　　Godly Living — An Essential Outward Sign To Society of A Well Ordered Church
Theme	SETTING THE CHURCH IN ORDER
	• involves the appointing of qualified leaders,
	• requires leaders who are sound in teaching and who model a Christian life style, and
	• necessitates leaders who exhort others to practical Christian living.

Key Words	sound (5), good works (6), good (11)
Key Events	none in focus

Purposes

- to give Titus authoritative backing in the eyes of the Cretan church,
- to give Titus perspective on leadership selection,
- to give Titus perspective on how leadership can best influence the situation — teaching and modeling,
- to encourage the Cretan believers to good works,
- to motivate outward behavior by focusing on the return of Christ.
- to model several mentoring styles: contemporary model, counselor, teacher, sponsor,
- to refute the legalistic heresy being propagated in Crete.

Why Important

Church leadership is needed everywhere at all times. This book points out its fundamental role. A church can not be established without it. For a church to be effective its people must be demonstrating Christian values in their lives. This comes when they are taught them, see them modeled by their leaders, and when they are held accountable to demonstrate them. This book also points out Eerdman's basic idea that the return of the Lord has always been the supreme motivation for consistent Christian living. This book in another cultural setting authenticates the concept of leadership selection dominantly by character — integrity is the key trait which is reflected in all the cultural descriptions. Both Ephesian culture and now this island culture, two varying cultures, show that integrity as reflected in specific cultural traits is the key issue of leadership selection. In addition, this book, Titus, emphasizes the importance of Word giftedness for leadership. Leaders have to know and use the word and influence their followers with it. This book encourages us to believe that high quality leaders are available in any culture no matter what the outward symptoms of the culture are (they are not described very complimentary in Titus).

Where it Fits[2]

In the redemptive drama Titus like Timothy occurs in Part II Salvation proclaimed and chapter 4, the church. Throughout this era God is inviting people everywhere (Acts 15:14) to be reconciled to Himself. His instrument for this is the church. When churches are started, where ever they are, there will always be a need for leadership. Titus shows that leadership is essential to a well ordered church. A church can not function well in society

---

[2.] Two frameworks are used to give overall perspective on where a book fits in the totality of the Bible. Framework 1 views the Bible as a whole as a redemptive drama and traces God's working both in what He says and what He does throughout the whole Bible. There is an Introduction, Chapter 1 The Making of a Nation, Chapter 2 The Destruction of a Nation, Chapter 3 Messiah, Chapter 4 The Church, and Chapter 5. Kingdom. Framework 2 views the Bible as a whole in terms of the development of the leadership concept. Six diverse leadership time periods include: 1. Leadership Roots (the patriarchal era); 2. Pre-Kingdom Leadership; 3. Kingdom Leadership; 4. Post-Kingdom Leadership; 5. N.T. Pre-Church Leadership; 6. N.T. Church Leadership.

unless it is well taught. The teaching must be practically oriented. The teaching involves explanation, demonstration, and application with accountability. Apostolic authority is important. Titus needs Paul's backing so that the Christians on Crete will listen to him. See **Article**, *Biblical Framework — The Redemptive Drama.*

Using the second framework for viewing the Bible as a whole, the leadership framework, Titus is seen to be in the sixth leadership era, the Church Leadership Era. This era is the one that we are presently in. Titus is definitely a book for today. Problems and opportunities seen in it are multiplied around the world today. See **Article**, *Six Biblical Leadership Eras — Overviewed.*

Leadership Lessons

1. APOSTOLIC LEADERSHIP FUNCTIONS

We surmise that Paul (along with Titus) founded this church. We have no other New Testament record to give us solid data on its founding. But since he *left* Titus behind to finish what he had begun, this is probably a valid assumption. He probably led most of these people to a saving knowledge of Christ. But they don't know much about following Christ. They have little or no Biblical information. Paul does not have a formal base to operate from, i.e. a position backed by a salary, a job description, or formal structure. And in addition, he himself was a cross-cultural worker in the Cretan situation, an alien to their island culture. He therefore operates not from a formal leadership relationship with the Cretan believers who seem to be scattered about in pockets around the island. Because he has founded this work, most likely backed by God-given authentication—signs and wonders, and miraculous conversions that have initially changed lives—he can operate as an apostle with these people.

Previously, in other New Testament church situations we have learned much about Paul's apostolic ministry. See leadership topic **Apostolic Functions** in 1 Timothy. See also **Article**, *Apostolic Functions.* This book of Titus gives us further insights on apostolic functions:

a. Apostles must appoint sound leaders if a church is to be healthy.

b. Apostles analyze needs in a situation and bring about training in basic teaching (sound doctrine) that can be applied to those needs in that culture. Initial knowledge of God through Christ does not guarantee growth to maturity.

c. Apostolic leadership must use modeling which flows from experience as a major leadership means for influencing followers.

d. Apostolic leadership does not have positional leadership but operates from a base dominantly using spiritual authority.

e. An apostolic leader can exercise strong leadership even without positional authority.

f. Apostolic leadership must know its Biblical truth very well and be able to defend such truth with authority.

g. Apostolic leadership should raise finances for Christian workers.

Interestingly enough, the miraculous is not stressed — usually thought of as a major indication of apostolic ministry. It is not *the power gifts* that are encouraged here but *word gifts*. Power is stressed all right but it is power in teaching that is emphasized. Strong leadership, i.e. highly directive (see **Article**, *Leadership Styles*), is stressed. This serves to reinforce three basic principle already noted in the Corinthian ministry that:

i. The Maturity Factor

The more mature the followers are, the more they recognize and follow spiritual authority.[3] The less mature they are the more likely they will not recognize spiritual authority, hence highly directive leadership styles must be used.

ii. Leadership Credibility

Apostolic leadership must demonstrate all of the means of recognized spiritual authority (gifted power, godly character, deep experiences with God) in order to have credibility in their leadership. Regardless of the level of maturity, the followers will inherently recognize some of these — in Titus' personal case, godly character is stressed as well as expertise in understanding God and God's revelation about how to live as a Christian.

iii. Confrontive

Apostolic authority must be confrontive in order to solve problems.
Titus is just the person to confront these new believers.

Leadership Principles / Values Suggested by this concept:

a. Apostolic leadership must authenticate its authority by demonstrated power from God, in this case by *life power* (Titus must model what victorious Christian living looks like in this culture) and by *gifted power* (Titus must teach powerfully in such a way that his teaching must be accepted and can not be refuted). See **Articles**, *Union Life — Intimacy With God*; *Power Gates*.

b. Apostolic authority must distinguish between core and peripheral issues both in doctrine and practice and bring corrective issues to doctrinal and behavioral situations which are heretical. The legalistic issues in Crete are core since they cut out the heart of the Gospel (see Galatians on this).

c. Apostolic authority must recognize that *problem solving* is a major thrust of its ministry.

---

[3] *Spiritual authority* from the standpoint of the follower, is the right to influence, conferred upon a leader by followers, because of their perception of spirituality in that leader. From the leader's perspective *Spiritual Authority* is that characteristic of a God-anointed leader, developed upon an experiential power base (giftedness, character, deep experiences with God), that enables him/her to influence followers through persuasion, force of modeling, and moral expertise. Paul, Timothy, and Titus did not hold a formal leadership position, like Bishop or other later recognized leadership title. Instead, they influenced using spiritual authority as a primary means. See **Article**, *Spiritual Authority — 6 Characteristics*.

    d.   Apostolic authority must be confrontive in order to solve problems.

    e.   Apostolic authority will always have edification of churches as a long term goal, even in the midst of problem solving. Paul's theme of *setting the church in order* points out three essentials of edification: leadership selection, life changing teaching, and impact on the surrounding culture in terms of changed lives.

2. MENTOR SPONSOR

The book of Titus shows us how Paul used his spiritual authority to give Titus backing he needed to do the job. A mentor sponsor is one who gives credibility and backing to a mentoree. See **Glossary**, *mentor sponsor.* Paul writes the book of Titus with that aim in mind. He wants the Cretan people to recognize that Titus represents him. "I left you in Crete to…"

Paul carefully weaves his theme of *applying the Gospel to life* throughout the epistle. But this *living the Christian life* flows out of being a Christian, the gracious work of God and not vice versa. He also openly makes it clear that Titus will appoint leaders and that Titus will teach the truth that Paul himself holds to. Thus he not only backs Titus but he has clarified the task that Titus will carry out.

Paul also sponsors Zenas and Apollos. In the very last portion of the epistle he raises money for them. Mentor sponsors also help mentorees with resources, when they can. See **Article**, *Mentoring — An Informal Training Model*; *Paul the Mentor; The Constellation Model.*

Leadership Principles / Values Suggested by this concept:

    a.   Mentor sponsors are needed especially to give authentication and credibility to ministry tasks carried out by their representatives.

    b.   Mentor sponsors need to clarify tasks for their mentorees.

    c.   Mentor sponsors link mentorees to resources.

3. LEADERSHIP TRANSITION / RELEASE

Leadership transition is one of the most important functions that older, more mature leaders must do. On the whole, biblical models for leadership transition are negative.[4] Only a handful of leadership transitions in the Bible are positive ones.[5] *Leadership transition* is the process whereby existing leaders prepare and release emerging leaders into the responsibility and practice of leadership positions, functions, roles, and tasks. *Leadership release* is the process whereby an existing leader deliberately encourages and allows an emerging leader to

---

[4.]   In the article on leadership transition, I list 18 leaders who were transitioned in to powerful influential roles or positions. Of these only 4 are positive transitions. There are many other leaders that I didn't mention which were poor transitions. Few there are of good transitions in the whole Bible.

[5.]   Of these important transitions, the three most positive include: Moses to Joshua (detailed information; can be studied); Elijah to Elisha (not much info on actual transition procedure); Barnabas to Paul (some info).

accept responsibility for and control of leadership positions, functions, roles, and tasks. Paul models well leadership transition in 2 Timothy where he passes his leadership mantle to Timothy and here in this book where he releases Titus for apostolic ministry. Titus has heavy responsibility given him. The guidelines are firm but he is left to carry it out on his own. Leaders must increasingly be released if they are to assume initiative for leadership. Paul models the release function and teaches it throughout the book in the guidelines he gives Titus. There is the mentor sponsoring of Paul. But it is Titus who is left to carry it out. See **Articles**, *Leadership Transition*; *Leadership Transitions — Timothy and Titus.*

Leadership Principles / Values Suggested by this concept:

a.   Effective leaders practice *progressive release* of emerging leaders by transitioning them into more responsible ministry in leadership tasks, major leadership func- tions, and finally leadership roles. See **Glossary**, *leadership tasks; leadership roles; three major leadership functions; leadership positions; progressive release.*

b.   Leadership transition should be exercised so that the emerging leader and the fol- lowers know that the transition has occurred and responsibility is now with the released leader. Paul's letter to Titus and letters to Timothy openly make clear the leadership transition.

4. LEADERSHIP STYLE — Pauline

Leadership style is the individual tendency of a leader to influence followers in a highly directive manner, directive manner, non-directive manner, or highly non-directive manner. It is that consistent behavior pattern that underlies specific overt behavior acts of influence pervading the majority of leadership functions in which that leader exerts influence. The style is the means that the leader uses in influencing followers toward purposes.

Of the 10 Pauline leadership styles previously identified, three are illustrated or implied in this book.

When dealing with problems leaders often have to come down with directive or highly directive leadership styles. Paul does so here using the *apostolic leadership style.* This style uses the fact that the leader founded the work as a lever for getting acceptance of influ- ence by the leader.   Paul assumes the role of delegated authority over followers and tells the Cretan believers what to do in terms of various issues (mostly Christian living).

One of the most important leadership styles illustrated in this book is the *confrontation style*—another highly directive leadership style. The *confrontation style* is an approach to problem-solving which brings the problem out in the open with all parties concerned, which analyzes the problem in light of revelation, and which brings force to bear upon the parties to accept recommended solutions. In this book there are several instances of this leadership style.

Note that highly directive leadership styles are used. This is often the case when a leader is faced with many problems or crises in a church and the followership is not very mature. Paul in his guidelines to Titus advocates highly directive leadership styles for Titus also.

In addition to these highly directive styles, Paul strongly commands Titus to influence by using the *imitator leadership style,* a highly indirect style. See **Glossary** for *leadership styles.* See **Article,** *Pauline Leadership Styles.* See also Clinton's *Coming To Conclusions on Leadership Style.*

Leadership Principles / Values Suggested by this concept:

a. Leaders must vary their leadership styles according to situation, personal ability, and follower maturity.

b. Problematic situations will frequently need highly directive leadership styles such as *father-initiator, apostolic, confrontation* in order to solve them and bring about unity and purpose in a situation.

c. The *imitation style* is a modeling style. We use this whether or not we want to. Paul goes a step further; he deliberately and proactively uses it as a means of influence and commands both Timothy and Titus to do so.

5. LEADERSHIP SELECTION/HIGH STANDARDS

Leadership selection is the life-long process of divine initiative and human recognition whereby a leader emerges. The process is punctuated with critical incidents, as viewed from a two-fold intermeshing perspective—the divine and the human. God selects a leader as indicated by various kind of shaping activities and human leadership affirms that selection, recognizing the shaping activities of God and working with God in that processing.

Paul lays out the guidelines for Titus to affirm in the initial outward selection of leaders in Crete. High standards for leadership must be held in all cultures. Paul tells Titus to appoint leaders with these qualifications, and he goes on to highlight integrity and its manifestations. He does not lessen the requirements because of the cultures' values that pervade. It is not, *get the best kind you can find*, but get *these kind*.

This notion of leadership selection is a critical on-going process that all church leaders should be involved in. Not only to meet their own present needs for ministry but for the on-going life of the church. Any ministry situation is just one generation away from becoming impotent, if it does not select, develop, and release emerging leaders into ministry.

One of the seven major lessons identified in the comparative study of effective leaders is this: *Effective leaders see leadership selection and development as a priority function in their ministry.* See **Articles,** *Leadership Selection; Seven Major Leadership Lessons.* Paul exemplifies this lesson.

Paul here (1:5-9) advocates top-down recruitment of potential leaders. The selection criteria focuses on two major qualities: (1) *character issues* — Paul advocates above reproach, an overall assessment by others concerning one's character. Individual character traits highlighted by Paul include: loyalty, ability to lead his own children in the Christian faith, not an arrogant, haughty, or egotistical person; even tempered; temperate with respect to alcoholic drinks; honesty; not in ministry to make money; a giving person; modeling godliness and a disciplined life. And (2) a *truth oriented person* — above all else, one who holds truth and demonstrates it in life and can refute unhealthy teaching. The implied emphasis is that the leader is a word gifted person.

Leadership Principles / Values Suggested by this concept:

a. Leadership selection and development is a responsibility of a leader.

b. Character qualities that demonstrate godliness, in the culture, should be the focus of one's selection criteria.

c. Leadership selection should include the ability to live out truth and defend truth — i.e. refute unhealthy teaching.

6. INTEGRITY/CHARACTER

The book of Titus reaffirms the importance of integrity as a necessary trait for a church leader (as seen also in 1 Timothy). Integrity is the top leadership character quality listed throughout the Bible.[6] *Integrity* is the consistency of inward beliefs and convictions with outward practice. It is an honesty and wholeness of personality in which one operates with a clear conscience in dealings with self and others. *Above reproach* is the general category that indicates that others see integrity in a leader. Paul gives a list of items which stand out in the Cretan culture to indicate integrity. Paul points out the negative ones they should avoid and the positive ones they must embrace.

Leadership Principles/ Values Suggested by this concept:

a. Character, not giftedness, is the foundation for leadership.

b. Each culture into which the Gospel is taken will have character traits which reveal what integrity is and is not.

c. Though character is foundational, giftedness must be able to enforce the rationale for character.

d. Leadership traits, other than character, may well vary from specific culture to specific culture (note God's comment on choosing David; note comments on Saul and later failure due to character issues).

See **Article**, *Integrity — A Top Leadership Quality.*

7. WORD GIFTEDNESS — A Leadership Necessity

In addition to character, the book of Titus stresses the importance of leaders understanding truth, defending it, living it, and passing it on to the church followers. These important functions require *word giftedness*. See **Articles**, *Giftedness* and *Developing Leadership Giftedness* for explanation of three clusters of spiritual gifts — Word, Power, and Love. Teaching giftedness (either natural ability, acquired skill or spiritual gift) would be required to carry out the admonitions that Paul gives. In addition, the spiritual gift of exhortation would be a natural complement to teaching and important to the application

---

[6]   All cultures recognize integrity as a leadership quality. But the indicators of integrity in a culture may vary. For example, the keeping of one's word (oaths, covenants, etc.) were extremely important to leaders of Israel in the Old Testament and were a top measure of integrity (see Saul's failures; Jephthah's so called rash vow, Joseph's final faith act, God's covenants with various leaders, etc.).

process of truth to life. For correction, the prophetic gift would aid. However, recognize how little giftedness is emphasized explicitly in the selection requirements as over against character. Yet, it does stand out here much more so than in Timothy's selection criteria list. See also 1Co **Key Leadership Insights**, *Topic — Giftedness.* See **Articles**, *Developing Giftedness; Spiritual Gift Clusters; Spiritual Gifts, Giftedness and Development; Apostolic Giftedness — Multiple-gifted Leaders.* See **Glossary**, word gifts, power gifts, love gifts, teaching, exhortation, prophecy.

Leadership Principles / Values Suggested by this concept:

a. Word giftedness (teaching, exhortation, prophecy) is important when bringing about change in a church situation where values must be addressed.

b. Word gifts, or complementary functions for them, should be developed in order to operate more effectively in bringing about value changes. A leader should develop knowledge, skills, and other perspectives which will enable giftedness to be used with effectiveness.

c. Modeling of truth emphatically supports the teaching of it. Leaders should proactively and deliberately use modeling to influence.

d. Giftedness should receive less stress in leadership selection and development than character building.

e. Gifts should be exercised with gifted power, that is, by faith in the Holy Spirit's empowerment of that giftedness. See **Glossary**, *gifted power.*

8. LEADERSHIP GUIDELINES

Paul indicates leadership guidelines throughout the book of Titus. These include:

1) *Plurality Of Leaders.* Titus shows us that at least in the churches in Crete there was a plurality of leaders. He is appointing multiple leaders. And these leaders are in dispersed localities. This possibly means that we have a regional church with a plurality of leaders. There also may have been more than one church leader for each local situation. How they related to one another is not given. Titus, himself, is operating as an apostolic leader with spiritual authority over these regional leaders.

2) *Qualifications for Leaders.* These focus on *character.* Paul's list of qualifications focuses on integrity and deals mainly with character though giftedness (teaching is mentioned) is at least strongly implied . Emphasis on selection is maturity in character, not riches, position, or ability. Selection of good potential/emerging leaders with character is the best preventive for avoiding bad leaders that later must be disciplined.

3) *Exteriority.* The spirituality factors of external testimony (*exteriority* — above reproach) and inner character (*interiority* — in the leader's life) must be kept in balance. Reputation without is crucial to a leader; a leader can sway followers and deceive them—but usually a bad character is recognized by non-followers external to the situation. Personal inward growth in a leader is a must and should lead to and be consistent with outward behavior. See **Article**, *Exteriority — A Must Spirituality Component for Leadership.*

4) *Integrity, Foundational.* Leadership character traits, in addition to abilities to influence people and traits thought of as leadership traits, should reflect integrity. Integrity is foundational to leadership.

5) *Pace Setting.* Leaders are pace setters. Their exemplary behavior sets the pace for followers. Their use of truth in daily living spills over to others.

See also the topic **Leadership Guidelines** given in 1 Timothy which have some of the above in common but also additional differing guidelines. Timothy is dealing with a much more complex situation and a much older church with its leadership already in place and traditions already well established. Paul was dealing with more leadership issues at Ephesus. Crete is relatively more straight forward.

Leadership Principles / Values Suggested by this concept:

a. Character is crucial to leadership.

b. Plurality of leadership can be used in church situations.

c. A foundational emphasis underlying leadership selection must be the identification of integrity, character, and traits of exemplary being and behavior in a culture. Leadership in a local church or regional church should be above criticism (as to character) by the surrounding culture.

d. Modeling of truth should be the norm for leaders.

e. An important facet of teaching others is giving them living examples to illustrate the teaching.

9. CONTEXTUALIZATION — A Major Leadership Problem in All Cultures

In Timothy Paul details just how complex leadership can be. In Titus the leadership issues are more straightforward, three basic ones. (1) The church needs sound leaders. (2) It needs leaders and people who know and obey truth in their own culture. This will require confrontation of cultural values out of line with this healthy living. (3) False teachers pushing Jewish legalistic ideas must be refuted.

These false teachers are introducing non-valid Jewish forms in the Cretan culture. Paul refutes these. All of his ministry has been involved with the notion of contextualization, which these Jewish legalists are botching. *Contextualization* is the process of taking something meaningful in one context and making it relevant to a new context. e.g. the Christian movement which began in a Jewish context had to be reinterpreted by Paul to a non-Jewish context, the Gentiles. Here in Crete, Biblical or revealed truth on how followers of God live, has to be applied to the Cretan situation. That is contextualization. Titus gives insights about how Christian living looks in this culture. Particularly some of the changes that must be made, if God is to be revealed in lives so that the culture can be impacted, are emphasized. Most of this contextualization is at value level and applying to orthopraxy, not doctrinal. However, much doctrinal truth is interwoven into the rationale for godly behavior. See **Article**, *Basic Ideas on Contextualization.* See **Glossary**, *contextualization.* See also Gilliland, *The Word Among Us* — especially the Clinton chapter on contextualizing leadership theory.

Leadership Principles / Values Suggested by this concept:

  a. Contextualization involves the application of Biblical truths given in some Biblical culture to a specific culture in which the leader is operating.

  b. When contextualizing Biblical truth to a cultural situation, aberrant values in the situation should be explicitly identified and compared or contrasted with their Biblical counterparts which have also been explicitly identified.

  c. Not all aberrant issues need to be dealt with at once. In a given situation an apostolic leader can usually identify those which are core — heretical, denying the Gospel message (orthopraxically, or orthodoxically), and those which are peripheral — problematic and needing attention but not necessarily heretical. The prior issues are dealt with immediately. Peripheral come later.

  d. Strong leadership will be needed in order to confront situations where change is needed.

  e. Contextualization needs to be done as early as possible in the life of a church. The longer a church (Ephesus church — Timothy situation) holds to and models cultural values at odds with Biblical truth, the harder it is to change. If Biblical values are contextualized and introduced early on (the Crete situation) in the church situation (everything is new anyway) the easier it will be to ground the church in Biblical truth (1 Ti 3:15).

  f. The notion of core and peripheral values is helpful in determining which values must be addressed first. See **Articles**, *Starting Point Plus Process; Principles of Truth.*

  g. Contextualization of doctrinal truth should be interwoven into the rationale for orthopraxic issues.

10. MENTORING — An Informal Training Model Within A Church Setting

Mentoring is a relational experience in which one person, the mentor, empowers another person, the mentoree, by sharing God-given resources. It is an informal training model very appropriate to training in a local church situation. Studies in mentoring have identified 9 different unique functions. A given mentor may be adept in several of these functions but not usually in all of them.

The mentoring functions advocated very strongly in the book of Titus include *contemporary modeling, mentor teaching,* and *mentor sponsoring.* It is *contemporary modeling* which is highlighted. Titus, older male leaders and older female leaders are commanded strongly *to model* for the younger believers in the church. In addition, the *mentor teacher* role is also commanded. While generally applicable to the same people as *contemporary modeling,* it is especially recommended to the older women who will mentor the younger women — how to live, be homemakers, display godliness as women (2:4). See **Articles**, *Mentoring—An Informal Training Model , Paul—Mentor, Paul—Developer,* See **Glossary**, *Contemporary Models, Mentor Teachers.*

Leadership Principles / Values Suggested by this concept:

a. Personal mentoring relationships allow for change of character and intimate meddling of the right sort.

b. Mentoring is a major means for developing people and leaders in a local church context.

11. REPUTATION OUTWARDLY / APPLICATION TO LIFE

Paul is concerned with what non-Chrisitans think (the impact of the Christian testimony of the Church) about followers of Jesus. He wants their daily testimony to be *above reproach.* This is true at Ephesus also where he references this concept several times (See 3:2, 7, 10; 4:12; 5:12, 14, 6:1 for references to outward testimony). In Titus, this outward testimony is referenced several times (See *truth that leads to godliness,* 1:1; *above reproach* 1:6; *reputation 1:7; No one should be able to malign the word of God because of their daily behavior,* 2:5; *attractive to others* 2:10; *may be careful to live out in daily life, testimonies which reflect this Goodnews, 3:8*).

What Paul is dealing with here is the concept of changed lives of believers who have seen the impact of God in their lives. In terms of spiritual growth, three spirituality components are in focus.[7]

i. **Exteriority** is the spirituality component that relates to living out the inner life. This component suggests overflow of interiority (ones vertical relationship with God and its impact on character and inner values) into life (the horizontal aspects of spirituality — its effects on our relationships with believers and unbelievers in the world in which we interact).

ii. **Spirit Sensitivity,** obeying the Holy Spirit Daily, is the spirituality component that embraces the realm of the Spirit. It reflects experience which recognizes the Holy Spirit in daily life. It essentially assesses the believer's sensitivity to Spirit life. It is an integrative component which relates centrality, interiority, and exteriority (3 important spirituality components) to life. Note the strong emphasis on the Holy Spirit in the book of Titus, much more so than in Timothy. A young church and new believers must learn early on the personal ministry of the Holy Spirit in their lives.

iii. **Fruitfulness,** being and doing what God intends, has two expressions: Inner (character — fruit of Spirit) and Outer (external fruit — results of giftedness and achievement for the Kingdom). It is the spirituality component that measures something of God's purposes for the believer and fulfillment as a human being. See **Glossary,** focused lives.

[7.]   *Spirituality* is the work of the Spirit in a leader's life which is indicated by the leader's, growing personal relationship with Christ (CENTRALITY), inner life with God (INTERIORITY), relationships with others in the body (COMMUNITY), Spirit-led and empowered ministry (UNIQUENESS), sensitive obedience to the Spirit daily (SPIRIT SENSITIVITY, EXTERIORITY), and by a character transformation toward Christ-likeness (FRUITFULNESS, DEVELOPMENT). The capitalized words represent 8 spirituality components. Three of these are being stressed here in Titus: SPIRIT SENSITIVITY, EXTERIORITY, and FRUITFULNESS. EXTERIORITY is the primary one stressed when dealing with above reproach, testimony before others, etc.

While Paul implies that these spirituality components are important for all in the church, one must note how much more so they are for a leader who is in the public eye. A leader can easily sway followers and deceive them—but usually a bad characteristic is more openly recognized by non-followers external to the situation. Personal inward growth in a leader is a must and should lead to and be consistent with outward behavior. See **Article**, *Exteriority — A Must Spirituality Component for Leadership; Adorning the Gospel — One's Personal Application of Truth; Principles of Truth.* See **Glossary** for definitions of spirituality components, *exteriority, centrality, interiority, fruitfulness, spirit sensitivity, uniqueness, community, development.*

Leadership Principles / Values Suggested by this concept:

a. Consistency between what one believes and how one behaves by all believers, is crucial if the church is to have impact on its surroundings (i.e. 1 Tim 3:15 become the pillar and ground of truth — Model Representatives of God's Truth. The church is God's foundational means for teaching, clarifying, and living out truth before the world.)

b. Outward behavior of believers should be a major attraction to the Gospel for unbelievers. If the Gospel can not change lives, why should it be advocated for others.

c. Leaders must take responsibility for changing the lives of their followers so that the Gospel becomes attractive to non-believers.

12. SECOND COMING — Motivation For Living Out Christian Beliefs

The passage, Titus 2:11-14, especially verse 13, is one of the strongest passages in the New Testament relating the second coming of Christ to present Christian testimony (see also 2 Ti 4:7,8; 1 Jn 3:1-3). The return of Christ was a major motivating factor of Paul's leadership. He advocates this for all leaders. See **Article**, *Motivating Factors for Ministry.*

Leadership Principles / Values Suggested by this concept:

a. A leader should use Christ's return as a personal motivating factor for life and ministry. One evidence of a leader's consciousness of Christ in a life or ministry is a love for the return of Christ.

b. Leaders should make explicit the motivating factors in their ministry. Paul certainly does so with this leadership topic.

13. CONFLICT — Separation Principle To Use

Where there are irreconcilable differences in orthodoxic or orthopraxic concerns — especially those bringing divisiveness in a situation, Paul commands shunning of the leaders bringing about the divisiveness. Warn a divisive person once, and then warn him a second time. After that, have nothing to do with him. Titus 3:10, 11. Compare this with advice given in the moral situation in 1 Co 3 and the advice given in 1 Th 5.

Leadership Principles / Values Suggested by this concept:

a. A leader should identify and clarify issues which may bring about division in a church. Those that are heretical must be dealt with first.

b. Reasonable efforts must be made by a leader to confront the divisive leader(s) to point out error. If after repeated efforts, there is nothing to be gained, the church should avoid altogether the one bringing about the division.

14. FINANCES — Paul Appeals for Zenas and Apollos

As in other epistles (see 1, 2 Co, Phm) Paul sponsors Christian workers (not himself, strangely enough), hoping, to link them up with financial resources to send them on their way in their itinerate ministries. He does not make a big issue of it but incidentally mentions the need of finances for Zenas and Apollos.

Leadership Principles/ Values Suggested by this concept:

a. Apostolic leaders should use their influence to help connect needy leaders with financial aid.

b. Apostolic leaders are not in ministry for money but they know its importance in getting Kingdom ministry done.

Titus

Apostolic Leadership

Verse by Verse Commentary

I. (ch 1:1-2)   Leadership — An Essential Basis for a Well Ordered Church

1:1[8]   I, Paul[9], am ministering as a servant of God and an apostle of Jesus Christ to help mature God's own chosen followers. I want them to know the truth that leads to godliness.[10]   **2** I want them to have a faith[11] and a knowledge grounded in an expectation of eternal life. God, who can not

---

[8]   Titus 1:1-4 is the salutation (the opening paragraph) to this letter. It follows the standard form of From/To/Greetings with some elaborating phrases and clauses in each section. Paul's salutations usually do several functions among which are: (1) claim's apostolic authority; (2) qualifies his ministry; (3) foreshadows (a good motivating technique) some major concept(s) he will deal with in the epistle; (4) does mentor sponsoring; (5) identifies the recipient(s) — usually with a unique name or phrase if a church; (6) sometimes gives his own personal state; (7) Greets, usually with some form of a blessing. Here Paul qualifies his ministry (ministering as a servant of God; to help mature God's own chosen believers), claims apostolic authority (apostle of Jesus Christ; at his appointed time revealed; God our Savior entrusted me), foreshadows what he will deal with (to know the truth that leads to godliness; to have a faith and a knowledge grounded in an expectation of eternal life; God our Savior); sponsors Titus (I write to you, Titus, one who is like my very own son because of our common faith. See also verse 5 which expands his sponsorship). See **Article**, *Paul's Salutations — Harbingers of His Epistles*.

[9]   Paul authored 13 epistles. See **Article**, *Time-Lines, The Apostle Paul*.

[10]   The truth that leads to godliness is the strongest foreshadowing (a thematic hint for the epistle) statement in the salutation (opening paragraph). Paul will develop this theme throughout the epistle. It keynotes a most important leadership function. Leaders must impact followers with truth from God which changes lives. They must use word gifts with impactful power. A second strong foreshadowing has to do with expectation. Looking forward to the fulfillment of eternal life which comes with Jesus' return. A third has to do with the character of God and the nature of the Christian life. Notice how these foreshadowing statements imply two of the purposes given in the Overview of Titus: to encourage the Cretan believers to good works, to motivate outward behavior by focusing on the return of Christ. See **Glossary**, salutation, gifted power, foreshadowing. See **Articles**, *Power Gates — Experiences That Renew and Enable Leaders; Figures and Idioms in the Bible*.

[11]   Faith here is most likely a *metonymy*. Faith, here means the whole Christian way of life and belief — which is by faith. Paul will later re-emphasize that the Christian way of life is by faith and not by works. God's grace enables one to live and believe the Christian truth. See **Glossary**, *Metonymy*.

lie,[12] promised this eternal life before the beginning of time. **3** At His appointed time,[13] He revealed His truth about this. God our Savior[14] entrusted me with this task[15] and commanded me to preach it. **4** I write to you, Titus,[16] one who is like my very own son because of our common faith.

[12.] Note *God who can not lie*. Paul is here emphasizing a trait of God which is important to the Cretan situation. This is *foreshadowing* a need he sees in Cretan behavior. If they are to live godly lives they must become like God, i.e. be truthful. Cretans were known for lying. Paul foreshadows what he will later explicitly demand. Cretans must experience truth that leads to godliness — especially becoming truthful in their everyday life.

[13.] Paul recognizes the importance of the *timing* of God in the redemptive drama. He also is implying that he, himself, was one who received revelation from God about the truth of salvation for Gentiles. See Eph 3:1-9; 1 Th 2:13 et al for further confirmation of revelation through Paul. See Gal 4:4 for concept of timing of God. Paul is aware of the timing macro: *God's timing is crucial to accomplishment of God's purposes.* See **Glossary**, *macro lessons; timing macro*. See **Articles**, *Macro Lesson, Defined; Macro Lessons—List of 41 Across Six Leadership Eras; God's Timing and Leadership.*

[14.] *God our Savior* is a special name for God used by Paul for emphasis and foreshadowing basic content he will elaborate on later in the epistle. This title for God is used in Titus 3 times (1:3; 2:10; 3:4). He uses it also two times in 1 Timothy (1:1; 2:3). He is emphasizing the source of salvation and its eternal significance. See **Article**, *God Our Savior — Paul's favorite Name for God in Later Life.*

[15.] Paul strongly implies his *sense of destiny*. He had a strong sense of appointment to ministry from God. See 1 Ti 1:1, 1:12, 2:7 and other salutations: Ro 1:1; 1Co 1:1; 2Co 1:1; Gal 1:1; Eph 1:1; Col 1:1; 1Ti 1:1; 2Ti 1:1; Tit 1:1. In 2Co this is identified as a Pauline leadership value called *divine appointment. Leaders ought to be sure that God appointed them to ministry situations.* Leaders need a strong sense of God's calling for their lives if they are to persevere and be effective over a lifetime. See **Glossary,** *divine appointment; sense of destiny.* See **Articles**, *Entrustment — A Leadership Responsibility; Paul — A Sense of Destiny.*

[16.] Titus is one of three mentorees very close to Paul (calls them all by the title *beloved son*). Titus is mentioned 15 times in Paul's epistles: 2Co 2:13; 7:6,13,14; 8:6,16,23; 12:18 (twice); 13:14 (some manuscripts); Ga 2:1, 3; 2Ti 4:10; Tit 1:4 ; 3:15 (some manuscripts). He was used by Paul as an Apostolic trouble shooter. A number of ministry tasks were given Titus. See **Glossary**, *ministry tasks.* See **Articles**, *Timothy, Beloved Son; Titus — Ministry Tasks; Titus — An Apostolic Worker; Apostolic Functions.*

5 The reason I left[17] you in Crete was that you might straighten out what was left unfinished[18] concerning church leadership. I directed you to appoint church leaders in every town.[19] **6**[20] A church leader must be above reproach.[21] He should be a one-wife kind of man — that is, a faithful person.[22] His children should be believers too. They should be obedient and not accused of wild behavior. **7** Since a person doing ministry is entrusted[23] with God's work, his reputation is very important. His character should be above reproach. He should not be overbearing. He must not be quick-tempered. Drunkenness is unthinkable. He must not be a violent person. He must have a reputation for honesty. He is not in the ministry for making money deceitfully.   **8** On the contrary, he is a giving kind of person showing hospitality. He loves what is good.

[17.] This implies that the two of them had been involved in a foundational ministry trip in which they had evangelized but had not yet formulated small groups and leaders.

[18.] This paragraph introduces the theme and first major idea for the whole book: **Setting The Church In Order,** meaning establishing the foundations for an effective, on-going, and life-giving church, involves the *appointing of qualified leaders.* Two other major ideas about establishing the foundations will be given in chapters 2 and 3.

[19.] A plurality of leaders is implied here for the whole island. There will be leader(s) for the scattered believers. How these leaders relate to each other is not given. See **Leadership Topic 8, Leadership Guidelines.**

[20.] For verse 5 especially, note how this describes a major purpose suggested in the **Overview**: *to give Titus authoritative backing in the eyes of the Cretan church.* Titus has Paul's backing to appoint leaders. Note also that verse 6-9 are fulfilling another purpose indicated in the overview: *to give Titus perspective on leadership selection.* See also **Leadership Topic 1, Apostolic Leadership Functions,** function a.

[21.] This *above reproach* statement, dealing with integrity, is the major assertion of this list of items. Verses 5-9 are most likely a list idiom. Following the standard method of an emphatic list, Paul highlights the first thing on the list as the most important thing. Other things on the list clarify and explain what the first item is or show how important it is. Here the first item has to do with character, (integrity). The next few items show negatively what Paul means by this above reproach trait (integrity). Paul then contrasts by giving positive things that integrity is. The negative traits are obviously cultural traits commonly seen on Crete. Paul is contextualizing the outworking of the Gospel in the Cretan society. These Cretan characteristics are off-base for Christian leaders. See **Glossary,** *list idiom.* See **Leadership Topics 5. Leadership Selection** and **6. Integrity/Character** and **9. Contextualization.** See **Article,** *Integrity, Basic Ideas on Contextualization.*

[22.] I agree with Peterson's interpretation on this clause. It is talking about loyalty, a quality needed in leadership, not polygamy or how many times a person has been married.

[23.] Paul sees leadership as a responsibility given by God. See **Article,** *Entrustment, A Leadership Responsibility.* Therefore, leaders represent God in one sense. Their reputation reflects on God. In a lesser sense, Paul will argue this same way for the followers in Crete.

He is self-controlled. He should have a reputation for being upright, demonstrating holiness and modeling a disciplined life. **9** He must hold firmly to the trustworthy message as it has been taught.[24] Thus he will be able to encourage others by good healthy teaching.[25] And he can refute[26] those who oppose this healthy[27] teaching.

10 The legalists, those especially advocating Jewish circumcision,[28] are a rebellious bunch. Their talk is as cheap as it is deceitful. **11** They must be silenced. Their negative teaching is having a disastrous effect. Whole households are being affected by it.[29] These teachers motives are questionable — they are in it dishonestly in order to

---

[24.] One wonders just how much has been taught and what Biblical materials they had for teaching.

[25.] Word gifts are implied here, especially teaching and exhortation. See **Glossary**, *word gifts, teaching, exhortation, prophecy.*

[26.] I have translated two words with one. The words — *exhort*, KJV, (SRN 3870 παρακαλεο) used in the sense of admonish and the word *convince*, KJV, (SRN 1651 ελεγχο) which means to expose, find fault with, to call to account, demand an explanation and/or correct in such a way as to bring shame upon the person convicted — were replaced with one word, *refute*. The word, *convince*, also carries the negative connotation of reprehending severely, chiding, and chastening, I think the one word, *refute*, carries these meanings. This kind of action by leaders requires strong word gifts. Paul is not asking a light thing here.

[27.] *Healthy*, KJV *sound* (SRN 5198 υγιαινο) is a key word. It essentially means sound or correct. and is translated by such words as sound, be sound, be whole, whole, wholesome, be in health, safe and sound. Physically, it means to be in good health. Metaphorically it describes followers of Jesus whose opinions are free from any mixture of error (orthodoxic issues) or those who behave uprightly (othopraxic issues). Paul uses this word 4 times in Titus (1:9, 13; 2:1, 2) and 4 times in 1,2 Timothy (1Ti 1:10; 6:3,; 2Ti 1:13; 4:3). This repeated emphasis in the last letters of Paul shows his concern for churches to be healthy in what they know and practice. Paul contrasts this good teaching with unhealthy legalistic teaching. See **Leadership Topic 7. WORD GIFTEDNESS — A Leadership Necessity.** See **Glossary**, *word gifts.*

[28.] Note here how another **Overview** purpose is being dealt with: *to refute the legalistic heresy being propagated in Crete.* Apparently these legalistic teachers are Cretan. Usually the legalistic teachers were Jewish folk who traveled around to where Paul had been and tried to proselytize folk. But here Paul attacks their character qualities as if they were Cretan.

[29.] One of the problems with a young church, like this church in Crete, is that its people are usually not well taught and are vulnerable to cultic movements. Apparently this was so here. And this unhealthy teaching was having a real impact.

make money.[30] **12** A quote from a Cretan prophet fits here. He said, "Cretans are always liars, evil brutes, lazy gluttons."[31] **13** I wish this weren't true.[32] Therefore, rebuke them sharply, so that they will have a healthy respect for truth and its application to life.[33] **14** They should pay no attention to Jewish myths or to the commands of those who reject the truth. **15** To the pure, all things are pure, but to those who are corrupted and do not believe, nothing is pure. In fact, both their minds and consciences[34] are corrupted. **16** They claim to know God, but by their actions they deny him.[35] They are detestable, disobedient and unfit for doing anything good.

[30.] Paul has clean hands here. Throughout his ministry he has bent over backwards to avoid having a reputation for making money via ministry. See especially 2 Co where he rigorously defends himself on this issue and Philippians where he shows his personal view on ministry and finances. See **Article**, *Finances — A Barrier To Finishing Well*.

[31.] Scholars disagree as to who is being quoted. Alford favors Epimenides.

[32.] However, no one disagrees with the actual description of a Cretan. Paul certainly highlights the antithesis of these bad characteristics when he exhorts to good living: be truthful people; be moderate; do good works.

[33.] See **Leadership Topic 11, Reputation Outwardly…**Application of truth exposed in church public ministry is one of the weakest elements of ministry in today's churches as well as at Crete. People need help in how to apply the word of God in their lives. See **Articles**, *Exteriority — A Must Spirituality Component for Leadership; Adorning the Gospel — One's Personal Application of Truth; Principles of Truth*.

[34.] Paul barely emphasizes conscience here in Titus. But it is a very important concept in the selection of leaders. Paul hits this hard in his letters to Timothy, written roughly in the same time period.

[35.] This key statement, *by their action they deny him*, typifies Paul effort to get through to the Cretan believers. He is saying, "Don't be like these people. You must live out what you believe. Your actions can deny the Gospel." This is indirectly reflecting his emphasis on the **Overview** purpose: *to encourage the Cretan believers to good works*. He will deal more directly with this *living out your faith* in chapters 2 and 3.

II. (Ch 2:1-14) Application Of Practical Teaching—An Essential Function Of A Well Ordered Church[36]

Titus 2:1 Your teaching must be solid,[37] through and through. **2** Teach the older men to be temperate, worthy of respect, self-controlled, and solid in what they believe.[38] They should demonstrate love and endurance.

3 Likewise,[39] teach the older women to be reverent in the way they live.[40] They should not falsely accuse others. They must not be addicted to wine. They must be able to pass on to others teaching that is good.
4 They should exhort

---

[36]   This section begins to develop the second and third major ideas about the theme. **Setting The Church In Order** requires leaders (1) who are sound in teaching and (2) who model a Christian life style and (3) necessitates leaders who exhort others to practical Christian living. Here Titus must model this in his leadership at Crete, in such a way, that the leaders can emulate him and followers will respond and live well. Note that Paul addresses all age groups of followers: older men (2:2) , older women (2:3), younger women (2:4) and younger men (2:6,7). A well established church has believers of all ages and gender living lives that make a difference. Non-believers can see examples that will encourage emulation. A leader in a local church situation has to be concerned with all age groups and gender and even classes.

[37]   This is our good friend *Healthy*, KJV *sound* (SRN 5198 υγιαινο) that occurred in 1:9. Paul repeats it twice in this context (2:1,2). This time I translate by *solid* (and reemphasize it by the qualifiers, through and through). Leaders must exhort and encourage personal application of truth from a solid base of truth. Again strong word giftedness is implied. See **Article**, *Word Disciplines and Bible Centered Leadership.*

[38]   Note the **Overview** purpose being developed: *to encourage the Cretan believers* (in this case the older men) *to good works*. Again Paul emphasizes consistency. Beliefs must affect behavior. He contextualizes things previously taught into the Cretan situation. Note the three areas: (1) temperate — an inward character trait; (2) worthy of respect — an outwardly recognized trait; (3) self-control — an inward discipline. These traits were missing, generally, in the Cretan culture. Paul is contextualizing biblical truth to their situation. By showing these kind of traits, Christian truth becomes attractive to non-believing Cretans. See **Glossary**, *interiority, exteriority, contextualization.* See **Articles**, *Adorning the Gospel — One's Personal Application of Truth; Basic Ideas on Contextualization; Principles of Truth.*

[39]   Paul continues to drive home his purpose *to encourage the Cretan believers* (in this case the older women) *to good works. Reverent in the way they live* translates the phrase *as becomes holiness* which is actually one Greek word (SRN 2412 ιεροπρεπέ). This is a *hapax legomena*, a one time appearing word. It essentially means living godly lives reflecting respect for God's holiness. Paul begins this context and ends it with strong exhortations to live lives that model Christian truth. See **Glossary**, *hapax legomena.* See **Article**, *Adorning the Gospel — One's Personal Application of Truth; Principles of Truth.*

[40]   Paul elaborates on *reverent in the way they live*. Three explanatory statements do this, contextualize for older women godliness in the Cretan situation. Note the three areas: (1) don't falsely accuse others; (2) don't be addicted to wine; (3) do pass on to other women the essence of godly living. Women are to influence women, a valid starting-point for the Cretan culture. Paul has previously given these truths (the tongue, temperance, gender leadership issues). Now he contextualizes them. See **Glossary**, *contextualization.* See **Articles**, *Starting Point Plus Process Model; Adorning the Gospel — One's Personal Application of Truth; Gender and Leadership; Basic Ideas on Contextualization; Principles of Truth.*

younger women to do their duty,[41] to love their husbands and children.[42] **5** They can emphasize that the young women exercise self-control, maintain purity in their marriage, be good homemakers, showing kindness, and a submissive spirit in their relationship to their husbands. No one should be able to malign the word of God because of their daily behavior.

6 Similarly, encourage the young men to be self-controlled.[43]   **7** Model for them by your

---

[41].   *Exhort to do their duty* is a phrase translating one word in the Greek (SRN 4993 σοφρονιζο). The KJV translates with the phrase *may teach to be sober.* In my opinion, four usus loquendi (local uses) are possible for this hapax legomena (one time only used word): 1) restore one to his senses; 2) to moderate, control, curb, discipline; 3) to hold one to his duty; 4) to admonish, to exhort earnestly. From the context which speaks of loving one's husband and children it seems most likely that use 3) do one's duty is the most likely interpretation. Nothing in the context seems to imply that the young women are out of their senses running amok with some weird behavior. Nor is there anything to indicate curbing or controlling or moderating. It is possible that they could be moving toward alcoholism, which is indicated for older women so that moderating could be a possible interpretation. It seems clear that the force of the statement indicates that use 4 is certainly a possibility — that is, exhort them earnestly to love their husbands and children. But I have chosen to interpret, exhort them to do their duty as wives, that is, love their husbands and children — a blended usus loquendi. See **Glossary,** *hapax legomena; usus loquendi.* See **Article,** *Adorning the Gospel — One's Personal Application of Truth; Principles of Truth.*

[42].   This is a famous verse used to emphasize the importance of women mentoring other women (the phrase *a Titus 2:4 woman* implies this; there are even organizations who teach women about mentoring and use this verse as their theme). Note in verse 5 the qualities that should be passed on to younger women: (1) self-control; (2) purity; (3) homemaking, (4) kindness, and (5) submission to their husbands. These are basically values and are more caught from modeling than taught as precepts. That is why Paul begins and ends this very tightly woven context the way he does. Paul is saying, "You must live your lives so as to impact the younger women around you." Paul begins this context, they should *be reverent in the way they live.* He closes this context, their lives must be consistent so that *No one should be able to malign the word of God because of their daily behavior.* This kind of consistent living will impact others, particularly the younger women who need these kind of models.

[43].   Notice that self-control is emphasized in for all ages, older men, older women, younger women, and younger men. Evidently that was a much needed behavior trait in the Cretan culture. The word here, KJV sober minded (SRN 4993 σοφρονεο), means in this context to exercise self-control with respect to one's passions — always an issue with young men.

own life.[44] Demonstrate what is good. Teach with integrity. Show that what you teach is important. **8** What you say should be irrefutable. Those who oppose you will have no grounds to condemn you. In fact, they will be embarrassed, because they can not deny what you have said and done.[45]

9 Teach slaves to be subject to their masters in everything. They should try to please their masters and not to talk back to them. **10** Slaves should not steal from their masters. Instead slaves should show that they can be fully trusted.[46] By these kind of attitudes and actions, slaves in every way will make the teaching about God our Savior attractive to others.[47]

---

44. Titus is a relatively young leader. His modeling of this self-control will impact others. Paul gives this same advice to Timothy (1 Ti 6:11).

45. Note verse 6-8. This is one of the great ministry challenges in the New Testament. Paul is using Goodwin's Expectation Principle with Titus. He believes in Titus and that Titus can competently do this. The modern day equivalent of this challenge would be, "You need to become a Bible Centered Leader!" See **Glossary**, *Ministry Challenge*; *Goodwin's Expectation Principle*; *Bible Centered Leader*. See **Article**, *Bible Centered Leader*.

46. The slavery institution was a terrible evil thing during this period of the Roman empire. Paul, in his letters to churches at this time, does not advocate abolishment of slavery. Instead he seeks to exhort both Christian slaves and Christian masters to better the situation via relationships and the application of Christian principles. In his individual letter to Philemon, Paul advocates the acceptance of Onesimus, a run away salve as a brother in the Lord — probably meaning a free man. What we see is the *starting-point-plus process model* in action. We also see the whole issue of deep processing in a life. A slave could be enabled to live a Christian life as a slave. But this would require great inward strength. But Paul believes it to be possible. From today's perspective one would like to see Paul come down heavily on the prophetic side to abolish slavery. But that was a battle Paul was not fighting. See **Glossary**, *deep processing*. See **Article**, *Starting Point Plus Process Model*. See also the leadership commentary on Philemon.

47. I have captured the verbal metaphor, *adorn the doctrine of God*, with its emphatic meaning- *will make the teaching about God our Savior attractive to others*. To live victoriously in such a terrible daily situation, like slavery was, would honor God in a way that would draw people to Him. People would see that following Jesus works out in life situations. If it can work out in this bad situation, it can work anywhere. This passage to Christians in awful situations challenges us (western Christians especially) today, who live in relatively prosperous and easy situations. See **Glossary**, *capture, metaphor*; See **Article**, *Figures and Idioms*.

11 God's salvation is real now, all can see it. His salvation graciously enables us to live well.[48]   **12** It teaches us to say "No" to ungodliness and worldly passions. It teaches us to say, "Yes" to living self-controlled, upright and godly lives in this present age.   **13** We do this while we wait for the blessed hope — the glorious appearing of our great God and Savior, Jesus Christ.[49]   **14** He gave himself for us to redeem us from all wickedness and to purify for himself a people that are his very own, eager to do what is good.[50]

15 These, then, are the things you should teach. Encourage and rebuke authoritatively. Don't let anyone put you down.[51]

[48.] This great summary passage, 2:10-15, condenses all that Paul has been saying to encourage the Cretan believers to do good works — i.e. live out the Christian life so others can see it and want it themselves. Note what he summarizes: 1) this Christian life is real, for now, not something in heaven; 2) it is God who enables us to live it; 3) we can live above the controlling authority of sin in our lives; 4) we can live Godly lives no matter how ungodly the culture. See **Article**, *Adorning the Gospel — One's Personal Application of Truth; Principle of Truth.*

[49.] Paul's purpose, *to motivate outward behavior by focusing on the return of Christ,* is seen strongly in this verse. As we wait for Christ's return, we will want to get ready for it. We do this by living the kind of lives He wants us to live. Paul is one of the great motivational leaders in the Bible. The second coming motivated him. See his closing word to Timothy in 2 Ti 4:7,8. It should motivate us. See **Article**, *Motivating Factors For Ministry; Motivating Principles: Pauline Influence.*

[50.] In this one verse is given the doctrinal rationale for Paul's admonitions to the Cretans about living out the Christian life. Jesus' work at the Cross is foundational. Leaders must always apply truth from a solid basis of truth. Paul does that here. The work on the cross enables — redeeming from wickedness and enabling toward pure lives and lives that demonstrate a heartfelt desire to do good in our world.

[51.] Titus has been well sponsored. He knows what he is to do. And Paul has clarified this openly in this letter which will be read by the Cretan believers. Paul closes this section by encouraging Titus in his leadership. Don't let any put you down (possibly because he was young; possibly because he was an outsider to the culture). Titus should lead authoritatively — strong apostolic leadership. Apostolic leadership does just that — lead with authority. See the leadership **topic 1. Apostolic Leadership Functions.** See also the **Articles**, *Apostolic Functions; Apostolic Giftedness — Multiple-Gifted Leaders.*

III. (Ch 3:1-11)[52] Godly Living — An Essential Outward Sign To Society Of A Well Ordered Church

Titus 3:1   Remind the people to be subject to rulers and authorities.[53] They should be obedient people and ready to do whatever is good.   **2** They should slander no one. They should be peaceable and considerate people. Humility toward all should be a hallmark of their changed lives.

[52.]   This entire chapter is devoted toward this purpose: *to encourage the Cretan believers to good works*. Glance again at the theme of the book of Titus. **Setting The Church In Order** involves the appointing of qualified leaders and requires leaders who are sound in teaching and who model a Christian life style and necessitates leaders who exhort others to practical Christian living. Chapter 1 dealt primarily with the appointing of qualified leaders. Chapter 2 dealt with leaders who are sound in teaching and who model a Christian life style. It also spilled over onto the 3rd major idea of exhorting followers to practical Christian living. Chapter 3 now takes that third idea and emphasizes in even more detail the notion of *practical Christian living*.

[53.]   Paul deals with subject of submission to governmental authority in more detail in Ro 13:1-7. Here in verses 1-3 the emphasis seems more to be on the corporate testimony. Christians as a whole, particularly in this island community where they would be watched and known, should be seen as those who obey governmental authorities and not as rebellious subject trying to overthrow the government. All of the characteristics in this context point out the notion that Christians as a whole group should be perceived by others as: 1) those having submissive and obedient attitudes toward government; 2) characterized as those who do good in society; 3) people who do not falsely accuse others (this notion of slandering seems to be prevalent in Cretan society; Paul has hit on it several times — truthfulness must be a Christian virtue that contextualizes to any culture); 4) peaceful people; 5) considerate people; 6) people characterized by humility (controlled strength). The question that comes to mind as one meditates on this passage is how can a leader like Titus actually bring about the notion of a Corporate testimony — Christians as a whole on the island of Crete. In this small island culture Christianity would be branded and known and watched and evaluated by those in the culture. So the corporate nature is there. But how to motivate groups so that their corporate testimony depicts the wonderful character qualities — that is the challenge of leadership. Today in most western societies the challenge is even greater — how to get the sense of corporate Christianity and how to get a corporate testimony. Christians are scattered in a diverse society. See **Glossary**, *corporate testimony*. See **Article**, *Corporate Characteristics of a Church — Impacting Society*.

3[54] At one time we too were foolish, disobedient, deceived and enslaved by all kinds of passions and pleasures. We lived in malice and envy, being hated and hating one another.   **4** But then the kindness and love of God our Savior appeared.[55] **5** He saved us, not because of righteous things we had done, but because of his mercy.[56] He saved us through a cleansing renewal in our inner life. We were renewed by the Holy Spirit.[57]

6 God provided us with this Spirit made available to us generously through the work of Jesus Christ our Savior.[58] 7 Now then, we have been made right with God due to His

---

[54.] When faced with a leadership challenge about a corporate testimony, like Paul has just given, 3:1-2, the question arises, "Is it even possible?" Paul, the master of motivational technique, answers, "Yes! As a matter of fact that is what has happened to me and those Christians who have accepted the message (note editorial we)." The use of personal testimony is always an effective motivator. "I have experienced it. I know it works!" Note too, again how Paul exhorts out of a solid base of truth. He explains the rationale behind living exemplary lives. It is based on the Cross, the intervention of God (note again Paul's use of this powerful term — God Our Savior). Paul is aware of the timing of God (kindness and love of God appeared). He roots the notion of transformed lives in the work of the Holy Spirit. This transformational work is a work of the Holy Spirit flowing out of the vicarious atonement — Christ death for us on the cross. See **Article**, *Motivating Principle: Pauline Influence.*

[55.] *Kindness and love appeared* probably are used as a metonymy. They stand for Jesus who appeared demonstrating God's kindness and love. His life and death showed us this kindness and love. Note too again the awareness of God's timing that Paul perceives. See **Glossary**, *metonymy*. See **Article**, *God's Timing and Leadership.*

[56.] Paul is careful to show that this salvation provided by God our Savior did not depend on the recipients being deserving of it. It was God's mercy that brought this salvation. So those being saved out of the Cretan culture can not say that they can't be saved because they are undeserving. All are undeserving. This fundamental notion then calls for a transforming work. Paul explains that in the next phrase describing the Spirit's inner work in a believer.

[57.] Paul pinpoints the transformational work by describing it as a work of the Holy Spirit. He uses a verbal metaphor. I have captured it with the words, cleansing renewal in our inner life. See **Glossary**, *metaphor*; *capture*. See **Article**, *Figures and Idioms in the Bible.*

[58.] Paul identifies the foundation for this renewing work—the work of Jesus on the cross.

gracious provision. We will become heirs. We have the hope of eternal life.[59] **8** What I am saying to you is the Gospel truth.   And I want you to stress these things, so that those who have trusted in God may be careful to live out in daily life, testimonies which reflect this *Goodnews*. These things are excellent and profitable for everyone.[60] **9** But avoid foolish controversies and genealogies and arguments and quarrels about the law, because these are unprofitable and useless.[61] **10** Warn a divisive person once, and then warn him a second time. After that, have nothing to do with him.[62] **11** You may be

---

[59.] Paul argues that we have, because of this renewing work of the Holy Spirit within us, a right standing with God. And this right standing with God is the basis on which we work out our right living. I am amazed at this over brief teaching on the work of the Spirit. Titus had quite a challenge — to explain this teaching in more detail and in such a way that people could appropriate it in a transformational way. But remember Titus knew all of Paul's teaching and would have been familiar with the Romans 3-8 concepts which deal with the work of the cross and the ministry of the Holy Spirit.. *We will become heirs. We have the hope of eternal life* is the anchor teaching of Romans 8. In terms of leadership perspectives, to operate as a leader bringing about transformational change in lives, we must know our Bibles well. There is a great need for Bible Centered Leaders. See **Glossary**, *Bible Centered Leader.* See **Article**, *Bible Centered Leader.*

[60.] For the last time Paul reinforces his notion, "You must live out what you believe. Your actions can deny the Gospel." Paul is emphasizing for a last time in this epistle, "Consistency in living out what you believe demands that you know the truth and let it transform your life so that it is seen all around you."

[61.] Verse 9 is dealing with the **Overview** purpose: *to refute the legalistic heresy being propagated in Crete.* Paul does not spend much attention to the actual heresy itself. Titus would have been familiar with it. Paul has dealt with it numerous times. His last time, done in more detail, occurs in his epistles to Timothy. A major function of apostolic leadership is to confront heresy (orthodoxic and/or orthopraxic) head on. The force of the confrontation in the book of Titus is largely orthopraxic. See **Article**, *Apostolic Functions.*

[62.] Paul's basic approach to confronting a heretical problem is twofold: 1) correct the damage of the heresy in the church by presenting the truth and/or modeling it; 2) confront the divisive person with the truth and give a chance for change. Give a reasonable time for the person to respond and make sure the person has understood (second time). If there is no positive response, then the person should be avoided by all in the church. The Amish and early Mennonites had a term for this — shunning. To be a part of a community and then to be ousted from it can have a powerful effect — maybe even redemptive (see 2 Co 2:5-11). See **Glossary**, *shunning.* See **Article**, *Shunning — Paul's Advice on This.*

sure that such a man is warped and sinful. He is self-condemned.[63]

12[64] As soon as I send Artemas or Tychicus to you, do your best to come to me at Nicopolis, because I have decided to winter there.   **13** Do everything you can to help Zenas the lawyer and Apollos on their way and see that they have everything they need.[65]   **14** Our people must learn to devote themselves to doing what is good, in order that they may provide for daily necessities and not live unproductive lives.[66]

15 Everyone with me sends you greetings. Greet those who love us in the faith. Grace be with you all.[67]

[63.]   Leaders need not feel guilty over this disciplinary action. The process has allowed for a response to correct the improper teaching or behavior and its effect. If the process has not brought about change then the discipline is applied. And there should be no guilt associated with it. However, there may yet be a change and one must be ready to forgive and respond later. See 2 Co 2:5-11 where the shunning process worked and the person ousted from the community was forgiven. See **Article**, *Shunning — Paul's Advice on This*.

[64.]   Paul's closing remarks generally deal with some personal requests and give incidental information about what is happening around him. That is true of this context, 3:12-14. Notice his use of personal names. Paul's ministry was very personal. Note how he is concerned for these colleagues. See **Articles**, *Paul — And His Companions; Paul — Developer*.

[65.]   Paul acts here as a mentor sponsor. He is attempting to raise financial support for Zenas and Apollos. He does this same function, supporting others, in the 2 Corinthian letters. See **Glossary**, *mentor sponsor*. See **Articles**, *Paul The Mentor; Finances — A Barrier To Finishing Well; Apostolic Functions — Comparison of Titus and Timothy*.

[66.]   Two positive benefits of leading productive Christian lives are: 1) Christians provide for the necessities of life in their own setting and are not a drain on society; 2) there is the availability of resources to support the advancement of Christian work elsewhere. Paul is certainly implying that here. Productive lives involves support of God work in the world.

[67.]   In his latter years Paul was more conscious of the concept of grace. The Greek word here is *grace*, (SRN 5485 χαριτι). Paul uses this in 1Ti, 2Ti and Tit in the sense of the enabling presence of God in a life so as to cause that one to persevere victoriously. I frequently translate grace by special enablement. The Titus 2:11,12 passage is using grace as a metonymy as I have commented on previously. But it also carries this sense of enablement. We can live the Christian lives that Paul calls for in Titus, because we have the grace of God working in us. A leader must experientially know this concept of grace if he/she is to lead with impact. It is interesting to see that all three great church leaders, Peter, Paul, and John close their writing ministry with words about grace. And all three seem to use it in the sense of the *enabling presence of God*. A leader will not make it to the end without knowing experientially this grace—the enabling presence of God. See *grace*, **Glossary**.

For Further Leadership Study

1. Study the mentoring roles that Paul works on in his relationship with Titus as illustrated in this book. What empowering tasks of a sponsor, counselor, teacher, or contemporary mentor are illustrated?

2. Titus is mentioned several times in the Pauline epistles (see especially 2 Corinthians and 2 Timothy). Paul uses an on-the-job training technique called a ministry task in Titus' development. A ministry task is an assignment recognized as from God which primarily tests a person's faithfulness and obedience but often also allows use of ministry gifts in the context of the task which has closure, accountability, and evaluation. The ministry task has a two-fold thrust — to develop the leader and to accomplish the task whatever it is. As the leader becomes more proficient the thrust of the task becomes more for the accomplishment of it and less for the development of the leader. Titus has four ministry tasks given (3 at Corinth and one in Crete). He is increasingly released in the tasks. This whole process is worthy of study.

3. Comparatively study the traits lists of 1 Timothy 3 and Titus 1 to see how culture affects the manifestation of integrity.

4. Study comparatively the kinds of leaders mentioned in 1 Timothy and Titus. Note which one is not present. Why?

5. What are the implications of the closing words for leadership selection and development? (note 3:12-14)

Special Comments

Again as in 1 Timothy this is a book dealing directly with leadership issues — more so on the corporate side of leadership while Timothy deals with the personal side, Timothy himself. The study of this book is a must for personal study and application and for teaching for the church. This book ought to be influential on a leader's foundations for ministry philosophy.

Notes:

Notes:

Titus

Apostolic Leadership

Commentary Articles

Table of Contents – Articles Referred To in Titus Commentary

Adorning the Gospel — One's Personal Application of Truth

Introduction

What we believe as followers of Christ ought to affect how we live. People should see in our lives an attractiveness. They should want what we as believers have. Paul, in giving Titus a major task in his apostolic role in Crete, uses figurative language to picture the challenge.

Titus 2:10 ...that they may adorn the doctrine of God our Savior in all things.

He is specifically applying this verbal metaphor[1] to slaves but it is clear from the tenor of his application of truth to young men, young women, older men and older women and especially the leaders of the church that the concept is being applied to all.

The verbal metaphor could be translated as,

> Titus 2:10 By these kind of attitudes and actions, slaves in every way will make the **teaching about God our Savior attractive to others.**

You can see that I have captured[2] the verbal metaphor, adorn the doctrine of God, with its emphatic meaning- will make the teaching about God our Savior attractive to others. To live victoriously in such a terrible daily situation, like slavery was, would honor God in a way that would draw people to Him. People would see that following Jesus works out in life situations — giving peace and stability where the situation promised anything else but. If it can work out in this bad situation, it can work anywhere. This passage to Christians in awful situations challenges us (western Christians especially) today, who live in relatively prosperous and easy situations. All believers should adorn the doctrine of God our Savior, that is, live daily lives in such a way as to make following Christ an attractive thing.[3]

---

[1] See **Glossary**, *metaphor*. See **Article**, *Figures and Idioms in the Bible*.

[2] *Capture* is a technical term used when talking about figures of speech being interpreted. A figure of speech or idiom is said to be captured when one can display the intended emphatic meaning of it in non-figurative simple words.

[3] While I don't have the actual data before me, I have heard it quoted (from well known Christian pollsters) by public rhetoricians, that Christians in the west, particularly in the United States, have divorce rates higher than that of secular folks. Other areas of behavior have also been mentioned which indicate that there is essentially no difference in daily living between Christians and non-Christians. I don't have hard evidence to believe this but the anecdotal evidence is strong.

Titus was strongly admonished to teach so as to change lives. His teaching was going against the cultural grain. Believers basically were living their lives not much differently from their neighbors in the culture.

Applying The Truth

Paul's admonitions to Titus to get the believers to apply truth included:

Titus

1:1   …I want them to know the truth that **leads to godliness.**

Titus 2:

2 Teach the older men to be **temperate, worthy of respect, self-controlled,** and solid in what they believe. They should **demonstrate love and endurance.**

3 Likewise, teach the older women to be **reverent in the way they live.** … No one should be able to **malign the word of God because of their daily behavior.**

6 Similarly, encourage the young men to be **self-controlled.** 7 Model for them by your own life.

9 Teach slaves to be subject to their masters in everything. They should try to please their masters and not to talk back to them.   10 Slaves should not steal from their masters. Instead slaves should show that they can be fully trusted. **By these kind of attitudes and actions, slaves in every way will make the teaching about God our Savior attractive to others.**

11 God's salvation is real now, all can see it. His salvation graciously **enables us to live well.** 12 It teaches us to say "No" to ungodliness and worldly passions. It teaches us to say, "Yes" to living self-controlled, upright and godly lives in this present age. … 14 He gave himself for us to redeem us from all wickedness and to purify for himself a people that are his very own, **eager to do what is good.**

Titus 3:

1   Remind the people to be **subject** to rulers and authorities. They should be **obedient** people and ready to **do whatever is good.**   2 They should **slander no one.** They should be **peaceable** and **considerate people. Humility** toward all should be a hallmark of their changed lives.

8 And I want you to stress these things, so that those who have trusted in God may be **careful to live out in daily life, testimonies which reflect this** *Goodnews.*

We do not know the effects of this apostolic ministry by Titus. However, we do know that Paul expected Titus to comply and for his ministry to affect the regional church in Crete.[4]

Adorning The Gospel Today

It is my opinion today, after observing many different church situations over a period of 36 years, that public ministry has very little effect on people. They neither remember much of what is said (taught or preached) on a given Sunday nor do they apply any truth from what is said. I am speaking generally. Of course, there are many exceptions to this generality.

Why is this? Let me suggest two basic reasons:

Reason 1.   Leaders do not know how to minister with Spirit-led application. Many know well how to expose truth, how to teach concepts. But few know how to minister with power what they have exposed. They do not sensitively with the Spirit see applicational breakthroughs on what they have just presented.

Paul gives good advice to Timothy for structuring public ministry.

13 Till I come, give attention to public reading of the Scriptures, to persuasive explanation (on them), and to teaching (of them).

He asserts a threefold formula for ministry: public reading of truth, explanation of it and application of it. Most public services in churches today have public reading of truth and may or may not have explanation of it but do not have any application of it. Application is hopefully left to the hearer. What is needed is a Spirit-led ministry time where the application of the Scripture is at least as much emphasized as the communication of it (the explanation).

Reason 2.   Hearers do not know they are supposed to apply truths to their lives. They need help to do this.

People in our modern church situations come to watch a performance — by the pastor and by the singing folks. They are not thinking of participating with God in the event, so as to meet God and have their lives changed. We as leaders must create values and an ambiance which teaches people to come expecting God to meet them and change their lives. And they must be conditioned to know that God will be working on changing them into the image of Christ over their lifetimes.

Practical suggestions

I want to give three suggestions that apply to the leaders of public ministry — more directly to the word ministers but also indirectly to the worship ministers.

Suggestion 1.   Learn how to bring closure to public presentations

Suggestion 2.   Have an applicational ministry time a-periodically.

---

4.   See **Article**, *Regional Churches and Plurality of Leaders*. Traditions tells us that Titus became the leader over this regional church. If that is true, his ministry must have been effective.

Suggestion 3.   Teach folks how to respond to truth by *modeling* for them, by *teaching* them about the importance of response, and by *giving them opportunity* to respond as well as *practical help* in learning to listen to and apply truth.

Let me briefly expand on each of these suggestions.

Suggestion 1. Closure

In *Having a Ministry That Lasts* I suggest to those wanting to become Bible Centered Leaders that they must work on their communication skills. One important component of a Bible Centered Leader is, one who uses the word with impact on followers. I suggest a framework for a communication event.[5] The final component of that communication model involves bring closure to the communication.

Definition   The *closure slot* is the final slot of the communication event which contains the various attempts by the communicator to move the hearers to a response (usually affective or conative)[6] that paves the way for use of the input in the future.

A communicator can learn basic skills to use in bringing about closure. These skills will usually supplement exhortation and teaching gifts. Each communicator must learn to bring closure in unique ways that fit his/her communication.[7] The point of this suggestion is that deliberate care needs to be taken to apply truth. As much time is probably needed to design good application as is needed to design the communication. And much faith is needed.

Suggestion 2. Ministry Times

Ministry times need to be deliberately built into public services.[8] Avoid too many repetitive applications such as invitations at the close. Overused methodologies usually lose their impact. I suggest a-periodic times of ministry application. Sometimes the thrust

---

5.   A communication event is made up of an attention getter slot, a lead in slot, the obligatory teaching or preaching information, a lead out slot, and a closure slot. It is the closure slot that is important for Spirit-led application to the hearts and lives of the hearers.

6.   Affect refers to the learning domain that deals with emotions and feelings. Conative refers to the learning domain that refers to the will or an appeal to decision making — a response of determination to follow through, to be committed.

7.   I have discovered, identified, practiced, and improved upon my ability to sensitively move with the Spirit in applying ideas from my communication events. For me, six different kinds of closure fit: 1. *Prayer*, either leader led or listener led; 2. *Special ministry time*, either leader focused (moving in revelatory information and power gifting), or listener focused in small groups or with special trained help who can minister in power; 3. Invitation — private, semi-private, open, public, or public with committal; 4. Application — Immediate in one-one-one interaction about an idea or specific application or small group interaction with an idea or specific application; 5. Application — Long Term Follow-Up by a challenge for development over a longer period of time or connecting to resources that will allow self-help or giving the first steps of a longer term application; 6. Blessing — individual in which a leader gets and pronounces a blessing as a word of faith for an individual or does the same thing for a group or the group exchanges blessings.

8.   What I am advocating in these suggestions applies to workshops and seminars and retreats and special meetings as well as regular on going ministries.

of an entire gathering can be dominantly ministry application. Vary your methodology and occasions for ministry application. But do make sure you have some from time-to-time.

Suggestion 3. Practical Help

Give practical helps and encourage accountability relationships for practical application. Early on, when I was being discipled, I was given two practical tools to help me learn to listen for God's speaking to me and to learn to apply truth in my life. Some self-starter types can apply things without any help. But most will not. So I suggest you provide practical tools to help. Two that I found helpful personally and which I use when I disciple others are,

1. the Listening Sheet

2. the Personal Application Sheet.

Listening sheets should be designed to fit the speaker and the hearers in a given situation. The principle involved is that people listen better if they are listening, looking for something. I will attach[9] a listening sheet that I have used in discipling others which follows that principle. But I want to stress, you should design your own to fit you or to fit the hearers you are ministering to.

My personal application sheet is very structured. To some, it seems rather mechanical. But I have found it useful. I use it in classes with mid-career leaders and they find it a refreshing change. Deliberate intent in application does not lessen the need to trust in God and be sensitive to the Spirit. In fact, it may help focus a person on what the Spirit wants to do.

To put teeth into application, a very good practical session is to suggest that folks have peer mentors who will hold them accountable for applying truth. Peer mentoring is a healthy thing that supports ministry application.

Conclusion

One thing we need today are stylish believers, those who adorn the teaching of God our Savior, that is, those who, make the **teaching about God our Savior attractive to others.**

Lets gets some stylish everyday clothes which catch the eyes of those around us.

---

[9]   See the *Personal Listening Sheet* which follows immediately after the conclusion section of this article.

SERMON OR TEACHING LISTENING SHEET

SPEAKER _____ TEXT OR PASSAGE _____

(use back of sheet for informal notes, then summarize what you have heard by answering the following questions)

1. What is he really saying? (Put the speaker's basic message into a one line summary statement)

2. Are there any illustrations worth retaining? Can I use any of his illustrations to explain truth?

3. List here any statements of truth that God shows you. Don't fail to capture any thought that God gives whether directly pertinent to what the speaker says or not.

4. Jot down the reference to any verse(s) God has impressed upon your mind. Give also the impression itself.

5. In what way(s) do you think God expects you to respond to the truth He has shown you?

PERSONAL APPLICATION WORKSHEET

Name _____

Date _____

1. List here the **TRUTH** that God is impressing upon your heart.

2. List here the **NEED** for this truth in personal terms. Give examples from recent experience showing your need for this truth.

3. List here your plans for **SPECIFIC USE** of the truth you have seen in terms of your needs.

4. List here some plan which will assure that you **FOLLOW THROUGH** on your application.

5. Claim a **PROMISE** from God for His enabling work in you for this application. Trust Him to do it.

Article 2

Apostolic Functions

Introduction

What do apostles do? Comparative studies in Ac, 1,2Ti and Tit reveal a number of functions that are symptomatic of apostles. But before looking at what apostles do, perhaps it is in order to examine some characteristics of apostolic workers such as giftedness, power bases used, leadership styles and leadership models. This will lay a good foundation for understanding apostolic functions.

Apostolic Giftedness

All apostolic workers have spiritual gifts as the focal element of their giftedness set.[10] But what spiritual gifts? First of all an apostle in this technical sense being examined in this article is one who has the gift of apostleship. Second, such leaders are often multi-gifted and include various power and word gifts. The below definitions refer to giftedness seen in apostles.

Definition   The *gift of apostleship* refers to a special leadership capacity to move with authority from God to create new ministry structures (churches and para-church) to meet needs and to develop and appoint leadership in these structures. **Its central thrust is Creating New Ministry.**

Definition   *Power gifts* refer to a category of spiritual gifts which authenticate the reality of God by demonstrating God's intervention in today's world. These include: tongues, interpretation of tongues, discernings of spirits, kinds of healings, kinds of power (miracles), prophecy, faith, word of wisdom, word of knowledge.

Definition   *Word gifts* refer to a category of spiritual gifts used to clarify and explain about God. These help us understand about God including His nature, His purposes and how we can relate to Him and be a part of His purposes. These include: teaching, exhortation, pastoring, evangelism, apostleship, prophecy, ruling, and sometimes word of wisdom,

---

[10]   *Giftedness set* refers to natural abilities, acquired skills, and spiritual gifts which a leader has as resources to use in ministry. *Focal element* refers to the dominant component of a giftedness set—either natural abilities, acquired skills, or spiritual gifts.

word of knowledge, and faith (a word of). All leaders have at least one of these and often several of these.

Frequently, in addition to power gifts which authenticate and validate an apostle's ministry, an apostle will have the gift of faith—which enables a strong projection of vision on others.[11]

What Power Bases Enforce Apostolic Functions?

Apostles use various power bases[12] to enforce their leadership influence. While, most would recognize spiritual authority as the ideal, they frequently use other forms since they often are dealing with immature followers in new works. A prioritized list of power forms seen in apostolic ministry would include personal authority, competent authority, coercive authority, induced authority—all laced with a sense of spiritual authority. Networking power often buttresses power used by apostolic workers.

What Leadership Styles Flow From the Power Bases?

Apostles frequently use highly directive leadership styles. A prioritized list of leadership styles seen in apostolic ministry includes: apostolic style, father-initiator, father-guardian, confrontation, indirect conflict, obligation persuasion, imitator. Highly indirect styles are used basically only with loyal trusted leaders.

What Leadership Models Dominate Apostolic Work?

Apostolic workers dominantly are driven by values underlying the stewardship model and the harvest model. Apostolic workers have a strong sense of calling and desire to accomplish for God. And for the most part this is directed toward the outward functions of the Great Commission as seen in the Harvest model. Servant, Shepherd, and Intercessor models are less seen in apostolic ministries.

Apostolic workers are dominantly task-oriented leaders with strong inspirational leadership. Usually apostolic workers lack relational leadership skills and must depend on others to supplement this or suffer the consequences of conflict, confrontation, and large back doors in their ministry as emerging workers leave them.

What Are Some Apostolic Functions?

Table 2.1 below lists seven major headings for apostolic functions observed in the N.T. Church Leadership Era. While there may be other apostolic functions these at least are highlighted in the Ac and epistles. I subsume a number of minor apostolic functions under these higher level categories.

[11.] Apostolic workers are strong leaders who use highly directive leadership styles. Those with the gift of faith obtain vision from God and can exercise strong inspirational leadership to motivate and recruit to the vision. They attract followers to their cause.

[12.] Wrong sees power in terms of a power holder, a power subject and the means the power holder uses to gain compliance from the power subject. Power base deals with the means. Force, Manipulation, Authority, and Persuasion are the general categories containing various power bases. See Dennis Wrong, **Power— Its Forms, Bases, and Uses**. San Francisco, CA: Harper and Row, 1979.

Table 2.1   Apostolic Functions

Function	N.T. Indication	Description/ Explanation
1. Start New Ministries	Paul and Barnabas, Ac 13; Paul Ac 16, 18	Paul and Barnabas inaugurate the missionary movement. Paul breaks open a new work in Europe and other new works in Asia. These are usually creative new approaches to ministry which challenge traditional approaches. Power ministry is often used to validate the apostle's ministry and authenticate God's existence, power, and presence. When starting new ministries whether churches, movements, organizations, apostolic workers attract followers due to their personality, competency, and power seen in ministry. Paul tried to start indigenized churches.[a] Most apostolic workers are driven by values underlying the Harvest Leadership model, though these values may be implicit.
2. Appoint Leaders	Paul and Barnabas do (1st missionary trip). Paul does this on all his missionary trips. Titus did this in Crete. Timothy does this in Ephesus.	Apostolic workers raise up leadership including selecting, developing and giving training that will develop these workers; they impart gifts as Paul did with Timothy; they appoint leaders in works. In fact, the basic message of Titus (and in 1,2Ti) concerns leadership selection and appointment. The basic message of the book of Tit (**Setting The Church In Order** involves the appointing of qualified leaders, requires leaders who are sound in teaching and who model a Christian life style, and necessitates leaders who exhort others to practical Christian living.) exemplifies this apostolic function and function 3.
3. Establish Works	Paul does this in Phillipi, Corinth, Ephesus, Rome and Crete.	Apostolic workers are concerned that ministries they have begun mature in the faith. They will send workers to solve problems, help develop leaders, and to teach and help followers mature. They will send helpful materials. They will exert influence through relationships to keep works going and growing. But establishing is secondary to creating new works. See the book of Tit.
4. Intercede for Works, both new and old	Paul does this for the churches he established.	Paul had a real burden for the churches he founded and worked with. *Beside outward circumstances pressing me, there is the inward burden, i.e. the anxiety and care, I feel daily for all the churches.* 2Co 11:28. Almost all apostolic leaders will have many values of the Intercessor Leader Model and will feel the responsibility of prayer for the works they associate with.
5. Combat Heresy[b] (both orthodoxy and orthopraxy)	Paul does this somewhat in Corinth and Crete and much in Ephesus. See also the Jerusalem conference, Ac 15.	1Ti is the comprehensive example of this apostolic function (four lines of heresy dealt with). Paul deals with potential heresy both in orthopraxy and orthodoxy. The practice of Christianity as well as the beliefs of Christianity can be heretical. Apostles are concerned with this. And apostles and so-called apostles themselves, frequently not accountable to others, can easily be the source of heresy. See 1,2Co.

6. Resource New Ministries and Old Ones	Paul and Barnabas Ac 11; Paul in 1Co, 2Co.	Apostolic workers raise finances for workers like Paul did for Timothy (1Co 16, 1Ti), Stephanus (1Co 16). They help out old works in special need. Paul had Philippian church giving to other churches. Had Corinthian churches giving to needs in Jerusalem. They also provide workers to help out in situations like Timothy, Titus, etc. Part of the resourcing includes knowledge, wisdom and findings from related experience. They also help those with resources understand both their freedom and responsibility to use these for the kingdom (1Ti).
7. Test New Ministries for Validity	Barnabas Ac 11	Barnabas is sent on a ministry task from the apostles in Jerusalem to test the Christianity in Antioch. Titus' ministry tasks had somewhat of this flavor in Crete as well.

a. An indigenized church has its own leadership from its own people and is organized to survive independently of outside leadership from other cultures and operates with appropriate forms, rites, and ministry fitting to its own culture.

b. Heresy refers to deviation from a standard, whether in belief (orthodoxy) or practice (orthopraxy). e.g. See 1Ti where both are present in the Ephesian church (as prophesied in Ac 20:30).

Conclusions

Apostolic functions involve the critical job of expanding ministry into new situations. Most apostolic workers identify strongly with values of the *Harvest Leadership model*. Without this expansion Christianity would die. Apostles exhibit strong gifts and strong leadership. Along with this strength goes the corresponding weakness of independence. Interdependence is needed—especially for accountability. Most apostolic workers do not have accountability for their ministries and hence abuses of power and heresies, both orthodoxic and orthopraxic, occur. A strong task-oriented leadership bias by most apostolic workers often lacks the needed balance of a relational leadership bias. Apostolic workers tend to build empires which they over control in a micro-managing manner. Needed is the indigenization function modeled by Paul, a very strong apostolic worker, which releases leadership and allows new leadership to function. But hats off to apostolic workers! They carry out the Great Commission. They want to reach the world!

See gifts of healings; discernings of spirits; exhortation; evangelism; faith; prophecy; ruling; teaching; word of knowledge; word of wisdom; coercive authority; competent authority; induced authority; personal authority ; spiritual authority; leadership styles; apostolic style; father-initiator; father-guardian; imitator; confrontation style; indirect conflict; obligation persuasion; harvest model, stewardship model, shepherd model, servant model, intercessor model; **Glossary**. *See* **Articles**, *Jesus-Five Leadership Models: Shepherd, Harvest, Steward, Servant, Intercessor; Developing Giftedness; Spiritual Gift Clusters; Spiritual Gifts, Giftedness, and Development. Pauline Leadership Styles; Value Driven Leadership. See For* **Further Study Bibliography**, *Clinton's* **Leadership Styles.**

Apostolic Functions — Comparison of Titus and Timothy

Introduction

In a previous article I identified 7 apostolic functions.[13] As I worked on the Titus leadership commentary I identified a new function that stood out because of the Cretan situation. I also identified three phases of apostolic ministry.[14] So this article is written not only to update the former article but also to compare which of these functions is seen in Titus ministry on Crete and Timothy's ministry in Ephesus and to draw out some comparative observations. All of the apostolic functions are seen in Paul's various ministries which involved different stints in all three phases of apostolic ministry.[15]

Apostolic Functions Updated

Below in Table 3.1 are given the previous 7 apostolic functions and the new function seen in Titus, function 8 — Contextualization.

Table 3.1 Apostolic Functions — Paul's, Timothy's and Titus

Function	Apostolic Thrust	Supplementary Gifts
1. Start New Works	pioneer new work	evangelism, power gifts
2. Appoint Leaders	leadership selection	basically an apostolic gifting function; sometimes word of knowledge, word of wisdom
3. Establish Works	leadership development; edification ministry with believers	teaching, exhortation, ruling
4. Intercede for Works, both new and old	release spiritual power in situations	faith, discernings of spirits, sometimes word of knowledge or word of wisdom
5. Combat Heresy[a] (both orthodoxy and orthopraxy)	correct and stabilize a deteriorating situation	exhortation, prophecy, teaching

---

[13.] See **Article**, *Apostolic Functions*.

[14.] See **Article**, *Apostolic Giftedness — Mulitple Gifted Leaders*.

[15.] Paul does have ministry in all three but dominantly in phase 1 ministries.

6. Resource New and and Old Ministries	resource apostolic ministries; give help to needy church situations	not clear
7. Test New Ministries for Validity	authenticate God's work	not clear
8. Contextualize[b] the Gospel to Cross-cultural Situations	apply truth to complex cultural situations	teaching, exhortation, sometimes prophecy

a. Heresy refers to deviation from a standard, whether in belief (orthodoxy) or practice (orthopraxy). e.g. See 1Ti where both are present in the Ephesian church (as prophesied in Ac 20:30).

b. See **Article**, *Basic Contextualion Principles*.

Comparison of Timothy and Titus's Apostolic Ministries

Three phases of apostolic ministry will work on differing apostolic functions:

Phase I. Ground Breaking Apostolic Work (like Paul in Thessalonica)

Phase II. Edification Work (like Titus in Crete)

Phase III. Corrective Work (like Timothy in Ephesus)

Table 3.2 Comparison of Apostolic Functions — Timothy and Titus

Function	Apostolic Thrust	Seen In Ministry
1. Start New Works	pioneer new work	neither
2. Appoint Leaders	leadership selection	seen in both
3. Establish Works	leadership development; edification ministry with believers	seen in both
4. Intercede for Works, both new and old	release spiritual power in situations	Paul models this in Timothy and commands Timothy to do so. Not seen in Titus.
5. Combat Heresy[a] (both orthodoxy and orthopraxy)	correct and stabilize a deteriorating situation	Timothy is combating at least 4 lines of heresy; Titus 2.
6. Resource New Ministries and Old Ones	resource apostolic ministries; give help to needy church situations	Paul does this in Titus. Titus does to (also did this at Corinth) gives Timothy advice on doing this in Ephesian situation.
7. Test New Ministries for Validity	authenticate God's work	neither
8. Contextualize the Gospel to Cross-cultural Situations	apply truth to complex cultural situations	Titus must do this. Cretan cultural has many values degrading from Christian testimony

a. Heresy refers to deviation from a standard, whether in belief (orthodoxy) or practice (orthopraxy). e.g. See 1Ti where both are present in the Ephesian church (as prophesied in Ac 20:30).

Conclusion

Apostolic ministries will vary due to local cultural situations and gifting of the apostolic leaders as well as the type of apostolic ministry being done, Phase 1, or 2, or 3. Timothy does apostolic functions 2, 3, 4, 5 and 6. Titus does apostolic functions 2, 3, 5, 6 and 8.

Timothy's situation was complex because it involved turning around a situation that had developed over 20 years. A major problem involved turning the leadership around — getting rid of leaders who were involved in heresy — both orthodoxic and orthopraxic. Four lines of heresy had to be combated.

Titus ministry was complicated in that he had to introduce values into a Cretan culture which had many counter values. His was a primitive situation in which new believers had a relatively small church base to work from. He too had to do leadership selection — to get leaders of integrity to help him model the needed changes.

Here is an observation on both their ministries. Neither were using or admonished to use power gifts. However, both were admonished to use the gifts they had with power — dominantly teaching, exhortation, and probably prophetical gifts.

Apostolic Giftedness — Multiple Gifted Leaders

Introduction

Breaking open new ground, like planting a church in a cross-cultural situation, will require a number of gifts. This can be done by a team which has the necessary gifts comprising the total needed in the situation.[16] One of the gifts needed for such new work is the apostleship gift. Another is the gift of evangelism. Sometimes power gifts will be needed in order to authenticate the work as being of God. As the work begins to succeed other gifts will be needed like teaching, exhortation, and pastoring. As a work ages it usually experiences ecclesiastical entropy — plateauing or worse, diverting from truth. Prophetical gifts, teaching gifts and exhortation gifts are desperately needed to embrace and correct this situation. Examples in the New Testament show apostolic ministries arising to help in all these situations.

Usually an apostolic leader will have multiple gifts, a gift-mix.[17] Teammates will come along side to provide other needed gifts, the apostolic support gifts.[18] In reading any of the Pauline epistles[19] or especially leadership books like Titus or 1, 2 Timothy or the book of Acts one needs an understanding of apostolic giftedness in order to read with an enlightened perspective. Such a perspective might also help to prevent certain excesses in apostolic ministries which may lead to leaders not finishing well. This article gives a quick

---

[16.] Different sets of gifts will be needed in different situations. More on this later.

[17.] *Gif-mix* refers to the set of spiritual gifts that a leader is exercising at a given time in his/her ministry. The broader term is *giftedness set* which includes natural abilities, acquired skills and spiritual gifts. In this article, we are restricting ourselves to spiritual gifts. See **Article**, *Developing Giftedness*. See **Glossary**, *spiritual gifts, gift-mix, giftedness set*, each of the individual spiritual gifts named in this article.

[18.] From 1973 to 1983 I did Biblical research on *spiritual gifts* and taught on spiritual gifts in a number of teaching roles. I published a book, **Spiritual Gifts**, which defined the gifts, from an exegetical and comparative study of them in the New Testament. From 1983 to 1993 we (my son began helping me in the research) did empirical research on giftedness in leaders. Around 500 contemporary leaders were studied. Out of that research came our present understanding of giftedness, a broader and more comprehensive treatment of how a leader operates. Of special interest was the whole notion of developing spiritual gifts. This research is written up in **Unlocking Your Giftedness** and forms the basis for much of this article.

[19.] Paul's epistles should be studied not only for content but to see what Paul is doing and how he is doing. Paul exercises apostolic ministry throughout his missionary career. An understanding of apostolic ministry and its giftedness is instructive for appreciating Paul's leadership.

overview of apostolic giftedness. Three phases of apostolic ministry will need differing sets of gifts:

Phase I. Ground Breaking Apostolic Work (like Paul and Barnabas in Thessalonica)

Phase II. Edification Work (like Titus in Crete)

Phase III. Corrective Work (like Timothy in Ephesus)

Leaders — Word Gifted

Apostleship, prophecy, evangelism, pastoring and teaching are often called the leadership gifts. Because of their nature and function, the exercising of these gifts are directly connected to exercising leadership influence. Some would not call these gifts but would call them offices. Because of the way that these gifts are listed in Ephesians 4, it is easy to see how this viewpoint is formed. In the Ephesians 4 passage, we believe that Paul is using metonymy as he wrote the text on spiritual gifts. We believe that he is referring to individuals who are gifted in apostleship, prophecy, evangelism, pastoring and teaching not just to apostles, prophets, evangelists, pastors and teachers who hold that office in the church.[20]

Is it possible to operate with these gifts without the *office* or official position? We believe that it is possible. In fact, we have observed many leaders operating in these gifts without the *official* title or position. Often, those positions were not available to these individuals because of things like denominational tradition, gender issues, or certain types of circumstances in their past. The fact that they were not in the position didn't stop them from exercising the leadership influence associated with the gift.

It is primarily these leadership gifts that have responsibility for maturing the body. Evidently they were needed to mature the church as described in Ephesians 4. Even if you don't believe them to be gifts you can ask yourself the question, what did each of these offices contribute to the maturing of the body? Even if the offices don't exist officially today, what functions did they represent? These functions will be needed today to mature the body. So what are these functions? They are essentially the thrust of certain spiritual gifts. Those central thrusts are essentially the functions that are needed to mature the body. Look at them!

1. The Apostolic Function — **CREATING NEW MINISTRY**
2. The Prophetic Function — **TO PROVIDE CORRECTION OR PERSPECTIVE ON A SITUATION**

---

[20]   We have some difficulties with the whole idea of these being just offices. What is the office of pastor? What kind of gifts would a person in that office have? What is the office of teacher? What kind of gifts would a person in that office have? What is the office of evangelist? What kind of gifts would a person in that office have? What is the office of prophet? What kind of gifts would a person in that office have? What is the office of Apostleship? What kind of gifts would a person in that office have? Why would these offices be in the church? If to equip and lead the body to maturity, is that not needed today? Has the church reached the full maturity described in Ephesians 4 so that we can do away with these offices and the gifts entailed in them? Why would some of them disappear and not all of them? Are just some of them needed to take the body to maturity?

3. The Evangelistic Function —   **INTRODUCING OTHERS TO THE GOSPEL.**
4. The Pastoring Function —   **CARING FOR THE GROWTH OF FOLLOWERS.**
5. The Teaching Function —   **TO CLARIFY TRUTH**

And to these we have added two other influence gifts — exhortation and ruling.

6. The Exhortive Function —   **TO APPLY BIBLICAL TRUTH**
7. The Ruling Function —   **INFLUENCING OTHERS TOWARD VISION.**

It is our contention that God is still following the Ephesians 4 mandate of equipping the body and developing it toward maturity. And these kinds of functions are still needed.

Implications

1. All seven of the functions listed above are needed to bring a balanced maturity to the body.
2. In general, over an extended time, no one of the functions should be overemphasized to the exclusion of others.
3. For a given contextual situation and for a given time, one or more of the functions may need to be overemphasized to meet crucial needs.

Phase I Apostolic Ministry — Initial Breakthroughs

The Acts of the Apostles traces Paul's pioneering ministry in a number of places including Cyprus, Iconium, Lystra, Derbe, Phillipi, Thessalonica, Berea, Athens, Corinth, and Ephesus. In these pioneer ministries Paul demonstrates apostolic gifting supplemented with various power gifts (word of knowledge, working of powers, gifts of healings, discernings of spirits, faith) to authenticate divine backing and various word gifts (dominantly teaching and exhortation with evangelism, occasionally prophecy) to start the edification process. Paul was very multi-gifted and needed to be since he is basically ushering in the church leadership era. He is an exemplar.

In the initial stages of a new work, power gifts validate the word gifts and bring about breakthroughs. Various word gifts initiate the growth process.

Phase II Apostolic Ministry — Edification Breakthroughs

Once a work gets going, apostolic leadership will usually transition leaders from the local setting in to do the edification work (especially pastoral gifting and ruling) needed to stabilize the embryonic work. In some situations, where much contextualization of the Gospel is needed, apostolic leadership will be necessary to get edification breakthroughs. This was the case for Titus in Crete. We do not know for certain Titus' giftedness set. But we do know that the demands that Paul gave him required strong teaching and exhortation gifts as well as the ruling gift. His apostolic gift gave him authoritative backing to contextualize the Gospel into the Crete situation with its values so counter to living out Gospel truth.

Phase III. Apostolic Ministry — Correction Breakthroughs

Timothy's work in Ephesus exemplifies apostolic ministry that is corrective in nature. The Ephesian church had stagnated, in fact, deteriorated following along the lines of Paul's prophetic warning to given to them in Acts 20. It was about 20 years old and had its own indigenous leaders at the time Timothy is sent in to correct the situation.[21] A number of heresies (orthopraxic and orthodoxic) needed to be countered. Timothy did this. Again we do not know for certain what Timothy's gift-mix was but we do know what was needed in addition to apostleship: teaching, exhortation, prophecy.

Apostleship Functions And Giftedness Needed

Elsewhere in two articles,[22] I have described some apostolic functions. Below I list these functions and suggest the apostleship gift and supplementary gifts needed to probably carry out the functions.

Function	Apostolic Thrust	Supplementary Gifts
1. Start New Ministries	pioneer new work	evangelism, power gifts
2. Appoint Leaders	leadership selection	basically an apostolic gifting function; sometimes word of knowledge, word of wisdom
3. Establish Works	leadership development; edification ministry with believers	teaching, exhortation, ruling
4. Intercede for Works, both new and old	release spiritual power in situations	faith, discernings of spirits, sometimes word of knowledge or word of wisdom
5. Combat Heresy[a] (both orthodoxy and orthopraxy)	correct and stabilize a deteriorating situation	exhortation, prophecy, teaching
6. Resource New Ministries and Old Ones	resource apostolic ministries; give help to needy church situations	not clear
7. Test New Ministries for Validity	authenticate God's work	not clear
8. Contextualize the Gospel to Cross-cultural Situations	apply truth to complex cultural situations	teaching, exhortation, sometimes prophecy

a. *Heresy* refers to deviation from a standard, whether in belief (orthodoxy) or practice (orthopraxy). e.g. See 1Ti where both are present in the Ephesian church (as prophesied in Ac 20:30).

In the following discussion I will suggest a basic core that is usually seen throughout apostolic ministry. Then I will show how it may be modified to fit the three phases of apostolic ministry. At this point, having discussed the apostolic functions and related giftedness, I want to suggest that frequently apostolic leaders easily recruit people to come alongside and work with them in an apostolic ministry. Such team members will usually

---

21. See **Article**, *Ephesian Church — Its Time-Line.*

22. See **Articles**, *Apostolic Functions*; Apostolic *Functions — Comparison of Titus and Timothy.*

be drawn for two very different reasons. Two patterns discovered in our giftedness research describes these reasons:

1. The Like-Attracts-Like Pattern
2. The Needs Pattern

The *like-attracts-like pattern* is a general giftedness pattern very helpful to a leader in assessing leadership selection and development. It asserts that potentially gifted emerging leaders are attracted to leaders because of gifts which they already have in potential or will receive. *The Needs Pattern*, much more rarely seen, asserts that emerging leaders recognize some glaring omissions in an apostolic leader in terms of giftedness and are drawn to help solve those needs. These emerging leaders have the needed gifts to supplement and support the apostolic ministry.

Definition   *Apostolic support* gifts refer to gifts that are needed in an apostolic work and are supplied by leaders drawn to the ministry.

This relieves the pressure on a given apostolic leader. Such a leader then does not have to have all the gifts needed in a situation.

Apostleship Giftedness — The Core

We can display a person's gift-mix and show the relationship between the various spiritual gifts that he/she operates in.[23] All leaders we have studied are multi-gifted. In our research we have commonly seen that certain gifts frequently supplement other gifts. Below I give the core Venn diagram for an apostolic worker. Then I modify it to fit the three phases of apostolic work.

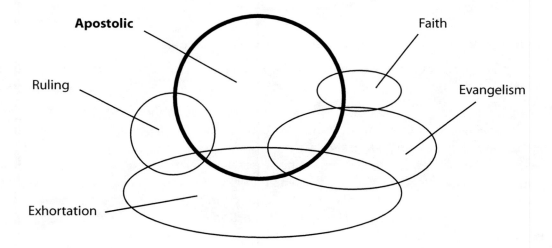

Figure 4.1 Venn Diagram — Apostolic Core

[23.] These are called Venn diagrams. See chapter 9 in **Unlocking Your Giftedness** for a detailed explanation of a Venn diagram and guidelines for constructing.

Of course in team situations, one or more of the gifts shown in the apostolic core may be dominantly supplied to the situation by some other team member. Frequently, in our giftedness research, the gift of faith accompanied the apostleship gift — especially in Phase 1 ministry.

For a Phase 2 ministry, like Titus' ministry in Crete, the apostolic core would be modified somewhat. The evangelism gift would usually be dropped off. In its place would be the teaching gift. Again, any of the peripheral gifts could be supplied by a team member. The *faith gift* may or may not be seen. The *ruling gift* takes on more of an influence as indicated by the larger bold faced line. Actually the book of Titus indicates a strong exhortation and teaching gift is needed.

Figure 4.2 Venn Diagram — Apostolic Core Modified for Phase 2

For a Phase 3 ministry like Timothy's ministry in Ephesus, the core would be modified again.

In the next diagram, Figure 4.3, notice the strong exhortation and/or prophetic gift. This is needed to correct the drift from known truth or practiced truth and to regain momentum. The teaching gift has to take on heightened use due to the clarification of heresy. The ruling gift drops off somewhat since there is indigenous leadership in place. However, leadership selection is usually needed to transition in leaders that can get the situation back on track. Old leaders, those immersed in the heresy and the stagnation will probably have to be moved on. The apostolic function of appointing leaders will be really needed.

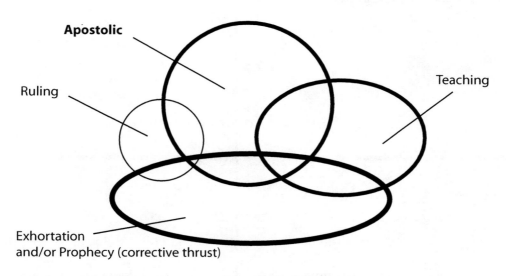

Figure 4.3 Venn Diagram — Apostolic Core Modified for Phase 3

Conclusion

Paul, Timothy, and Titus model for us apostolic ministries. Paul was powerfully multi-gifted as can easily be demonstrated from Luke's historical narrative in Acts. The gift-mix of Timothy and Titus is not demonstrated. But from the functions they had to perform in their ministries, certain things about gifts can be inferred.

Perspective is needed on apostolic ministry and apostolic giftedness. In the fervor of a powerful movement, like the present day emphasis on apostolic leaders, it is easy to be carried away pragmatically by tides that tug away from Biblical anchors. This article is a start to analyzing apostolic ministry and giftedness. The varying gift needs in terms of the basic three phases provides some anchors.[24] The concept of apostolic support gifts, another anchor, takes some of the pressure off of an apostolic worker. They do not have to have it all.

---

[24]. In terms of the barriers to finishing well it is easy for present day apostolic ministries to fall into the traps of five of the six barriers: abuse of power, financial impropriety, family neglect, sexual impropriety, pride. This basically relates to lack of accountability of powerful apostolic leaders.

Basic Ideas on Contextualization

Introduction

In previous material[25] I have defined the basic notion of contextualization,

Definition   *Contextualization* is the process of taking something meaningful in one context and making it relevant to a new context. e.g. the Christian movement which began in a Jewish context had to be reinterpreted by Paul to a non-Jewish context, the Gentiles.

In Crete, Biblical or revealed truth on how followers of God should live, has to be applied to the Cretan situation. That is contextualization. The book of Titus gives insights about how Christian living should look in this culture. Particularly some of the changes that must be made , are emphasized. That is, if God is to be revealed in lives so that the culture can be impacted. Most of this contextualization is at value level and applying to orthopraxy, not doctrinal. However, much doctrinal truth is interwoven into the rationale for godly behavior.

Theoretical Contextualization

For a fuller treatment of contextualization I recommend Gilliland's (editor)classical treatment of it in *The Word Among Us.*[26] In that work I suggest some guidelines in transferring leadership theory from one culture to another. Graphically the model for contextualizing is shown in Figure 5.1.

---

25.   See **Topic 9. Contextualization** in the Titus Overview. See also comments on verses in Titus (1:6; 2:2,3; 3:1).

26.   See *The Word Among Us — Contextualizing Theology for Mission Today,* Dean S. Gilliland, editor, 1989, Dallas: Word Publishing.

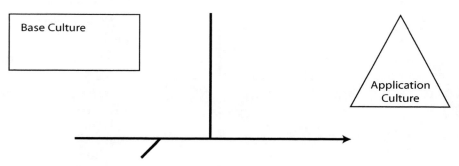

Transferring things from one culture to another:
Dynamics Involved
- appropriateness
- relevance
- modifications
- feedback
- ownership

Figure 5.1   Three Elements in the Contextualization Problem

When we talk about contextualization in Crete, with Titus' apostolic ministry, we are talking about taking Biblical truth, from the base culture in which it was applied in the Bible, and transferring it into the application culture, Cretan culture.

Several questions reflect the dynamics involved in such a transfer.

1. Are the concepts (biblical truth) being transferred appropriate for the application culture?
2. Does it meet a need?
3. What modifications are needed to make it appropriate and relevant?
4. Does its use in the application culture give feedback that may affect the ideas being transferred?

Thus one basic issue of contextualization is the possible transfer and necessary modification of conceptual ideas from the base culture to the application culture.

In terms of dynamics, how does Paul's contextualization efforts stack up when he tells Titus to apply Gospel truth to the Cretan situation.

How about appropriateness? when Paul seeks to transfer Biblical truth, in the Cretan example — usually truth he has written to other churches previously, Paul assumes appropriateness. As a general rule, in the Bible when something is seen to be applied to multicultural situations, different peoples, and over different time spans, one can assume that it is appropriate (moving toward absolutes). That is the case with the applicational/ behavioral truth that Paul apples to the Cretan situation.

How about relevance? Paul demonstrates his thorough knowledge of the Cretan culture when he describes it and when he picks behavioral issues to confront. In Paul's mind the truth he is applying is relevant and desperately needed if the church is to have any impact on its surrounding culture.

How about modifications or feedback? These dynamics are not addressed in the letter, at least we don't have any indications or implications that they are.

How about ownership? This is the critical dynamic for Titus. He must get leaders and the whole spectrum of followers (young men, young women, older men, older women) to buy into these transformational life changes. Ownership, the practical aspects of contextualizing usually presents the greatest challenge to contextualization. Paul gives Titus lots of ideas about this including modeling and teaching it with power.

In the Cretan situation false teachers are introducing non-valid Jewish forms into the newly forming Cretan Christian culture. Paul refutes these. All of his ministry has been involved with the notion of contextualization. Paul was chosen as the major person who would move Christian truth from a Jewish movement into various Gentile cultures. Paul was bi-lingual/bi-cultural. He was trained in both Hebrew and Greek thought. He was gifted with revelatory gifts. He was the *idea person* to contextualize God's redemptive truth so that it could reach out to the whole world. He has experienced the truth that he applies. He knows its power. He has seen it work in various cultures.

Some Contextualization Issues in Crete

Paul is concerned with the impact of this regional church in Crete. He wants it to have a corporate testimony that impacts Cretan society. He is therefore concerned with the transformational process of the Gospel being worked out in lives. The whole *adorning the gospel idea* is applied across the board to the members of this regional church. Table 1 shows some of the issues in Crete that Paul felt should be addressed by Biblical truth. Remember, Paul has seen this Gospel change lives all over the Roman empire in various cultures (see especially 2 Co 5:17 for a statement of the transforming nature of the Gospel). He knows the power of the Gospel to transform lives (Ro 6-8; see 1 Co 6:9-11). He knows the work of the Holy Spirit in folks who have experienced the Spirit's renewing work (Tit 3:5-8). Paul knows that God will work in these lives. This experience leads him to address issues at Crete. He commands Titus to confront these issues. Table 5.1 identifies a number of issues that Paul addressed.

Table 5.1   Issues in Crete that Paul Addressed

Topic	Location	Addressed Elsewhere
General — Godliness	Tit 1:1 and throughout	Php — Paul models this; Eph 4-6; Ro 12-15; 1 Co throughout; Gal 4-6
Integrity in leadership especially as reflected in numerous qualities in the culture: loyalty; leadership in the home; overbearing attitude of leaders; control of temper; control of self with regard to acoholic beverages; honesty; guileless; generosity/ hospitable; lover of good things; self-controlled in general; disciplined life	Tit 1:6-9	1Ti 3; his own personal model — see especially Ac 24:16; see also Php 4:8,9; Eph 5
legalism being introduced by Judiazer converts	Tit 1:10-11; 3:9	See also Gal and 1 Ti where this kind of problem was dealt with

lying, drawn by evil things, lazy, not in control of physical appetites	Tit 1:12	See Eph 4 especially on tongue; see 1 Co 8-10 and Ro 14 on disputed practices and self-control
older men: temperate, self-control, worthy of respect; demonstrating love; perseverance — staying with the Christian life	Tit 2:1	general qualities addressed elsewhere; see godliness above
older women/ younger women: godly daily testimonies; not slandering others — gossiping; not addicted to wine; exercising self-control; purity in marriage relationship; model good homemaking; kindness; submissive spirit; older women to model these qualities for younger women	Tit 2:3-5	general qualities addressed elsewhere; see godliness above
younger men: self-control, especially sexual passion;	Tit 2:6,7	see especially 1 Ti 4-6 advice to Timothy
slaves; subjection (non-rebellious); not to steal; be trustworthy;	Tit 2:9,10	see Eph 5 and model of Onesimus in Phm
all believers subjection to governmental authority; not slandering others; humility as a major characteristic	Tit 3:1,2	Ro 13

I have only briefly touched *places elsewhere*, column 3, that show where Paul has given these same truths he is applying at Crete. The point I am making is that this truth Paul is applying is done so in multi-cultural contexts and therefore has validity in terms of the appropriateness dynamic of contextualization.

Some Contextualization Principles — Three Overview Guidelines

When we come to study any of the epistles that Paul has written, we can never forget that we are studying truth already applied to some given culture. We must use our hermeneutics to understand what was said and the truth of it as applied to that specific situation. Out of that we then contextualize how that truth fits our own situations. I have described the hermeneutics I use to do that in other material.[27] I have also described how I get at the principles of truth in other material.[28] Three basic overview guidelines to use in contextualizing biblical truth include:

1. Use sound hermeneutics to identify the transcultural principles from the given Bible material, applied already to some culture. This is the base culture[29] (preliminary for getting at relevance, modifications dynamics).

[27.] See *Having A Ministry That Lasts*, Appendix G which details my hermeneutical system. See also individual self-study manuals available from Barnabas Publishers: *Word Studies; Parables; Hebrew Poetry; Figures and Idioms.*

[28.] See *Leadership Perspectives.* See also **Article**, *Principles of Truth.*

[29.] One of the great works dealing with transcultural issues of Bible material is C.H. Kraft's, *Christianity in Culture*, Orbis Books.

2. Recognize the need for whatever of this truth applies to your current situation, the application culture (appropriateness dynamic).[30]

3. Seek to communicate it in an impactful way to your culture — the application culture (ownership dynamic).

I have identified some basic observations on contextualization. Some of these are just observations. Some are principles. And some are values.

Leadership Principles / Values Suggested by this concept:

a. Contextualization involves the application of Biblical truths given in some Biblical culture to a specific culture in which the leader is operating.

b. When contextualizing Biblical truth to a cultural situation, aberrant values in the situation should be explicitly identified and compared or contrasted with their Biblical counterparts which have also been explicitly identified.

c. Not all aberrant issues need to be dealt with at once. In a given situation an apostolic leader can usually identify those which are core — heretical, denying the Gospel message (orthopraxically, or orthodoxically), and those which are peripheral — problematic and needing attention but not necessarily heretical. The prior issues are dealt with immediately. Peripheral come later.

d. Strong leadership will be needed in order to confront situations where change is needed.

e. Contextualization needs to be done as early as possible in the life of a church. The longer a church (Ephesus church — Timothy situation) holds to and models cultural values at odds with Biblical truth, the harder it is to change. If Biblical values are contextualized and introduced early on (the Crete situation) in the church situation (everything is new anyway) the easier it will be to ground the church in Biblical truth (1 Ti 3:15).

f. The notion of core and peripheral values is helpful in determining which values must be addressed first. See **Articles**, *Starting Point Plus Process; Principles of Truth.*

g. Contextualization of doctrinal truth should be interwoven into the rationale for orthopraxic issues.

---

[30] See my materials on deriving principles of truth in **Leadership Perspectives**.

Conclusion

Let me summarize some of what I have been saying. You must recognize contextualization issues and how to deal with them in your own ministry. You have to be aware of the notion of base cultures (in the Bible and your cultural interpretation of the Bible) and your application culture. You should know your application culture well. Then, make sure you:

1. Identify carefully the base cultural truth which you need to transfer.

2. Compare this base cultural truth with the applicational culture form of it or its negation of it.

3. Make sure that the base cultural truth is defanged of its inappropriate cultural overhangs, that is, make sure the base cultural truth has been generalized for cross-cultural application.

4. Modify the base cultural truth so that it is generalized and appropriate for various cultures.

5. Recognize the ownership problems in applying the base cultural truth into the applicational culture.

6. Recognize the various levels of the different truths you are transferring. Choose the core issues first, rather than peripheral. Core and periphery will vary due to the situational needs in the Application culture.

If you live in the United States, you will be dealing with major issues in the future, driven by our culture (increasingly less biblically informed): like euthanasia; genetics/ ethics; abortion; many gender issues; racial reconciliation issues; power issues — control of information; financial issues — church and state; and many others that I can not think about as I write this. My point is you will have to go to the Bible and find out what are the transcultural truths that apply (what base cultures given in) and how can you apply them to your applicational culture. Thank God, we have models in the Bible for contextualizing truth.

Article 6

Bible Centered Leader

Introduction

Where would you go in the O.T. if you wanted to look at a description of a Bible centered leader? Where would you go in the N.T. if you wanted to look at material about a Bible Centered Leader. Here is where I would go.

Table 6.1   Bible Centered Material O.T./ N.T.

Old Testament	Psalm 1, 19, 119
New Testament	2 Timothy 2:15; 3:16-17

Glance quickly at Psalm 1 and feel its impact about how important it is to base a life on God's word.[31]

1. O, how happy is the person
   who hasn't based his conduct on the principles of the ungodly
   Nor taken his stand in the way of sinners,
   Nor taken his place with an assembly of scoffers!

2. But it is in the law of the Lord that he takes his delight;
   And on His law he keeps thinking day and night.

3. And he will be like a tree planted by the side of streams of water,
   That yields its fruit in its season;
   Its leaves also do not wither;
   And whatsoever he attempts, succeeds

4. Such is not the case with the ungodly,
   But they are like the chaff which the wind scatters.

5. Because of this, the ungodly will not be able to maintain themselves when
       the judgment comes,
   Nor sinners, with righteous people.

[31.]   An adaptation of Leupold's work. See **For Further Study Bibliography** section.

6. For the Lord watches over (knows intimately) the way of the righteous;
   But the way of the ungodly is headed toward destruction.

What is A Bible[32] Centered Leader? According to this passage, Psalm 1, give above here is a definition.

Definition   A *Bible centered leader* is one who:

1. Gets his/her counsel on life matters from other Bible centered leaders.
2. Delights in the Word of God and lets it permeate his/her soul.
3. Will persevere joyfully and with stability through out life (figure of tree/ rooted deep in water).
4. Will be watched over by God and will prosper. That is the bent of the life.

Now glance at two passages taken from 2Ti. These were given to a relatively young leader, Timothy, probably in his early 30s. I have reversed the order of these passages so you can see the challenge first and then the appropriate response next.

2 Timothy 3:16,17 The Guarantee

Every Scripture inspired of God is profitable for teaching, for setting things right, for confronting, for inspiring righteous living, in order that God's leader be thoroughly equipped to lead God's people.

That is quite a challenge for any leader. My response to that choice and one which is encouraged by Paul himself is:

2 Timothy 2:15 The Proper Response to the Guarantee

Make every effort to be pleasing to God, a Bible Centered leader who is completely confident in using God's Word with impact in lives.

From these two passages and from reading 1Ti and 2Ti in general, I would define a Bible centered leader as,

Definition   A *Bible centered leader* is one who:

1. studies the word of God in order to use it confidently and proficiently, and
2. recognizes that inspired Scripture will equip him/her for a productive leadership ministry.

A Bible Centered Leader Defined

Here is my own definition, derived from a comparative study of several Bible charac-

---

32. I am using Bible loosely to mean what is known of God's word; I realize the Psalmist was limited in terms of how much of God's word was available. I also am assuming that a Bible centered leader is first of all a person centered in God. The word of God becomes a central part of centering one self in God. So I am not talking about some one who is simply technically proficient in knowing the Word but one whose life is centered in God and as such wants to hear from God.

ters and numerous passages stating the importance of the **Word of God**.

Definition   A *Bible Centered leader*

- refers to a leader whose leadership is informed by Biblical leadership values,

- has been shaped personally by Biblical values,

- has grasped the intent of Scriptural books and their content in such a way as to apply them to current situations,

- and who uses the Bible in ministry so as to impact followers.

Note carefully the meaning of each of the concepts:

Table 6.2   Bible Centered Leader Components Explained

Concept	Meaning
Bible centered	A person who is centered on God and recognizes that hearing from God involves seeing the Word of God as being very important.
Leadership informed from the Bible	Recognizes that the Bible itself will have much to say about leadership (one thrust of the words equipped to lead in 2Ti 3:16,17). Further, it means recognizing leadership issues from the Bible like that which is given in this Titus Commentary.
Has been shaped personally by Biblical values	The Bible has been used by God to change the life of the leader. That is one reason such a leader can use it confidently. He/she knows it has life changing power in it.
Has grasped the intent of Scriptural books and their content in such a way as to apply them to current situations,	A thorough understanding of books in the Bible allows for the application of dynamic principles where they fit current situation.
Uses the Bible in ministry so as to impact followers	The Bible contains authoritative truth. When used it will change lives.

Conclusion

Take comfort in the **Guarantee** and **Your Response** to it.

2 Timothy 3:16,17 The Guarantee
Every Scripture inspired of God is profitable for teaching, for setting things right, for confronting, for inspiring righteous living, in order that God's leader be thoroughly equipped to lead God's people.

2 Timothy 2:15 Your Response To the Guarantee
Make every effort to be pleasing to God, a Bible Centered leader who is completely confident in using God's Word with impact in lives.

Become a Bible Centered leader. It will take a lifetime of discipline. But it is worth it. It will revolutionize your life and ministry.

Constellation Model

Introduction

One of the major lessons[33] identified from a comparative study of many effective leaders is,

> **Effective Leaders See Relational Empowerment As Both A Means And A Goal Of Ministry.**

Both Jesus and Paul demonstrated this leadership principle in their ministries. In fact, both used mentoring as a means for applying this principle in their ministries. Jesus dominantly mentored in a small group context. Paul mentored both with individuals and in a small group context.

Definition *Mentoring* is a relational experience in which one person, the mentor, empowers another person, the mentoree, by sharing God-given resources.[34]

Stanley researched leadership relationships for a number of years. From his observations on various kinds of mentoring relationships as well as his observations on leaders who finished well and who did not, he postulated a principle.[35]

---

33. Seven such lessons have been identified: (1) Effective Leaders View Present Ministry in Terms Of A Life Time Perspective. (2) Effective Leaders Maintain A Learning Posture Throughout Life. (3) Effective Leaders Value Spiritual Authority As A Primary Power Base. (4) Effective Leaders Who Are Productive Over A Lifetime Have A Dynamic Ministry Philosophy. (5) Effective Leaders View Leadership Selection And Development As A Priority Function In Their Ministry. (6) Effective Leaders See Relational Empowerment As Both A Means And A Goal Of Ministry. (7) Effective Leaders Evince A Growing Awareness Of Their Sense Of Destiny.

34. See the nine mentor roles: mentor discipler, mentor spiritual guide, mentor coach, mentor counselor, mentor teacher, mentor sponsor, mentor contemporary model, mentor historical model, mentor divine contact, **Glossary**. The apostle Paul demonstrated many of these roles in his relationships with team members and others in his ministry. See **Articles**, *Paul—the Developer; Paul—The Mentor*. For further follow-up study, see Stanley and Clinton **Connecting** for a popular treatment of mentoring. See Clinton and Clinton **The Mentor Handbook** for a detailed treatment of mentoring.

35. Paul Stanley, at this writing, is an International Vice President for the Navigators, a Christian organization heavily involved in developing laborers for the Kingdom. Mentoring is heavily used in Navigator ministries. Stanley would never call this theorem by his name, but I have taken the liberty to do so, since he was the discoverer of it and taught it to me.

Stanley's Thesis

> **Over A Lifetime A Christian Leader Needs A Balanced Relational Network With other Christian Leaders Who Will Help Him/Her And Vice Versa.**

What did he mean by a balanced relational network with Christian leaders? By it Stanley was saying that four kinds of relationships are needed over a lifetime:

> *Upward Help:*
> A Christian Leader needs to relate to Christian Leaders more experienced in the Christian life who will help them in their growth and give needed perspective as well as help them be accountable for growth.

> *Lateral Help:*
> A Christian Leader needs to relate to Christian Leaders who are peers in the Christian life who will share, care, and relate so as to encourage them to persevere.

> *Downward Help:*
> A Christian Leader needs to relate to younger emerging leaders who he/she can help to grow.

Stanley was talking about mentoring relationships. Both he and I have observed that over a lifetime, effective leaders who finished well experienced from five to 30 or more mentoring relationships for limited periods of time in their lives. Mentoring is one of the five major enhancement factors that accompany leaders who finish well. [36]

The Constellation Model

> The popular name for the graphic representation of Stanley's thesis is *The Constellation Model*. Figure 7.1 shows this graphic representation.

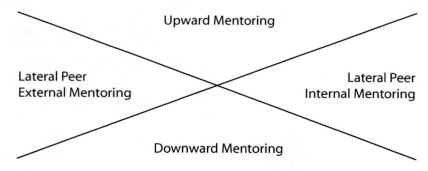

Figure 7.1   The Constellation Model

[36.]   See **Articles**, *Finishing Well—Five Enhancement Factors; Finishing Well—Six Characteristics.*

Upward mentors dominantly bring strategic accountability and perspective to a relationship. When you have an *upward mentor* you are being mentored by someone else. *Lateral peer mentoring*, internal, means a mentoring relationship with someone in the same organization or someone coming from basically the same background as you. Such a mentor knows you and your organization fairly well. Confidential things can be shared. Accountability for each other is expected. An internal lateral mentor is roughly at the same stage of maturity as you. Lateral peer mentoring, external, means a relationship with some one from a very different background than you and a very different ministry experience. Such a person can bring objectivity to you and you to that person, since you will frequently ask the question, "Why do you do it that way?" Accountability and perspective are expected in such a relationship. Downward mentoring means that you are helping someone not as far along as you, at least in the area of the mentoring expertise. Such a relationship benefits both participants. The person being mentored of course receives the empowerment of the mentoring. The person doing the mentoring often experiences two things: (1) reality checks (mentorees frequently ask embarrassing questions about whether or not something is true for you); (2) a fresh injection of faith—often a by-product of being around a younger Christian is that they are not so cynical about things and trust God in ways that an older mentor used to do.

Each of the nine mentoring relationships can fit into any of the quadrants of *The Constellation Model*. Table 7.1 briefly lists the nine relationships.

Table 7.1 Nine Mentoring Relationships That May Happen in the Four Quadrants

Type	Definition
mentor discipler	A *mentor discipler* is one who spends much time, usually one-on-one, with an individual mentoree in order to build into that mentoree the basic habits of the Christian life. It is a relational experience in which a more experienced follower of Christ shares with a less experienced follower of Christ the commitment, understanding, and basic skills necessary to know and obey Jesus Christ as Lord.
mentor spiritual guide	A *spiritual guide* is a godly, mature follower of Christ who shares knowledge, skills, and basic philosophy on what it means to increasingly realize Christ-likeness in all areas of life. The primary contributions of a Spiritual guide include accountability, decisions, and insights concerning questions, commitments, and direction affecting spirituality (inner-life motivations) and maturity (integrating truth with life).
mentor coach	Coaching is a process of imparting encouragement and skills to succeed in a task via relational training.
mentor counselor	A *mentor counselor* is one who gives timely and wise advice as well as impartial perspective on the mentoree's view of self, others, circumstances, and ministry.
mentor teacher	A *mentor teacher* is one who imparts knowledge and understanding of a particular subject at a time when a mentoree needs it.
mentor sponsor	A *mentor sponsor* is one who helps promote the ministry (career) of another by using his/her resources, credibility, position, etc. to further the development and acceptance of the mentoree.

mentor model (contemporary)	A *mentor contemporary model* is a person who models values, methodologies, and other leadership characteristics in such a way as to inspire others to emulate them.
mentor model (historical)	A *mentor historical model* is a person whose life (autobiographical or biographical input) modeled values, methodologies, and other leadership characteristics in such a way as to inspire others to emulate them.
mentor divine contact	A person whose timely intervention is perceived of as from God to give special guidance at an important time in a life. This person may or may not be aware of the intervention and may or may not have any further mentoring connection to the mentoree.

Closing Observations

1. Mentoring relationships that fill the four quadrants are usually limited in time and are not permanent. They happen and meet a need and then terminate after the empowerment. The relationship may endure and be rekindled later for mentoring effectiveness.

2. A given leader will not necessarily have mentoring relationships in all the quadrants at once. But over a lifetime mentoring in each of the quadrants brings balance.

3. Internal lateral peer mentoring usually stresses relationship, accountability and perspective rather than specific mentoring relationships.

4. Upward mentors are harder to find as a leader matures and ages in life. This is because fewer and fewer leaders are upward to a mature leader.

5. A leader with a strong learning posture will take proactive steps to find mentoring.

A closing exercise that is often used at mentoring workshops involves having leaders draw a constellation diagram and have them fill in names of mentors and types of mentoring that they have experienced in the past, even if the mentoring was not deliberate or formal. I have them try to think through each of the four quadrants. Then I ask them to re-do the diagram and put in current mentoring relationships they are experiencing. Finally I ask them to draw a final diagram with the kind of profile they would like to have over the next year or two. These diagrams are called Constellation Profiles.

What does your Constellation Profile look like now?

Corporate Characteristics of a Church — Impacting Society

Introduction

It is clear in Paul's final written words to his two close mentorees, Timothy and Titus, that Paul is deeply concerned with the corporate testimony of local churches in their surrounding societies. His dream for the church in Ephesus is indicated in these thematic verses.

1 Timothy

14 These things I am writing to you hoping to come to you shortly: 15 But if I am delayed, you will know how you should handle yourself the house of God, which is the church of the living God, **the pillar and ground of the truth.**

This great truth statement forms the basis for the thematic subject for the whole book of Timothy—**Leading, God's People, As Model Representatives of God's Truth.** That is what Paul repeatedly emphasizes to Timothy. A full statement of his theme in that first letter to Timothy is,

Theme   **Leading God's People, As Model Representatives Of God's Truth,**
- requires confrontation against false doctrines and practices,
- involves selection of quality local leadership,
- demands personal development as a leader, and
- outworks itself in meeting social needs for the believers.

 Notice the subject. It is dealing with a church which impacts its society. The church, here basically a local or regional church,[37] is God's foundational means for teaching, clarifying, and living out truth before the world.

And just as emphatically his dream for the church in Crete is indicated in the thematic statement of the book as a whole. Note especially the second and third major idea, where my italics emphasize crucial ideas.

[37.] See **Article,** *Regional Churches and Plurality of Leaders.*

Theme   **Setting The Church In Order**
- involves the appointing of qualified leaders,
- requires leaders who are sound in teaching and who *model a Christian life style*, and
- necessitates leaders who exhort others to *practical Christian living.*

Paul's concern for impacting the Cretan society revolves around believers demonstrating what the Christian life is all about. And doing it in an attractive way.

From a comparative study of these two apostolic epistles, one can derive some characteristics of a church which corporately impacts the society around it.

Some Corporate Characteristics of Effective Churches

Churches which are impactful and effective in their societies should reflect the basic themes and emphases of these two letters to Paul's apostolic successors. Here are some things that should be in place.

1. They should have leaders who are selected on the basis of character and who have testimonies above reproach both within and without the church. Credibility of leadership depends on this.
2. They should have leaders who are personally growing and changing and modeling this growth with their followers. Their modeling of consistency in the Christian life is one of their most powerful means of influencing their followers (and indirectly influencing the society around them).
3. Such leaders must be able to teach and defend the Christian faith in such a way as to have a transformational influence upon their followers.
4. Such leaders must be able to root out heresies within their church settings so that there church has a consistent truth basis upon which to build. That is, a church must clean up its own act so that its basic understanding and practice of truth is not heretical.
5. Its followers must be practicing truth in such a way as to make it attractive to non-believers. Lives which reflect peace, joy, self-control and purpose in the midst of life's difficult situations will attract. People leading productive lives with inner attitudes reflecting God's impact on their lives will impact folk in the society around them.
6. The church must take care of its own. Followers saved out of a sinful society will have many problems. Churches must corporately find ways to solve these problems not only to meet the needs of their people but to model what Christian community is all about.
7. Churches must not only reflect God's truth in their own midst but also without — so what is modeled inwardly in terms of taking care of its own, must also spill over to those outside the church. This will demonstrate God's love.

Conclusion

While there may be many other corporate characteristics of a church that impacts society, the above certainly are important. Two things are clear in these last two instructive epistles in the Church Leadership Era.

1. Paul is concerned with the testimony of the church before the world. He wants it to impact. He wants it to be the foundational means of demonstrating God's truth to the world around it.

2. Paul emphasizes the importance of consistent living among leaders and followers as the most important means for influencing the society around them. In the Timothy epistle he is concerned with Timothy's own personal testimony. He also is concerned with the leaders of that church at Ephesus. They must be people of character who demonstrate lives of integrity. He wants followers in the church to demonstrate godliness. In the Titus epistle the same emphases are given. Titus must teach and model Christian truth and do it in such a way as to bring about behavioral change in the followers: young men, young women, older men, older women. He must also appoint leaders of integrity who will stand out character-wise, in the Cretan island society.

While emphasizing the doctrinal truth of salvation,[38] repeatedly in both epistles, it is surprising that Paul does not emphasize evangelistic outreach as the primary way of reaching the world. Nor does he emphasize power ministry. Instead he emphasizes that believer's changed lives in their society will be the bridge to reaching them.[39]

He himself evangelized. He himself demonstrated power ministry in order to authenticate his breakthroughs in new ministry to cross-culturally different folks. But his emphasis in teaching in all his epistles (apart from correcting doctrinal error) is on getting believers to demonstrate transformed lives flowing from their relationship with God.

If our churches are to,

> be **Model Representatives Of God's Truth** (the Timothy theme),

then we must,

> **Set our Churches In Order** (the Titus theme).

Paul was deeply concerned with the corporate testimony of local churches in their surrounding societies. We as leaders, should be too.

[38.] Paul certainly has his theology straight about salvation. And it is really important to him — note the numerous aside references to these doctrinal emphases in 1 Ti and the whole notion of God Our Savior in Titus. But he is emphasizing the formation of a base from which evangelistic outreach can happen.

[39.] Word gifts and love gifts seem to be emphasized, rather than power gifts.

Developing Giftedness — Paul's Advice To Timothy

Paul was concerned for Timothy's development. This concern flows throughout 1,2Ti. Table 9.1 lists passages and developmental implications. The central thrust of development—contained in 2Ti 2:15; 3:16,17—concerns developing his word gifts.[40]

Table 9.1   Paul's Advice To Timothy—Developmental Implications

Passage	Implications for Development
1Ti 4:6-10	• Foundational teaching in the Scriptures forms the basis for development. • Spiritual disciplines promote growth and have implications for the here and now and eternity. • Teaching foundational truth is a means of growth. A teacher learns far more than the learners.
1Ti 4:11-16	• Modeling growth and its end result—maturity provides a younger leader with the foundation for influencing others. • The public reading of Scriptures , appropriate for situations (with the study of them in private to see that they are appropriate) is a major means of development. • Development of public oratorical skills are necessary for a leader who applies Scripture with persuasive power. • Development of one's spiritual gift is a responsibility of a leader. • Development in a leader should be recognized by followers. • A leader is ultimately responsible for his/her own personal growth and for development of ministry. • To ignore development is to open oneself to danger—plateauing at the least and being set aside from leadership at the most.
1Ti 6:11-16	• Development implies growth in character as revealed by such things as integrity, holiness, faith, love, steadfastness, gentleness. • Development will involve appropriation of the resources of the Christian life so as to make them practical in life.
2Ti 1:3-10	• A foundational heritage pattern forms an advantageous basis for development. • A leader must develop and use a spiritual gift or lose his/her influence via that gift.

[40.] *Word Gifts, Power Gifts, Love Gifts* describe corporate gifting. Primary *Word Gifts* include apostleship, prophecy, evangelism, pastoral, and exhortation. See **Glossary**. See **Articles**, *Spiritual Gift Clusters; Spiritual Gifts, Giftedness and Development.*

2Ti 19	2:14-	• One goal of development of one's word gifts involves study and use of the Word of God with power. **The motivating factor for this is pleasing God in how the Word of God is used.**
2Ti 26	2:20-	• Purity is a major character developmental goal. A leader with **purity** as a hallmark will be especially used by God. • **Gentleness** is a second major character developmental goal. A gentle leader wins opponents by persuasion.
2Ti 17	3:10-	• Development in the Scriptures involves experiential demonstration of them in the life and breeds confidence in a leader. • The Foundational Heritage pattern should have as a major developmental goal the grounding of a young person in the Word. This grounding has great effect when the models themselves live out the Word. • **The Bible is the primary tool for developing a leader. It can develop a leader completely for leadership, that is, who studies and uses it.**

Paul was a mentor (counselor, spiritual guide, teacher, model) who was concerned with development for Timothy—of particular concern was his grounding in the Scriptures.

See *Heritage Pattern*; **Glossary**. See **Article**, *Bible Centered Leader*.

Entrustment — A Leadership Responsibility,
The Notion of a Leadership Stewardship

In the midst of a trial Paul makes an astonishing statement.

> Yet I am completely confident. For I know whom I have believed, and am persuaded that he is able to keep that which was entrusted[41] to me until that day. 2Ti 1:12

What was entrusted to him?

> ...which is in harmony with the glorious gospel of the blessed God, which was entrusted to me. 1Ti 1:11

> And this is why I was established[42] as a preacher, and an apostle. I speak the truth in Christ, and lie not; a teacher of faith and truth to the Gentiles. 1Ti 2:7

> So I was divinely chosen[43] as a preacher, and an apostle, and a teacher. 12 For this reason I am suffering [in prison]. 2Ti 1:11

Paul viewed his call to ministry and its ensuing destiny as a special leadership task. He would take the Gospel to the Gentiles. This task was an entrustment.

Definition | A *leadership entrustment* is the viewing of one's call to leadership and its ensuing ministry as a trust, something committed or entrusted to

---

41. Paul viewed his leadership ministry as something entrusted to him—a leadership stewardship—that he was to use and fulfill. He also recognized that God would protect him in the carrying out of that trusteeship until it was finished. Finally, he knew he would have an accounting for it (That Day). One could not have this view nor the confidence about it without a strong sense of destiny—a major *leadership committal*, see **Glossary**.

42. Again, an assertion of divine assignment from God. established (SRN 5087 ἐτέθην) carries the sense of appointing or ordaining as was seen in putting in 1:12. See also 1:1 Apostle by the commandment of God and also the Pauline salutations: Ro 1:1; 1Co 1:1; 2Co 1:1; Gal 1:1; Eph 1:1; Col 1:1; 1Ti 1:1; 2Ti 1:1; Tit 1:1. These also strongly assert a divine calling. Leaders need a strong sense of God's calling for their lives if they are to persevere and be effective over a lifetime.

43. The heart of a ministry that is effective begins here. This is a statement of a *leadership committal*, see **Glossary**—a response to God's call on a life for leadership. It is a *sense of destiny* experience, *a spiritual benchmark*, which a leader can always look back to and be bolstered in ministry. See **Article**, *Spiritual Benchmarks*.

one to be used or cared for in the interest of God, who has given the trust. It is a leadership stewardship.

Paul ties his entrustment back to his destiny call. Further, he is certain that God will protect that entrustment. Four Pauline leadership values embedded in these forceful quotes include:

1. Paul believed that God had entrusted to him his leadership task to preach the Gospel to the Gentiles.
2. Paul believed that he was accountable to God for that entrustment.
3. Paul believed that he must guard that entrustment.
4. Paul believed that God would protect him until that entrustment was finished.

Further, Paul saw Timothy's ministry as an entrustment—an entrustment that he as an Apostolic leader had been involved in imparting.

> This command I am entrusting to you, son Timothy. It is based on the prophecies which were given about you. These words should encourage you to fight on bravely. 1Ti 1:18

> Don't keep on neglecting your spiritual gift, which was given to you by prophecy in conjunction with the laying on of the hands of the leaders. 1Ti 4:14

> Dear Timothy, guard what has been entrusted to you. Avoid worldly and fruitless discussions and false tenets of "so called science." 1Ti 6:20

> Guard carefully what was entrusted to you with the help of the Holy Spirit who lives within us. 2Ti 1:14

As leaders today, we should take away several lessons from this brief introduction of entrustment.

Lesson 1.   We should be sure of our call—the stronger is our call and our sense of divine establishment in our ministry, the better.

Lesson 2.   We should see our ministry as a leadership stewardship.

Lesson 3.   We should confidently trust God to preserve us in our ministry till He has done what He wants to do through us.

Lesson 4.   We may, with God's leading, responsibly pass on to others a leadership trust.

See **Articles**, *Destiny Pattern; Spiritual Benchmarks; Paul—A Sense of Destiny; Apostolic Functions—Derived from 1,2 Timothy and Titus.*

Article 11

Exteriority — A Must Spirituality Component for Leadership

Introduction

When Paul gives his leadership selection criteria in Ephesus and Crete, his stress is on an external testimony that is above reproach. Note the boldfaced phrases.

1 Timothy 3

1 This is a reliable saying, "If anyone aspires to leadership oversight, that one desires a good work." 2 Such a church leader then **must be exemplary in moral conduct:** e.g. the husband of one wife, calm and collected in spirit, discreet, modest, a hospitable person, able to teach; 3 not a drunkard, not belligerent, not one open to shady deals for money. Other qualities include: one who is gentle, not hotheaded, not money-hungry; 4 ruling well one's own household, having obedient and reverent children. 5 For if anyone can not rule a household, how can that person take care of the church of God? 6 Not a new believer, who can easily become proud and condemned by the devil. 7 But instead**, a good reputation with outsiders**; lest reproach allow entrapment by the devil.

8 Similarly a lesser church leader should have **good character,** not deliberately deceptive with words, not a drunkard, not one open to shady deals for money. 9 One who has a clear understanding of the deep things of the faith with a clear conscience. 10 Primarily, these men should be carefully scrutinized; they should minister well, being above board in their ministry. 11 Similarly, women leaders should have **good character,** not prone to slander others, marked by restraint in satisfying desires, can be trusted with anything. 12 Let those who minister be faithful spouses, ruling their children and their own households well. 13 For they that have ministered well are making progress toward leadership and gain great boldness in the faith which is in Christ Jesus.

Titus 1

5 The reason I left you in Crete was that you might straighten out what was left unfinished concerning church leadership. I directed you to appoint church leaders in every town. 6 A church leader must be **above reproach.** He should be a one-wife kind of man — that is, a faithful person. His children should be believers too. They should be obedient and not accused of wild behavior. 7 Since a person doing ministry is entrusted with God's

work, his reputation is very important. His character should be above reproach. He should not be overbearing. He must not be quick-tempered. Drunkenness is unthinkable. He must not be a violent person. He must have a reputation for honesty. He is not in the ministry for making money deceitfully. 8 On the contrary, he is a giving kind of person showing hospitality. He loves what is good. He is self-controlled. He should have a reputation for being upright, demonstrating holiness and modeling a disciplined life. 9 He must hold firmly to the trustworthy message as it has been taught. Thus he will be able to encourage others by good healthy teaching. And he can refute those who oppose this healthy teaching. teaching.

Throughout the books of 1 Ti and Titus, Paul is not only concerned with leaders testimonies in the surrounding culture but also the other believers, the followers. His repeated exhortations challenge to living out in daily life what they know to be true.

Paul is concerned throughout 1 Timothy for how a Christian or a Christian leader is perceived without. Notice the emphases in 1 Timothy. Paul is concerned with what outsiders think about believers.

1 Timothy 5

7 Strongly urge what I am saying that widows may be beyond criticism. 8 But if any provide not for his own, and most of all, for those of his own family, that one has denied the faith, and is worse than a non-believer.

12 They are judged, because they have rejected their first faith.

14 I would prefer that the younger women marry, bear children, manage their households, give no opportunity for opponents to speak reproachfully.

1 Timothy 6

1 Slaves, under the yoke, must consider their own masters deserving of proper respect, that the name of God and [his] teaching not be spoken evil of.

Notice also the strong admonitions to live outward consistent lives in Titus.

Titus

1:1 ...I want them to know the truth that leads to godliness.

Titus 2

2 Teach the older men to be temperate, worthy of respect, self-controlled, and solid in what they believe. They should demonstrate love and endurance.

3 Likewise, teach the older women to be reverent in the way they live. ... No one should be able to malign the word of God because of their daily behavior.

6 Similarly, encourage the young men to be self-controlled. 7 Model for them by your own life.

9 Teach slaves to be subject to their masters in everything. They should try to please their

masters and not to talk back to them.   10 Slaves should not steal from their masters. Instead slaves should show that they can be fully trusted. **By these kind of attitudes and actions, slaves in every way will make the teaching about God our Savior attractive to others.**

11 God's salvation is real now, all can see it. His salvation graciously **enables us to live well.** 12 It teaches us to say "No" to ungodliness and worldly passions. It teaches us to say, "Yes" to living self-controlled, upright and godly lives in this present age. ... 14 He gave himself for us to redeem us from all wickedness and to purify for himself a people that are his very own, **eager to do what is good.**

Titus 3

1   Remind the people to be **subject** to rulers and authorities. They should be **obedient** people and ready **to do whatever is good.**   2 They should **slander no one.** They should be **peaceable** and **considerate people.** **Humility** toward all should be a hallmark of their changed lives.

8 And I want you to stress these things, so that those who have trusted in God may be **careful to live out in daily life, testimonies which reflect this** *Goodnews.*

Paul is deeply concerned that leaders have an outward testimony that is consistent with the truth they claim to believe. Followers too must live daily lives that are consistent.

Spirituality Components

Leaders need to be growing spiritually[44] all their lives. Spirituality mentors use a set of components that help assess and set direction for spiritual growth.[45] Table 11.1 lists these spirituality components.

[44.] *Spirituality* is the work of the Spirit in a leader's life which is indicated by the leader's: growing personal relationship with Christ (CENTRALITY); inner life with God (INTERIORITY); relationships with others in the body (COMMUNITY); Spirit-led and empowered ministry (UNIQUENESS); sensitive obedience to the Spirit daily (SPIRIT SENSITIVITY, EXTERIORITY), and by a character transformation toward Christ-like-ness (FRUITFULNESS, DEVELOPMENT).

[45.] See Chapter 4, Active Mentoring — Spiritual Guide, in **The Mentor Handbook,** a Barnabas Publications offering. These components are detailed there. Mentoring as a *spiritual guide* is a process in which a godly mature follower of Christ relates to a younger believer and shares knowledge, skills, and basic philosophy on what it means to mature in spirituality in such a way as to bring about significant growth in spirituality and free the younger believer to advance in a personal relationship with God.

Table 11.1   Spirituality Components

Component	Major Thrust of the Component
1. CENTRALITY (A Christ-centered life)	This component focuses on one's personal relationship with and experience of Christ. It assesses personal experience with the person and work of Christ.
2. INTERIORITY (development of the inner life)	This component looks at the development of the inner life — vertical aspects of spirituality with God — the devotional life and disciplines of silence, solitude, fasting, and prayer help.
3. EXTERIORITY (living out the inner life)	This component suggests overflow of interiority into life — the horizontal aspects of spirituality — its effects on our relationships with believers and unbelievers in the world in which we interact.
4. SPIRIT SENSITIVITY (obeying the Holy Spirit Daily)	This component touches the realm of the Spirit; It reflects experience which recognizes the Holy Spirit in daily life. It essentially assesses the believer's sensitivity to Spirit life. It is an integrative component which relates centrality, interiority, and exteriority to life.
5. UNIQUENESS (developing along gifted lines)	This spirituality component recognizes that each spirituality model will be tailored by the Spirit to fit a believer. While there are some common factors there is much that will differ. Each new believer's giftedness, personality, gender, and spiritual history will be part of his or her spirituality model. No two spirituality models are the same.
6. COMMUNITY (recognizing the interdependence of God's people)	This component blends exteriority, interiority and Spirit sensitivity so that the checks and balances of Christian community both constrain and stretch the growing believer toward development and use of giftedness for others.
7. FRUITFULNESS (being and doing what God intends)	Inner (character — fruit of Spirit) and Outer (external fruit — results of giftedness and achievement for the Kingdom) measure of God's purposes for the believer and fulfillment as a human being.
8. DEVELOPMENT (continuing to grow throughout life)	This integrative spirituality component suggests that there should be ongoing progress in every spirituality component through life. It refers to evaluation, affirmation, and feedback which helps assess progress in any component and ultimately toward conformity to Christ.

The Exteriority Component

While it is important that a leader be progressing in all these spirituality components, it is most important that a leader be developing the exteriority component. Let me explain this component a bit more.

Introduction

James points out (James 1:22) that anything that is real for a believer should be reflected in life behavior. Exteriority is the spirituality challenge which keeps interiority, primarily a vertical focus on God, from being the only focus. Real changes in personality, behavior and relationship to God should have effect in our horizontal relationships with others.

Definition   *Exteriority* refers to the outward testimony to the inner life and refers to a lifestyle, a spiritual tone, that others sense and see which is consistent with the inner depth being experienced. (syn: outward testimony, horizontal spirituality)

Figure 11.1   Exteriority Continuum

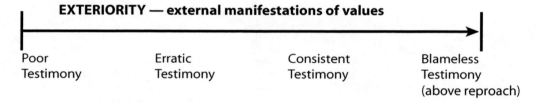

EXTERIORITY — external manifestations of values

| Poor Testimony | Erratic Testimony | Consistent Testimony | Blameless Testimony (above reproach) |

Example

1 John 2:6 exhorts that a believer who claims to be in Christ must walk as he walked. That is, an observed outward manifestation, confirms a real inward relationship (interiority).

Example

Onesiphorus, 2 Timothy 1:16

Example

Dorcas, Acts 9:36

Example

Barnabas, Acts 11:24

Comment

The application sections of the Pauline epistles (e.g. Ephesians 4-6, Romans 12-15) always stress the outworking of the Christian relationship. That is, exteriority is the natural outward manifestation of the inward relationship with God in Christ.

Comment

Paul's requirements for leaders have the phrases *above reproach* (1 Timothy 3:2,) and a *good reputation with outsiders* (1 Timothy 3:7) and *blameless* (Titus 1:7). The point being emphasized is that leaders model or set an example of what Christianity is and their observed behavior by believers and non-believers ought to be consistent with what a Christian ought to be.

Development along the exteriority continuum is a must for a leader. It is not an option. While leaders are not perfect they must be above reproach. A life of integrity, which is what above reproach entails is necessary if a leader is to have credibility to influence followers.

Conclusion

Some suggestions:

1. You probably can benefit from having a peer mentor hold you accountable in basic EXTERIORITY.

2. Why don't you have the peer mentor take the Exteriority continuum and assess where the believers who are your followers would put you on the continuum?

3. What is more important, most likely, is, where would the unbelievers put you on the continuum?

4. Recognize that your own personal evaluation is probably not where either believers or unbelievers will put you.

Why don't you take the little exercise that follows. This will help you start thinking about EXTERIORITY. And why don't you get your peer mentor to read your exercise and evaluate it from his/her perspective.

See **Glossary,** *mentoring*; See **Articles,** *Abiding — 7 Symptoms; Conscience — Paul's Use of; Finishing Well — 6 Characteristics; Integrity — A Top Leadership Quality; Union Life — Intimacy With God.*

Exteriority Exercise

1. Consistency between a person's inner values and external behavior is the essence of this spirituality component. Ephesians 4-6 is full of exhortations concerning exteriority and consistency in Christian living. Read through these chapters and highlight every phrase which deals with exteriority.

2. Now place beside each of these phrases, on a scale of 1-10, where you think you are in each of these exteriority phrases you jotted down. 1 means you are not doing it at all, 10 means you are doing it very well. Hopefully, you will be able to get a peer mentor to do the same thing so that you can check your self-analysis with his/her analysis.

3. From your list of phrases pick out the top three phrases you need to work on. Have your peer mentor do this also. Compare your lists.

Figures and Idioms In The Bible

Introduction to Figures

All language is governed by law—that is, it has normal patterns that are followed. But in order to increase the power of a word or the force of expression, these patterns are deliberately departed from, and words and sentences are thrown into and used in unusual forms or patterns which we call figures. A figure then is a use of language in a special way for the purpose of giving additional force, more life, intensified feeling and greater emphasis. A figure of speech is the author's way of underlining. He/She is saying, "Hey, take note! This is important enough for me to use a special form of language to emphasize it!" And when we remember the fact that the Holy Spirit has inspired this product we have— the Bible—we are not far wrong in saying figures are the Holy Spirit's own underlining in our Bibles. We certainly need to be sensitive to figurative language.

Definition   A *figure* is the unusual use of a word or words differing from the normal use in order to draw special attention to some point of interest.

For a figure, the unusual use itself follows a set pattern. The pattern can be identified and used to interpret the figure in normal language. Here are some examples from the Bible. I will make you fishers of people. Go tell that fox. Quench not the Holy Spirit. I came not to send peace but a sword. As students of the Bible we need to be sensitive to figures and know how to interpret and catch their emphatic meaning.

Definition   A figure or idiom is said to be *captured* when one can display the intended emphatic meaning in non-figurative simple words.

One of the most familiar figures in the Bible is Psalm 23:1. The Lord is my shepherd. I shall not lack. *Captured*: God personally provides for my every need.

E.W. Bullinger, an expert on figurative language, lists over 400 different kinds of figures. he lists over 8000 references in the Bible containing figures. In Romans alone, Bullinger lists 253 passages containing figurative language. However, we do not need to know all of those figures for the most commonly occurring figures number much less than 400. Figure 12.1 below lists the 11 most common figures occurring in the Bible. If we know them we are well on our way to becoming better interpreters of the Scripture. In fact, you can group these 11 figures under three main sub-categories, which simplifies learning about them.

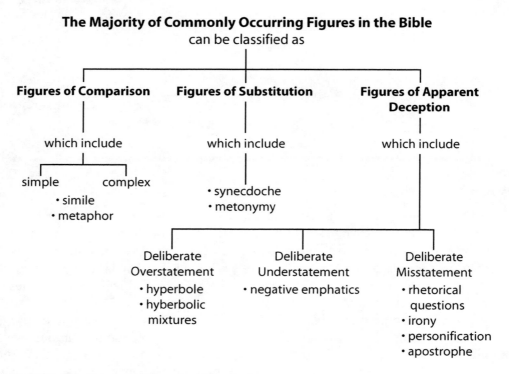

Figure 12.1 Eleven Common Figures of Speech

Table 12.1 below gives these 11 figures of speech, a Scriptural reference containing the figure, and the basic definition of each of these figures.

Table 12.1 Eleven Figures in the Bible Defined

Category Figure	Scriptural Example	Definition
Figures of Comparison: 1. Simile 2. Metaphor	simile—Isa 53:6 metaphor—Ps 23:1	A *simile* is a stated comparison of two unlike items (one called the real item and the other the picture item) in order to display one graphic point of comparison. A *metaphor* is an implied comparison in which two unlike items (a real item and a picture item) are equated to point out one point of resemblance.
Figures of Substitution 3. Metonymy 4. Synecdoche	metonymy—Ac 15:21 Moses for what he wrote synecdoche—Mt 8:8 roof for the whole house.	A *metonymy* is a figure of speech in which (usually) one word is substituted for another word to which it is closely related in order to emphasize something indicated by the relationship. A *synecdoche* is a special case of metonymy in which (again usually) one word is substituted for another to which it is related as, a part to a whole or a whole to a part.

Figures of Apparent Deception— Deliberate Over-statement: 5. Hyperbole 6. Hyperbolic mixtures	hyperbole—1Co 4:14-16 ten thousand instructors hyperbolic mixture—2 Sa 1:23 swifter than eagles, stronger than lions	A *hyperbole* is the use of conscious exaggeration (an over-statement of truth) in order to emphasize or strikingly excite interest in the truth. Hyperbole is sometimes combined with other figures such as comparison and substitution. When such is the case it is called a *hyperbolic mixture* figure.
Figures of Apparent Deception— Deliberate under-statement: 7. Negative emphatics	negative emphatics—Mk 12:34 not far = very near	A figure of *negative emphasis* represents the deliberate use of words to diminish a concept and thus call attention to it or the negating of a concept to call attention to the opposite positive concept (I have deliberately merged two figures, litotes and tapenosis into one because of the basic sameness of negative emphasis).
Figures of Apparent Deception— Deliberate Mis-statement: 8. Rhetorical questions 9. Irony 10. Personification 11. Apostrophe	rhetorical question—1Ti 3:5 irony—2Co 12:13 personification—Heb 4:12 apostrophe—1Co 15:55	A *rhetorical question* is a figure of speech in which a question is not used to obtain information but is used to indirectly communicate, (1) an affirmative or negative statement, or (2) the importance of some thought by focusing attention on it, or (3) one's own feeling or attitudes about something. *Irony* is the use of words by a speaker in which his/her intended meaning is the opposite of (or in disharmony with) the literal use of the words. *Personification* is the use of words to speak of animals, ideas, abstractions, and inanimate objects as if they had human form, character, or intelligence in order to vividly portray truth. *Apostrophe* is a special case of personification in which the speaker addresses the thing personified as if it were alive and listening.

I have developed in-depth explanations for all of the above figures. I have developed study sheets to aid one in analysis of them. Further I have actually identified many of these in the Scriptures and captured a number of them.[46]

Introduction to Idioms

Idioms are much more complicated that figures of speech.

Definition   An *idiom* is a group of words which have a corporate meaning that can not be deduced from a compilation of the meanings of the individual words making up the idiom.

What makes idioms difficult is that some of them follow patterns while others do not. For the patterned idioms, like figures, you basically reverse the pattern and capture the idiom. Table 2 lists the patterned idioms I have identified in the Bible.

---

[46]. See my self-study manual, **Interpreting the Scriptures: Figures and Idioms**.

Table 12.2   Thirteen Patterned Idioms

Idiom	Example	Definitive Principle/ Description
Three Certainty Idioms: 1. Double certainty (pos/neg) 2. Fulfilled (promised/proposed) 3. Prophetic past	double certainty—1Ki 18:36 fulfilled—Ge 15:18 prophetic past—Jn 13:31	*double certainty*—a negative and positive statement (in either order) are often used to express or imply certainty. *fulfillment*—in the fulfillment idiom things are spoken of as given, done, or possessed, which are only promised or proposed. *prophetic past*—in the prophetic past idiom the past tense is used to describe or express the certainty of future action.
4. Superlative (repetitive superlative)	Ge 9:25 servant of servants Isa 26:3 peace, peace = perfect peace 2Ti 4:7	The *Hebrew superlative* is often shown by the repetition of the word. Paul uses a variation of this by often using the noun form and a verb form of the same word either back to back or in close proximity. (the good struggle I have struggled).
5. Emphatic comparisons	1Pe 3:3,4	This takes three forms: *absolute for relative:* one thing (importance or focus item) is emphasized as being much more important in comparison with the other thing (the denial item). Form not A but B really means A is less important than B. *relative for absolute:* One thing is positively compared to another when in effect it is meant to be taken absolutely and the other denied altogether. *abbreviated emphatic comparisons:* Half of the comparison is not given (either the focus item or denial items). Half of the statement is given. the half missing is an example of ellipsis and is to be supplied by the reader.
6. Climactic arrangement	Pr 6:16-19 Ro 3:10-18	To emphasize a particular item it is sometimes *placed at the bottom of a list* of other items and is thus stressed in the given context as being the most important item being considered.
7. Broadened kinship	Ge 29:5	Sometimes the terms son of, daughter of, mother of, father of, brother of, sister of, or begat, which in English imply a close relationship have a much wider connotation in the Bible. Brother and sister could include various male and female relatives such as cousins; mother and father could include relatives such as grandparents or great-great-grandparents, in the direct family line; begat may simply mean was directly in the family line of ancestors.
8. Imitator	Ge 6:2, 11:5	to indicate that people or things are governed by or are characterized by some quality, they are called *children of* or a *son of.* or *daughter of* that quality.
9. Linked noun	Lk 21:15	Occasionally two nouns are linked together with a conjunction in which the second noun is really to be used like an adjective modifying the first noun.
Indicator Idioms: 10. City indicator 11. List indicator 12. Strength Indicator	city indicator La 1:16, daughter of Zion list indicator Pr 6:16, these 6 yea 7 Strength indicator 1Sa 2:1,10	*city indicator*—idiomatic words, daughter of or virgin of or mother of. *list indicator*—2 consecutive numbers—designates an incomplete list of items of which the ones on the list are representative; other like items could be included. *strength indicator*—a horn denotes aggressive strength or power or authority.
13. Anthropomorphism	Lk 11:20	In order to convey concepts of God, *human passions, or actions, or attributes are used to describe God.*

In addition, to the patterned idioms there are a number of miscellaneous idioms which either occur infrequently or have no discernible pattern. I have labeled 32. Their meaning must be learned from context, from other original language sources, or from language experts' comments, etc.

Table 12.3   Fifteen Body Language Idioms

Name	Word, Phrase, Usually Seen	Example	Meaning or Concept Involved
1. Foot gesture	shake off the dust	Mt 10:14, Lk 9:5 et al	have nothing more to do with them
2. Mouth gesture	gnash on them with teeth; gnashing of teeth	Ps 35:16; 37:12 Ac 7:54 et al	indicates angry and cursing words given with deep emotion and feeling
3. Invitation	I have stretched forth my hand(s)	Ro 10:21; Pr 1:24; Is 49:22	indicates to invite, or to receive or welcome or call for mercy
4. New desire	enlighten my eyes, lighten my eyes	Ps 13:3; 19:8; 1Sa 14:29; Ezr 9:8	to give renewed desire to live; sometimes physical problem sometimes motivational inward attitude problem
5. Judgment	to stretch forth the hand; to put forth the hand	Ex 7:5; Ps 138:7; Job 1:11	to send judgment upon; to inflict with providential punishment
6. Fear	to shake the hand, to not find the hand, knees tremble	Is 19:16; Ps 76:8	to be afraid; to be paralyzed with fear and incapable of action.
7. Increase punishment	to make the hand heavy	Ps 32:4	to make the punishment more severe
8. Decreased punishment	to make the hands light	1SA 6:5	to make punishment less severe
9. Remove punishment	to withdraw the hands	Eze 20:22	to stop punishment
10. Repeat punishment	to turn the hand upon	Is 1:25	to repeat again some punishment which was not previously heeded
11. Generosity	to open the hand	Ps 104:28; 145:16	to generously give or bestow
12. Anger	to clap the hands together	Eze 21;17; 22:13	to show anger; to express derision
13. Oath	to lift up the hand	Ex 6:8; 17:16; De 32:40; Eze 20:5,6	to swear in a solemn; take an oath; an indicator of one's integrity to consider worthy to be accepted; to accept someone or be accepted by someone
14. Promise	to strike with the hands (with someone else)	Pr 6:1; Job 17:3	become a co-signer on a loan; to conclude a bargain
15. Accept	to lift up the face	Nu 6:26; Ezr 9:6; Job 22:26	to consider worthy to be accepted; to accept someone or be accepted by someone

Table 12.4   Fourteen Miscellaneous Idioms

Name	Word, Phrase, Usually Seen	Example	Meaning or Concept Involved
1. Success	tree of life	Pr 3:18; 11:30; 13:12; 15:4	idea of success, guarantee of success, source of motivation to successful life
2. Speech cue	answered and said	Mt 11:25; 13:2 and many others	indicates manner of speaking denoted by context; e.g. responded prayed, asked, addressed, etc.
3. Notice	verily, verily	Many times in Jn	I am revealing absolute and important truth; give close attention (this is a form of the superlative idiom)
4. Time	___ days and ___ nights	Jn 1:17; Mt 12:40; 1Sa 30:11; Est 4:16	any portion of time of a day is indicated by or represented by the entire day
5. Lifetime	forever and ever	Ps 48;14 and many others	does not mean eternal life as we commonly use it but means all through my life; as long as I live
6. Separation	what have I to do with you	Jn 2:4; Jdg 11;12; 2Sa 16:10; 1Ki 17;18; 2Ki 3;13; Mt 8:29; Mk 5:7; Lk 8:28	an expression of indignation or contempt between two parties having a difference or more specifically not having something in common; usually infers that some action about to take place should not take place
7. Reaction	heap coals of fire	Ro 12:20; Pr 25:21	to incur God's favor by reacting positively to a situation in which revenge would be normal
8. Orate	open the mouth	Job 3:1	to speak at great length with great liberty or freedom
9. Claim	you say	Mt 26:25,63,64	means it is your opinion
10. Excellency	living, lively	Jn 4:10,11 Ac 7:38; Heb 10:20; 1Pe 2:4,5; Rev 1:17	used to express the excellency of perfection of that to which it refers
11. Abundance	riches	Ro 2:4; Eph 1:7; 3:8; Col 1:27; 2:2	used to describe abundance of or a great supply
12. Preeminence	firstborn	Ps 89:27; Ro 8:29; Col 1:15, 18; Heb 12:23	special place of preeminence; first place among many others
13. Freedom	enlarge my feet; enlarge	2Sa 22:37; Ps 4:1; 18:36	freed me; brought me into a situation that has taken the pressure off, taken on to bigger and better things
14. Reverential respect for	fear and trembling	Ps 55:5; Mk 5:33; Lk 8:47; 1Co 2:3; 2 Co 7:15; Eph 6:5, Php 2:12	describes an attitude of appropriate respect for something. The something could be God, could a person, or could be a combination including some process. Sometimes indicates confronting a difficult situation or thing with a strong awareness of it and possible consequences

Again I would recommend you refer to my manual **Figures and Idioms** to see the approach for capturing the patterned idioms.

Figures and Idioms should be appreciated, understood, and should be interpreted with emphasis. Hardly any passage which is any one of the seven leadership genre will be without some figure or idiom.

Finances, Pauline Perspectives on
A Barrier to Finishing Well

Introduction

One of the startling findings in our studies of leadership emergence theory[47] is a negative one. *Few leaders finish well.* Once this was seen, research shifted to find out why leaders don't finish well. Six barriers to finishing well were identified:

Barrier 1. Finances—their Use And Abuse
Barrier 2. Power—its Abuse
Barrier 3. Pride—which Leads To Downfall
Barrier 4. Sex—illicit Relationships
Barrier 5. FAMILY—Critical Issues
Barrier 6. Plateauing.

This article is dealing with Barrier 1. Finances—their Use And Abuse.

Leaders, particularly those who have power positions and make important decisions concerning finances, tend to use practices which may encourage incorrect handling of finances and eventually wrong use. A character trait of greed often is rooted deep and eventually will cause impropriety with regard to finances. Numerous leaders have fallen due to some issue related to money. Some Biblical examples standout like Gideon's golden ephod in the Old Testament and Ananias and Sapphira's deceitful giving in the New Testament. Paul, the leader exemplar in the New Testament Leadership Era had a lot to say about leadership and finances.

Paul had a value,

Label	Value Statement
Financial Integrity	A Christian leader must handle finances with absolute integrity.

This value stood him in good stead. Paul finished well. Paul was very careful about finances. This was not a barrier to trap him. He was cautious, maybe overly cautious with

---

47. Leadership emergence theory is a framework for viewing how God develops leaders over a lifetime. My research has involved the study of more than 1500 leaders, including Biblical leaders, historical leaders, and contemporary leaders.

regard to leadership and finances. His careful attention to finances and their handling paid off. His general guidelines can help us today.

Pauline Passages Dealing With Finances

Table 13.1 displays a number of passages. Paul talks either directly or indirectly about finances and leadership. Scan this list. Then I will print out the Biblical context of each of these and make some explanatory comments about them.

Table 13.1 Pauline Passages On Finances and Leadership

From 1 Corinthians: 9:3-22, 16:1-4, 16:5-7, 16:10, 11, 15-18
From 2 Corinthians: 2:16b, 17, 8:16-24, 12:14, 15
From Galatians 6:6
From Philippians 4:14-20
From 1 Timothy 3:2b-5, 3:6, 5:9-16, 17-20, 6:6-10
From 2 Timothy 2:3-7
From Titus1:10, 11
From Titus 3:12-14

Paul's remarks are scattered throughout his letters. Only a couple of passages are large contexts: 2 Co 8 and 1 Co 9. These two were teaching that was concentrated on special aspects of giving and financial support. The rest are incidental small ideas tucked away in the midst of other things. But a careful review of each can lead to some useful observations, guidelines, principles and values.

1 Co 9:3-22

3 When people criticize my leadership, here is how I respond. 4 Don't we have a right to be given food and drink because of our work? [We sure do] 5 Don't we have the right to take along a Christian wife, like the other apostles, the brothers of the Lord, and Peter? [Sure we have that right] 6 Or are Barnabas and I the only ones who have to work to support our own ministry? [No] 7 Who ever goes to war at his own expense? [No one] Who plants a vineyard and does not eat of its fruit? [No one] Or who tends a flock and does not drink of the milk of the flock? [No one]

8 Is this just human reasoning? [No] Doesn't the Old Testament law say the same also? [Yes, it does] 9 For it is written in the law of Moses,

"You shall not muzzle an ox
while it treads out the grain."

Is it just oxen God is concerned about? [No] 10 Wasn't He also speaking to us? [Yes] No doubt it is for our sakes, this is written. The person who plows and the person who reaps should do their work in anticipation of getting a share of the crop. 11 If we have sown spiritual seed among you, is it too much to expect to reap material benefits? [I don't think so] 12 If others have the right to expect benefits for ministering to you, don't we have an even greater right? [yes, we do; but here is my point!]

Nevertheless we have not used this right. We have had to put up with lots in order not to hinder the gospel of Christ. 13 Don't you know that those working in the temple have a share of the sacrifices brought to the altars? [for their meals] 14 In the same way, the Lord has commanded that those who preach the gospel should get their living from it. 15 But I have not used this right, nor do I now write these things in order to claim these rights. I would rather die first than impose these rights. 16 I have no right to boast because I preach the Gospel. I am compelled to do so due to my calling. What an awful thing it would be if I didn't preach the Gospel! 17 For if I did my ministry out of my own desire, I would deserve to be rewarded. But I do it because it has been given me as a trust. 18 Do I get any reward then? [You bet] I get satisfaction when I preach the Gospel without charging anyone. This certainly keeps me from abusing my authority and demanding my rights.

19 Since I am not under obligation to anyone I am free to minister; yet I have made myself a slave to all in order to win as many as possible. 20 With the Jews I live like a Jew to win them. When I am with those who strictly follow the law, I do too, even though I am free from the law. 21 In the same way, when I am with Gentiles who do not have the Jewish law, I identify with them as much as I can in order to win them. I do not discard God's law but I do obey the law of Christ. 22 With those weak in the faith I become weak like them in order to win them. I can adapt to different situations that I might save some of them by any means.

Comment On 1 Co 9:3-22

Paul has used this large buildup of rhetorical questions[48] to show that he has a right to expect financial remuneration from these Corinthians to whom he has done a fundamental work in bringing the Gospel to them. Now he makes his point. "I gave up this right in order not to hinder the Gospel being received by you." He thus models the guideline of giving up a right for the better good that he has just taught on in chapter 8. He will come back to this support problem in chapter 16.

Paul is in this contextual flow dealing with two of the major barriers to a leader finishing well: (1) financial issues, (2) abuse of power. He is careful to avoid being trapped by either one.

There is an implication here. I am not paid by people; therefore they can't order me around. NLT captures this as, *This means I am not bound to obey people just because they pay me...*

Paul's flexibility in adapting to Jewish and non-Jewish situations implies: (1) He has a core (law of Christ) which he holds on to but he also has a lot of give and take in peripheral things; (2) More importantly, he can give up his rights with regards to these peripheral issues, like finances which to others may seem core. He does this in order to get the best hearing possible for the Gospel. When he speaks of being weak, he means on some disputed practice on which he, himself, has freedom. But he can give up that right[49]

---

48. Rhetorical questions are figurative language. See **Article**, *Figures and Idioms in the Bible.*

1 Co 16:1-4

1 Now concerning the collection for the Church in Jerusalem— do what I told the churches in Galatia to do. 2 On the first day of every week each one of you should put some money aside, in proportion to what you have earned. That way there will be no need for special collections when I come. 3 And when I come, I will send the ones you approve, along with letters of recommendation, to take your liberal offerings to Jerusalem. 4 If appropriate, I may also accompany them.

Comments on 1 Co 16:1-4

Notice, Paul advocates proportionate giving, not a tithe. Note also the systematic giving.

Note the special care to maintain integrity with regard to finances; more than one person who these Corinthians know will be handling these finances. See also 2Co 8:18-21 for another reference to this integrity guideline. Paul is audacious—asking for money from this problem filled church. He expands on this quick teaching on giving in 2Co 8,9. Note he implies that the Galatian church is following his orders about giving—a motivating lever to challenge the Corinthians. In 2Co 8,9 he again uses this comparative motivational technique, there using the Philippian church.

1 Co 16:5-7

5 Now I will come to you after I have been to Macedonia—for I do intend to go through Macedonia. 6 And it could be that I will stay awhile, or maybe even spend the whole winter with you. And then you may *send* me on my journey, wherever I go. 7 For I do not wish to only have a short visit. I hope to spend a longer time with you, if the Lord permits.

Comments on 1 Co 16:5-7 1 Co 16:10, 11

When Paul uses Send (SRN 4311 προπεμπο) he means to send him off and fit him out with the requisites for a journey—i.e. resources, money, whatever. See also verse 11 where Paul uses this same word to urge the Corinthians to financially back Timothy.

1 Co 16:10, 11

10 Now if Timothy comes, treat him with respect. He is doing the work of the Lord, just like me. 11 Don't look down on him. But send him on his journey in peace, so that he will come back to me. I am waiting for him with the brothers.

Comments on 1 Co 16:10, 11

Paul is here acting as a mentor sponsor for Timothy. Not only does he strongly ask for Timothy to be treated with respect, he also asks that they send (SRN 4311 προπεμπο) him

---

49.   A *disputed practice* a practice for which a Christian has freedom to do, from a Biblical and conscience standpoint, but for which other Christians feel is wrong for whatever reasons, a matter of conscience for them. Essentially it deals with the notion of Christian liberty. Some would see the practice as legitimate for a Christian, others would not. Paul gives guidelines on how to approach disputed practices in 1Co 8-10 and Ro 14. See my major paper on this, *Disputed Practices*.

off—that is, give him financial backing. Young leaders in Asian and African setting often do not get respect for their leadership since the cultures respect age and tend to want older leaders.

1 Co 16: 15-18

15 You know that Stephanas and his family were the first Christians in Greece. They have dedicated themselves to serving Christians. 16 I urge you, fellow Christians that you respect their leadership, and others like them who also serve. 17 I am glad that Stephanas, Fortunatus, and Achaicus came. They have made up for your lack of help. 18 For they have encouraged me just like they did you. These men deserve to be honored.

Comments on 1 Co 16: 15-18

Again as with Timothy in 16:10,11, Paul acts as a mentor sponsor, this time for Stephanus. This time raising financial support.

Paul gives a slight admonition about lack of support for himself—a problem being repeatedly dealt with in these closing remarks.

2 Co 2:16b, 17

16b And who could claim sufficiency for such a task? 17 For I am not like many, using God's word to make money. I speak in utter sincerity as one sent by God, a minister accountable to God.

Comments on 2 Co 2:16b, 17

Using (SRN 2585 καπηλεύοντες) is a word which means peddle or sell something for profit (with negative connotations; putting something over on the buyer). Paul accuses several groups of doing this. See the heretical teachers in Ephesus and on Crete.

2 Co 8:16-24

16 I thank God for giving Titus the same enthusiasm for you that I have. 17 He not only responded to my challenge but he did it because he himself wanted to. 18 We are sending with him a brother, highly respected by all the churches for his work in proclaiming the Good News 19 He was appointed by the churches to travel with us as we take this gift to Jerusalem. This service of love brings the Lord glory and shows that we really want to help.

20 We want to be very *careful in handling this gift* and *avoid any criticism*. 21 We want to do what is right, not only in the sight of the Lord but in the sight of everyone.

22 And we are sending along another brother who has been thoroughly tested on many occasions. He has always been eager to help. He is now even more eager to help because of his increased confidence in you. 23 Titus is my partner in my work with you. The other brothers going with him represent the churches and are honoring Christ. 24 So show them your love. Prove to all the churches that our boasting about you was justified.

Comments on 2 Co 8:16-24

Of the six barriers to leaders finishing well, improper handling of finances, whether deliberately or just carelessly done, is probably the number three barrier: 1. illicit sexual relationships, 2. abuse of power, and 3. money problems, in that order. Usually two and three go together. Financial issues often waylay a leader. Note the special care to maintain integrity with regards to finances that Paul suggests in 1 Co 16:3,4 and Ac 11:27-30.

2 Co 12:14, 15

14 I am ready to come to you, for the third time. And I am not going *to be a burden for you.* I don't want your money; I want you. For children shouldn't have to support parents. Parents should take care of their children. 15 I will very gladly spend all I have and all that I am in order to help you. Though it seems the more I love you, the less you love me.

Comments on 2 Co 12:14, 15

When Paul says be a *burden for you,* he means try to obtain money for my own needs. Paul was above board on any issues regarding his personal finances. Note how carefully he states over and over that he did not take finances from them. Obviously he had been accused of this by the false apostles. And probably just as obvious, he is accusing these apostles of doing that very thing. That is why he is so clear about his own finances.

Gal 6:6

But let the ones being taught in the Word share with their teachers.

Comments on Gal 6:6

Followers, who recognize spiritual authority in a leader and who have been helped by that leader's ministry in their lives will naturally be generous and help that leader with financial resources. They will need to do this voluntarily since a leader with spiritual authority will never exploit that authority for his/her personal benefit.

Php 4:14-20

14 However, I am glad you shared with me in my hardship. 15 Now you Philippians know also, that in the beginning of the gospel, when I departed from Macedonia, no church gave me gifts of money; but you did! 16 For even in Thessalonica you sent twice to meet my needs. 17 I say these things not because I desire a gift. But I desire fruit that may abound to your account. 18 But I have all, and abound. I am full, having received of Epaphroditus the things which were sent from you, an aroma of a sweet smell, a sacrifice acceptable, well pleasing to God. 19 But my God *shall supply all your need* according to his riches in glory by Christ Jesus. 20 Now unto God and our Father be glory for ever and ever. Amen.

Comments on Php 4:14-20

This is a passage on corporate giving. See also 1Co 9:1-19, Gal 6:6 and 2Co 8,9 for other Pauline teaching on giving. The first two references are dominantly referring to leaders; the third one gives principles for individuals giving in a corporate situation. Followers, who recognize spiritual authority in a leader, and who have been helped by that leader in their lives will naturally be generous and help that leader with financial resources. They will need to do this voluntarily since a leader with spiritual authority will never exploit that authority for his/her personal benefit. The Philippians were just such a sensitive church. They appreciated Paul's ministry.

This is a conditional promise.[50] Those who give sacrificially can claim it. The Philippians could claim this great promise, because they have fulfilled the conditions of it. Most people who want to claim this promise don't meet the conditions—those who sacrificially given to others.

1 Ti 3:2b-5

2b These things teach and urge strongly. 3 If anyone teaches differently, and doesn't agree with this solid teaching, true teaching right from our Lord Jesus Christ, which flows from godliness, 4 then that one is proud, knows nothing, and has an unhealthy focus on questions and argumentative things. This leads to envy, strife, slander, evil suspicions, 5 as well as useless occupation of people whose minds are corrupt. They are no longer concerned with truth but using religion to make money.

Comments on 1 Ti 3:2b-5

Here we are talking about using ministry as a means for making money and duping people.

In 1Ti 3:3 (money problems), 1Ti 3:6 (pride), and 1Ti 5:2 (illicit sexual relationships), I have noted three of the six barriers commonly seen as those which waylay leaders from finishing well. Timothy had his work cut out for him at Ephesus. Here money is mentioned again. Two others are hinted: family problems—the character traits for leaders states that positively leaders must rule their families well (3:4,5, 12)—and plateauing (4:14). The only barrier missing is abuse of power.

1 Ti 3:6

Other qualities include: one who is gentle, not hotheaded, not money-hungry…

Comments On 1 Ti 3:6

Paul is describing leadership traits that Timothy should use in selecting leaders for the church in Ephesus. A leader who is in ministry for money (that is, money-hungry) can easily be led into lack of financial integrity. Lack of integrity with finances, specifically, and money matters, in general, is identified as one of the six major barriers to finishing well.

1 Ti 5:9-16

9 Don't put a widow on the widow's list who is younger than sixty. Further she should having been a loyal wife— 10 A reputation for good works. She should have brought up

---

[50].   See **Glossary**, promise. See **Article**, *Promises of God*.

her children well. She should have lodged strangers, and she should have washed the saints' feet. She should have assisted those in deep trouble. She should be a good worker.

11 But the younger widows refuse (to put on the list): for when they have strong desires to marry they turn away from Christ. 12 They are judged, because they have rejected their first faith. 13 Further they idle away their time, wandering about from house to house; and not only idle, but gossiping and minding others' business saying things which they ought not. 14 I would prefer that the younger women marry, bear children, manage their households, give no opportunity for opponents to speak reproachfully 15 For some are already turned aside after Satan. 16 If any Christian woman has relatives who are widows, she must take care of them, and keep the church from being burdened; It should take care of widows who are alone and needy.

Comments on 1 Ti 5:9-16

This is a social problem that the Ephesian church faced. While we as a church may not face this exact problem it is instructive to note how Paul advises solving it. Paul solves it contextually. His solution fit the Ephesian situation. It was concerned with the testimony of these widows in the Ephesians context. It is careful application.

1 Ti 5:17-20

17 Church leaders that are exercising good leadership should be *evaluated as worthy of double pay*—especially the ones who are working hard teaching the word. 18 For the scripture says, Don't muzzle the ox that is treading out the corn. And, The laborer is worthy of his reward. 19 Don't listen to an accusation against a leader unless it is backed by two or more witnesses. 20 Those leaders that are sinning rebuke before all, that others also may fear.

Comments On 1 Ti 5:17-20

Two implications are worth noting. (1) Leaders should be recompensed for their ministry. Those doing exceptional ministry, especially word oriented ministry should be amply rewarded. (2) There are differing functions of elders—ruling, teaching.

This is an important leadership principle. Accusations against leaders must be carefully examined. There should be strong confirmation where wrongdoing is involved. Note also in vs 20 that those found in the wrong should be publicly rebuked. This serves as part of the disciplinary action to restore the leader and to warn others. It also serves to guard the credibility of leadership. Today both of these guidelines are avoided. Frequently, accusations which are unfounded are given which destroy a leader even if later proved wrong. And very seldom is there public discipline of a leader found in the wrong.

Note that the principle concerning accusation occurs in a context dealing with money.

1 Ti 6:6-10

6 But a godly life with contentment is riches indeed. 7 For we brought nothing into this world, and it is certain we can carry nothing out. 8 So we should be content to have the food and clothing we need. 9 But those that set their hearts on becoming rich, can be eas-

ily trapped by foolish and harmful desires, which lead to ruin and destruction. 10 For the love of money is the root of all evil. Some have sought this and have strayed from the faith, and suffered deep grief because of it.

Comments on 1 Ti 6:6-10

Here Paul gives some solid teaching about money. Though useful, it can not rule our lives. Contentment (SRN 841 αὐταρκείας) refers to an inner attitude satisfied with its lot, an inner sufficiency. Riches (SRN 4200 πορισμος) translates a word meaning source of gain, or a means to gain, or gain). Indeed (SRN 3173 μέγας) simply means great or a lot. The idea being, there is an inner source of satisfaction that a godly person has which is far better than worldly riches.

Strayed from the faith is a repeated theme in 1 Ti (See also 1:6, 20; 5:11, 15; 6:10). This is a major problem that pastors and apostolic workers will face—especially in situations of radical conversions. The setting of ones heart on becoming rich can have disastrous result, even though reached.10 For the love of money is the root of all evil. Some have sought this and have strayed from the faith, and suffered deep grief because of it. This desire for money (or the power it can bring) can easily sidetrack a leader or a Christian follower.

2 Ti 2:3-7

3 So endure hardness, as a good soldier of Jesus Christ. 4 If you go on a military expedition you can't get enmeshed in civilian life or you won't please your commanding officer. 5 And if a person competes to win an athletic crown, that one follows the rules or else will not be crowned. 6 A hard working farmer ought to be the first to enjoy the harvest. 7 Consider these analogies and the Lord will help you understand them.

Comments on 2 Ti 2:3-7

I think these three analogies are applied directly to Timothy's situation. The *soldier illustration* is a warning for Timothy not to get sidetracked (this is repeatedly admonished in 1Ti also); the *athlete illustration* warns that it will take discipline to pull off the ministry. Timothy must maintain integrity (play by the rules) as he faces the Ephesian problems. The *farmer illustration* probably goes to the heart of the lack of financial support for Timothy. No leader likes to have to push his own situation where finances are concerned. 1Ti 5:17,18 also dealt with this. Timothy was not being supported. Paul says, "You need to be."

Tit 1:10, 11

10 The legalists, those especially advocating Jewish circumcision, are a rebellious bunch. Their talk is as cheap as it is deceitful. 11 They must be silenced. Their negative teaching is having a disastrous effect. Whole households are being affected by it. These teachers motives are questionable — they are in it dishonestly in order to make money.

Comments on Tit 1:10, 11

Paul has clean hands here. Throughout his ministry he has bent over backwards to avoid having a reputation for making money via ministry. See especially 2 Co where he rigorously defends himself on this issue and Philippians where he shows his personal view on ministry and finances.

Tit 3:12-14

12 As soon as I send Artemas or Tychicus to you, do your best to come to me at Nicopolis, because I have decided to winter there.   13 Do everything you can to help Zenas the lawyer and Apollos on their way and see that they have everything they need.[51]   14 Our people must learn to devote themselves to doing what is good, in order that they may provide for daily necessities and not live unproductive lives.[52]

Comments on Tit 3:12-14

Paul acts here as a mentor sponsor. He is attempting to raise financial support for Zenas and Apollos. He has done this previously for Timothy and Stephanus. He does this same function, supporting others, in the 2 Corinthian letters. This is an apostolic function, raising money to help support groundbreaking/ pioneering ministry.

Pauline Observations, Principles and Values About Finances

Finances can be a blessing and a curse. Having or not having wealth is not the issue. It is the stewardship of resources that is the major issue. What they are used for is what is significant. There are dangers of having financial resources—they can subtly turn away trust from God to trust in the resources. Paul admonishes to use resources well.

Leadership Principles / Values Suggested by this concept:

a. Money can not be trusted as a source of power or security.
b. Money must be appreciated as coming from God.
c. The use of money to bring enjoyment is valid.
d. Money ought to be a strong power base useful to do good for people.
e. Learning to use money wisely for God's kingdom work will allow a person to experience a reality in their Christian life.

Pauline Observations, Principles and Values About Fund Raising

Churches and parachurch organizations have financial needs just like any other organization in society.   These needs must be met.   How leaders influence followers with

---

51. Paul acts here as a mentor sponsor. He is attempting to raise financial support for Zenas and Apollos. He does this same function, supporting others, in the 2 Corinthian letters. See **Glossary**, *mentor sponsor*. See **Articles**, *Paul The Mentor; Finances — A Barrier To Finishing Well; Apostolic Functions — Comparison of Titus and Timothy.*

52. Two positive benefits of leading productive Christian lives are: 1) Christians provide for the necessities of life in their own setting and are not a drain on society; 2) there is the availability of resources to support the advancement of Christian work elsewhere. Paul is certainly implying that here. Productive lives involves support of God work in the world.

respect to meeting these needs is important. Paul demonstrates this delicate matter in 2Co 8,9. Paul also sponsors Christian workers (not himself, strangely enough), hoping, to link them up with financial resources to send them on their way in their itinerate ministries. He does not make a big issue of it but incidentally mentions the need of finances for various workers like Timothy, Stephanus, Zenas and Apollos.

Some observations concerning his raising money for various ministry things include:

Leadership Principles / Values Suggested by this concept:

a. A major motivational technique[53] relates the issue of giving to the issue of absolute surrender. True freedom to give flows from a life given to God.
b. Another motivational technique involves competitive comparisons with others who are poorer and yet give beyond expectations.
c. Willingness to give, not the amount given, is the criterion for giving.
d. Resources in the wider body of Christ will include surplus and great need. Where there is surplus giving should shift resources to needs.
e. Integrity in the handling of money is essential.
f. Apostolic leaders should use their influence to help connect needy leaders with financial aid.
g. Apostolic leaders are not in ministry for money but they know its importance in getting Kingdom ministry done.

Pauline Observations, Principles and Values About Giving

Chapters 8 and 9 in 2 Co give us the most comprehensive treatment of N.T. Church giving. I am certain that Paul was deeply affected by his mentor, Barnabas, concerning giving. See Ac 4:36,37; 11:27-30. Paul advocates giving to help fellow churches in need. He also advocates giving to help Christian workers (see comments above on this in 1Co 9, 16 as well as Php 4:10-17). His strong exhortations on giving highlight a number of principles which I have identified below.

Leadership Principles / Values Suggested by this concept:

a. Christians should be led of God to give (purpose in their hearts).
b. Christians should give proportionately as God has blessed them (as opposed to the O.T.'s various tithes given out of duty).
c. Christians should give as generously as they can.
d. Christians should give joyfully out of what they have, fully expecting God to bless it beyond its intrinsic worth.
e. Christians should give to those in need out of their extra that God has supplied; they can expect the same thing to happen when they have need.
f. Christians should expect God to give them more than their needs which they can then give generously.

53.　See **Article**, *Motivating Principles: Pauline Influence.*

   g.   Collections should be done systematically over time to be ready when needed.

   h.   God receives honor and praise and thanksgiving from many who are helped.

   i.   Those helped will remember the givers in prayer with affection;

   j.   There should be integrity in the handling of money given for various needs. Multiple parties of trustworthy people should be involved in the handling. This helps insure integrity.

Pauline Observations, Principles, Values Ministers Receiving Money

A leader's ministry is worthy of remuneration. This is not a big thing with Paul. But a leader who is effective should not be ashamed of reward for having done effective ministry. (2 Ti 2:6,7)

Leadership Principles / Values Suggested by this concept:

   a.   Leaders deserve remuneration for effective ministry.

   b.   Leaders need not be ashamed of this fact but should assume it as a God-given resource.

Conclusion

Forewarned is forearmed. There are many other reasons why leaders don't finish well—usually all related to sin in some form. Money issues have trapped many leaders and taken them out of the race. Leaders who want to finish well, Take heed! The bottom line value from Paul's teaching and modeling on leadership and finances is,

Label	Value Statement
Financial Integrity.	A Christian leader must handle finances with absolute integrity.

  Most cultures will have guidelines on what integrity with respect to finances is. Make sure you, like Paul, have clean hands with regards to money issues.

Gender and Leadership

Introduction

I referred to a perspective, *the starting-point-plus-process model*, when I commented on slavery in Phm. In the article describing the *starting-point-plus-process model*, I mentioned that the model applied to women in leadership as well as to slavery and marriage, both institutions in which God moved from less ideal held views to His ideals over long periods of time. It probably will apply as well to other issues, once they come into focus. For it describes how God works with people, graciously dealing with them to bring them to maturity. He begins where they are and moves them toward the ideal.

Basically the starting-point-plus-process model[54] has four major assertions.

1. Assuming a valid faith-allegiance response,[55] God allows for a range of under-standing of Himself and His will for people, for He starts *where people are* rather than demanding that they immediately conform to His ideals.
2. This range of understanding of God can assume a *variety of potential starting points* anywhere from sub-ideal toward ideal perception of God and His ways.
3. God then initiates a process which involves a *revelational progression* from a sub-ideal starting point toward the ideal. This on-going process often takes long time periods with small gains along the way.
4. This process of beginning with a range of sub-ideal starting points of perception and behavior and moving by revelational progression from the sub-ideal toward the ideal can be applied to any doctrine of Scripture and any Scriptural treatment of behavioral patterns.

Most of the cultures represented in the O.T. and N.T. have a sub-ideal starting point concerning leadership and the female gender. Most of these cultures were largely male-dominated cultures. This is an acceptable starting point, though sub-ideal.[56] People, who within these cultures accept God as their only God and His salvation, can be worked with to move toward the ideal. In this case of gender and leadership, that ideal is gifted leaders

---

54. This model is adapted from C.H. Kraft's work, *Christianity and Culture*.
55. That is, an acceptable starting place. By a faith-allegiance response I mean a valid decision to place God as top priority in a life—a trusting response for God's salvation and work in a life.

contributing to God's work, regardless of gender. Exceptions to the cultural norms as seen in the O.T. and N.T. which are blessed by God only serve to enforce what I am saying about movement toward an ideal.[57]

Leadership and Giftedness—The Ideal

A leader is a person with God-given capacity and a God-given burden who is influencing specific groups of people towards God's purposes for them. Comparative studies of leaders identified the concept of leaders being word-gifted. Study of giftedness throughout the N.T. church era indicated that people receive word gifts without regard to gender. That is, the Holy Spirit gives leadership gifts to male and females who are part of the body of Christ. Because of the work of the Cross both males and females are accepted into the body of Christ. Both are endowed with gifts from the Holy Spirit. The ideal is simply stated.

> **A gifted body operating interdependently allows the gifts of all its people to be used by God to mature the body and to expand it by bringing in new believers from the environment around it.**

Paul—Well Ahead of His Time

By the time of Paul's ministry, God had already begun strong movement toward the ideal. Jesus' ministry, in the Pre-Church Leadership Era inaugurated the movement toward the ideal by elevating the status of women in general.[58] Paul carried it further, co-ministering with women in local church situations, and sponsoring them elsewhere.[59]

When Paul describes selection of leaders to Timothy, even in a male dominated culture, he describes the characteristics for leaders not only in male terms but also in terms allowing for females.[60] For Paul the problem of female leaders is not so much theological (he is free here) but cultural (he recognizes that cultures may not be ready for it nor women in those cultures ready for it).

The so-called objections[61] to women in leadership in 1Co and 1Ti are not dealing with women as leaders, that is, giving a theological argument against women in leadership, but represent special cultural situations in which church behavior is not proper. Paul is correcting the church situations.

---

56. I am assuming the ideal of a gift based leadership church in which the Holy Spirit gives gifts that are needed to people without gender bias. People with leadership gifts should lead. This is a theological argument based on the nature of the church and the ministry of the Holy Spirit in the church. I also am aware of the ideal described in Gal 3:28.

57. Deborah is a case in point in the O.T. Priscilla, Phoebe, Syntyche, Euodias, Junia, Tryphena, and Tryphosa are fellow workers with Paul and are indications of movement toward the ideal.

58. Luke's Gospel is particularly instructive along these lines. Jesus reaches out to gentiles and women upon numerous occasions in Luke's Gospel. See also, **Article**, *Jesus—Circles of Intimacy—A Developmental Technique.*

59. See Ro 16:1,2 where Paul sponsors Phoebe as a minister of the Gospel.

60. See Peterson's translation, in **The Message**, of 1Ti 3 where he recognizes female leadership in the contextual flow. I agree with his interpretation.

Conclusion

Both males and females, who are gifted with leadership gifts, bring advantages to leadership because of their genders. Both are needed to see a full range of effective leadership in churches. Should Christ's Second Coming be delayed, we will see further movement toward the ideal in these next years. Once God has moved His people to the ideal, looking back, they wonder how they could have ever held such sub-ideal positions as were held (think back on slavery and marriage). So it will be with gender and leadership.

See *giftedness; word gifts;* **Glossary.** See **Article,** *Starting-Point—Plus—Process Model.* **See For Further Study Bibliography,** Clinton positional paper entitled, *Gender and Leadership,* an extended treatment of this subject which also gives the author's journey and paradigm shifts which brought about this present understanding.

---

61. I have studied all of these objections in depth. I have also read many present day authors who come down on both sides of the fence—those dead set against women as leaders and those who see women as leaders. I would expect that Paul would have written a very clear context placing men as leaders and showing that women cannot lead if that were the nature of the case. It is not. And Paul did not. His so called anti-women-in-leadership passages are really dealing with cultural church problems specific to those situations (Corinth, Ephesus). In my comments in the **Leadership Insights** in Eph I even give a paraphrase of the 1Ti 2 passage which reflects this notion of a specific cultural problem.

God our Savior — Paul's Favorite Title in Latter Ministry

Introduction

Sometimes when you are studying something comparatively you notice things that otherwise would be missed. For example, if you are studying the Apostolic Ministry Epistles — 1, 2 Timothy and Titus — and reading them over and over and comparing things you might notice some things about Paul in his old age. Like his tendency in 1 Timothy to get sidetracked from his main purpose and throw in little doctrinal comments. Or like repeated phrases in these books.

As to the sidetracking doctrinal asides in 1 Timothy (1:17; 2:3-6; 3:16; 6:15,16), I note how fundamental and core they are. They deal with fundamental things like God and salvation. The harvest model is carried strongly in the asides. The shepherd model is carried in the epistle as a whole, but the asides deal with God, His purposes, His character, His desire for people to know his salvation. I see Paul as he ages, making sure that the fundamentals that he started with are in clear and in focus.

As to the repeated phrases, one such is Paul's favorite title for God in these Apostolic Epistles — *God our Savior*. The same is true of the repeated phrase for God that Paul uses — God our Savior. It is dealing with a fundamental core truth.

Passages With God Our Savior

Glance below at the passages that use this phrase for God.

Table 15.1　Paul's Use of God our Savior — Passages

Passage	Verses
1 Ti 1:1,2	1 Paul, an apostle of Jesus Christ by the commandment of **God our Savior**, and the Lord Jesus Christ, which is our hope; 2 Unto Timothy, my own son in the faith: Grace, mercy, and peace, from God our Father and Jesus Christ our Lord.
1 Ti 2:1-7	1 Consequently, I strongly urge that, first of all, requests to God, prayers, intercessions, and giving of thanks, be made for all people. 2 Do so for kings, and for all that are in authority, that we may lead a quiet and peaceable life in all godliness and seriousness. 3 For this is good and acceptable in the sight of **God our Savior**, 4 who would wish for all people to be saved, and to come unto the knowledge of the truth. 5 For there is one God, and one mediator between God and mankind, the man Christ Jesus, 6 who gave himself a ransom for all, to be testified in due time. 7 And this is why I was established as a preacher, and an apostle. I speak the truth in Christ, and lie not; a teacher of faith and truth to the Gentiles.
Tit 1:1-4	1 I, Paul, am ministering as a servant of God and an apostle of Jesus Christ to help mature God's own chosen followers. I want them to know the truth that leads to godliness. 2 I want them to have a faith[a] and a knowledge grounded in an expectation of eternal life. God, who can not lie, promised this eternal life before the beginning of time. 3 At His appointed time, He revealed His truth about this. **God our Savior** entrusted me with this task and commanded me to preach it. 4 I write to you, Titus, one who is like my very own son because of our common faith.
Tit 2:9-10	1 I, Paul, am ministering as a servant of God and an apostle of Jesus Christ to help mature God's own chosen followers. I want them to know the truth that leads to godliness. 2 I want them to have a faith and a knowledge grounded in an expectation of eternal life. God, who can not lie, promised this eternal life before the beginning of time. 3 At His appointed time, He revealed His truth about this. **God our Savior** entrusted me with this task and commanded me to preach it. 4 I write to you, Titus, one who is like my very own son because of our common faith.
Tit 3:1-5	Remind the people to be subject to rulers and authorities. They should be obedient people and ready to do whatever is good. 2 They should slander no one. They should be peaceable and considerate people. Humility toward all should be a hallmark of their changed lives. 3 At one time we too were foolish, disobedient, deceived and enslaved by all kinds of passions and pleasures. We lived in malice and envy, being hated and hating one another. 4 But then the kindness and love of **God our Savior** appeared. 5 He saved us, not because of righteous things we had done, but because of his mercy. He saved us through a cleansing renewal in our inner life. We were renewed by the Holy Spirit.

a.　Faith here is most likely a metonymy. Faith, here means the whole Christian way of life and belief — which is by faith. Paul will later re-emphasize that the Christian way of life is by faith and not by works. God's grace enables one to live and believe the Christian truth. See **Glossary**, *Metonymy*.

Conclusion

I want to draw out two implications from the use of this phrase by Paul.

Implication 1.	As we as leaders age we should find that our distinction between core and peripheral issues firms up. We will probably have less core things and more peripheral than we did when we were younger. But our core becomes more of an emphasis for us. You can see this with Paul. Basic truth about God, especially His saving ability gets highlighted in these Apostolic Epistles.

Implication 2.	We, as leaders, need to recognize the importance of our phrases we use for God. They should be indicative of what God is to us. Our people need to know that we know God in certain important ways. Our phrases we use to describe God will do this.

God our Savior is a special name for God used by Paul for emphasis. In the salutation to Titus it foreshadows basic content he will elaborate on later in the epistle. In general, Paul, when using this phrase, is emphasizing God as the Source of Salvation, from the past, in the present and in the future.

God's Timing and Leadership

Introduction

What do these verses have in common?

Joseph's birth:

> And God remembered Rachel, and God hearkened to her, and opened her womb. 23 And she conceived, and bore a son; and said, God hath taken away my reproach: 24 And she called his name Joseph; and said, The LORD shall add to me another son. Gen 30:22

Jesus Ministry:

> But when the fullness of the **time** was come, God sent forth his Son, made of a woman, made under the law, 5 To redeem them that were under the law, that we might receive the adoption of sons. Gal 4:4

From John Quoting Jesus:

> John: Jesus said unto her, Woman, what have I to do with thee? my **hour** is not yet come. Jn 2:4

> Then Jesus said unto them, **My time** is not yet come: but your time is always ready. Jn 7:6

> I am not going to the feast, yet; for **my time** is not yet full come. Jn 7:8

> Then they sought to take him: but no man laid hands on him, because his **hour** was not yet come. Jn 7:30

> These words spoke Jesus in the treasury, as he taught in the temple: and no man laid hands on him; for his **hour** was not yet come. Jn 8:20

> And Jesus answered them, saying, The **hour** is come, that the Son of man should be glorified. Jn 12:23

> Now is my soul troubled; and what shall I say? Father, save me from this **hour**: but for this cause came I unto this **hour**. Jn 12:27

> Now before the feast of the passover, when Jesus knew that his **hour** was

come that he should depart out of this world unto the Father, having loved his own which were in the world, he loved them unto the end. Jn 13:1

All have to do with God's timing. One of the major macro lessons first seen in *the Patriarchal Leadership Era* and then in every other leadership era thereafter states,

God's timing is crucial to the accomplishment of God's purposes.[62]

Effective leaders are increasingly aware of the timing of God's interventions in their lives and ministry. They move when he moves. They wait. They confidently expect. Leaders must learn to be sensitive to God's timing. God's direction includes *What, How, and When*. All are important.

This is a leadership lesson that all leaders must learn. Strong leaders, such as apostolic leaders desperately need to learn this. Such leaders usually have a strong sense of destiny. Such leaders usually have a strong vision they want to accomplish. Often these strong leaders tie their vision to some prophecy or other revelatory word. While they may know the *what* and even the *how* of the vision they may well be off in the *when*. They often move ahead of God's timing. God's timing is crucial. Less bold and forceful leaders also need to learn about God's timing. Frequently, they lag behind God's timing. What can we learn from some Bible characters about God's timing?

Thirteen Bible Characters and God's Timing

Table 16.1 lists thirteen Bible characters and implications about God's timing.

Table 16.1   Thirteen Bible Characters and God's Timing Across the Leadership Eras

Character	Era	Timing Issue	Observations/ Lessons
Abraham/ Sarah	Patriarchal	Birth of Isaac/ Israel's deliverance 400 years later	Isaac: *The promises of God include what, how, and when.* Abraham and Sarah only knew what. The *how* they tried to manipulate. The *when*—they went ahead of God. God was true to his promise. The *what, how, when* all came together. God's timing was crucial. Israel's Promised Deliverance from Egypt: Sometimes God's timing is well beyond a leader's own lifetime. Such a promise can enable one to live with hope and faith though they may never see the fulfillment of that promise.
Jacob/ Rachael	Patriarchal	Birth of Joseph	Joseph's birth, as to timing was important. The birth order was necessary to God's purposes for him—both favored status and his brothers jealousy. The time of birth was important; he was to deliver in 39 years. *Manipulation of God's timing can bring problems. Manipulation begets manipulation.*
Joseph	Patriarchal	Fulfillment of Certainty Guidance—2 Dreams	Throughout the Joseph narrative timing is important (dreams at 17; caravan; in jail with two of Pharaoh's servants; God's dreams about drought, etc.) Most important lesson. *The way up is often down and may take a long time for God to accomplish.*

---

62.   See **Articles**, *Macro Lessons—Defined; Macro Lessons—List of 41 Across Six Leadership eras.*

Moses	Pre-King-dom	Deliverance of Israel from Egypt	Deliverance from Egypt: Moses was a strong leader who went ahead of God to deliver Israel from Egypt. He learned a major lesson that strong leaders often learn—The Death of a Vision. *A strong ego leader must surrender a vision and give it back to God. God will bring it about in his own way and timing. Don't move ahead of God. Make sure the how of guidance is God's how.* Crossing the Red Sea: *The when of God's guidance is crucial. It takes faith to believe in exact timing of God's intervention.* Failure to Enter the Land: *Failure to heed God's intervention time can bring long term ramifications—* 40 years in the desert, loss of a generation Going in to the land: *God's progressive timing has underlying reasons behind it. Development of an armed force takes time.*
Joshua	Pre-King-dom	Generational leadership/ Capture of Jericho/ Gibeon (flesh act)	Desert Wandering: *A leader often pays a price due to followership. A leader needs time to enculterate and be enculterated to a new generation of followers.* Crossing the Jordan: They could have crossed in non-flood season without God's help. They needed this God intervention for courage and to give Joshua spiritual authority. The three days they camped beside the flood waters built anticipation and fearfulness. Fall of Jericho: *The How and When must be obtained from God in a major achievement.* Gibeon: *Moving ahead of God, making a decision in the flesh with hearing from God and then asking God to approve your decision often results in major negative ramifications that you must live with.*
Caleb	Pre-King-dom	Generational Leadership; Fulfillment of Promise	Desert Wandering: *Leaders who model whole hearted obedience to God can impact a new generation with the importance of believing God and obeying Him.* Land: *The promises of God will be fulfilled in His timing. Respond with courage.*
Samuel	Pre-King-dom	Moving from decentralized leadership to a Kingdom	Sons: *The what of God's intervention is as important as the when and how. Samuel's sons were not God's answer to the leadership need.*: Saul: *Obedience to God's timing is necessary. Failure to obey God as to His timing may well imply lack of integrity and an eventual setting aside by God.*
David	Kingdom	Made King	Uniting the Kingdom: *Time is involved even when the what is known.*
Hezekiah	Kingdom	Sickness Unto Death/ Babylonian Envoy (flesh act)	Changing God's Timing: *Hezekiah's prolonged life brought ramifications he probably didn't foresee. The birth of Manasseh occurred in this time.* Babylonian envoy: *To move ahead of God, make a decision without consulting God, can bring ramifications (later Babylonian captivity). To be safe in one's own generation may well bode problems for future generations.*
Daniel	Post-King-dom	70 Years Captivity Fulfilled	Learning Posture: *Daniel's maintaining a learning posture, studying the Scriptures, brought out the what and when and hints as to the how of God's plans. God's timing is exact. He will fulfill His promises on time.*

Jesus	Pre-Church	The Cross	World Scene: *The timing was perfect for Jesus' birth.* Sensitivity: *Jesus was sensitive to God's timing for his life, throughout his ministry. He never went ahead; he never lagged behind. Jesus models perfectly the whole notion of what, when, and how in following God's plans.*
Peter	Church	Impulsive Actions; Coming of Holy Spirit	Impulsive: *Peter's tendencies to move too quickly throughout the disciples training serves as a negative model.* See Jesus' reactions and training of Peter. Pentecost: *God's promise of power was fulfilled exactly on time. Waiting was involved.* Lagging Behind: *The church failed to expand. God brought persecution to get them to expand.*
Paul	Church	Reaching of Gentiles/ Kings	Antioch Call: *A leader may be called upon to do something at a time (when is clear—release my Servants for the ministry to which I have called them). But the what and how are hazy. The what and when may be revealed over time.* Macedonian call: *God's timing may involve pre-preparation about the what and how. The move to Europe involved a pre-prepared receptive group ready to hear and respond.*

Reasons For Delay In Timing

In a number of the Biblical examples given above God delayed what He was going to do. Some possible reasons for delay include:

a. **Dealing With a Strong Ego Leader**—The *Death of a Vision* as seen in Moses' case involved dealing with the right vision but the wrong motivation, wrong power base, and wrong timing.

b. **God's Working out of other purposes**—In the promise to Abraham (400 years), God pointed out that He was dealing with the nations in the land and that their iniquity was not yet full. That is, He was giving them time to repent. That time wasn't up yet when Moses made his first attempt at deliverance.

c. **Foundational Character Shaping**—Moses' isolation period brought about a humility in character (Nu 12:3) which made him a pliable vessel in God's hands. He would need this humility because God would reveal power through his ministry which could be dangerous with a strong unfettered ego leader.

d. **Remedial Training**—God is doing remedial training. He is giving time for certain disciplines to be built in the life of the leader. Moses was a desert leader. He learned about desert disciplines as a shepherd wandering over desert land taking care of sheep.

Reasons To Move Fast in God's Timing

Just as some leaders have a tendency to move too fast and God has to delay their actions, some leaders move too slowly. Why should leaders move faster? Here are some reasons:

a. **Windows of Opportunity**—God knows that sometimes the needed action must take place within a certain time period or an opportunity to accomplish something may be lost.

b. **Networks/ onward guidance**—Sometimes the timing is such that obedience will connect to other things God has set up. The next piece of guidance will open up after obedience. To not move will be to miss it. Following an unusual, apparently hurried intervention may lead to a series of people or events and give guidance that would not previously have been dreamed of.

c. **God's Doing**—Sometimes God moves a leader to action before things are apparently ready because He wants all to know that He alone is responsible and He alone will get credit for the results. That is, sometimes God has something happen fast because it would be impossible for it to happen unless God alone brought it about.

Four Implications of the Timing Lesson

Four observations can be drawn from a comparative study of God's timing with biblical leaders:

1. **Ramifications.** Moving ahead of God's timing in guidance or in carrying out some aspect of ministry may accomplish the task, yet, it will most certainly bring ramifications which will require remedial training and the repetition of incidents to teach us the dependence lesson.

2. **Guidance.** The *what*, *how*, and *when* are the major elements of guidance. We need clarity on all three. It is the *when* that is most in focus on the timing macro lesson.

3. **Sensitivity.** We must be sensitive to the Spirit in our lives. Timing can refer to daily interventions or long term guidance decisions. In either case we need to be sensitive to the Spirit. Seemingly small issues may turn out to be pivotal points. This implies that we as leaders especially need to develop the Spirit sensitivity component of the Spirituality model.

4. **Negative Preparation and Flesh Act.** We need to be thoroughly familiar with these two process items including the various illustrations of them in Scripture so we will respond more quickly and carefully to incidents which God is using for this kind of processing. A *flesh act* means making a decision based on fleshly wisdom and moving ahead without getting God's guidance. *Negative preparation* refers to numerous negative happenings in the life. These may well be used by God to move a leader out of a situation.

Conclusion

Look again at the basic lesson.

God's Timing Is Crucial To Accomplishment Of God's Purposes.

Moses learned this lesson the hard way. But he learned it well. The latter stages of his desert leadership reflect his increased sensitivity to God's timing. The question is,

> Are You Sensitive To God's Timing In The Little Things Of Daily Ministry As Well As The Big Things Of Major Guidance?

Some final advice should be noted, especially for major guidance decisions.

1. **Triple Confirmation.**   Where possible never make a major decision unless you are clear on the *what*, the *how*, and the *when* of the issues. Should you be unclear on any, then it may be best to wait. Certainty guidance via double confirmation or divine contact should be sought on all three issues: what, when, how.

2. **Presumption.** Be careful of presuming to know God's intents on some aspects of ministry without clearing with Him first. Simply attempting to get His approval after the fact may prove fatal in the long run.

3. **Patterns.** Study the concept of timing in the Bible and identify patterns of sensitivity to God's timing. Note what to avoid as well as what to assert. Go back through the vignettes associated with the leaders given in Table 1. Study them carefully and learn first hand what you need to know about God's timing and your leadership.

Let me repeat in closing. *Effective Leaders Are Increasingly Aware Of The Timing Of God's Interventions In Their Lives And Ministry.* They Move When He Moves. They Wait. They Confidently Expect. Leaders must learn to be sensitive to God's timing. God's direction includes *What, How,* and *When*. All are important.

See *flesh act; negative preparation; pivotal point; double confirmation; divine contact;* **Glossary.**

Integrity — A Top Leadership Quality

Introduction

I have been repeating a number of times in the leadership commentary, for a number of books, a major leadership principle.

Ministry flows out of being.

Being is a term describing a number of factors which refer to the inner life and essence of a person. It refers to at least the following, but is not limited to them: (1) intimacy with God; (2) character; (3) personality; (4) giftedness; (5) destiny; (6) values drawn from experience; (7) conscience, and (8) gender influenced perspectives. The axiom, ministry flows out of being means that one's ministry should be a vital outflow from these inner beingness factors.

It is integrity, the rudder that steers character, that I want to highlight in this discussion. Consider the following two words:

1. deception   noun 1.The use of deceit. 2.The fact or state of being deceived. 3. A ruse; a trick. [adapted from The American Heritage Dictionary of the English Language, Third Edition, 1992.] **Synonyms:** trickery, gulling, lying, juggling, craftiness. **Antonyms:** sincerity, frankness, honesty, openness, truthfulness, trustworthiness, genuineness, earnestness, innocence, candor, veracity, verity, probity, fidelity.

2. integrity   The uncompromising adherence to a code of moral, artistic or other values which reveals itself in utter sincerity, honesty, and candor and avoids deception or artificiality (Adapted from Webster). **Synonyms:** honesty, virtue, honor, morality, uprightness, righteousness. Antonyms: deception, dishonesty, corruption, infidelity.

The words are opposite.

Few leaders finish well.[63] Most major failures in ministry are dominantly rooted in spiritual formation issues (spirituality) rather than ministerial formation and strategic formation issues.[64] Most of these failures can ultimately be traced to basic failures of integrity.[65] Leaders who fail often do not have integrity but instead have some sort of deception about at least some of their leadership. On the other hand, leaders who finish well, across the board are leaders of integrity.

Let me remind you of the definition of a Christian leader: A Christian leader is a person with a God-given capacity and a God-given responsibility who is influencing a specific group of God's people toward God's purposes for the group. You cannot influence a group very effectively if they don't trust you. And if you are suspected of trickery, gulling, mendacity, juggling, craftiness—they won't trust you and you won't lead them.

At the heart of any assessment of biblical qualifications for leadership lies the concept of integrity—that uncompromising adherence to a code of moral, artistic or other values which reveals itself in utter sincerity, honesty, and candor and avoids deception or artificiality. So if we want to be leaders who finish well we want to be people of integrity. What is integrity? How do we get it?

Definition   *Integrity,* the top leadership character quality, is the consistency of inward beliefs and convictions with outward practice. It is an honesty and wholeness of personality in which one operates with a clear conscience in dealings with self and others.

God develops integrity in leaders. It is at the heart of character. A repeated observation on leaders whom God developed and used for his purposes resulted in the following helpful definition.

Definition   An *integrity check* refers to the special kind of shaping activity (a character test) which God uses to evaluate heart–intent, consistency between inner convictions and outward actions, and which God uses as a foundation from which to expand the leader's capacity to influence. The word check is used in the sense of test—meaning a check or check-up.

---

63. Of the Biblical leaders for whom there is evidence about finishing well, about one in three finish well. Probably it is even less for contemporary leaders if anecdotal evidence means anything. What do I mean by finish well? I have identified six characteristics of finishing well from a comparative study of leaders who finished well. A given leader will not necessarily demonstrate all six but at least several. These six characteristics include the following: (1) They maintain a personal vibrant relationship with God right up to the end. (2) They maintain a learning posture and can learn from various kinds of sources—life especially. (3) They manifest godliness (especially Christ-like attitudes and behavior) in character as evidenced by the fruit of the Spirit in their lives. (4) Truth is lived out in their lives so that convictions and promises of God are seen to be real. (5) They leave behind one or more ultimate contributions. (6) They walk with a growing awareness of a sense of destiny and see some or all of it fulfilled.

64. *Spiritual formation* is the shaping activity in a leader's life which is directed toward instilling godly character and developing inner life (i.e. intimacy with God, character, values drawn from experience, conscience). *Strategic formation* is the shaping activity in a leader's life which is directed toward having that leader reach full potential and achieve a God-given destiny. *Ministerial formation* is the shaping activity in a leader's life which is directed toward instilling leadership skills, leadership experience, and developing giftedness for ministry.

65. Studies of leaders who have failed to finish well has identified six major barriers to their finishing well. These include: finances—their use and abuse; power—its abuse; inordinate pride—which leads to a downfall; sex—illicit relationships; family—critical issues; plateauing. At the very heart of most of these major barriers lies an integrity issue.

I'll come back to this notion of an integrity check and give detailed information on it. But first think with me about Biblical leaders and the notion of integrity.

Biblical Leaders of Integrity

If I were to ask you to name the top two O.T. leaders who demonstrated integrity, who would you suggest? If I were to ask you to name the top two N.T. leaders who demonstrate integrity, who would you suggest?

My top two O.T. leaders who demonstrated integrity are Joseph and Daniel. My top two N.T. leaders who demonstrated integrity are Jesus and Paul (Barnabas is a close second behind Paul).

Both Joseph and Daniel exemplify leaders who were tested by God as to their integrity and passed with flying colors. Joseph in Gen 39 refuses to have an affair with Potiphar's wife. He sees this as wrong. In fact, he states that to do so would be sin against God. God honors this stand and later elevates Joseph to the top administrative post in Egypt (under the Pharaoh). Daniel in Da 1 is tested as to integrity with regard to eating food unacceptable to a Jew. He stands on his convictions. He too is blessed by God and becomes a high administrator under Nebuchadnezzar and eventually becomes the number one administrator under Darius. Jesus throughout his whole ministry demonstrates integrity, always showing unity between outward practice and inward conviction. (See especially the Satanic temptations in Mt 4.) Paul writes a whole epistle defending his integrity. He was being accused of all kinds of deception: lying, craftiness, dishonesty, trickery. The book of 2Co reveals Paul's answers to the accusations of deception. A major Pauline leadership value emerges in 2Co.

Label	Statement of Value
Integrity and Openness	*Leaders should not be deceptive in their dealings with followers but should instead be open, honest, forthright, and frank with them.*

Paul, throughout 2Co, refutes the accusations of deception in his leadership and lays out for us many principles underlying integrity in a leader.

Paul's instruction to Timothy in 1Ti about leadership qualifications should be noted here. His qualifications for leaders includes character and conscience. Paul's list of qualifications focuses on integrity and deals mainly with character not giftedness. See his three lists[66] in 1Ti 3:1-7; 8-10; 11-13. All three lists emphasize integrity. And this integrity should be seen by those outside the church as well as those within.

---

[66]. These three lists are apparently list idioms in which the initial item on the list is the main assertion and other items illustrate or clarify the primary item. If so, then the major leadership trait is integrity, a moral characteristic implying a consistency between inner and outer life. The items on the list would then illustrate in the Ephesian culture what moral character, integrity, looks like. So then these items in themselves are not necessarily universal characteristics for a leader but are indicative of what moral character and integrity look like in this culture. The obligatory item is inner integrity, moral character. Paul concludes this small section in vs 7 by returning to this important idea to reemphasize it. This is repeated in descriptions of the lesser leader lists described in vs 8-10, 11-13. Note especially vs 8 and 11. See *list idiom*, **Glossary.**

Integrity Check Revisited

God uses life situations to test and build up the inner character of a leader. Integrity is one of the main qualities God shapes in a leader. The *integrity check* is a major way this happens. From comparative study (e.g. Daniel in Da 1,5; Shadrach, Meshach, and Abednego in Da 3; Joseph in Gen 39; Abraham in Gen 24; Jephthah in Jdg 11; Paul in Ac 20:22,23 and many others), a list of kinds of integrity checks can be identified. And their use by God can be suggested. Table 17.1 gives the kinds of integrity checks. Table 17.2 lists their uses.

Table 17.1 Kinds of Integrity Check

Label	Explanation
temptation (conviction test)	An integrity check frequently is given to allow a leader to identify an inner conviction and to take a stand on it. Such a stand will deepen the conviction in the leader's life. Can a leader really take a stand on some conviction?
restitution (honesty testing)	Some integrity checks force a leader to make right things done wrong in the past, particularly those with on-going ramifications. This is particularly seen in money matters where in the past someone was defrauded. Will a leader be honest, especially about the past?
value check (ultimate value clarification)	Situations frequently force leaders to think through their beliefs about something so that they can identify explicitly a value(s). This value once identified can be evaluated. It can be used more strongly. It may be modified. It may be discarded as not really valid. Can a leader identify the underlying value in a situation?
loyalty (allegiance testing)	God must be first in a life. Frequently, other things become first in a leader's life with perhaps it not even being known by the leader. God can bring to light those things which take His rightful place in our hearts and lives. Who is really first in our lives?
Guidance (alternative testing— a better offer Holy Spirit led choice to some decision)	Frequently a leader is led by God to declare for a certain thing (a ministry, a choice, some option). It is clear that God has led the leader to that choice. After making the choice God may well bring an alternative which looks easier or better simply to test the follow-through on the original decision. Can a leader stick to God's former sure guidance when other challenging guidance comes along?
conflict against ministry vision (guidance/faith testing)	Frequently, a leader will be led into a situation and even have followers support in it. But down the line in the midst of the decision being worked out, particularly when negative ramifications arise, followers or others will oppose the situation. Conflict arises. Note that conflict is a mighty weapon in the hand of God. Usually this integrity check will enforce faith in the leader. Can a leader maintain guidance and believe God will under gird some ministry vision?
word conflict or obedience conflict (complexity testing usually in guidance)	Sometimes a leader will get a word from God or be challenged to obey God in some particular way. Usually this has to do with guidance. Conflict arises as in the previous description. Can a leader trust in his/her ability to hear from God? Or will a leader obey, even if conflict arises?

Table 17.2   The Ways that God Uses Integrity Checks

Identifying Label	Why It Is Used
Follow Through	to see follow-through on a promise or vow
Deepening Burden	to insure burden for a ministry or vision
Edification	to allow confirmation of inner-character strength
Faith Builder	to build faith
Value Clarifying	to establish inner values very important to later leadership which will follow
Lordship	to teach submission
Warnings	to warn others of the seriousness of obeying God

Often the integrity check happens completely unknown to people around the leader. That is because of its inward nature. The secondary causes may be events, people, etc. They may not even know that they are sources. The primary causal source is inward through the conscience. The Holy Spirit shapes the conscience.[67]

There is a three step pattern to an integrity check which is passed positively: (1) the challenge to consistency with inner convictions, (2) the response to the challenge, and (3) the resulting expansion. Sometimes the expansion may be delayed or take place over a period of time but it can definitely be seen to stem from the integrity check. Delayed expansion is seen in Joseph's classic test with Potiphar's wife. Immediate expansion is seen in Daniel's wine test.[68]

There is also a three part pattern to an integrity check which is failed: (1) the challenge to consistency with inner convictions, (2) the response to the challenge, and (3) the remedial testing. God will frequently repeat an integrity check until a leader gets it or will take more drastic action. Instead of remedial testing there may be discipline, or setting aside from ministry, or even death.

Conclusion

Character is crucial to leadership. Integrity is the foundational trait of character in a leader. Let me summarize some observations, principles and values suggested by the importance of integrity in a leader.

a. Ministry flows out of being of which character is a major component and integrity the dominant necessary leadership trait within character.

b. Leaders without character cannot be trusted and will be followed only to the extent that they have coercive power to back up their leadership claims.

c. A leader must be conscious of what others think of him/her, character-wise. Integ-

---

[67]. Conscience refers to the inner sense of right or wrong which is innate in a human being but which also is modified by values imbibed from a culture. This innate sense can also be modified by the Spirit of God. See **Article**, *Paul's Use of Conscience.*

[68]. See *testing patterns, positive and negative,* **Glossary**. See **Article**, *Daniel Four Positive Testing Patterns.*

rity is universal and occurs in every culture as a notion. But it will take on cultural manifestations peculiar to a culture that demonstrate to those in the culture what integrity is.[69]

d. A leader must seek to have a testimony respected by others (within the bounds of God's ministry assignments).[70]

e. Even though the source of some character trial may be Satanic, a leader should use it to purge impure character traits and rest in God's overriding purposes through the testing.[71]

f.   A leader should recognize that character integrity checks will be used by God as foundational training for increased usefulness.[72]

Do the people you influence see you as deceptive or a person of integrity? Do the people outside your ministry see you as deceptive or a person of integrity? Conscience is the inner governor of character—and especially integrity. Remember Paul's challenging statement.

> Because I believe in an ultimate accounting before God, I make every effort always to keep my conscience clear before God and man. Ac 24:16

[69.] For example, oath-keeping was a high value of integrity in the Hebrew O.T.

[70.] Paul repeats this notion over and over in 1Ti when advising Timothy about his consulting ministry with the Ephesian church.

[71.] Job shows us that behind the apparent things happening to us there may be an unseen spiritual source causing it (Satanic). But even where bad things happen, God can use them to shape character.

[72.] A basic understanding of integrity checks can aid one in recognizing much earlier and giving a godly response to them. Forewarned is forearmed.

Leadership Lessons— Seven Major Lessons Identified

From comparative study of over 1200 leader case studies, seven major leadership lessons have emerged. These leadership lessons are listed below with a brief explanation, a value suggested which flows from the lesson, reasons why important, a Biblical and a contemporary example and some suggestions for follow-up.

1. Lifetime Perspective

Effective Leaders View Present Ministry in Terms Of A Lifetime Perspective.

Explanation: Leaders who recognize the big picture for their lives have a jump start on surviving present circumstances which may be both negative and overwhelming. A leader needs to recognize the notion of developmental phases over a lifetime and boundaries transitioning between them. He/she needs to understand the shaping activity of God over a lifetime. If such a leader also knows the basic goal toward which God is moving, he/she can respond to present day shaping for maximum benefit. In general, a leader knowing what it means to finish well, determines to have that for his/her life. That leader recognizes the barriers to finishing well: 1. lack of financial integrity, 2. sexual impropriety, 3. abuse of power, 4. family related problems, 5. problems with pride, 6. plateauing. That leader recognizes the factors that will promote a good finish: 1. a learning posture, 2. mentoring help, 3. renewal experiences, 4. disciplines, 5. a lifelong perspective. A leader thus armed can perceive what is happening today from a sovereign mindset. In short, it allows the leader to go through present happenings because of the hope of the future and knowledge that God is in them.

Value Suggested: A leader ought to gain perspective on what is happening today in his/her life by interpreting it in the light of his/her whole lifetime and God's overall purposes in it.

Why Important: 1) Few leaders finish well. Perspective is one of the enhancements that can help a greater number of leaders finish well. 2) Making it through tough times in leadership may well depend on gaining perspective. Without perspective, a longer range viewpoint on what is happening, few leaders will persevere through hard times. 3) A critical difference between leaders and followers is perspective. The difference between leaders and more effective leaders is better perspective. Effective leaders will be broadening their perspective.

Biblical Examples: Jesus, Paul

Contemporary Example: Billy Graham

Suggestions for Follow-Up: Read Clinton's **The Making of a Leader** for a popular treatment of a lifetime perspective on a leader's development. See also the ***Article** Time-Lines—Defined for Biblical Leaders*. See Graham's autobiography, **Just As I Am.**

2. Learning Posture

Effective Leaders Maintain A Learning Posture Throughout Life.

Explanation: The ability to learn from the Bible, current events, people, reading, ministry experience, and other sources in such a way as to affect one's leadership is fundamental to being an effective leader. Flexible leaders usually do have a good learning posture (has to do with an attitude, a mental stance toward learning). Inflexible leaders are not usually active learners. God will bring into a leader's life necessary information and wisdom to meet leadership situations if that leader is open to learning. Leadership is dynamic. Changing situations demand that a leader be constantly learning. One of the five major factors identified with leaders who finish well is a good learning posture.

Value Suggested: A leader ought to be continually learning from a wide variety of sources in order to cope effectively with life and ministry.

Why Important: A good learning posture is one of the enhancements toward a good finish. It is also the key to ministry insights, paradigm shifts, and other leadership lessons that can make the difference in effective on-going leadership.

Biblical Examples: Daniel, the classic Old Testament leader, models an exemplary learning posture. The Apostle Paul does the same in the New Testament.

Contemporary Examples: Watchman Nee (Chinese church/para church leader who died in prison in the early 70s); A. J. Gordon, Baptist pastor in Boston area and developer of one of the first flagship churches in the U.S. (1836-1895). Examples from today include Phil Yancey, Hans Finzel and Robertson McQuilkin.

Suggestions for Follow-Up: See Kinnear's book on Nee, **Against The Tide.** See For Further Study Bibliography, Clinton's chapter 3 on A.J. Gordon in **Focused Lives.**

3. Spiritual Authority

Effective Leaders Value Spiritual Authority As A Primary Power Base.

Explanation: Spiritual authority is the right to influence conferred by followers because of their perception of spirituality in a leader. It is that characteristic of a God-anointed leader which is developed upon an experiential power base that enables him/her to influence followers through: 1) Persuasion, 2) Force of modeling, and 3) Moral expertise. Spiritual authority comes to a leader in three major ways. First as leaders go through deep experiences with God they experience the sufficiency of God to meet them in those situations. They come to know God more intimately by experiencing Him. This experiential knowledge of God and the deep experiences with God are part of the experiential acquisition of spiritual authority. A second way that spiritual authority comes is through a life which models godliness. When the Spirit of God is transforming a life into the image of Christ, those characteristics of love, joy, peace, long suffering, gentleness, goodness, faith, meekness, temperance carry great weight in giving credibility. They show that the leader is consistent inwardly and outwardly. A third way that spiritual authority comes is through gifted power. When a leader demonstrates gifted power in ministry —that is, a clear testimony to divine intervention in the ministry—there will be spiritual authority. While all three of these means of developing spiritual authority should be a part of a leader, it is frequently the case that one or more of the elements dominates. Ideally spiritual authority is the major influence means used with mature followers. Other power bases such as coercion, inducement, positional, and competence may have to be used as well as spiritual authority because of lack of maturity in followers. Mature followers will recognize spiritual authority. Leaders who command and demand compliance are not using spiritual authority.

Values Suggested: 1) Leaders should respond to God's processing in their life so as to let spiritual authority develop as a by-product of the processing. 2) Leaders ought to recognize and use spiritual authority whenever they can in their ministry.

Why Important: Leaders who rely on privilege and power associated with a position tend to abuse power in their ministry. Spiritual authority counters the abuse of power. Spiritual authority honors God's maturity processes in followers.

Biblical Examples: Moses, Jesus, Paul

Contemporary Examples: Henrietta Mears, Bible teacher/ entrepreneur (1890-1963); Watchman Nee (Chinese church/para church leader who died in prison in the early 70s). John Wimber was a leader who especially had spiritual authority because of gifted power.

Suggestions for Follow-Up: See For Further Study Bibliography, Clinton's chapter 8 on Mears in Focused Lives and teaching by Nee on this subject, Spiritual Authority.

4. Dynamic Ministry Philosophy

Effective Leaders Who Are Productive Over A Lifetime Have A Dynamic Ministry Philosophy.

Explanation: An unchanging set of core values and a changing set of peripheral values comprise a dynamic ministry philosophy. Such a ministry philosophy expands due to a growing discovery of giftedness, changing leadership situations, and greater understanding of the Scriptures. A leader's discovery of his/her giftedness and development of the same takes place over 10 to 15 years of ministry. Continued discovery will bring about issues of ministry philosophy not previously seen or anticipated. The same is true of the Scriptures. A leader will continue to master the Word over a lifetime. New input will lead to new philosophical values which will add to, clarify, or even replace earlier philosophical values which now become less important. Finally, leaders will usually move through three or four very different ministry situations over a lifetime. Each new situation will demand discovery of new leadership values. But a leader will also have some core values which continue throughout all phases. This core will also expand as new critical leadership values are added. But that leader will also have numerous periphery leadership values which will change, come and go, over a lifetime.

Value Suggested: A leader ought to identify core and peripheral leadership values under girding his/her leadership philosophy and be ready to adapt and changes these over a lifetime.

Why Important: Ministry essentially flows out of being. A conglomerate of factors make up one's being including (but not limited to): intimacy with God, personality, gender, giftedness, character, and values (convictions) learned via ministry experience. One's ministry philosophy emerges from those values. Hence, if we are to operate in terms of who God has made us to be, we must increasingly become explicitly aware of the values that under gird our leadership.

Biblical Examples: Joseph, Habakkuk (generally prophetic ministry demands a ministry that is value based), Paul.

Contemporary Examples: G. Campbell Morgan, British pastor and international Bible teacher (1863-1945), Warren Wiersbe, Billy Graham.

Suggestions for Follow-Up: See **Article**, *Value Driven Leadership*. See also **For Further Study Bibliography**, Clinton's chapter 5 on Morgan in **Focused Lives**.

5. Leadership Selection And Development

Effective Leaders View Leadership Selection And Development As A Priority Function In Their Ministry.

Explanation: God raises up future leaders in present ministries. A major responsibility of Christian leaders is to partner with God in the on-going selection and development of leaders. The processes of identifying and developing leaders is both a means and an end. It is an end in itself by producing new leaders. But it is also a means for stimulating life in the ministry that is doing it. Emerging leaders also bring new life to a ministry. Strong leaders usually attract emerging leaders to themselves who are potentially like-gifted. Leaders should recognize this pattern and proactively respond to it by developing those potential leaders so attracted. Leaders who fail to recognize, select, and develop emerging leaders in their ministry miss out on personal growth that comes through this experience. They may almost be guaranteeing a weak future ministry that is overly dependent upon themselves.

Value Suggested: Leaders ought to be involved in the selection and development of emerging leaders.

Why Important: No work of God can last long that is not producing new leaders. Any work of God is only one generation away from nominality and mediocrity. New leadership emerging offsets nominality and plateauing ministry.

Biblical Examples: See Jesus ministry in the Gospels. See Paul's ministry. Both of these leaders selected and developed leaders.

Contemporary Examples: Robert Jaffray (1873-1945), Christian Missionary and Alliance missionary to Indo-China and Indonesia. Howard Hendricks. Paul Stanley. Alan Andrews.

Suggestions for Follow-Up: See For Further Study Bibliography, Clinton's chapter 6 on Jaffray in **Focused Lives**.

6. Relational Empowerment

Effective Leaders See Relational Empowerment As Both A Means And A Goal Of Ministry.

Explanation: Personal relationships between a leader and followers allow for interdependence in the body. Leaders need the feedback that comes through personal relationships with their followers. Leaders should be developing body life (reciprocal living—the one-another commands) as a major goal. This kind of behavior in a group provides a base from which all kinds of development can occur. For example, personal relationships will develop which will lead to mentoring. Mentoring is probably the best informal means for developing followers and especially emerging leaders. It is in the context of close, accountable, personal relationships that younger leaders can be encouraged and truly empowered.

Value Suggested: A leader ought to view personal relationships as a Biblical and critical priority in ministry both for developing ambiance for growth and for empowering others via mentoring methods.

Why Important: Mentoring is one of the most appropriate means of developing followers and challenging emerging leaders. Modeling, one form of mentoring, is one of the most important influence means. Personal relationships form the seedbed for both mentoring and modeling.

Biblical Examples: Jesus, Paul

Contemporary Examples: Henrietta Mears (1890-1963); Dawson Trotman (1906-1956), founder of the Navigators, Howard G. Hendricks, Paul Stanley, Bill Hull.

Suggestions for Follow-Up: See **Articles** *Reciprocal Living—The One-Another Commands; Paul the Mentor; Mentoring—An Informal Training Model; Paul—Modeling As An Influence Means*. See **For Further Study Bibliography,** Clinton's chapter 8 on Mears in **Focused Lives.** See Skinner's book, **Daws—The Story of Dawson Trotman, Founder of the Navigators.** See Clinton and Clinton, **The Mentor Handbook.** See Stanley and Clinton, **Connecting.**

7. Sense Of Destiny

Effective Leaders Evince A Growing Awareness Of Their Sense Of Destiny.

Explanation: A sense of destiny is an inner conviction arising from an experience (or a series of experiences) in which there is a growing awareness that God has His hand on a leader in a special way for special purposes. This typically happens along a three-fold destiny pattern: destiny preparation, destiny revelation, and destiny fulfillment. That is, a leader is usually unaware of preparation items as they happen, but in retrospect can reflect and see how God was preparing for a destiny. The sense of destiny deepens as God begins to unfold more clearly life purpose, role, and strategic guidance. And finally some or all of the destiny is fulfilled. Leaders become gradually aware of a destiny with God as He continues to shape them over a lifetime.

Value Suggested: A leader ought to be sensitive to destiny shaping activities in his/her past and present, and be anticipating their future implications. This awareness informs decision making reflecting partnership with God toward fulfilling that destiny.

Why Important: No Biblical leader greatly used by God failed to have a strong sense of destiny. A strong sense of destiny will buttress a leader to persevere toward a strong finish.

Biblical Examples: Abraham, Joseph, Moses, Jesus, Paul. Joseph, Moses, and Paul vividly demonstrate the threefold pattern of destiny preparation, destiny revelation and destiny fulfillment.

Contemporary Examples: Samuel Logan Brengle (1860-1936), Salvation Army Stalwart, Bill Bright.

Suggestions for Follow-Up: See Article *Destiny Pattern*. See **Glossary** for *destiny pattern; destiny processing; sense of destiny.* See also these same concepts in **Clinton's Leadership Emergence Theory Manual.** See Clarence Hall's work, **Samuel Logan Brengle, Portrait of a Prophet.** See **For Further Study Bibliography,** Clinton's chapter 4 on Brengle in **Focused Lives.**

Conclusion

Not all these lessons appear in a specific example of an effective leader. Some leaders exemplify three or four of them, others five or six and in a few cases all seven. But they are certainly goals for which to strive. It is not clear whether these lessons are by-products of effective leaders or causes of them being effective. Hopefully they are some of both so that if we deliberately try to put these in our lives they will improve our effectiveness.

Note: All articles listed in the Suggestions for Follow-Up section are contained in this **Handbook.** See the **For Further Study Bibliography** for full citations of books or manuals.

Leadership Levels
Looking At A Leadership Continuum: Five Types Of Leaders

Introduction

It is helpful to differentiate leaders in terms of some criteria. Several can be constructed. One typical example looks at Christian leadership in a church or denomination or parachurch organization. The primary criterion involves sphere of influence.[73] This typology of leaders along the continuum helps us pinpoint three major problems leaders face as they emerge from low level influence to high levels. These problems will repeatedly be faced around the world as the church emerges: 1. The Experience Gap, 2. The Financial (Logistics) Barrier, 3. The Strategic (Psychological) Barrier

Five Types of Leaders Along An Influence Continuum

Examine Figure 19.1 below which presents a continuum of leaders based on sphere of influence and shows some potential problems along the way.

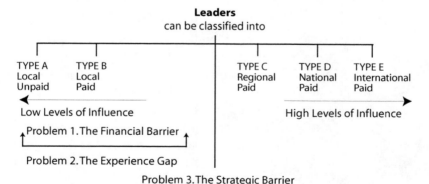

Figure 19.1   Five Types of Leaders — Expanding Sphere of Influence / Three Problems

---

73. *Sphere of influence* refers to the totality of people being influenced and for whom a leader will give an account to God. The totally of people influenced subdivides into three domains called direct influence, indirect influence, and organizational influence. Three measures rate sphere of influence: 1. Extensiveness—which refers to quantity; 2. Comprehensivenes—which refers to the scope of things being influenced in the followers' lives; 3. Intensiveness—the depth to which influence extends to each item within the comprehensive influences. Extensiveness is the easiest to measure and hence is most often used or implied when talking about a leader's sphere of influence.

Table 19.1 further identifies each of the types of leaders.

Table 19.1   Five Types of Leaders Described

Type	Description
A	These are volunteer workers who help local churches get their business done. Low level workers in a Christian organization, who do clerical work or other detailed staff administration work, fit this level of influence also.
B	Paid workers in small churches like pastors of small congregations or pastors of multi-congregations fit here. Sometimes these are bi-vocational workers having to supplement their salaries with outside employment. Associate pastors on staff in a larger church also have this same level of influence. Paid workers doing administrative work in a Christian organizations have the equivalent level of influence from an organizational standpoint.
C	This level of influence includes senior pastors of large churches who influence other churches in a large geographic area (e.g. via Radio/TV ministry, Pastor Conferences, separate organization promoting the pastor's publications, workshops, etc.). It also includes leaders in Christian organizations or denominations who are responsible for workers in a large geographic region.
D	These include senior pastors of large churches who have national influence usually via organizations created by them to promote their ministry. Denominational heads of a country would fit here too. Professors in prestigious seminaries which train high level leaders and are writing the texts which others use would fit here too. Some influential Christian writers might fit here.
E	Heads of international organizations with churches in various countries and or missionaries in many countries fit here. Some influential Christian writers might fit here. Leaders at this level dominantly do strategic thinking. Often Type E leaders will control large resources of people, finances, and facilities. They will have very broad personal networks with other international leaders and national leaders. They will often be on boards of very influential organizations.

It should be explicitly stated here that there is no inherent value attached to any of the types. That is, a Type E leader is not better than a Type A leader. All of the various types are needed in the church and mission organizations. More types A and B are needed than Type E leaders. The type of leader we become depends on capacity that God has given and God's development of us toward roles which use that capacity. To be gifted for Type B leadership and to aspire for Type D is a mismanagement of stewardship. So too, to be gifted for Type E and yet remain at Type C. None of the types are better than any other. All are needed. We need to operate along the continuum so as to responsibly exercise stewardship of our giftedness and God's development of our leadership. Bigger is not better. Appropriate is best.

Problem 1. The Financial Barrier

Problem 1, also called the *Logistics Barrier* or the *Lay/Clergy Dilemma*, deals with finances.[74] In most situations where a church is emerging, a need for workers who can devote their full time and giftedness to accomplish ministry goals will arise. In the Chris-

---

74. Leaders who hold to the major leadership lesson on selection and development, as a value, will face this problem repeatedly as they seek to find ways to move leaders along in development. That lesson (Effective leaders view leadership selection and development as a priority function) carries with it some heavy responsibility.

tian enterprise there are non-professional workers, people doing necessary work in churches. There are para-professional workers, those who give their most energy to church work and have some developed giftedness but who support themselves financially with some sort of secular job. And finally there are semi-professional workers. Some leaders get partial pay for their Christian work. When a worker moves from non-professional, para-professional, or semi-professional status to full time paid Christian worker, that is, workers move from Type A to Type B, he/she will face the financial barrier. How can such workers be financed? [75]Many potential leader stumbles over this barrier and never makes it in to full time ministry (and perhaps because of discouragement, drops out of ministry altogether). Paul was dealing with this problem in 1Co 16 when he exhorts the Corinthians about finances for Christian workers-his own self (subtlety given), Timothy, and Stephanus.

Additional Problems with Problem 1 Moving Across the Financial Barrier

There is a tendency, which I call, *The Projection Tendency,* to seek to pressure effective Type A leaders to *go full time*. The idea involves the subtle implication that full time Christian leaders are more dedicated to God than lay leaders.

There is another minor problem involved in moving from Type A to Type B leadership. I call it *The Expectation Problem*. When leader cross the logistics barrier, it involves a major status change for leaders. Laity perceive full time Christian workers differently than lay leaders. Movement from Type A to Type B leadership means that people will view them differently (perhaps have higher expectations of them) even though their roles may not change.

Problem 2. The Experience Gap

Problem 2, also called the pre-service training problem, basically deals with a modern problem. Where churches have spread in a given geographical area, training institutions like seminaries and Bible colleges have also emerged. Normally, as a church is emerging, leaders are trained on-the-job and take on more responsibility as they are ready for it. But once there is a large number of churches and larger individual churches, people who are untrained on the job and with little or no leadership experience go to these training institutions and in a short period of time are academically trained (sort of) for ministry. They then attempt to enter ministry at Type B or higher level if they can. They don't have the experience for it. So we have people leading at levels they are not experienced to lead. A similar but not identical problem is being dealt with in 1Ti where Paul is seeking to give Timothy, a younger worker, to be accepted by older leaders, the Ephesian elders. The problem is not exactly the same, since Timothy did have experience—but the culture did not respect younger leaders. *The Experience Gap* is a double problem in some cultures since they respect age and experience, and training institutions turn out potential leaders who fit neither requirement.

---

75.   This is a major problem that will be faced around the world as the model which arose in the 19th and 20th centuries in countries with financial resources, that is, at least one full time paid pastor per congregation, goes by the by. Bi-vocational workers will most likely dominate in the early part of the next century.

Problem 3. The Strategic Barrier—Its Two Problems

Problem 3, also called the *ministry focus problem*, deals with a giftedness/ responsibility problem seen in leaders who move from Type C ministry to Type D or E ministry. That is, they become leaders who do less direct ministry and more indirect ministry. Heads of organizations with a big sphere of influence face this problem. Direct ministry means dominantly using word gifts to influence people directly. Indirect ministry means leaders who are now helping or directing other leaders in direct ministry but are themselves not primarily doing direct ministry. Usually leaders who rise to these levels do so because they were successful in direct ministry at lower levels of influence. Simply because they were effective at that lower level doing direct ministry depending on their word gifts does not insure that they will be successful at a higher level not dominantly using their word gifts. In short, they are not trained for the functions at the higher level. And what is more startling, little or no formal training exists to develop leaders to do these higher level leadership functions.

A second problem arises, *psychological loss*. It has to do with satisfaction in ministry. When one is doing direct ministry and dominantly using word gifts, there is a constant feedback of things happening in lives which gives affirmation and satisfaction. At higher levels most leaders are doing leadership functions like problem solving, crises resolution, structural planning, and strategizing. These functions do not reward one in the same way as direct ministry. They do not receive the same satisfaction in doing these things and getting little affirmation as they did when they effectively did direct ministry.

Two things can help overcome these two problems. One, leaders should be trained for the higher level functions, dominantly by mentoring from leaders who are doing them well, and then transitioned into them. Two, the psychological loss perceived by leaders crossing the strategic barrier can also be addressed in at least the following two ways that I have observed in leaders at high level. One, they can from time to time do forays back into direct ministry which bring satisfaction that was experienced previously. Two, they can learn to see that what is being accomplished has broader potential and more far reaching results than their former direct ministry which had to be sacrificed in accepting the higher level of leadership. This requires strategic thinking and an application of the servant leadership model at a higher capacity level. Paul's later ministry dealt with this strategic barrier problem. Most of his latter ministry was indirect. Note his epistles are largely indirect ministry. He is helping other leaders deal with their issues—problem solving, dealing with crises, etc. He is not out there teaching and preaching directly. Note he got strategic eyes—see 2Co 11:28,Then besides all this, daily, I am burdened with my responsibility for the churches.

Conclusion

Types of leaders, that is, levels of leadership, are distinguished not to imply that bigger is better but to indicate that problems will be faced as leaders develop to higher levels of leadership. Further, leadership issues will vary noticeably with the different types. Types D and E are much more concerned with leadership means/resources, items of organizational structure, culture, dynamics, and power. They are multi-style leaders. They are more concerned with leadership philosophy and with strategic thinking. They know they will have heavy accountability to God in these areas. They are concerned with macro-contextual factors. Because leadership functions vary greatly along the continuum, different training is needed for each type. Informal/non-formal training focusing on skills for direct ministry is needed for Types A/B and should usually be in-service. All three modes (informal, non-formal, and formal) are needed to provide skills and perspectives for Types C, D, and E. In-service and interrupted in-service should dominate for Types C, D, and E.

See *sphere of influence, pre-service training, in-service training, word gifts, mentoring definitions, leadership styles, formal training, non-formal training, informal training,* **Glossary**. See **Articles,** *Pauline Leadership Styles; Training Modes—When They Fit.*

Leadership Selection

Introduction

A major lesson identified from a comparative study of leaders[76] challenges to the core,

Effective Leaders View Leadership Selection and Development as a priority function.

This value dominated Christ's ministry. To instill an on-going movement Christ had to inculcate his values in a band of leaders who would continue to propagate his movement. And he had to train them well in order for them to carry on. This he did. *Selection and Development* are stressed in Christ's Ministry.[77] Paul held to this value very strongly in his ministry.[78] What should we know about leadership selection and development if we want to have this important value in our lives? Two things will help us: (1) terminology that describes what happens and (2) an overall time perspective integrating the things that happen. [79]

Leadership Selection—The Basic Concept Defined

When God touches a life for leadership, there will be indications that can be recognized by observant Christian leaders. Mature leaders who know the importance of leadership selection and development are constantly on the lookout for just such recognition features. They want to partner with God in what He is doing to raise up emerging leader-

---

76. Seven such lessons have been identified: (1) Effective Leaders View Present Ministry in Terms Of A Life Time Perspective. (2) Effective Leaders Maintain A Learning Posture Throughout Life. (3) Effective Leaders Value Spiritual Authority As A Primary Power Base. (4) Effective Leaders Who Are Productive Over A Lifetime Have A Dynamic Ministry Philosophy. (5) Effective Leaders View Leadership Selection And Development As A Priority Function In Their Ministry. (6) Effective Leaders See Relational Empowerment As Both A Means And A Goal Of Ministry. (7) Effective Leaders Evince A Growing Awareness Of Their Sense Of Destiny. It is the fifth one I am exploring in this article.

77. See Bruce's, **The Training of the Twelve**, a famous treatise dealing with Jesus' approach to leadership selection and development. See also, **Articles**, *Jesus—Circles of Intimacy, A Developmental Technique; Jesus—Recruiting Techniques.*

78. Whereas both selection and development are seen equally well in Jesus' ministry, development dominates Paul's ministry. See **Articles**, *Paul—And His Companions; Paul—Mentor; Paul—Modeling as An Influence Means.*

79. To really appreciate leadership selection over a lifetime one needs to have a thorough grasp of leadership emergence theory.

ship. The process of God's selection, the recognition and affirmation by human leadership, and the subsequent development comprise what leadership selection is all about.

Definition   *Leadership selection* is the life-long process of divine initiative and human recognition whereby a leader[80] emerges.

Leadership selection describes a life-long recognition process which is punctuated with critical incidents, as viewed from a two-fold intermeshing perspective—the divine and the human. The process starts from earliest symptomatic indications of a leader emerging. It continues right on up to maturity. God will continue to select a leader throughout his/her lifetime. Mature selection involves God strategically guiding the leader on to a focused life. But note this is a threefold interactive process: (1) God is involved; (2) the leader is involved; and (3) other human leadership is involved. God gives confirmation to the selection of a leader via others leaders as well as directly to that leader.

The Ministry time-line is shown below in Figure 20.1 highlights the three fold interactive process. The Divine perspective involvement occurs above the time-line. The entries below the line portray some of the human interactions—both the individual leader's processing and what other human leaders see and confirm.

Figure 20.1 The Leadership Selection Process Viewed Pictorially Over a Time-line

---

[80].   The definition of leader used in this commentary pre-supposes the divine element of leadership selection. A leader is a person with God-given capacity and God-given responsibility who is influencing a specific group of God's people toward God's purposes.

[81].   See **Article,** *Time-Line, Defined for Biblical Leaders.* The time-line shown here is a generic time-line used to assess where a leader is in development over a life time. The four phases represent segments correlating to development in a life. Each phase to the right represents a more mature stage. General ministry is a time of learning for the leader. God is doing more in the leader's life than through him/her. Focused ministry is a time of efficient ministry. The leader knows his/her own giftedness and uses it well—a time of tactical ministry. Convergent ministry represents a time of strategic ministry. If Focused Ministry can be described as doing things right then Convergent Ministry means doing the right things right. It is a time of strategic accomplishment.

Human Recognition Vantage Point

1. Response to God
2. Potential Seen
3. Emerging Leader Symptoms, Word Gifts/ Obedience Attitude
4. Challenge Toward Expectations
5. Foundational Patterns
6. Foundational Ministry Pattern
7. Like — Attracts-Like Gift Pattern
8. Ministry Entry Patterns
9. Give Affirmation
10. Transitional Training Patterns
11. Mentoring
12. Giftedness Development Pattern

Figure 20.1 The Leadership Selection Process Viewed Pictorially Over a Time-line cont.

Illustrations from Jesus' and Paul's Ministry

Table 20.1 illustrates important leadership selection concepts in Jesus own life, Paul's own life and in their ministry.

Table 20.1   Leadership Selection Concepts Illustrated

Concept	Illustration
Divine 1. (Pre-birth Call)	See Gal 1:15—indication in Paul's life; See also Samuel; Samson; John the Baptist.
Divine 2. Destiny Unfolding	See **Article**, *Destiny Pattern*, for Paul's destiny unfolding.
Divine 3. Giftedness/ Leadership Potential Engendered	Php 3:4-6 Paul's advancement before conversion—indications of great potential. Apollos—Ac 18:24-26;
Divine 4. Call	Jesus ministry: See Jn 1 for call of John, Andrew, Simon Peter, James, Philip, Nathanael. For (repeated) call trace the phrase, *follow me*: see Mt 4:19; 8:22; 9:9; 16:24; 19:21; Mk 2:14; 8:34; 10:21; Lk 5:27; 9:23; 9:59; 18:22; Jn 1:43;12:26.
Divine 5. Processing: focal incidents/ strategic guidance	See Section, **Biblical Leaders Time-Lines** where critical incidents are shown along time-lines. See Paul's Time-Line; See Jesus' Time-Line. See *critical incident*, **Glossary**.
Human 1. Response to God	See Paul, Ac 9, 22, 26—conversion story; Ac 13 further ministry call; Ac 16 further call to Europe. All show Paul's response well.
Human 2. Potential Seen	See Timothy Ac 16:2.
Human 3. Emerging Leader Symptoms, Word Gifts/Obedience/Attitude	Obedience and Attitudes seen in lives of Paul's companions. But symptoms of Word Gifts not seen in a detailed way in Biblical examples. This selection observation arises from many contemporary case studies.
Human 4. Challenge Toward Expectations	See Paul's writings to Timothy for numerous illustrations of this. See especially the concept of Goodwin's Expectation principle, 2Ti 1:5;
Human 5. Foundational Patterns	See Timothy for Heritage pattern; see Titus for Radical Conversion;

Human 6. Foundational Ministry Pattern	See Lk 16:10 for Jesus teaching on this. Faithfulness in ministry leads to other ministry. Illustrated in ministry assignments given Timothy and Titus.
Human 7. Like — Attracts-Like Gift Pattern	Difficult to see in Biblical characters because of lack of details but seen repeatedly in contemporary case studies.
Human 8. Ministry Entry Patterns	The most important ministry entry pattern *self-initiated creation of new ministry structures* is seen repeatedly in Paul's life.
Human 9. Give Affirmation	This is demonstrated repeatedly in Paul's life and ministry.
Human 10. Transitional Training Patterns	The transitional training in-service pattern is seen repeatedly in both Jesus' and Paul's training of emerging leaders.
Human 11. Mentoring	Jesus mentors in a group context with occasional personal mentoring with Peter, James and John. Paul demonstrates mentoring at group level and many illustrations of individual mentoring. Both Jesus and Paul move along into partnering with God in developing leaders via deliberate proactive intervention in lives via mentoring.
Human 12. Giftedness Development Pattern	Not seen in Biblical examples because of lack of details. But seen in numerous contemporary case studies.

Observations on Leadership Selection

Observations flowing from this leadership selection model include:

1. The on-going operation of a movement, organization, or church require leadership selection and development. To ignore selection is to cut off the next generation of leaders. To ignore development is to provide a big back door whereby your recruited leaders leave and are developed by others.

2. To partner with God in leadership selection and development effectively, a leader needs to be very familiar with developmental theory—that is, how a leader develops over a lifetime.[82] Or to say it another way, the more familiar you are with how God develops a leader the more you will be sensitive to when you can intervene in a godly way to help develop that leader.

3. Rarely will all 17 selection elements be seen in a given individual. Some are missing altogether. Others are more prominent. The list was synthesized from comparative study of many leaders.

4. The prime responsibility for leadership selection and development is God's. But an important secondary responsibility involves God's use of other human leaders to select and develop leaders. Without human affirmation of God's call in a life, a potential leader is subject to only internal subjective discernment of God's working. Self-deception can run rampant. External human recognition and affirmation is desperately needed to protect both an individual leader and those he/she will influence.

5. Progressive calls over a lifetime (see Jesus ministry with his own and God's dealing with Paul) highlight the concept of selection taking place over a lifetime.

[82.] My leadership emergence theory has developed over the past 19 years. It views how God develops a leader over a lifetime. All of the concepts alluded to in the leadership selection model of this article are defined or described in leadership emergence theory. See **For Further Study, Bibliography**, the manual, **Leadership Emergence Theory**.

Conclusion

No strategic thinking leader will overlook this important leadership value,

> **Effective Leaders View Leadership Selection and Development as a priority function.**

No effective leader can carry out all the functions that need to be done to select and develop. But every leader can look for and join with other leaders who can help carry out this important function. Needed are recruiter specialists, early developer specialists, strategic developers. Recruiters hook potential leaders. Early developer specialists develop efficiency in a maturing leader. Strategic developers develop effectiveness in mature leaders.

See *progressive calling,*   **Glossary.** See **Articles,** *Developing Giftedness; Destiny Pattern; Divine Affirmation in the Life of Jesus; Entrustment—A Leadership Responsibility; Focused Life; Foundational Patterns; God's Shaping Processes With Leaders; Impartation of Gifts; Integrity—A Top Leadership Quality; Isolation Processing—Learning Deep Lessons from God; Jesus—Circles of Intimacy—A Developmental Technique; Leadership Lessons—Seven Identified; Leadership Continuum—Five Types of Leaders; Ministry Entry Patterns; Paul—Sense of Destiny; Paul—And His Companions; Paul—Deep Processing; Paul—Developer; Paul—Mentor; Spiritual Benchmarks; Spiritual Gifts, Giftedness and Development; Training Models—When They Fit.*

Leadership Transitions

Background/ Definitions

An important macro lesson discovered in the Pre-Kingdom Leadership Era is stated as:

15. Transition[83] **Leaders must transition other leaders into their work in order to maintain continuity and effectiveness.**

This lesson was discovered during Moses' leadership. His transition of Joshua into leadership over a long period of time stands out as the classical model for transitioning a leader into an important leadership role.

Transition times in movements, organizations and churches are hard, complex times. How leaders transition new leaders into leadership can make or break the on-going ministry. It is a special time of problems and opportunities. The process is best understood when viewed along a continuum.

Definition — *Leadership transition* is the process whereby existing leaders prepare and release emerging leaders into the responsibility and practice of leadership positions, functions, roles, and tasks.

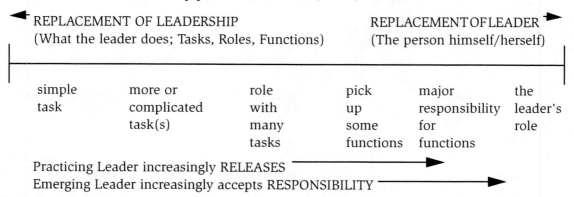

Figure 21.1   Leadership Transition Continuum

---

83.   This is number 15 of 41 macro lessons listed over the six leadership eras. See **Article**, *Macro Lessons, List of 41*.

Continuum Definitions

Definition	A *task* is an observable assignment of usually short duration.
Definition	A *role* is a recognizable position which does a major portion of the ministry. It probably has several ongoing tasks associated with it.
Definition	*Leadership functions* is a technical term which refers to the three major categories of formal leadership responsibility: task behavior (defining structure and goals), relationship behavior (providing the emotional support and ambiance), and inspirational behavior (providing motivational effort).
Comment	Each of these major leadership functions has several specific sub-functions.
Definition	*Leadership release* is the process whereby an existing leader deliberately encourages and allows an emerging leader to accept responsibility for and control of leadership positions, functions, roles, and tasks.
Definition	*Overlap* is that unique time in a leadership transition when the emerging leader and existing leader share responsibility and accountability for tasks, roles, and functions.
Definition	*Tandem training* describes the training technique during overlap used by an existing leader with an emerging leader.

Let me comment on the two extremes on the continuum. On the right of the continuum is the maximum limit of leadership transition, that is, the leader himself/ herself is replaced totally from the leadership situation. The emerging leader thus becomes the new leader and is totally responsible for the leadership situation. On the left is the minimum, the present leader turns over some small piece of leadership, e.g. a simple task. In between the two extremes, various levels of transition are experienced.

The process across the continuum is simply described. As one moves across the continuum faithful performance of simple tasks leads to increasing responsibility such as a role. Faithful or successful accomplishment of a role will lead to greater responsibility—usually wider roles and responsibility for important functions of the ministry as a whole.

Two tendencies have been observed as the transition process goes on. As you move from left to right on the continuum, the present leader is increasingly releasing more tasks, functions and finally major responsibility for the ministry. This is signified by the arrow moving toward the right. The function of release is a difficult one for most leaders. The tendency is to either *over-control* on the one hand (*authoritarian defensive posture*), or to *give too much responsibility without adequate supervision* or transitional training on the other (*the quick release posture*). The first tendency suffocates emerging leaders and frustrates them in their attempt to grow and assume leadership. Such a posture usually drives them out of the organization to another ministry where they can be released. The second tendency overwhelms them and usually insures failure in their first attempt at leadership. This can be discouraging and cause some to decide not to move into leadership in ministry.

The rate at which the release should occur ought to depend on the ability of the emerging leader to pick up responsibility for it and not an authoritarian posture or a quick release posture. The arrow moving to the right demonstrates that the emerging leader should be picking up responsibility for the tasks, roles, or functions. As this is done, the leader should be releasing.

Overlap is the time in which both the leader and emerging leader are working together in an increasing way to release and accept responsibility. Overlap can occur anywhere along the continuum.

Tandem training allows the younger leader to share the learning experiences of the older leader via modeling, mentoring, apprenticeship, or internships so as to leapfrog the younger leader's development.

Leadership Transitions In The Bible

There are numerous instances in Scripture of leadership transitions. Most are not ideal as suggested by the transitional continuum. The Moses/Joshua transition which took place over an extended time does follow the description given above of the transitional continuum. It is one of the positive models of leadership transition in the Scriptures. Another positive model occurs in the New Testament—that of Barnabas and Saul. Other leadership situations in Scripture are worthy of study, mostly for the negative lessons and identification of the items on the transitional continuum that are missing. Table 21.1 lists some of the instances of Scripture that provide data for observing the positive and negative effects of leadership transitions — be they good or bad.

Table 21.1   Examples of Leadership Transitions in Scripture Providing Insights

Joseph (sovereign transition)	David/Absalom (aborted)
Moses (sovereign transition)	David/Solomon (negative)
Moses/Joshua (tandem transition)	Elijah/Elisha (minimum)
Joshua/? (none)	Daniel (sovereign)
Jephthah (other judges—negative)	Jesus/disciples
Eli/sons (negative)	Apostles/deacons (Acts 6)
Samuel (sovereign transition)	Barnabas/ Paul (leader switch)
Samuel/Saul (modified negative)	Acts 20 Paul/Ephesian elders
Saul/David (negative)	Paul/ Timothy (2Ti)

Probably the best leadership transition to observe in which the continuum concepts are more readily seen involves Moses' transition of Joshua into leadership.

10 Steps In Moses/Joshua Transition

In the Moses/Joshua transition several steps, stages, or discernible events can be ordered. These give insights into why the transition was successful and led to a great leader being raised up to follow a great leader. Table 21.2 lists observations which suggest why the transition was successful.

Table 21.2. Observations on the Moses/ Joshua Leadership Transition

Step	Label	Description
1	Definite Leadership Selection	There was deliberate and definite leadership selection. Moses chose Joshua. Joshua came from a leading family with leadership heritage (note the march order in Exodus — his grandfather prominent). Notice Moses' lack of Nepotism; see comment which follows these steps.
2	Ministry Task	Moses gave him ministry tasks with significant responsibility: a. First, select recruits and lead battle among the Amalekites who were harassing the flanks of the exodus march. b. Second, spy out the land (probably one of the younger ones to be chosen). Moses checked Joshua's: (1) faith, (2) faithfulness, (3) giftedness (charismatic ability to lead) with these increasing responsibilities.
3	Spirituality/ Tandem Training	Moses included Joshua in his own spiritual experiences with God. Joshua had firsthand access to Moses' vital experiences with God. Moses took him into the holy of holies, frequently into the tabernacle into the presence of God and up on the mountain when he was in solitude alone with God. This was tandem training in spirituality using mentoring as the means of training.
4	Leadership span	Moses recognized the complexity of the leadership situation toward the end of his life. He knew Joshua could not do it all. When transitioning him into leadership he saw that Joshua was a charismatic militaristic leader who needed a supportive spiritual leader. He set Eleazar up as the spiritual leader. He publicly did this—bolstered Eleazar in the eyes of the people, recognized Joshua's strengths and weaknesses. Moses knew that any leader coming into his position would have trouble—most likely could not fill his shoes; he would need help. Actually Joshua developed real spiritual authority and became a spiritual leader in terms of inspirational leadership.
5	Public Recognition	Moses recognized the importance of followers knowing whom he had appointed to be the next leader. No ambiguity. No scramble of leaders for that position after Moses' death. He settled it ahead of time and gave a public ceremony stipulating his backing of Joshua.
6	New Challenge	The new leader following an old leader must not look back and compare. One way of overcoming this tendency is to have a big challenge, a new task not done by the old leader. There was a big task to do. It would be his own contribution—possess the land.
7	Divine Affirmation	The new leader needed to know not only that Moses had appointed him as leader but that God had confirmed this appointment. Dt 31:14-18 and Joshua 1 point out Joshua's experiences personally with God concerning the appointment.
8	Public Ceremony	Not only must there be personal assurance that God has appointed him/her but there must be public recognition of this. God gives this in Joshua 3 (note Joshua 3:7: "What I do today will make all the people of Israel begin to honor you as a great man, and they will realize that I am with you as I was with Moses." See also Joshua 4:14: "What the Lord did that day made the people of Israel consider Joshua a great man. They honored him all his life, just as they had honored Moses.")

| 9 | Initial Success | A leader moving into full responsibility needs an initial success that can bolster spiritual authority and demonstrate that the leader can get vision from God in his/her own right. Joshua's experience with the Captain of the Lord's Army was a pivotal point that did this. It gave him vision — tactical plan with strategic implications. Its success came early on and stimulated followers. With it there was assurance that brought closure to the whole transition experience. |
| 10 | Initial Failure | A final thing that ensured a successful transition was the early failure at Ai. Leaders must know they are not infallible. They must trust God in their leadership. An early failure after initial success was a major deterrent to pride, showed the moral implications of godly leadership, and the notion that leaders must always move followers along toward God's purposes for them in God's way. |

Commentary On Moses/Joshua Transition

Is this model transferable? Peculiar dynamics occur in this model. Its uniqueness may preclude its application in other situations. There was a long period of overlap due to the disciplining of the people in the wilderness. Joshua essentially led the next generation—not his own. A mighty expectation existed for the new task that challenged everyone. Joshua was a home-grown leader from a leadership heritage who had proved himself in many ways. He was a charismatic/military leader with a good spiritual track record of sensing and obeying God. Certain of the underlying ideas of these observations will probably be applicable even if the overall dynamics are not identical.

Notice that Moses avoids the problem of nepotism.[84] Joshua was hand-picked early for leadership. Yet when the final transition time arrived, Moses did not just assume that Joshua was the Lord's choice but sought the Lord's confirmation. And when it came *he did all he could to give Joshua the best chance of success*. This leadership transition is the most successful in Scripture. Moses was well aware that if his ministry was to be established beyond his lifetime as he wished (Psalm 90:17), providing leadership for it was necessary. He certainly exemplifies the *continuity* or *transition* macro-lesson.

Transition   **Leaders must transition other leaders into their work in order to maintain continuity and effectiveness.**

Four implications about leadership transition should be noted.

1. *Continuity.* No ministry can be expected to continue well without deliberate transition efforts.
2. *Nepotism.* Rarely can a leader replace his/her father/ mother with the same leadership effectiveness. The appropriate leader, gifted for the job, is the proper selection.
3. *Best Start.* Whenever leaving a ministry, insure that the next leader has the best possible chance of success.

---

[84]. It is not clear but it appears from hints given that Moses really had family problems and probably was separated from his family for extended times during his desert leadership. His sons are never prominently mentioned anywhere. His wife and children visit him when Jethro comes. So perhaps he was never tempted to try to place them in leadership as many charismatic leaders do today.

4. *Models*. Study negative and positive Biblical models for guidelines. The positive models include Moses/ Joshua, Elijah/ Elisha, Jesus/ Disciples, Barnabas/ Paul, Paul/Timothy. A particularly negative one to see is Solomon/ Rehoboam.

See *leadership transition, leadership functions, leadership release, overlap, tandem training.*, **Glossary**. See **Article**, *Regime Turnover*.

Leadership Transitions —Timothy and Titus

Introduction

On the whole, leadership transitions in the Bible have not been done very well. An important macro lesson discovered in the Pre-Kingdom Leadership Era is stated as:

15. Transition[85] **Leaders must transition other leaders into their work in order to maintain continuity and effectiveness.**

This lesson was discovered during Moses' leadership.[86] His transition of Joshua into leadership over a long period of time stands out as the classical model for transitioning a leader into an important leadership role. Imagine trying to step into Moses' shoes, arguably the greatest Old Testament leader. That was a tough job, yet, Joshua did it and made his own unique contribution to the redemptive drama. Well imagine again, stepping into Paul's shoes.[87] Again, who could do this. Well, I am going to suggest that two men did, Timothy and Titus. And again, like Moses' work, the transition process was extended over a long time and involved lots of hands-on co-ministry with Paul.

Transition times in movements, organizations and churches are hard, complex times. Such was the case with Moses and Joshua. And such was the case with Paul and his two close mentorees, Timothy and Titus.

How leaders transition new leaders into leadership can make or break the on-going ministry. It is a special time of problems and opportunities. The process is best understood when viewed along a continuum.

Definition   *Leadership transition* is the process whereby existing leaders prepare and release emerging leaders into the responsibility and practice of leadership positions, functions, roles, and tasks.

This article will offer some observations of Paul transition of two leaders, Timothy and

---

[85.] This is number 15 of 41 macro lessons listed over the six leadership eras. See **Article**, Macro Lessons, List of 41.

[86.] See **Article**, *Leadership Transitions*, for a detailed explanation of the Moses/Joshua transition model.

[87.] Arguably this is an even tougher task since the Church Leadership Era is so complex with dispersed leadership all over the globe and no one structure permeating all followers.

Titus, into ministry. The leadership transition continuum will be used to assess Timothy's and Titus' transitions.

Leadership Transition Continuum

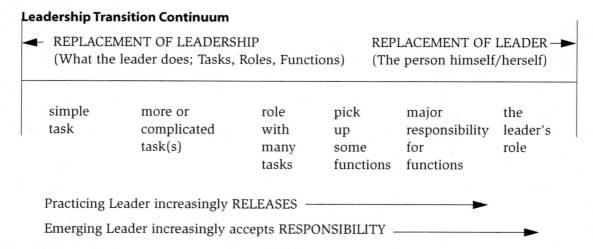

Figure 22.1   The Leadership Transition Continuum

In order to understand the continuum, several concepts must be defined.

Definition   A *task* is an observable assignment of usually short duration.

Definition   A *role* is a recognizable position which does a major portion of the ministry. It probably has several ongoing tasks associated with it.

Definition   *Leadership functions* is a technical term which refers to the three major categories of formal leadership responsibility: task behavior (defining structure and goals), relationship behavior (providing the emotional support and ambiance), and inspirational behavior (providing motivational effort).

Comment   Each of these major leadership functions has several specific sub-functions.

Definition   *Leadership release* is the process whereby an existing leader deliberately encourages and allows an emerging leader to accept responsibility for and control of leadership positions, functions, roles, and tasks.

Definition   *Overlap* is that unique time in a leadership transition when the emerging leader and existing leader share responsibility and accountability for tasks, roles, and functions.

Definition   *Tandem training* describes the training technique during overlap used by an existing leader with an emerging leader.

Let me comment on the two extremes on the continuum. On the right of the continuum is the maximum limit of leadership transition, that is, the leader himself/ herself is replaced totally from the leadership situation. The emerging leader thus becomes the new leader and is totally responsible for the leadership situation. On the left is the minimum, the present leader turns over some small piece of leadership, e.g. a simple task. In between the two extremes, various levels of transition are experienced.

As one moves across the continuum, faithful performance of simple tasks leads to increasing responsibility, such as a role. Faithful or successful accomplishment of a role will lead to greater responsibility — usually wider roles and responsibility for important functions of the ministry as a whole.

Two tendencies have been observed as the transition process goes on. As you move from left to right on the continuum, the present leader is increasingly releasing more tasks, functions and finally major responsibility for the ministry. This is signified by the arrow moving toward the right. The function of release is a difficult one for most leaders. The tendency is to either *over-control* on the one hand (*authoritarian defensive posture*), or to *give too much responsibility without adequate supervision* or transitional training on the other (*the quick release posture*). The first tendency suffocates emerging leaders and frustrates them in their attempt to grow and assume leadership. Such a posture usually drives them out of the organization to another ministry where they can be released. The second tendency overwhelms them and usually insures failure in their first attempt at leadership. This can be discouraging and cause some to decide not to move into leadership in ministry.

The rate at which the release should occur ought to depend on the ability of the emerging leader to pick up responsibility for it and not an authoritarian posture or a quick release posture. The arrow moving to the right demonstrates that the emerging leader should be picking up responsibility for the tasks, roles, or functions. As this is done, the leader should be releasing.

Overlap is the time in which both the leader and emerging leader are working together in an increasing way to release and accept responsibility. Overlap can occur anywhere along the continuum. Tandem training allows the younger leader to share the learning experiences of the older leader via modeling, mentoring, apprenticeship, or internships so as to leapfrog the younger leader's development.

Paul's Leadership Transitions Efforts With Timothy and Titus Figure 22.2 shows the leadership transition continuum. On it I have placed Timothy and Titus beside each item on which I have indications or implications that Paul worked on transition items with them.

Leadership Transition Continuum

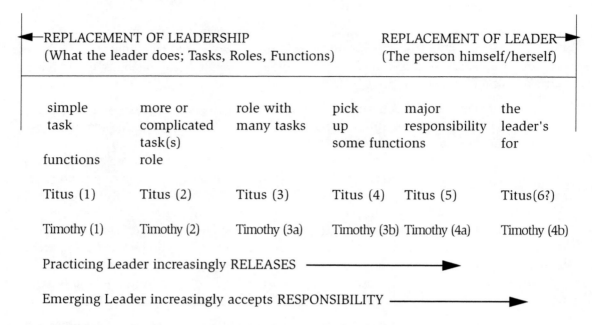

←**REPLACEMENT OF LEADERSHIP**			**REPLACEMENT OF LEADER**→		
(What the leader does; Tasks, Roles, Functions)			(The person himself/herself)		
simple task functions	more or complicated task(s) role	role with many tasks	pick up some functions	major responsibility	the leader's for
Titus (1)	Titus (2)	Titus (3)	Titus (4) Titus (5)		Titus(6?)
Timothy (1)	Timothy (2)	Timothy (3a)	Timothy (3b) Timothy (4a)		Timothy (4b)

Practicing Leader increasingly RELEASES ──────────────▶

Emerging Leader increasingly accepts RESPONSIBILITY ──────────────▶

Figure 22.2   Timothy and Titus — Transition Functions Done

Legend for Figure 22.2

Titus (1) Titus goes with Paul to Galatia. This was a critical contextualization issue (see Galatians 2:1,3). Later Titus would have to do contextualization work with the believers on Crete.

Titus (2) Ministry Task 1.[88] Titus initiates giving for Jerusalem project in Corinthian church.

Titus (3) Ministry Task 2. Titus was sent to Corinth to ascertain accountability; He was to take disciplinary measures depending on how they were responding. This was part of Paul's dealing with the crises in his ministry stemming from the attempts within the Corinthian church to reject his apostolic leadership.

Titus (4) Ministry Task 3. Titus is resent to Corinth to 1. complete the Jerusalem project, 2. test loyalty to Pauline authority, and 3. follow-up on discipline. The results of this are not known. However, the inclusion of 2 Corinthians in the canon is probably indicative of a successful completion of this task.

Titus (5) Ministry Task 5. Titus is sent to Crete. Titus transitions into apostolic Leadership with his major ministry task at Crete. It involved: 1. the appointment of leaders, 2. the grounding in teaching of the believers in this regional church, 3. the modeling of a Christian lifestyle and the 4. establishing of mission giving. Here the thrust is on appointing

---

[88].   A *ministry task* is an assignment from God which primarily tests a person's faithfulness and obedience but often also allows use of ministry gifts in the context of a task which has closure, accountability, and evaluation. It is one of 51 shaping activities, called process items, describing how God develops a leader. Titus had 5 of these that we can identify. See **Article**, *Titus and Ministry Tasks*.

leadership which will model a Christian lifestyle in the Cretan context. The exact outcome is not known but tradition indicates it was successful. See Titus 3:15 footnote in which Titus is implied as having an important role in Crete. It is clear from the letter that Titus is released to operate in full apostolic ministry in Crete.

Timothy (1) Philippian Ministry Task

Timothy (2) Stayed behind in Berea with Silas (stabilizing believers probably); Goes with Erastus on an Errand into Macedonia for Paul (not clear exactly what they did); Goes to Troas (with team) probably to set up things for Paul's coming there. Sent to Thessalonica with multiple tasks involving building up the group.

Timothy (3a) Lots of overlap time with Paul in Corinth (would receive most of Paul's Teaching); Paul mentions Timothy in Ro 16 showing he was fully versed with a theology of redemption, etc.

Timothy (3b) Sent to Corinth. Co-ministry with Paul in writing Corinthian letters. Sent to clarify Paul's teaching. Co-writes letter to Colossians.

Timothy (4a) Ephesus Timothy sent to Ephesus. Full orbed ministry there, apostolic. Appoints leaders, etc.

Timothy (4b) Ephesus In 2nd Timothy, it is clear Paul is handing the baton over to Timothy. Did Timothy pick it up — see Heb 13:23

Some Comparisons — Moses and Paul, Leadership Transition

Both Moses and Paul were at least relatively successful in transitioning in leaders to carry on their ministries. Remember the basic goal in leadership transition is have leaders who will carry on ministry so as to maintain *continuity* and *effectiveness*. Remember the transition macro lesson.

Transition **Leaders must transition other leaders into their work in order to maintain continuity and effectiveness.**

Moses and Paul did this. What were the common things they did?

1. They spent lots of personal time with their mentorees.

2. They co-ministered so that others saw they were associated in leadership.

3. They sponsored their mentorees so that it was known that they backed them and that these mentorees represented them.

4. They publicly named these mentorees as successors.

What were the differences in their transition processes?

Moses ministered to the same followers over a long period of time, facing the same obstacles in the same geographical locale. Continuity was easier since all the followers knew Joshua and observed the many tasks and responsibilities he did over the years. Joshua, the leader being transitioned in, was of the same language and culture as the followers. It was clear that Joshua and Moses basically had the same values about leadership. And Moses was able to have an official public ceremony inaugurating Joshua's forthcoming leadership with the important followers present.. Continuity was assured since it was clear that there was a top position, a role, and Joshua was to fill it.[89]

Paul, on the other hand, had an itinerant non-on-going leadership/ relationship with lots of different groups of followers in different cultures and geographical locales. In addition, he did not have a formal position as a leader over any of these groups. His leadership was basically determined by spiritual authority alone. So to transition new leaders in, he had to make sure these new leaders had spiritual authority with the followers. Paul did this in four major ways:

1. He *embedded his leadership values* in these mentorees so that he could rest assured that what ever ministry they faced in the future, they would carry on ministry similar to the way he did it. He used mentoring, particularly that of discipler, spiritual guide, coach, teacher and contemporary model to insure the embedding of values. He had strong personal relationships with his mentorees. He was transparent with them. He was vulnerable with them. He made sure they knew how he thought and lived. While we don't have as much evidence of this with Titus as with Timothy we can assume it, knowing that Titus was traveling a lot with Paul.

Notice this excerpt in his final letter to Timothy which shows this personal relationship and its impact for embedding values.

2 Timothy 3

10 But you fully know my teaching, my lifestyle, my purpose in life, my faith, my steadfastness, my love, my endurance.[90] 11 I was persecuted at Antioch, at Iconium, at Lystra; I endured those persecutions. Yet the Lord delivered me out of them. 12 And indeed all who will live godly lives—in union with Christ Jesus—will suffer persecution. 13 But evil people and impostors will go from bad to worse. They will deceive others, and they will be deceived themselves.[91] 14 But, as for you, stay with that which you have experientially learned. You are confident of it because you know who you have learned it from.[92] 15 From early childhood[93] you have known the holy scriptures.[94] They have given you the wisdom to accept

---

89. Moses' situation is closer to an organizational situation than was Paul's. In today's ministries, organization transition has its dangers. See **Article**, *Regime Turnover*.

90. This, vs 3:10-17, is one of the great passages on a mentoring relationship. Here you have the mentor, Paul, describing a very personal, open, transparent, vulnerability in his mentoring with Timothy. The mentoring types of teacher, counselor, and contemporary model are reflected in this intense passage, appealing to Timothy. *See mentor, mentor teacher, mentor counselor, mentor model,* **Glossary**. See **Articles**, *Mentoring— An Informal Training Model; Paul the Developer*.

91. Any leader can be blindsided by self-deception. One of Paul's antidotes is to recognize good models who have experientially confirmed truth for you (verse 14). When you differ from them you are in danger of self-deception. See *modeling, contemporary models*, **Glossary**.

92. Trustworthy models are needed early on in the life of a developing leader. This is particularly true when transitioning into ministry and/or when facing a new situation. But it is also true that leaders will need various kinds of mentoring all of their lives; comparative case studies have shown that effective leaders will have from 10-25 important mentoring experiences throughout their lifetime. See *mentor*, **Glossary**.

93. The foundational heritage pattern is referred to here, highlighting one of its advantages (vs 15). Also one who is familiar with the Scriptures, even just the facts of them, has a jump start on learning the Scriptures for use in ministry once the call of God on a life is received. See *heritage pattern*, **Glossary**.

salvation through faith which is in Christ Jesus. 16 Every scripture inspired by God is profitable for teaching, for reprimand, for correction, for leading one to righteous living.[95] 17 That a person of God may be equipped, completely ready[96] to do well.[97]

Did Paul embed his important values? One incidental comment in the Philippian letter indicates that Paul was very confident that his values had taken with Timothy.

Philippians 2

19 But I trust the Lord Jesus will let me send Timothy shortly,[98] that I also may be encouraged when I know what is happening to you. 20 For I have no one like-minded,[99] who will naturally care for what is happening to you. 21 For all seek their own, not the things which are Jesus Christ's. 22 But you know his proven character,[100] that, as a son with the father,[101] he has served with me in the gospel. 23 So I hope to send him shortly, as soon as I shall see how it will go with me.

Those words *like-minded and who will naturally care for what is happening to you*, say it all. Paul knew Timothy had those basic leadership values that he himself had.

[94.] Paul is here referring to the O.T. Scriptures which can be expanded today to include the N.T. Scriptures as well. See *Bible centered leader*, **Glossary**. See **Article**, *Vanishing Breed*.

[95.] This verse has as its intent, not the doctrine of the inspiration of Scripture, but that every inspired (God breathed) Scripture has usefulness for equipping Timothy for his leadership (and by extension other leaders). See *Bible centered leader*, **Glossary**. See **Article**, *Vanishing Breed*.

[96.] This is an instance of the superlative (i.e. repetitive idiom) being used. *Completely ready* (SRN 1822 ἐξηρ-τισμένος) is a combination of two words, one an intensifying preposition and a root word which is a derivative of *equipped*, (SRN 739 ἄρτιος). So what we have here is equipped, thoroughly equipped, that is, really really equipped. I captured it using *equipped, really ready*. My concepts 1 and 2 of the Bible centered leader flow from this verse:(1) whose leadership is being informed by the Bible and (2) who personally has been shaped by Biblical values. See *superlative idiom, capture, Bible centered leader*, **Glossary**,

[97.] Seeing that this admonition is given to a leader in a leadership situation, I don't think I am far wrong to paraphrase this passage as follows. *Every Scripture inspired of God is profitable for (1) leadership insights* (doctrine), *(2) pointing out of leadership errors* (reproof), *(3) suggesting what to do about leadership errors* (correction), *(4) for highlighting how to model a righteous life* (instruction in righteousness) *in order that God's leader* (Timothy) *may be well equipped to lead God's people* (the special good work given to the young leader Timothy). (Clinton paraphrase—slanted toward Timothy's leadership situation).

[98.] Timothy and Titus and others were often sent on ministry trips. These trips served a twofold function—training of those sent and accomplishment of the given mission. See *ministry task*, **Glossary**. See **Articles**, *Paul—and His Companions; Timothy—A Beloved Son in the Faith*.

[99.] This word, *like-minded* (SRN 2473, ἰσόψυχον) is a strong relational word. Paul's leadership value of personal relationships in ministry reach their high point in his relationship with Timothy. See also verse 22, the phrase, *as a son with the father*. Paul felt ministry ought to be very personal. Stated more generally for all leaders, *Leaders should view personal relationships as an important part of ministry, both as a means for ministry and as an end in itself of ministry*. Leaders best pass on values when they have a strong relationship like this one. See 2Ti 3:10-17, fn 3:10. See *leadership value*, **Glossary**. See **Article**, *Timothy—A Beloved Son in the Faith*.

[100.] This Greek word for proven *character* (SRN 1382 δοκιμην) highlights the foundation of a leader. Integrity and proven character are the essential traits of a leader. See fn 1Ti 3:2. See *integrity*, **Glossary**. See **Article**, *Integrity—A Top Leadership Quality*.

[101.] Here we see again Paul's strong leadership value of personal relationships as part of the ministry. Of all the people he lists in his letters, nearly 80, only three does he call sons in the faith—Timothy, Titus, Onesimus. Timothy was closest. See **Article**, Timothy, *A Beloved Son in the Faith*.

2. He co-ministered with his mentorees in a *team setting* as well as *individually* over long periods of time. He made sure others knew of this co-ministering.

3. Paul was very *deliberate in his training efforts*. His word to Timothy (2 Ti 2:2) was indicative of a value he himself possessed. His mentor teaching, contemporary modeling and in particular, use of ministry tasks were three powerful ways that he trained his team members

4. *Functional Equivalent of Moses' public ceremony.* Moses was able to have an official public ceremony in which Joshua was ordained to lead in Moses stead. Paul did not have that luxury. But he did the functional equivalent. The second letter to Timothy and the letter to Titus on Crete were the functional equivalents of Moses' public ceremony with Joshua. They were written proof to these dispersed followers that Paul was tapping Timothy for leadership in Ephesus and Titus in Crete.

If you want your ministry to live on beyond you, then embed your values in leaders who can carry them on. Co-minister with them so that others perceive your high view of them. Train them, with much on-the-job practice. Mentor them. Find ways to let it be known that they represent you.

Conclusion

Glance again at the transition macro lesson.

15. Transition   **Leaders must transition other leaders into their work in order to maintain continuity and effectiveness.**

Any ministry is just one generation away from obsolescence if something is not done to maintain continuity. No ministry can be expected to continue well without deliberate transition efforts. Work on leadership transition and practice it at every level of ministry you are involved it. See it as a process that you are working at all the time. And when you are bringing closure to a given leadership transition effort, insure that the next leader has the best possible chance for success. Do what you can to sponsor that transitioning leader into your vacated role.

We need some good contemporary leadership transitions. Let yours be one of these needed case studies.

Macro Lesson—Defined

Macro Lessons inform our leadership with potential leadership values that move toward the absolute. We live in a time when most do not believe there are absolutes. In my study of leadership in the Bible, I have defined a leadership truth continuum which recognizes the difficulty in deriving absolutes but does allow for them.[102] Figure 23.1 depicts this.

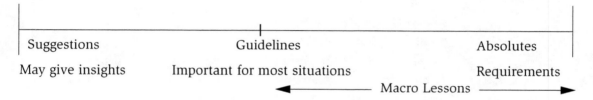

Figure 23.1   Leadership Truth Continuum / Where Macro Lessons Occur

Introduction to Macro lessons

In the *Complexity Era* in which we now live,[103] the thrust of leadership theory has moved, toward the importance of leadership values. The questions being asked today are not as much what is leadership (the leadership basal elements—leader, followers, and situations) and how does it operate (leadership influence means—corporate and individual) as it is why do we do what we do (leadership value bases). The first three eras (Great Man, Trait, and Ohio State) answered the question, "What is leadership?" The Contingency and early part of the Complexity Era answered the question, "How do we do it?" Now we are grappling with, "Why do we lead? or What ought we to do?" We are looking for leadership values. A leadership value is an underlying assumption which affects how a leader behaves in or perceives leadership situations. They are usually statements that have *ought* or *must* or *should* in them. Macro-Lessons are statements of truth about leadership

---

102. See Clinton, **Leadership Perspectives** for a more detailed explanation of the continuum and for my approach to deriving principles from the scriptures. See **Article**, *Principles of Truth.*

103. A study of leadership history in the United States from 1850 to the present uncovered 6 Eras (an era being a period of time in which some major leadership theory held sway): 1. Great Man Era (1840s to 1904); 2. Trait Theory (1904-1948); 3. Ohio State Era (1948-1967); Contingency Era (1967-1980); Complexity Era (1980-present). See Clinton, *A Short History of Leadership Theory.* Altadena, Ca.: Barnabas Publishers.

which have the potential for becoming leadership values. These macro-lessons are observations seen in the various leadership eras in the Bible. Many of these became values for numerous Bible leaders. These macro-lessons move toward the right (requirement, value) of the leadership truth continuum.

What is a macro lesson?

Definition   A *macro-lesson* is a high level generalization

- of a leadership observation (suggestion, guideline, requirement), stated as a lesson,

- which repeatedly occurs throughout different leadership eras,

- and thus has potential as a leadership absolute.

Macro lessons even at their weakest provide strong guidelines describing leadership insights. At their strongest they are requirements, or absolutes, that leaders should follow. Leaders ignore them to their detriment.

Examples:

Prayer Lesson: If God has called you to a ministry then He has called you to pray for that ministry.

Accountability: Christian leaders ought always to minister with a conscious view to ultimate accountability to God for their ministry.

Bible Centered: An effective leader who finishes well must have a Bible centered ministry.

Macro Lessons are derived from a comparative study of leadership in the Six Leadership Eras. These Six Leadership Eras and number of macro lessons identified are shown in Table 23.1.

Table 23.1 Leadership Eras and Number of Macro Lessons

Leadership Era	Number of Macro Lessons
1. Patriarchal Era	7
2. Pre-Kingdom Era	10
3. Kingdom Era	5
4. Post-Kingdom Era	5
5. Pre-Church Era	9
6. Church Era	5

I have identified 41 macro lessons, roughly 5 to 10 per leadership era. When a macro-lesson is seen to occur in varied situations and times and cultural settings and in several leadership eras it becomes a candidate for an absolute leadership lesson. When that same generalization becomes personal and is embraced by a leader as a driving force for how that leader sees or operates in ministry, it becomes a leadership value.

The top three Macro Lessons for the four O.T. Leadership Eras are listed in Table 23.2.

Table 23.2 Top Three Macro Lessons in O.T. Leadership Eras

Priority	Era	Label	Statement
1	Pre-Kingdom	Presence	The essential ingredient of leadership is the powerful presence of God in the leader's life and ministry. (*Therefore a leader must not minister without the powerful presence of God in his/her life.*)
2	Patriarchal	Character	Integrity is the essential character trait of a spiritual leader. (*Therefore, a leader must maintain integrity and respond to God's shaping of it.*)
3	Pre-Kingdom	Intimacy	Leaders develop intimacy with God which in turn overflows into all their ministry since ministry flows out of being. (*Therefore a leader must seek to develop intimacy with God.*)

Table 23.3 gives the top three Macro Lessons for the two N.T. Leadership Eras.

Table 23.3 Top Three Macro Lessons in N.T. Leadership Eras

Priority	Era	Label	Statement
1	Church	Word Centered	*God's Word must be the primary source for equipping leaders and must be a vital part of any leader's ministry.*
2	Pre-Church	Harvest	*Leaders must seek to bring people into relationship with God.*
3	Pre-Church	Shepherd	*Leaders must preserve, protect, and develop those who belong to God's people.*

You will notice that some of these macro lessons are already described in value language (should, must, ought) while others are simply statements of observations. I have put in italics my attempt to give the value associated with the observation.

Comparative study across the six leadership eras for macro lessons makes up one of the seven leadership genres, i.e. sources for leadership findings from the Bible.

Macro Lessons— List of 41 Across Six Leadership Eras

Macro Lessons inform our leadership with potential leadership values that move toward the absolute. The following are the 41 lessons I have identified as I comparatively studied the six different leadership eras for leadership observations.

No.	Label	Era	Statement of Macro Lesson
1.	Blessing	Patriarchal	God mediates His blessing to His followers through leaders.
2.	Shaping	Patriarchal	God shapes leader's lives and ministry through critical incidents.
3.	Timing	Patriarchal	God's timing is crucial to accomplishment of God's purposes.
4.	Destiny	Patriarchal	Leaders must have a sense of destiny.
5.	Character	Patriarchal	Integrity is the essential character trait of a spiritual leader.
6.	Faith	Patriarchal	Biblical Leaders must learn to trust in the unseen God, sense His presence, sense His revelation, and follow Him by faith.
7.	Purity	Patriarchal	Leaders must personally learn of and respond to the holiness of God in order to have effective ministry.
8.	Intercession	Pre-Kingdom	Leaders called to a ministry are called to intercede for that ministry.
9.	Presence	Pre-Kingdom	The essential ingredient of leadership is the powerful presence of God in the leader's life and ministry.
10.	Intimacy	Pre-Kingdom	Leaders develop intimacy with God which in turn overflows into all their ministry since ministry flows out of being.
11.	Burden	Pre-Kingdom	Leaders feel a responsibility to God for their ministry.

12.	Hope	Pre-Kingdom	A primary function of all leadership is to inspire followers with hope in God and in what God is doing.
13.	Challenge	Pre-Kingdom	Leaders receive vision from God which sets before them challenges that inspire their leadership.
14.	Spiritual Authority	Pre-Kingdom	Spiritual authority is the dominant power base of a spiritual leader and comes through experiences with God, knowledge of God, godly character and gifted power.
15.	Transition	Pre-Kingdom	Leaders must transition other leaders into their work in order to maintain continuity and effectiveness.
16.	Weakness	Pre-Kingdom	God can work through weak spiritual leaders if they are available to Him.
17.	Continuity	Pre-Kingdom	Leaders must provide for continuity to new leadership in order to preserve their leadership legacy.
18.	Unity	Kingdom	Unity of the people of God is a value that leaders must preserve.
19.	Stability	Kingdom	Preserving a ministry of God with life and vigor over time is as much if not more of a challenge to leadership than creating one.
20.	Spiritual Leadership	Kingdom	Spiritual leadership can make a difference even in the midst of difficult times.
21.	Recrudescence	Kingdom	God will attempt to bring renewal to His people until they no longer respond to Him.
22.	By-pass	Kingdom	God will by-pass leadership and structures that do not respond to Him and will institute new leadership and structures.
23.	Future Perfect	Post-Kingdom	A primary function of all leadership is to walk by faith with a future perfect paradigm so as to inspire followers with certainty of God's accomplishment of ultimate purposes.
24.	Perspective	Post-Kingdom	Leaders must know the value of perspective and interpret present happenings in terms of God's broader purposes.
25.	Modeling	Post-Kingdom	Leaders can most powerfully influence by modeling godly lives, the sufficiency and sovereignty of God at all times, and gifted power.
26.	Ultimate	Post-Kingdom	Leaders must remember that the ultimate goal of their lives and ministry is to manifest the glory of God.

27.	Perse-verance	Post-Kingdom	Once known, leaders must persevere with the vision God has given.
28.	Selection	Pre-Church	The key to good leadership is the selection of good potential leaders which should be a priority of all leaders.
29.	Training	Pre-Church	Leaders should deliberately train potential leaders in their ministry by available and appropriate means.
30.	Focus	Pre-Church	Leaders should increasingly move toward a focus in their ministry which moves toward fulfillment of their calling and their ultimate contribution to God's purposes for them.
31.	Spirituality	Pre-Church	Leaders must develop interiority, spirit sensitivity, and fruitfulness in accord with their uniqueness since ministry flows out of being.
32.	Servant	Pre-Church	Leaders must maintain a dynamic tension as they lead by serving and serve by leading.
33.	Steward	Pre-Church	Leaders are endowed by God with natural abilities, acquired skills, spiritual gifts, opportunities, experiences, and privileges which must be developed and used for God.
34.	Harvest	Pre-Church	Leaders must seek to bring people into relationship with God.
35.	Shepherd	Pre-Church	Leaders must preserve, protect, and develop God's people.
36.	Movement	Pre-Church	Leaders recognize that movements are the way to penetrate society though they must be preserved via appropriate ongoing institutions.
37.	Structure	Church	Leaders must vary structures to fit the needs of the times if they are to conserve gains and continue with renewed effort.
38.	Universal	Church	The church structure is inherently universal and can be made to fit various cultural situations if functions and not forms are in view.
39.	Giftedness	Church	Leaders are responsible to help God's people identify, develop, and use their resources for God.
40.	Word Centered	Church	God's Word is the primary source for equipping leaders and must be a vital part of any leaders ministry.
41.	Complexity	All eras	Leadership is complex, problematic, difficult and fraught with risk—which is why leadership is needed.

See Also **Article** *Macro Lessons—Defined.*

Mentoring—An Informal Training Model

Training Modes

Today's training can be categorized under three modes as shown in Figure 25.1.

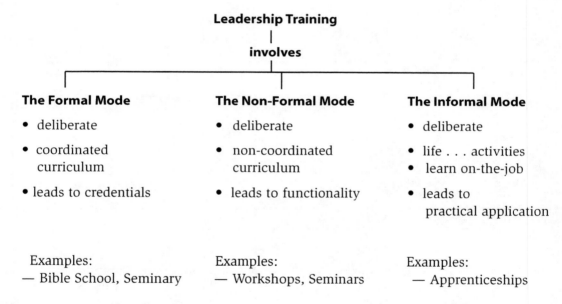

Figure 25.1   Three Training Modes

Mentoring as a training means, while definitely informal in its essence, can be applied to any of the three modes.

Jesus and Paul used the informal training mode as their major training methodology. On-the-job training, modeling, cultural forms of apprenticeships and internships were used. But dominantly it was mentoring which was the primary informal means of training.

Mentoring Defined

Definition | *Mentoring* is a relational experience in which one person, the mentor, empowers another person, the mentoree, by a transfer of resources.

Empowerment can include such things as new habits, knowledge, skills, desires, values, connections to resources for growth and development of potential. We[104] have identified a number of mentoring functions. Table 25.1 identifies nine mentoring functions we have categorized.

Table 25.1 Nine Mentor Functions

Type	Central Thrust
1. Discipler	Basic habits of the Christian life dealing with hearing from God and talking with God; operating in a fellowship of Christians; learning to minister in terms of giftedness; learning to get input from God.
2. Spiritual Guide	Evaluation of spiritual depth and maturity in a life and help in growth in this.
3. Coach	Skills of all kind depending on the expertise of the coach
4. Counselor	Timely and good advice which sheds perspective on issues and problems and other needs.
5. Teacher	Relevant knowledge that can be used for personal growth or ministry or other such need.
6. Sponsor	Protective guidance and linking to resources so that a leader reaches potential.
7. Contemporary Model	Values impactfully demonstrated in a life that can be transferred and used in one's own life.
8. Historical Model	Values demonstrated in a life and inspiration drawn from that life so as to encourage ongoing development in ones own life and a pressing on to finish well.
9. Divine Contact	Timely Guidance from God via some human source.

Mentoring is a relational experience. Five dynamics are involved: attraction, relationship, responsiveness, accountability, empowerment. The more each of these dynamics are in place the more impactful is the empowerment. Table 25.2 gives the essence of each of the dynamics.

---

[104].   My son, Dr. Richard W. Clinton, my colleague Paul Stanley, and I have all been busily researching and using mentoring in our own personal ministries. See *Connecting* by Stanley and Clinton. See The *Mentor Handbook* by Clinton and Clinton.

Table 25.2   Five Mentoring Dynamics

Dynamic	Responsibility of	Explanation
attraction	both mentor and mentoree	A mentoree must be attracted to a mentor—that is, see something in the mentor that is desired in his/her own life; A mentor must be attracted to a mentoree and see potential value in working with the mentoree—that is, development of potential for the mentoree is a worth while investment of time and energy.
relationship	both mentor and mentoree	A mentor must build the relationship with a mentoree and vice versa. The stronger the relationship the more likely that the responsiveness and the accountability functions will take place naturally instead of forced.
responsive-ness	mentoree	The mentoree must respond to the mentor's suggestions and growth projects. Faithfulness in carrying out assignments is a major trait of responsiveness. The mentor is responsible to help the mentoree grow. The mentoree is responsible to respond/submit to the mentor's plan and methodology for growth.
accountabi-lity	mentor	The mentor is responsible to evaluate how the mentoree is doing and to hold the mentoree accountable for following suggestions for growth, for doing what is asked, etc
empower-ment	mentor domi-nantly; mentoree secondarily	Both mentor and mentoree should evaluate and recognize empowerment out of the relationship. The mentor knows and has the best perspective to evaluate empowerment. But the mentoree also should recognize growth in his/her life.

All of these dynamics do not always appear in fullness in the different relationships. They are necessary for the intensive mentoring functions (heavy face-to-face time commitments are usually involved): discipling, spiritual guide, coaching. All do not have to be present in the occasional mentoring functions: counseling, teaching, sponsoring. Empowerment can happen even when all the dynamics are not present. However, the stronger the five dynamics, even in occasional mentoring, the more impactful will be the resulting empowerment. In the passive mentoring functions—contemporary modeling, historical modeling, and divine contact—attraction is present, responsiveness is present and empowerment takes place. But relationship and accountability are essentially missing.

Both Jesus and Paul used mentoring. They had individual relationships with trainees. But they also combined individual mentoring relationships with training of groups.

Mentoring relates directly to two of the seven major lessons observed in comparative study of effective leaders.

> **Effective leaders view leadership selection and development as a priority function in their ministry.**

> **Effective leaders see relational empowerment as both a means and a goal of ministry.**

Mentoring will be one of the dominant forces in the training of emerging leaders in the years to come.

Article 26

Motivating Factors For Ministry

Introduction

What motivated Paul to be and do—to be what God intended him to be and to accomplish what God intended him to accomplish? Some factors which motivated Paul, who is our major model for leadership in the **Church Leadership Era**, are given below. Many of these same factors should motivate leaders today.

Factors That Motivated Paul

Table 26.1 lists motivating factors observed in the Pauline epistles (exceptions, I have not yet done Ro, Gal, Eph, Col, 1,2Th. Probably some new factors might emerge but the major ones will have been identified from the epistles included in the table below).

Table 26.1   Motivational Factors for Paul's Ministry

Factor	Where Observed	Explanation
1. Finishing Well; (Achieving/ Becoming/ Fulfilling Life Purpose)	2Ti 4:7,8; 1Co 9:24-27; 1Ti 6:11,12; 2Ti 4:6; Php 3:14.	Paul is the classic N.T. case of a leader finishing well. Christ is still Lord of His life. He is ministering looking for the return of Christ. All six characteristics of a good finish are indicated. (a) His relationship with God via Christ is still warm and personal. (1Ti 4:17). (b) He evinces a learning posture (1Ti 4:13). (c) He has been shaped by the Holy Spirit over his lifetime into the image of Christ. That is, he demonstrates Christ-likeness (1Ti 4:16). (d) He lives by Biblical convictions, his faith intact (2Ti 4:7). (e) He is leaving behind a legacy. His ultimate contributions include those associated with saint, stylistic practitioner, mentor, pioneer, writer, promoter. To finish well, go the full distance, to finish his course all were drives under lying Paul's motivation for ministry. Principles: a. Present ministry should always be seen in the light of a whole life of ministry and particularly the end of ministry, a good finish. A good thought question, "In what way is my present shaping circumstances going to affect my finish?" b. One's sense of destiny guides toward and highlights a good finish. c. An anticipation of the Lord's return is a major motivating factor for a leader to minister well and finish well.

2. Return of Christ (and the Ultimate Accountability associated with it)	2Ti 4:7,8 (see also Tit 2:11-13). Php 1:6,10; 2:16; 4:1; 2Th 2:2; 2Co 1:14; 5:10,11; 11:30; 1T 6:14; 2Ti 4:8; many others	Paul always ministered with a conscious view to ultimate accountability to God for their ministry. Paul was conscious of a future day in which God would hold him and others accountable for their actions (see 1:16, 4:8, 4:14). This is more fully developed in 2Co and 1, 2Th but is affirmed in many epistles. (See especially He 13:17). Principles: a. Leaders will be held accountable for their ministry efforts. b. Leaders will be rewarded for their positive achievements in ministry. c. A final accountability is one motivating factor for a leader.
3. Giftedness (especially the Apostolic Functions with it)	1Co; 1Ti; 2Co 11:4	Paul exemplifies all of the apostolic functions. For example, a number of his epistles were written in part to correct heresy. His word giftedness dominated all that he did: apostleship, teaching, evangelism, and sometimes pastoring. His giftedness was a major factor in motivating and directing/ guiding him into ministry.
4. Confidence in the Gospel	2Co 3:12; (see also Ro 1:16); 1 Co 6:11.	Confidence in the power of the Good News about Christ is a strong motivating factor leading to bold ministry. Paul spoke boldly because he had experienced the power of the Gospel in lives. He saw people delivered from sins and from addictive sin.
5. Burden for Ministry	2Co 2:4; 2Co 11:28;	Paul, like Moses, had a heavy calling on his life. This calling gave him a burden which drove him to reach Gentiles and to do the apostolic functions he did with them. His strong concerns for those he influenced are interwoven throughout all he does. He exemplifies the double thrust of burden—downward toward ministry with those he was influencing and upward, answering to God for them.
6. Resurrection	1Co 15; 2Co 4:14; Php 3:10;	Paul was driven to know that there was a life after death. His conversion experience convinced him that it was real. From then on, he was obsessed with realizing this for his own life; particularly he wanted to experience resurrection power in his ministry.
7. Handling God's Word appropriately	2Ti 2:15; 2Co 4:2; 2Ti 3:16,17	Paul used the Word of God with great impact. He maintained integrity in how he handled the Word. Knowing the Word of God and used it properly with impact in ministry was a motivating guideline for Paul.
8. Eternal Realities	2Co 4:18	Paul viewed present problems, pressures, physical problems as being bearable in the light of eternity. He always ministered looking forward to resurrection life. He saw these kinds of things *as negative preparation* making him ready and longing for heaven and eternal reality.
9. Love	1Co 12:29; 13; 2Co 5:14	Paul believed that love should be a major underlying motivating and driving force for using giftedness and for ministry in general. His love for Christ compelled him in ministry.

Conclusion

What motivates you in ministry? Strangely absent from Paul's motivation was a drive for prestige, power, or money—factors driving numerous present day leaders.

See *negative preparation*, **Glossary**.

Article 27

Motivating Principles — Pauline Influence

Introduction

Paul was a powerful leader who influenced numerous people and churches in *the Church Leadership Era*. What principles or techniques did he use? Following are given some observations (some are statements of principles; others are techniques) which Paul used to motivate individuals and churches. Many of these same principles/techniques can be used by leaders today. Paul is the major model for leadership in the **Church Leadership Era**.

Paul's Motivational Principles and Techniques

Table 27.1 lists some principles/ techniques observed in the Pauline epistles on how Paul motivated followers. Not all the Pauline epistles were considered; Missing would be Ro, Gal, Eph, Col, 1,2Th. Probably some new factors might emerge but the major ones will have been identified from the epistles.

Table 27.1   Paul's Motivational Principles and Techniques

Principle/ Technique	Where Observed	Explanation
Goodwin's Expectation Principle	1Ti 6:11; 2Ti 1:5 et al	Principle: Paul uses the dynamic under lying Goodwin's expectation principle—emerging leaders tend to live up to the genuine expectations of leaders they admire.
Teach For Results	1Ti 1:5	Principle: True teaching ought to result in people who have love, a pure heart and a genuine faith. Paul contrasts this result with the heretical teachers who are producing argumentative people.
Prophecy	1Ti 1:18; 4:14	Principle: Paul recalled a prophecy about a spiritual gift made over Timothy in order to motivate Timothy to use that gift with impact. He recalled a prophecy about Timothy living the Christian life.
Touchstone	1Ti 6:11,12	Principle: Use public committals as a motivating factor for continuing on in the Christian life. Public committals on major decisions form a touchstone.

Heritage	2Ti 1:5	Principle: Paul affirmed a foundational heritage for Timothy in order to exhort him to move on in faith (like his mother and grandmother).
Get It On the Agenda	1Co 1:1, 4, 5;	Principle: Paul often subtly introduced subjects he would later deal with in depth. Later when he began to deal with the subject the hearers were already somewhat primed for it.
Future/ Hope	1Co 1:4-9;	Principle: Inspirational leaders point toward the future and what God will do in order to give followers hope.
Competition	1Co 16:1, 4; 2Co 8:1-5, 24; 9:1,2;	Principle: Paul compares churches with churches always pointing out the strengths of churches in order to motivate the other churches to attain that level.
Absolute Surrender	2Co 8:5	Principle: Paul challenged believers to commit themselves totally to God. From that standpoint, then he could motivate them to give freely of all kinds of their resources. Without it, at best he would get some grudging help.
Openness	2Co 8:8	Principle: Paul was open and above board even about using motivational techniques. He would sometimes explain his motivational technique.
Modeling/ Jesus	2Co 8:9; Php 2:1-11.	Principle: Paul appealed to Jesus as a model to motivate followers of Jesus to emulate that modeling.
Spiritual Authority	2Co 12:19;	Principle: Paul used strong authoritative techniques but always in line with spiritual authority which seeks the best for the ones being helped.
Foreshadowing	2Co 12:21.	Principle: Paul lays out for them a future scenario that could happen should they not follow his advice. And he promises to back this scenario up with power.
Modeling/ Jesus	See Php	Principle: One of Paul's strongest motivating means is the modeling in his own life. Over and over this is stressed throughout all his epistles. Paul knows it is a motivating force.
Accountability	Php 2:16; 3:17.	Principle: Paul uses his own ultimate accountability to motivate followers.

Conclusion

Paul demonstrates several techniques for motivating followers, especially the Corinthians. Leaders are people with God-given capacities and a God-given burden who are influencing a specific group of people toward God's purposes for them. Influence is the key word. And motivational techniques are means of exerting that influence. Motivation in this case is even more difficult since Paul is confronting a problem church in which a minority are not responding to him. Paul uses several means of motivating which I have given in the table above. However, let me summarize the more important ones. Motivational Leadership Principles/ Observations include:

a. Goodwin's Expectation Principle, a social dynamic usually dealing with individuals, which recognizes that emerging leaders will usually rise to the level of expectancy of someone they respect, is applied by Paul to a group situation of followers.

Paul states his personal positive outcome expectancies for the churches (see especially the Corinthians, both concerning their giving and their following of his exhortations).

b. Paul uses the gift of exhortation throughout all his books, deliberately, openly, and with clear application to situations. See footnotes identifying the gift of exhortation in use.

c. Paul uses a form of comparative competition. He describes what other churches have done with respect to giving (in a rather positive ideal description) in order to set expectancies for giving from the churches (both Philippians and Corinthians).

d. Paul tells churches that he has said great things about their giving to other churches. Their failure to give would make them lose face in the eyes of these other churches.

e. In the Corinthian case, Paul commissions a delegation from one of the churches which has given and been used as a model to go to Corinth to be part of the group that will administer the gift.

f. Paul uses Jesus as a model of giving and as a model for humility and putting others first.

g. Paul uses coercive authority (threatens to exercise spiritual power to correct situations if people do not respond voluntary) backed by a personal visit to motivate.

h. Paul uses well reasoned out logic in giving solutions to issues and defending his own character.

i. In the Corinthian case, Paul uses irony (sometimes bordering on sarcasm), often, in order to force the Corinthians to see their positions on things and to challenge them to respond.

Paul motivated people—even in very complex and problematic situations. An awareness of some of his techniques might prove helpful to leaders today who must motivate followers in equally if not more complex and problematic situations.

Pauline Leadership Styles

Introduction

Consider the fundamental definition for leader given in this commentary.

Definition   A *leader* is a person with God-given capacity and God-given responsibility who is influencing a specific group of people toward God's purposes.

How does one influence? Leadership style is one measure of how a leader influences. Paul again sets an example for leaders in the N.T. Church Leadership Era.

In Php, I point out that Paul uses the maturity appeal (opening salutation) and imitation modeling leadership styles (throughout the book, see especially Php 4:9). In Phm, I show how Paul uses several leadership styles: father-initiator (Phm 19), maturity appeal (Phm 9), and obligation persuasion (Phm 8-21).   In1Co and 2Co I repeatedly make comments on Paul's leadership styles. In 1Co I point out his Father-initiator style (4:14,15), his Apostolic leadership style (9:1,2), his confrontation style (1Co 5:1-5), his indirect conflict leadership style (1Co 5:1-4) and his imitator leadership style (1Co 4:16). In 2Co I point out maturity appeal (6:9,10), obligation persuasion (8:8), Father-initiator (2Co 10:14). Paul is a multi-style leader—a very modern concept in leadership style theory. What is a multi-style leader? Some definitions are needed in order to understand leadership style. Then I will move on to examine Pauline leadership styles.

Definition: The *dominant leadership style* of a leader is that,
1. highly directive or
2. directive or
3. non-directive or
4. highly non-directive

consistent behavior pattern that underlies specific overt behavior acts of influence pervading the majority of leadership functions in which that leader exerts influence.

This concept of leadership style can be shown in picture format. Figure 28.1 which follows lays out the four basic behavioral tendencies.

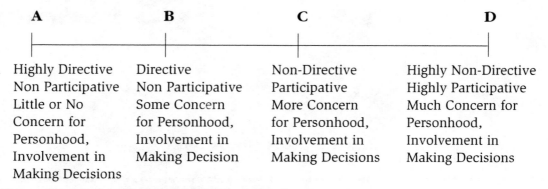

Figure 28.1 Influence Behavior Along a Continuum

Leadership style, deals with the individual behavioral expression a leader utilizes in influencing followers. This individual expression includes methodology for handling crises, methodology for problem solving, methodology for decision making, methodology for coordinating with superiors, peers and subordinates, methodology for handling leadership development. The individual methodology for a specific leadership act or series of acts can often be labeled as well as identified on the Directive—Non-Directive continuum.

My study of Paul's influence identified ten styles. These were given specific labels. Paul was multi-styled[105] in his approach to influencing followers. The styles are not defined exclusively. That is, there is some overlap of concepts between different styles. Let me describe the ten styles I labeled.

Ten Pauline Styles Observed

1. Apostolic Style

Where a person demonstrates with self-authenticating evidence that he/she has delegated authority from God—that is, there is a sense of spiritual authority about the leadership—then that person can use the apostolic leadership style.

Definition: The *apostolic leadership style* is a method of influence in which the leader

- assumes the role of delegated authority over those for whom he/she is responsible,

- receives revelation from God concerning decisions, and

- commands obedience based on role of delegated authority and revelation concerning God's will.

A synonym for this style is the command/demand style. This style is implied in 1Th 5:12, 13. "And I want you, fellow Christians, to personally know the leaders who work among you, and are over you in the Lord, and warm you. Lovingly honor them for their work's sake." It is implied in 1Ti 5:17: "Church leaders that are exercising good leadership should

---

105.   Doohan, a noted author on Pauline leadership also concludes that Paul is multi-styled. See Helen Doohan, *Leadership in Paul*. Wilmington, Del.: Michael Glazier, Inc., 1984.

be evaluated as worthy of double pay—especially the ones who are working hard teaching the word." Another example implying this style is seen in Heb 13:17: "Obey those leaders who are set over you. Submit to their leadership. For they watch for your souls, as those who must give account. And they want to do so with joy and not with grief. Make it worth their while." This style is also seen in 1Th 2:6; even though Paul chooses not to command obedience, he asserts that he could have done so as was his apostolic right. The essence of the apostolic style is the legitimate right from God to make decisions for others and to command or demand their compliance with those decisions.

This style with its top-down command/demand approach is considered the most highly directive leadership style.

2. Confrontation Style

Many leaders try to avoid problems, particularly those involving troublesome people and those carrying heavy emotional ramifications. The basic rationale seems to be, "this is a tough problem; if I try to do anything about it I'm going to incur wrath, maybe have my character maligned, lose some friends and be drained emotionally. Perhaps if I just ignore it, it will go away by itself." For some problems, perhaps this is a good philosophy; time does give opportunity for a clearer perspective, for healing, and for indirect conflict to occur. But for most problems, leaders must confront the problem and parties involved directly. At least this seems to be the approaches exemplified in Jude, John, Peter, and Paul in their Scriptural writings.

Definition: The *confrontation leadership style* is an approach to problem solving

- which brings the problem out in the open with all parties concerned,

- which analyzes the problem in light of revelational truth,

- and which brings force to bear upon the parties to accept recommended solutions.

This style is usually seen in combination with other styles. Seemingly, the majority of cases emphasize *obligation-persuasion* as the force for accepting the solution, but *apostolic* force is also seen in the Scriptures. The book of Jude is an example. Several of the leadership acts in the book of 1Co utilize this style. Paul also uses this style in the Philippian church. See the problem between Euodia and Synteche. This style, like the apostolic style, is highly directive since the solutions to the problems are often the leader's solutions.

3. Father-Initiator Style

Paul resorts to this leadership style when exerting his influence upon the Corinthian church. He is establishing his authority in order to suggest solutions to some deep problems in the church.

Definition: The *father-initiator leadership style* is related to the apostolic style which uses the fact of the leader having founded the work as a lever for getting acceptance of influence by the leader.

In 1Co 4:14, 15 Paul writes, "14 I do not write these things to shame you, but as my beloved children I warn you. 15 For though you might have ten thousand Christian teachers, you only have one father in the faith. For I became your spiritual father when I preached the Gospel to you." Paul uses the father-initiator style in this case." Note in this example the force of the two powerful figures: the absolute for the relative in verse 14 and the hyperbole in verse 15.

The father-initiator style is closely related to the obligation-persuasion style, in that obligation (debt owed due to founding the work) is used as a power base. However it differs from obligation-persuasion in that more than persuasion is used. The decision to obey is not left to the follower. It is related to the apostolic style in that it is apostolic in its force of persuasion.

This style is highly directive/directive style.

4. Obligation-Persuasion Style

One method of influencing followers over which you have no direct organizational control involves persuasion. The leader persuades but leaves the final decision to the follower. A particularly powerful technique of persuasion is obligation-persuasion in which normal appeal techniques are coupled with a sense of obligation on the part of the follower due to past relationship/experience with the leader. Such a leadership style is seen with Paul's treatment of the Onesimus/Philemon problem.

Definition: An *obligation-persuasion leadership style* refers to an appeal to followers to follow some recommended directives which

- persuades, not commands followers to heed some advice;
- leaves the decision to do so in the hands of the followers, but
- forces the followers to recognize their obligation to the leader due to past service by the leader to the follower;
- strongly implies that the follower owes the leader some debt and should follow the recommended advice as part of paying back the obligation; and finally
- reflects the leader's strong expectation that the follower will conform to the persuasive advice.

The classic example of this is illustrated in the book of Philemon. Paul uses this style in combination with other styles in 1,2Co also.

This is a directive style. The expectation is high, though the actual decision to do so passes to the follower.

5. Father-Guardian Style

This style, much like the nurse style, elicits an empathetic concern of the leader toward protection and care for followers.

Definition: The *father-guardian style* is a style which is similar to a parent-child relationship and has as its major concern protection and encouragement for followers.

Usually this style is seen when a very mature Christian relates to very immature followers. 1Th 2:10, 11 illustrates this style. "You know it to be true, and so does God, that our behavior toward you believers was pure, right, and without fault. You know that we treated each one of you just as a father treats his own children. We encouraged you, we comforted you, and we kept urging you to live the kind of life that pleases God, who calls you to share in his own Kingdom and glory."

Usually this style is directive, but because of the caring relationship between leader and follower and the follower maturity level it does not seem directive, since influence behavior always seem to have the follower's best interest at heart.

6. Maturity Appeal Style

The book of Proverbs indicates that all of life is an experience that can be used by God to give wisdom. And those who have learned wisdom should be listened to by those needing yet to learn. Maturity in the Christian life comes through time and experience and through God-given lessons as well as giftedness (see *word of wisdom gift*, **Glossary**). Leaders often influence and persuade followers by citing their *track record* (learned wisdom) with God.

Definition: A *maturity appeal leadership style* is a form of leadership influence which counts upon

- Godly experience, usually gained over a long period of time,
- an empathetic identification based on a common sharing of experience, and
- a recognition of the force of imitation modeling in influencing people in order to convince people toward a favorable acceptance of the leader's ideas.

Heb 13:7 carries this implication: "Remember your former leaders who spoke God's message to you. Think back on how they lived and died and imitate their faith."

See also 1Pe 5:1–4, 5–7 where Peter demonstrates maturity appeal. "I, an elder myself, appeal to the church elders among you. I saw firsthand Christ's sufferings. I will share in the glory that will be revealed. I appeal to you to be shepherds of the flock that God gave you. Take care of it willingly, as God wants you to, and not unwillingly. Do your work, not for mere pay, but from a real desire to serve. Do not try to rule over those who have been put in your care, but be an example to the flock. And when the chief Shepherd appears, you will receive the glorious crown which will last."

Paul's description of his sufferings as an Apostle (2Co 11:16–33) and experience in receiving revelation (2Co 12:1–10) are exemplary of the maturity appeal style leadership.

This style moves between the categories of directive to non-directive depending on how forcefully the desired result is pushed for.

7. Nurse Style

In 1Th 2:7, Paul uses a figure to describe a leadership style he used among the Thessalonian Christians. The figure is that of a nurse. It is the only use of this particular word in the N.T., though related cognates do occur. The essential idea of the figure is the gentle cherishing attitude of Paul toward the new Christians in Thessalonica with a particular emphasis on Paul's focus on serving in order to help them grow.

Definition: The *nurse leadership style* is a behavior style characterized by gentleness and sacrificial service and loving care which indicates that a leader has given up "rights" in order not to impede the nurture of those following him/her.

The primary example is given in 1Th 2:7, "But we were gentle among you, even as a nurse cherishes her children." Paul commands an attitude of gentleness to Timothy in 2Ti 2:24–25. "24 The Lord's servant must not quarrel; instead be gentle unto all, skillfully teaching and being patient, 25 gently instructing those opponents. Perhaps God will give them opportunity to repent and see the truth."

The nurse style is similar to the father-guardian style in that both have a strong empathetic care for the followers. It differs in that the father-guardian style assumes a protective role of a parent to child. The nurse role assumes a nurturing focus which will sacrifice in order to see nurture accomplished.

The nurse style is non-directive.

8. Imitator Style

Paul seemed continually to sense that what he was and what he did served as a powerful model for those he influenced. He expected his followers to become like him in attitudes and actions. It is this personal model of *being* and *doing* as a way to influence followers that forms part of the foundational basis for spiritual authority.

Definition: The *imitator style* refers to a conscious use of imitation modeling as a means for influencing followers. It reflects a leader's sense of responsibility for what he/she is as a person of God and for what he/she does in ministry with an expectant view that followers must and will and should be encouraged to follow his/her example.

Paul emphasizes this in Php 4:9 which illustrates this leadership style. "9 Those things, which you have both learned, and received, and heard, and seen in me, do—and the God of peace shall be with you. A second Pauline illustration is seen in 2Ti 3:10,11. 10 "But you fully know my teaching, my lifestyle, my purpose in life, my faith, my steadfastness, my love, my endurance. 11 I was persecuted at Antioch, at Iconium, at Lystra; I endured those persecutions. Yet the Lord delivered me out of them." Paul goes on to give the response he expects of Timothy based on this imitation modeling and maturity appeal.

The whole book of Php emphasizes this influential methodology as being one of the most powerful tools a leader can use to influence followers. This style is highly non-directive.

9. Consensus Style

Decisions which affect people's lives and for which leaders must give account require careful spirit-led consideration. One leadership style approach to decision making involves consensus decision making. This style is often used in coordination situations where ownership is desired. Cultures which stress group solidarity, such as many of the tribes in Papua New Guinea, see this style used frequently by leaders.

Definition: *Consensus leadership style* refers to the approach to leadership influence which involves the group itself actively participating in decision making and coming to solutions acceptable to the whole group. The leader must be skilled in bringing diverse thoughts together in such a way as to meet the whole group's needs.

In a consensus style there is much give and take in arriving at decision. Unless there is a *check in the spirit* which prohibits an agreement, the final decision carries the weight of the entire group and thus will *demand* all to follow through on implications and ramifications which follow. James apparently gives a consensus decision reflecting the entire group's corporate will in the Ac 15 decision. Note this decision was identified as Spirit-led. The Ac 6 decision concerning distribution of good to widows is an example of both of consensus (within the plurality of Apostles) and apostolic (commanded to the followers) leadership styles.

This style is highly non-directive.

10. Indirect Conflict Style

A powerful style for dealing with crises and problem solving involves the concept of dealing with *first causes*, that is, the primary motivating factors behind the problem rather than the problem itself. This style recognizes that spiritual conflict is behind the situation and must be dealt with before any solution will take hold. The parties directly involved may not be aware that the leader is even doing problem solving. A leader who uses this approach must be skilled in prayer, understand spiritual warfare and either have the gift of discerning spirits or access to a person with that gift.

Definition   The *indirect conflict leadership style* is an approach to problem solving which requires discernment of spiritual motivation factors behind the problem, usually results in spiritual warfare without direct confrontation with the parties of the problem. Spiritual warfare is sensed as a necessary first step before any problem solving can take place.

See the context of Mt 16:21–23 especially verse 23: "Get away from me Satan. You are an obstacle in my way, because these thoughts of yours don't come from God, but from man." This is an example of indirect conflict leadership style. Mk 3:20–30 gives the underlying idea behind this style. See especially verse 27: "No one can break into a strong man's house and take away his belongings unless he first ties up the strong man; then he can plunder his house." See also Eph 6:10–20, especially verse 12: "For we are not fighting against human beings but against the wicked spiritual forces in the heavenly world, the rulers, authorities, and cosmic powers of this dark age."

Conclusions

I think the following are worth noting because they point out what I have been attempting to do in this section dealing with biblical styles, most of which come from Pauline material.

1. I have demonstrated how to use the generic (directive/non-directive continuum) as the overarching umbrella on which to pinpoint specific leadership-style behaviors.

2. I have identified 10 different Pauline leadership styles.

3. These 10 models of specific styles are transferable to many situations which we as leaders face today.

4. I have indicated that Paul's leadership style was multi-styled.

5. I have pointed out that Paul was a flexible leader who matured in his leadership as he grew older and was able to change to meet change to meet changing situations.

Current leadership style theories differ on whether or not a leader can actually change his/her leadership style. My own observations recognize that some leaders are flexible and can change. Others are not. Perhaps the ideal is a flexible leader who can change. But where this is not possible, then a leader who dominantly uses a certain leadership style should be placed in a situation where that style fits. Directive styles fit best with immature followers who need that direction. As followers mature the leadership styles should move to the right on the directive-non-directive continuum. This allows for follower maturity and for emerging leaders to arise.

Paul — A Sense of Destiny

Introduction

The Apostle Paul had a strong sense of destiny. You see it all over the pages of his epistles. One of the major leadership lessons[106] that emerged from a comparative study of effective leaders concerned the concept, sense of destiny.

Effective leaders evince a growing sense of destiny over their lifetimes.[107]

You will notice reminders of Paul's sense of destiny sprinkled throughout my leadership commentary notes on the Pauline Epistles. He exemplifies in the N.T. Church Leadership Era the importance of a sense of destiny. Such an awareness stabilizes a leader, encourages perseverance, and becomes a Pole Star to shed directive light in major decisions about guidance.

Definition   A *sense of destiny* is an inner conviction arising from an experience or a series of experiences in which there is a growing sense of awareness that God has His hand on a leader in a special way for special purposes.

Definition   *Destiny processing* refers to the shaping incidents or means God uses to instill this growing sense of awareness of a destiny is called **destiny processing.**

It is through these shaping activities of God that a leader becomes increasingly aware of God's Hand on his/her life and the purposes for which God has intended for his/her leadership. This processing causes a sense of partnership with God toward God's purposes for the life and hence brings meaning to the life.

---

106. Seven such lessons have been identified: (1) Effective Leaders View Present Ministry in Terms Of A Life Time Perspective. (2) Effective Leaders Maintain A Learning Posture Throughout Life. (3) Effective Leaders Value Spiritual Authority As A Primary Power Base. (4) Effective Leaders Who Are Productive Over A Lifetime Have A Dynamic Ministry Philosophy. (5) Effective Leaders View Leadership Selection And Development As A Priority Function In Their Ministry. (6) Effective Leaders See Relational Empowerment As Both A Means And A Goal Of Ministry. (7) Effective Leaders Evince A Growing Awareness Of Their Sense Of Destiny. It is this last one I am exploring in this article.

107. This is a major key to an effective ministry. No Bible leader who had an effective ministry failed to have a sense of destiny. Paul is the exemplar in the N.T. Church Leadership Era. Over and over again in his epistles, Paul's makes statements that reflect on his understanding of his destiny with God.

A sense of destiny and accompanying destiny processing form the seedbed for life purpose—not only the driving force behind our lives but the defining essence of it. When a leader surrenders to God, in terms of an all out commitment to be the leader God wants, a whole process begins in which that leader begins to discover for what purposes he/she was uniquely created. **Life purpose** represents the descriptive label that characterizes the underlying motivational thrust(s) that energizes a given leader to be and do and around which life begins to center. It becomes that overall centralizing ideal or accomplishment or task to which all of a leader's life is committed. **Life purpose** is the most important of four focal issues which define the focused life.[108]

Definition   A *life purpose* is a burden-like calling, a task or driving force or achievement, which motivates a leader to fulfill something or to see something done.

Paul and The Destiny Pattern

Paul exemplifies the N.T. church leadership prototype for the destiny pattern as seen in Figure 29.1 below.

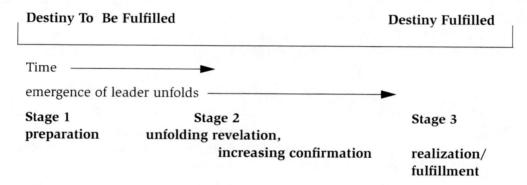

Destiny To Be Fulfilled   **Destiny Fulfilled**

Time

emergence of leader unfolds

Stage 1   Stage 2   Stage 3
preparation   unfolding revelation,
                                increasing confirmation   realization/
                                                             fulfillment

Figure 29.1   Unfolding of Destiny in 3 Basic Stages

The destiny experiences can be related generally to these three stages as categorized below in Figure 29.2.

---

108.   A *focused life* is a life dedicated to exclusively carrying out God's unique purposes through it, by identifying the focal issues, that is, life purpose, major role, effective methodology, or ultimate contribution, which allows an increasing prioritization of life's activities around the focal issues, and results in a satisfying life of being and doing. The 4 focal issues—life purpose, major role, effective methodology, or ultimate contribution—are discovered over a lifetime.

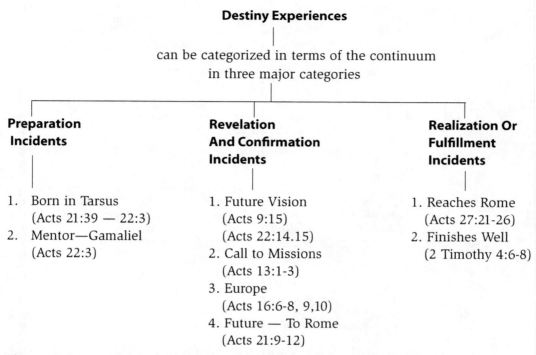

Figure 29.2   Paul's Destiny Processing and Three Fold Destiny Pattern

Paul's Destiny And Ensuing Life Purpose—Progressively Seen

Paul progressively grasped his sense of destiny. God used a number of special events over time to build into Paul a more detailed awareness of his sense of destiny.

Definition   A *prime critical incident* is a special intervention (could be a series over time) in which God gives a *major value* that will flow through the life or will give *strategic direction* to narrow the leader's life work.

1. Some produce a dominant value which pervades the leader's ministry philosophy.
2. Some pinpoint a key strategic directional factor.
3. Some do both.

Table 29.1 gives Seven prime critical incidents in the life of Paul. I synthesize how each of these progressively fed into Paul's life purpose.

Table 29.1   Paul's Life Purpose Unfolding

Incedent	Label/ Scripture	Life Purpose
C_1	Damacus Road	My life purpose is to serve the risen Lord Jesus by witnessing to what he has shown me and will show me to Jews, Gentiles, and Kings.

C_2	Barnabas Sponsors Acts 9	My life purpose is to serve the risen Lord Jesus by witnessing to what he has shown me and will show me to Jews, Gentiles, and Kings. **I know I am to be a part of expanding Jesus' work begun in Jerusalem.**
C_3	Barnabas sponsors in Antioch Acts 11	My life purpose is to serve the risen Lord Jesus by witnessing to what he has shown me and will show me to Jews, Gentiles, and Kings. I know I am to be a part of expanding Jesus' work begun in Jerusalem. **It will involve working with a team and development of local groups of Christians.**
C_4	Apostolic Call/ Acts 13	My life purpose is to serve the risen Lord Jesus by witnessing to what he has shown me and will show me to Jews, Gentiles, and Kings. I know I am to be a part of expanding Jesus' work begun in Jerusalem. It will involve working with a team and development of local groups of Christians. **Further, I know that I will be in an itinerant ministry, having been sent by the Holy Spirit, confirmed by other leaders, to witness to Gentiles on Cyprus.**
C_5	Conflict and the Jerusalem Council/ Gospel Clarified Acts 15	My life purpose is to serve the risen Lord Jesus by witnessing to what he has shown me and will show me to Jews, Gentiles, and Kings. I know I am to be a part of expanding Jesus' work begun in Jerusalem. It will involve working with a team and development of local groups of Christians. Further, I know that I will be in an itinerant ministry, having been sent by the Holy Spirit, confirmed by other leaders, to witness to Gentiles on Cyprus. **I will be the primary person who will contexualize truth into Gentile situations. Occasionally, I will also speak truth into Jewish situations.**
C_6	European/ Western Gentiles Acts 16	My life purpose is to serve the risen Lord Jesus by witnessing to what he has shown me and will show me to Jews, Gentiles, and Kings. I know I am to be a part of expanding Jesus' work begun in Jerusalem. It will involve working with a team and development of local groups of Christians. Further, I know that I will be in an itinerant ministry, having been sent by the Holy Spirit, confirmed by other leaders, to witness to Gentiles on Cyprus, **Asia Minor and Europe. My ministry will thus be widespread, an itinerant ministry among Gentiles.** I will be the primary person who will contexualize truth into Gentile situations. **I know that my ministry will be pioneering, breaking open new situations to western Gentiles as well as others.** Occasionally, I will also speak truth into Jewish situations.
C_7	Destiny in Rome Via Jerusalem Persecution Acts 21	My life purpose is to serve the risen Lord Jesus by witnessing to what he has shown me and will show me to Jews, Gentiles, and Kings. I know I am to be a part of expanding Jesus' work begun in Jerusalem. It will involve working with a team and development of local groups of Christians. Further, I know that I will be in an itinerant ministry, having been sent by the Holy Spirit, confirmed by other leaders, to witness to Gentiles on Cyprus, Asia Minor and Europe. My ministry will thus be widespread, an itinerant ministry among Gentiles. I will be the primary person who will contexualize truth into Gentile situations. I know that my ministry will be pioneering, breaking open new situations to western Gentiles as well as others. Occasionally, I will also speak truth into Jewish situations. **I know I am destined to give my witness to Christ before high rulers.**

Conclusion

Paul finished well. One reason, he led a focused life. At the heart of that focus was the sense of destiny that drove him on to serve God. He struggled a good struggle. He finished his course. He fulfilled his life purpose. He stands as a model for us.

> 6 As for me, I am ready to be sacrificed. The time for me to depart this life is near. 7 I have run a good race.[109] I have fulfilled my God-given destiny.[110] I still have my faith intact. 8 And now for my prize, a crown of righteousness. The Lord, the righteous judge, will award it to me at that day. And not to me only, but unto all those who eagerly await his return.[111]

---

[109]. Literally, this is *the good struggle I have struggled*, a use of the superlative repetitive idiom. The two words for struggle are the noun form and verb form from which we derive our words agony and agonize and refer to an Olympic athlete who is disciplining himself for a marathon or other event.

[110]. Fulfilled my destiny, literally I have finished or completed (SRN 5758 τετέλεκα) a perfect action, i.e. already done it with on going results, my course (SRN 1408 δρόμον). Course, used three times in the N.T., refers to life's destiny, the pathway set before one to do. The destiny pattern usually follows a threefold pattern: destiny preparation, destiny revelation, and destiny fulfillment. This idea of already completing it is the use of a certainty idiom, the prophetic past. It is so certain that he speaks of it in the past tense as if it had already happened. See Ac 20:24 where Paul states his desire to finish his course. See also, Ac 13:25 where the same word refers to John the Baptist's having finished his course. See certainty idiom, prophetic past, sense of destiny, destiny preparation, destiny revelation, destiny fulfillment, **Glossary. See Articles,** *The Destiny Pattern.*

[111]. Vs 4:6-8 show that Paul finished well. He is the classic case of a N.T. church leader finishing well. All six characteristics of a good finish are seen: (1) vibrant personal relationship with God; (2) have a learning posture; (3) Christ-likeness in character; (4) live by Biblical convictions; (5) leave behind ultimate contributions; (6) fulfill a sense of destiny. One of the major leadership contributions of 2Ti is this challenge to finish well, which Paul models. See *modeling,* **Glossary. Article,** *Finishing Well—Six Characteristics.*

Paul—And His Companions

Introduction

Paul developed leaders. He did this through teaching, modeling, and on-the-job training. A comparative study of his relationships with numerous leaders reveals that he exemplifies a number of mentoring roles: discipler, spiritual guide, coach, teacher, contemporary model, sponsor. He operated as a mentor with individuals. He also mentored in a team context.

Several Pauline leadership values[112] under girded this drive to develop leaders.

> Leaders Must Be Concerned About Leadership Selection And Development.
>
> Leaders Should View Personal Relationships As An Important Part Of Ministry.
>
> A Christian Leader Ought To Have Several Life Long Mentorees Who He/She Will Help Over A Lifetime To Reach Their Potential In Leadership.

And the following two major lessons are the foundation for the above three.

> Effective Leaders View Leadership Selection And Development As A Priority In Ministry.
>
> Effective Leaders View Relational Empowerment As Both A Means And A Goal In Ministry.

This article simply points out that Paul had a personal ministry. Paul developed many leaders, his companions in ministry. It also seeks to exhort us by example.

Paul's Companions

Luke's *we sections* in Ac points out that Paul frequently had a team with him. A num-

---

[112]. A *leadership value* is an underlying assumption which affects how a leader perceives leadership and practices it. Leadership values contain strong language like should, ought, or must. Must statements are the strongest.

ber of the people listed below actually traveled on teams with Paul. Others were in ministry with him in various locales. Still other were acquaintances he thought highly of. But all of them had some personal relationship with Paul. Table 30.1 lists the many folks Paul related to personally. Many of them were leaders.

Table 30.1   Paul's Companions—Reflected in His Epistles

Who	Vs	Comments
Achaicus	1Co 16:17, 24	One of three men who brought Paul financial support when he was in Philippi, from the Corinthian church. Also one of three men who were present when the first letter to the church at Corinth was penned. So, he along with the other two probably supplied Paul with lots of information about the church at Corinth.
Ampliatus	Ro 16:8	A close friend in the church at Rome.
Andronicus	Ro 16:7	An apostle and Christian before Paul. Was in prison probably with Paul. Paul calls him a kinsman but whether this is a brother in Christ or physically is not certain.
Apelles	Ro 16:10	A Christian friend well thought of by Paul in the church at Rome. In his greeting he gives affirmation for this person.
Apollos	Seen 10 times in Ac, 1Co, Tit	A strong Christian worker and well known as a public rhetorician, mighty in the Scriptures. Was mentored by Priscilla and Acquilla. Associated with the church at Corinth. Late in Paul's ministry, when Titus was in Crete, Paul asked Titus to raise funds in Crete to support Apollos.
Apphia	Phm 2	A female Christian, probably the wife of Philemon. Paul loved her dearly and thought highly of her in his greeting in the Phm letter.
Aquila	Ac 18:2, 18, 26; Ro 16:3, 1Co 16:19; 2Ti 4:19.	A Jewish believer married to Priscilla. They were persecuted under Claudius and driven out of Rome. A tentmaker by trade he and his wife associated with Paul (bi-vocational; financial support) and were taught by him in the Christian faith. They were teammates with Paul and made a ministry trip with him. Paul affirmed them to the church at Rome as co-ministers with him and as those who had saved his life—putting their own lives on the line. Priscilla and Aquila apparently had house churches where ever they went. They were in Ephesus when Timothy went there to do apostolic consulting work.
Archippus	Col 4:17; Phm 1,2	A Christian worker well thought of by Paul. He ministered in the church at Colossee and in the church in Philemon's home. Paul calls him a fellow soldier—a beautiful compliment.
Aristarchus	Ac 19:29; 20:4; 27:2	A fellow preacher with Paul. He was persecuted in Ephesus. He traveled on one of Paul's teams from Ephesus to Turkey. Also accompanied Paul to Rome. Suffered in prison with Paul. Mentioned in Phm as a fellow worker.
Aristobulus	Ro 16:10	A Christian friend well thought of by Paul in the church at Rome. In his greeting he gives affirmation for this person.
Artemas	Tit 3:12	On Paul's team when he wintered in Nicopolis, late in Paul's ministry. Probably sent as a messenger to Titus on Crete.
Asyncritus	Ro 16:14	One of several Christians at Rome that Paul greeted warmly. Most likely a small group leader since he greets not only him but the Christians with him. See *Ro 16:14* Salute **Asyncritus**, Phlegon, Hermas, Patrobas, Hermes, and the brethren which are with them.

Barnabas	Mentioned 33 times; Many times in Ac; 1Co 9:6, Ga 2:1,9, 13 ; Col 4:10	A mentor sponsor of Paul who brought Paul into the work at Antioch. He led the first missionary team (Paul and his nephew John Mark). Paul became the leader of that team when it moved from Cyprus to Asia minor. Barnabas continued to sponsor Paul with the Jerusalem church. His generosity and giving values impacted Paul. He and Paul had a falling out and split before Paul's second missionary journey. Paul still thought highly of him as seen by his mentioning him in 1Co.
Cephas	1Co 1:12; 3:22; 9:5; 15:5; Gal 1:18; 2:9, 11, 14.	Paul uses this name for Peter several times. Paul recognized and respected Peter as the leader of the Jewish Christian movement. He also clashed with Peter concerning contextualizing the Gospel. Peter respected Paul and recognized that God had revealed truth through him—Scriptural truth.
Claudia	2Ti 4:21	A Christian at Rome. Paul mentions her in his last words to Timothy in 2Ti. She is probably a local house church leader or small group leader since Paul singles our her name and then says also all the Christians. Probably among those Christians giving support to Paul in Rome.
Clement	Php 4:3	A fellow Christian worker with Paul in Phillipi. Paul ask the unnamed pastoral leader at Philippi to aid Clement.
Crescens	2Ti 4:10	Crescens was part of a team around Paul in his second Roman imprisonment. He is mentioned as having left Paul. The context is not clear whether he was on some mission or left for some other reason.
Crispus	Ac 18:8; 1Co 1:14	He was the chief ruler of the Jewish synagogue at Ephesus. Paul led him to Christ. And Paul baptised him. Crispus led his family to the Lord, always a difficult thing with Jewish people.
Demas	Col 4:10; Phm 24; 2Ti 4:10	Demas was part of a team around Paul in his second Roman imprisonment along with Luke and Titus. He is mentioned as having deserted Paul to go to Thessalonica. The context indicates this was not pleasing to Paul. He loved this present world (does that mean he didn't want to be martyred with Paul or that he loved worldliness?)
Epaphroditus	Php 2:25; 4:18	Took a gift from the Php church to Paul while Paul was in prison. He helped Paul while Paul was imprisoned. Nearly died of some sickness. He was a fellow Christian worker with Paul. Paul sponsored him to the Philippians.
Epaphras	Col 1:7; 4:12; Phm 23.	A fellow minister of the Gospel, from the church in Colosse and probably sent out by them. Paul speaks very highly of him calling him a faithful servant of Christ, an intercessor praying for the maturity of the church at Colosse. He was also a fellow prisoner with Paul.
Epenetus	Ro 16:5	Paul speaks highly of this Christian calling him beloved and identifying him as the first Christian in the Achaia (region surrounding Corinth). Probably was in Rome at the time of Paul's writing the Roman epistle.
Erastus	Ac 19:22; Ro 16:23; 2Ti 4:20	He was a missionary with Paul, on one of his traveling teams on his third missionary journey. He was a city treasurer at Corinth so a man of influence. He is mentioned as staying in Corinth when Paul was in prison the second time in Rome. He was one of several people, probably a support team for Paul, who heard Paul dictate the letter to the Romans. One of the team took the dictation.

Eubulus	2Ti 4:21	A Christian at Rome. Paul mentions him in his last words to Timothy in 2Ti. He is probably a local house church leader or small group leader since Paul singles our his name and then says also all the Christians. Probably among those Christians giving support to Paul in Rome.
Eunice	2Ti 1:5	Timothy's mother. A woman of real faith whom Paul highly respected. She gave Timothy a foundation in the O.T. Scriptures and modeled a life of faith and piety for him.
Euodias	Ph 4:2,3	A woman who co-labored in the Lord with Paul at Philippi. She was having problems with another woman, Syntyche, in the church at the time Paul wrote the Php epistle. He spoke highly of her as he entreated her to make up her differences with Syntyche.
Fortunatus	1Co 16:17,24	One of three men who brought Paul financial support when he was in Philippi, from the Corinthian church. Also one of three men who were present when the first letter to the church at Corinth was penned. So, he along with the other two probably supplied Paul with lots of information about the church at Corinth.
Gaius	Ro 16:23; 1Co 1:14	Gaius was led to Christ and baptized by Paul in the city of Corinth. Later Paul stayed in his home, at the time of the writing of the epistle to the Romans. Gaius was part of a small group of people that heard Paul dictate the letter to the Romans.
Hermas	Ro 16:14	A Christian at Rome that Paul greeted warmly. Most likely a small group leader since he greets not only him but the Christians with him.
Hermes	Ro 16:14	A Christian at Rome that Paul greeted warmly. Most likely a small group leader since he greets not only him but the Christians with him.
Hermo-genes	2Ti 1:15	He is described as one who has turned away from Paul.
Herodion	Ro 16:11	A Christian at Rome that Paul greeted warmly. Paul identified him as a kinsman (spiritual or other, it is not clear).
Jason	Ro 16:21	Maybe a relation of Paul. One of a privileged group who heard Paul dictate the letter to the church in Rome (Timothy, Lucius, Jason, Sosipater, Tertius, Gaius, Erastus and Quartus).
John Mark (Marcus)	Ac 12: 25; 13:5, 13; 15:37, 39; Col 4:10; Phm 24; 2Ti 4:11; 1Pe 5:13	Also called Mark or John. John Mark was a relative of Barnabas (most likely a cousin or nephew). He was on Barnabas and Paul's missionary team which went to Cyprus. He quit the team when it went on to Asia minor. Paul would not have him on his second missionary journey. Paul and Barnabas split over this. Later he went with Barnabas back to Cyprus and Paul took Silas with him on his 2nd missionary journey. Later Paul received him back and sponsored him. Mark also served with Peter and is the author of the Gospel of Mark.
Julia	Ro 16:15	A Christian woman at Rome greeted warmly by Paul. Probably a local church leader since Paul also mentions the saints that are with her.
Junia	Ro 16:7	A female apostle and Christian before Paul. Was in prison probably with Paul. Paul calls her a kinsperson but whether this is a sister in Christ or physically is not certain.

Linus	2Ti 4:21	A Christian at Rome. Paul mentions him in his last words to Timothy in 2Ti. He is probably a local house church leader or small group leader since Paul singles our his name and then says also all the Christians. Probably among those Christians giving support to Paul in Rome.
Lois	2Ti 1:5	Timothy's grand mother. A woman of real faith whom Paul highly respected. She along with Timothy's mother Eunice gave Timothy a foundation in the O.T. Scriptures and modeled a life of faith and piety for him.
Lucius	Ro 16:21	One of a privileged group who heard Paul dictate the letter to the church in Rome (Timothy, Lucius, Jason, Sosipater, Tertius, Gaius, Erastus and Quartus). He could possibly be the prophet who was at Antioch in Ac 13:1 when Paul and Barnabas received their great sense of destiny call to missions.
Luke	2Co 13:14; Col 4:14; 2Ti 4:11; Phm 24	Luke was called the beloved physician. He was on one of Paul's traveling teams, the second missionary journey. He went to Rome with Paul (including the shipwreck). He ministered faithfully to Paul in his imprisonments. He authored the Gospel of Luke and the book of Acts. Both these writings reflect the deep impact that Paul made on Luke.
Mary	Ro 16:6	A Christian at Rome who was noted for her ministry of helps to Paul.
Narcissus	Ro 16:11	A Christian at Rome who Paul greeted warmly. Probably a small group leader or house church leader as Paul also mentions his household (could be only his kin or a housechurch set up).
Nereus	Ro 16:15	A Christian at Rome that Paul greeted warmly. Probably a local church leader since Paul also mentions the saints that are with him.
Nymphas	Col 4:15	Said to have been a wealthy and zealous Christian in Laodicea. Hosted a house church and was probably a small group leader.
Olympas	Ro 16:15	A Christian at Rome that Paul greeted warmly. Probably a local church leader since Paul also mentions the saints that are with them.
Onesimus	Col 4:9, 18; Phm 10, 11;	A runaway slave whom Paul led to the Lord while he was in prison in Rome. After some mentor discipling, Paul sent him back to his master, Philemon, a Christian who had a church in his home. This was a challenge both to Onesimus and Philemon, showing the power of the Gospel to break up a major social institution, slavery. Tradition had it that Onesimus became a very influential church leader in the region.
Onesiphorus	2Ti 1:16; 4:19	This man ministered unashamedly to Paul during his second imprisonment. He was probably a small group leader or elder in the work at Ephesus.
Patrobas	Ro 16:14	A Christian at Rome that Paul greeted warmly. Most likely a small group leader since he greets not only him but the Christians with him.
Persis	Ro 16:12	A Christian woman at Rome. Paul uses the word beloved in describing her and that she labored much in the Lord's work.
Philemon	Phm 1. See whole book.	A wealthy landowner in the Colosse region. He became a Christian under Paul's two year teaching ministry at Ephesus. Philemon hosted a house church. Paul asked him a special favor—to take back a runaway slave named Onesimus. He gave strong affirmation to Philemon for his Christian testimony.
Philologus	Ro 16:15	A Christian at Rome that Paul greeted warmly. Probably a local church leader since Paul also mentions the saints that are with him.

Phlegon	Ro 16:14	A Christian at Rome that Paul greeted warmly. Most likely a small group leader since he greets not only him but the Christians with him.
Phoebe	Ro 16:1	A fellow leader, female, in the church at Corinth. Paul sponsored her to the church in Rome.
Phygellus	2Ti 1:15	He is described as one who turned away from Paul.
Priscilla	Ac 18:2, 18, 26; Ro 16:3, 1Co 16:19; 2Ti 4:19.	A Jewish woman, a believer married to Acquila. They were persecuted under Claudius and driven out of Rome. A tentmaker by trade he and his wife associated with Paul and were taught by him in the Christian faith. They were teammates with Paul and made a ministry trip with him. Paul affirmed them to the church at Rome as co-ministers with him and as those who had saved his life—putting their own lives on the line. Priscilla and Aquila apparently had house churches where ever they went. Their final ministry was in Ephesus. They were in that church when Timothy went there to do apostolic consulting work. Priscilla was apparently the word gifted person of the pair.
Pudens	2Ti 4:21	A Christian at Rome. Paul mentions him in his last words to Timothy in 2Ti. He is probably a local house church leader or small group leader since Paul singles our his name and then says also all the Christians. Probably among those Christians giving support to Paul in Rome.
Quartus	Ro 16:23	One of a privileged group who heard Paul dictate the letter to the church in Rome (Timothy, Lucius, Jason, Sosipater, Tertius, Gaius, Erastus and Quartus).
Rufus	Ro 16:13	A Christian at Rome. Paul makes a strong destiny statement about him. He also praises Rufus' mother whom he addresses as his own mother—so close was the relationship.
Sosipater	Ro 16:21	One of a privileged group who heard Paul dictate the letter to the church in Rome (Timothy, Lucius, Jason, Sosipater, Tertius, Gaius, Erastus and Quartus).
Sosthenes	1Co 1:1	Co-authored 1Co with Paul. A respected leader in Corinth. He most likely filled Paul in on many issues of the church situation at Corinth.
Stachys	Ro 16:9	A Christian in Rome greatly loved by Paul.
Stephanas	1Co 16: 15, 17, 24	One of three men who brought Paul financial support when he was in Philippi, from the Corinthian church. Also one of three men who were present when the first letter to the church at Corinth was penned. So, he along with the other two probably supplied Paul with lots of information about the church at Corinth. Paul asks the Corinthian church to support this man who has gone into full time ministry.
Silvanus	2Co 1:19; 1Th 1:1; 2Th 1:1	A Roman citizen and fellow missionary. A part of Paul's traveling team. Co-authored two books, 1,2Th. A respected leader by Paul.
Syntyche	Php 4:2,3	A woman who co-labored in the Lord with Paul at Philippi. She was having problems with another woman, Euodias, in the church at the time Paul wrote the Php epistle. He spoke highly of her as he entreated her to make up her differences with Euodias.
Tertius	Ro 16:22	One of a privileged group who heard Paul dictate the Roman epistle (Timothy, Lucius, Jason, Sosipater, Tertius, Gaius, Erastus and Quartus).

Timothy	Occurs 31 times	The most intimate follower of Paul. Traveled with him on many missionary trips. Was sent on ministry trips for Paul. Best known for his apostolic consultation ministry at Ephesus. One of a privileged group who heard Paul dictate the letter to the church in Rome (Timothy, Lucius, Jason, Sosipater, Tertius, Gaius, Erastus and Quartus). Received two special letters while at Ephesus which reveals the mentoring relationship between Paul and Timothy. These two letters are the top two leadership books in the N.T. Church Leadership Era. In 2Ti Paul passes the baton of leadership over to Timothy.
Titus	Occurs 15 times	Next to Timothy, Paul's closest worker. He was given some of the toughest ministry assignments including one at Corinth dealing with finances and authority problems. He also was given an apolstolic assignment in Crete. The book of Tit written to sponsor him is the third most important book on leadership in the N.T. Church Leadership Era.
Trophimus	2Ti 4:20	He was one of a small group of people close to Paul during Paul's second imprisonment. He became sick and was left at Miletum.
Tryphena	Ro 16:12	A Christian woman in Rome who was described as a worker for the Lord.
Tryphosa	Ro 16:12	A Christian woman in Rome who was described as a worker for the Lord
Tychicus	Eph 6:21, 24; Col 4:7, 18; 2Ti 4:12; Tit 3:12	A Christian worker, part of Paul's support team during his second imprisonment. He also was involved in transcribing and carrying the Ephesian and Colossian letters and traveled with Onesimus as he carried the Philemon letter. Tychicus was well thought of by Paul—described as a beloved brother. He was sent on a mission to Ephesus during the time of the writing of 2Ti.
Urbanus	Ro 16:9	A Christian worker in Rome who had helped Paul in the past (financially or ministry wise—unclear).
Zenas	Tit 3:13	A lawyer whom Titus was to bring to Paul.

Some Observations

Several important observations from Paul's co-ministry and relationship with others should be noted.

1. Paul believed in affirmation both public and private. Affirmation is one of the strongest means a leader has in encouraging emerging workers. Frequently, affirmation involves use of Goodwin's Expectation Principle: *Emerging leaders tend to live up to the genuine expectations of leaders they respect.* Paul not only affirms but challenges through the affirmation.

2. Paul personally related to leaders all up and down the levels of leadership: local church members, lay leaders in general, bi-vocational leaders at small group level, local church elders, fellow bi-vocational workers, full time workers of regional influence, leaders of Christian movement in Jerusalem, etc. He was at home with kings, ambassadors, and with common folk.

3. Paul used networking power as a means of strong influence in numerous leadership ways. He could not have accomplished all that he did with out all kind of help from people whom God had given to him in relationships.

4. Most of Paul's companions, whom he knew at one time or another and supported him, stayed faithful to him. Only a very small few are said to have fallen away from him.

5. A number of Paul's companions were women who ministered in local church situations. Paul did not have a problem with women in ministry (at least from a giftedness or theological standpoint; yes, there were cultural problems).

Conclusion

Paul certainly sets a standard for those who would invest personally in the lives of others. He exemplifies one who held this important value.

Leaders Should View Personal Relationships As An Important Part Of Ministry.

Leaders today with their thoughts on bigness and success may well miss this most important aspect of ministry.

Paul — Developer Par Excellence

Introduction

Paul selected and trained leaders. No matter where he was or what actual ministry he was actively pursuing he was always developing those around him. He demonstrates, forcefully, two of the major leadership lessons observed from comparative studies of effective leaders.[113]

> **Effective leaders view leadership selection and development as a priority in their ministry.**
>
> **Effective leaders see relational empowerment as both a means and a goal of ministry.**

Paul was a developer of leaders.

Two Pauline leadership values explain this bent for Paul. A leadership value is an underlying assumption which affects how a leader perceives leadership and practices it. Let me state them first as Pauline leadership values and then generalize them for possible application in other leader's lives.

Value 1	Leadership Development
Statement of Value	Paul felt he must identify potential leadership and develop it for ministry in the church.
Generalized	Leaders must be concerned about leadership selection and development.

[113.] I have identified seven which repeatedly occur in effective leaders: 1. Life Time Perspective—Effective Leaders View Present Ministry In Terms Of A Life Time Perspective. 2. Learning Posture—Effective Leaders Maintain A Learning Posture Throughout Life. 3. Spiritual Authority—Effective Leaders Value Spiritual Authority As A Primary Power Base. 4. Dynamic Ministry Philosophy—Effective Leaders Who Are Productive Over A Lifetime Have A Dynamic Ministry Philosophy Which Is Made Up Of An Unchanging Core And A Changing Periphery Which Expands Due To A Growing Discovery Of Giftedness, Changing Leadership Situations, And Greater Understanding Of The Scriptures. 5. Leadership Selection And Development—Effective Leaders View Leadership Selection And Development As A Priority Function In Their Ministry. 6. Relational Empowerment—Effective Leaders See Relational Empowerment As Both A Means And A Goal Of Ministry. 7. Sense Of Destiny—Effective Leaders Evince A Growing Awareness Of Their Sense Of Destiny. See the **Article**, *Leadership Lessons—Seven Major Identified*.

Value 2	Personal Ministry
Statement of Value	Paul saw that in his own life he should use personal relationships as a strong means for doing ministry.
Generalized	Leaders should view personal relationships as an important part of ministry.

These two values are at the heart of being a developer.

Defining a Developer

What is a developer? Let me define it.

Definition	A *developer* is a person with a mentoring bent who readily sees potential in an emerging leader and finds ways to help move that emerging leader on to becoming an effective leader.

Developers are mentors who have a variety of mentoring methods. Mentoring is a relational experience in which one person, the mentor, empowers another person, the mentoree, by a transfer of resources. The resources which empower can be habits, skills, perspectives, specific advice, training, connection to other resources, etc.

What does it take to be a developer? It takes the ability to do several key mentoring functions. A developer is a mentor who usually uses three or more of the following mentoring functions effectively in developing people:

Mentor Function	*Basic Empowerment*
Discipler	basic habits of Christian living
Spiritual Guide	perspective on spiritual growth
Coach	basic skills usually related to doing ministry
Counselor	perspective and advice to meet situational and growth needs
Teacher	basic information that applies to the emerging leader's situation
Model	demonstrates values and skills for possible emulation
Sponsor	watches over the mentorees development and makes sure doors are open for development to potential

Paul operated in all the above mentor functions. This is best seen in his developing ministry with Timothy. Frequently, his development involved a traveling team ministry using on-the-job experience. Leaders whom he worked with and developed include: Priscilla, Acquila, Timothy, Titus, Luke, Silas, Epaphras, Archippus, John Mark, Aristarchus, Philemon, Onesimus and many others.

Developers are concerned about the future of ministry. Paul was. Paul represents the most prominent leader in the *Church Leadership Period*. He is an important model. We need to learn from his life. Paul The Developer sets the pace for us, concerning leading with a developmental bias.

No organization or church will last long with effectiveness if it is not developing people. Churches and Christian organizations, without exception, need developers. What should they do? They should identify developers, reward developers, help the developers develop themselves, and help promote mentoring relationships so that these developers not only have access to emerging leaders but are encouraged in behalf of the organization or church to develop people. And keep it simple. No programs. Just relationships.[114]

See Also **Articles**, *Leadership Lessons—Seven Major Identified; Pauline Leadership Values; Mentoring—An Informal Training Model; Timothy A Beloved Son of the Faith; Paul—and His Companions; Leading With A Developmental Bias.*

---

[114]. Most developers need the freedom to move a mentoring relationship along the most natural lines for developing it. They can work within programs of development which are broad enough to let them freely identify mentoring needs and pursue them.

Paul—Mentor for Many

Paul was an outstanding mentor. He used mentoring as a major means of developing leaders. Mentoring is a relational experience in which one person, called the mentor, empowers another person, called the mentoree, by a transfer of resources. Empowerment can include such things as new habits, knowledge, skills, desires, values, connections to resources for growth and development of potential. We[115] have identified a number of mentoring functions. Usually any given leader will not be an ideal mentor and perform all of the mentoring functions. Instead a given leader will usually be proficient in three or four of the mentor functions. The set of mentoring functions that a leader uses in ministry is called his/her mentor-mix. It is easiest to demonstrate that Paul was an outstanding mentor by illustrating his mentoring relationship with Timothy.

Table 32.1 identifies the nine mentoring functions:

Table 32.1   Nine Mentor Functions

Type	Central Thrust
1. Discipler	Basic Habits of the Christian Life dealing with hearing from God and talking with God; operating in a fellowship of Christians; learning to minister in terms of giftedness; learning to get input from God.
2. Spiritual Guide	Evaluation of spiritual depth and maturity in a life and help in growth in this.
3. Coach	Skills of all kind depending on the expertise of the coach.
4. Counselor	Timely and good advice which sheds perspective on issues and problems and other needs.
5. Teacher	Relevant knowledge that can be used for personal growth or ministry or other such need.
6. Sponsor	Protective guidance and linking to resources so that a leader reaches potential.
7. Contemporary Model	Values impactfully demonstrated in a life that can be transferred and used in one's own life.

[115.] My son, Dr. Richard W. Clinton, my colleague Paul Stanley, and I have all been busily researching and using mentoring in our own personal ministries.

| 8. Historical Model | Values demonstrated in a life and inspiration drawn from that life so as to encourage on-going development in ones own life and a pressing on to finish well. |
| 9. Divine Contact | Timely Guidance from God via some human source. |

Paul over the course of his 30 + years in ministry demonstrated almost all of the nine functions. With Timothy, as seen in the Acts and the two epistles to Timothy, several of the mentoring functions can be seen. Figure 1 gives Paul's Mentor-Mix[116] in a pictorial format. This is called a Venn diagram. Each separate oval represents a mentor function. The larger the size of a symbol the more important it is. Overlap of symbols indicates some of both functions taking place. Non-overlap of a symbol with other symbols indicates exclusive manifestation of the symbol. Table 32.2 takes these mentor functions and indicates where the mentoring function is indicated in the Scriptures and perhaps some empowerment.

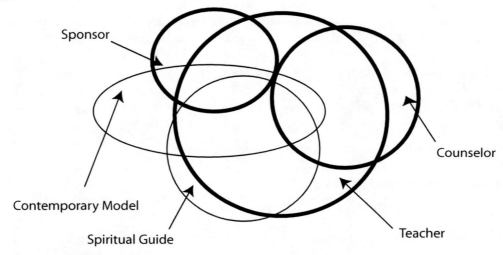

Figure 32.1   Paul's Mentor-Mix with Timothy

From the Venn diagram in Figure 32.1 it can be seen that the three most important mentor functions (indicated by the heavier lines) that Paul did with Timothy were teacher, Counselor, and sponsor. He also models and gives spiritual advice for Timothy's own growth.

Table 32. 2   Mentor Functions of Paul With Timothy

Kind	Where Seen	Empowerment
Teacher	Ac 16, 17, 18, 19, 20; 2Ti 3:10 Ro 16:21; 1Co 4:17; 2Co 1:19	Timothy was familiar with all of Paul's teaching from the Scriptures. For example, he heard the teaching on the material that was later incorporated as Romans given at Corinth; he was present for the dictation of the book of Romans. He spent hours on the road with Paul and chatted with him.

---

116. Mentor-mix refers to the set of mentoring functions that a leader demonstrates in his/her ministry over time—not necessarily seen at any one given time but over a lifetime.

Counselor	1,2Ti are laced with words of advice	1Ti ch 1,2 Paul's advice on major problems in the church, 1Ti ch 3 Paul's advice on local leadership selection, 1Ti ch 5 Paul's advice on the problem of widows and discipline of leaders.
Sponsor	1,2Ti	He is listed by Paul as co-author (a sponsoring function) of six epistles (See 2Co 1:1; Php 1:1; Col 1:1; 1Th 1:1; 2Th 1:1, Phm 1:1). The material in 1,2Ti is dominantly written with a view to the church there reading it and knowing that Paul was giving Timothy instructions for that church.
Model	2Ti 3:10-17; Php	Philippians gives Paul's comprehensive treatment of his use of modeling.
Spiritual Guide	1,2Ti	See especially 1Ti 4 Paul's personal advice to Timothy on How to Handle Himself.—especially maintaining the balance of developing self and developing ministry.. See also 2Ti 1;3-10 on developing giftedness.

Five Features of Paul's Mentoring

Table 32.3 below lists five features noticeable in Paul's mentoring or that supplemented his mentoring.

Table 32.3 Five Features About Paul's Mentoring

Feature	Explanation
Personal Value	Paul often talked straight from the heart to those he ministered to. He illustrates one of his strongest leadership values when he does that. And this is even more true in his mentoring relationships. A *leadership value* is an underlying assumption which affects how a leader behaves in or perceives leadership situations. Paul felt ministry ought to be very personal. Stated more generally for all leaders, *Leaders should view personal relationships as an important part of ministry both as a means for ministry and as an end in itself of ministry.* In his epistles Paul names almost 80 people by name—most of whom he ministered with or to or in some way they ministered to him. Of the five dynamics of mentoring (attraction, relationship, responsiveness, accountability, empowerment) relationship was Paul's strong suit. And with Timothy relationship is seen more clearly than any of Paul's companions. See **Article**, *Timothy, A Beloved Son in the Faith.* Principle: *The development of a personal relationship between a mentor and mentoree will increase the effectiveness of the mentoring.*
Took People With Him; On-the-Job training.	Whenever possible, Paul never went into ministry alone. He almost always took someone with him—frequently, one he had a mentoring relationship with, one who he was developing as a leader. Principle: *Modeling as a major means of influencing or developing emerging leaders best happens in on-the-job training.*
Teams	Whenever possible, Paul took more than one person with him. He used teams of people. And he would send various team members on important errands. See **Article**, *Paul and His Companions.* Note especially the *we sections* in Acts 16 etc.. See also the number of folks around in Romans 16:20-22 (Timothy, Lucius, Sosipater, Tertius, Gaius, Erastus, Quartus) when he dictated the letter.

Little/Big; Ministry Tasks	Paul used the basic principle of the Luke 16:10 little/ big: *The one faithful in little things will be faithful in bigger things*. Give people little things to do and if they are faithful in them, give them bigger things to do. This was especially true of the ministry tasks given Titus and Timothy. A *ministry* **task** is an assignment from God which primarily tests a person's faithfulness and obedience but often also allows use of ministry gifts in the context of a task which has closure, accountability, and evaluation. See Titus' five ministry tasks (3 in Corinth 1 in Crete and 1 in Dalmatia). As the person grows the ministry task moves more from the testing of the person's faithfulness toward the accomplishment of the task.
Goodwin's Expectation Principle	Goodwin's expectation principle states, *Emerging leaders tend to live up to the genuine expectations of leaders they respect*. A well respected leader can use this dynamic to challenge younger leaders to grow. The challenge embodied in the expectation must not be too much or the young leader will not be able to accomplish it and will be inoculated against further challenges. The challenge must not be too little or it will not attract. It must be a genuine expectation. Paul uses this with Timothy, Philemon, and Titus several times (see fn 1Ti 6:11 . See fn 2Ti 1:5).

The end result of mentoring is the empowerment of the mentorees. Luke, Titus, Timothy, Philemon, Onesimus, Archippus, Priscilla, Phoebe and many others attest to the power of Paul's mentoring. And of all of Paul's mentoring functions, probably the most effective was the modeling. Note in his mentor-mix how modeling subtly interweaves itself throughout every other mentoring function. Paul personally related to numerous leaders to develop them. He left behind a heritage—men and women who could continue to lead and carry out his life purpose and use his values in their lives and ministry.

See **Articles**: *Paul the Developer; Paul and His Companions*. For more detailed study see Stanley and Clinton 1992, **Connecting**. Clinton and Clinton 1993, **The Mentor Handbook.**

Paul's Salutations — Harbingers of His Epistles

Introduction

I distinctly remember in my eleventh grade English class when I first ran into the word harbinger. It was in a poem by now long forgotten,

A robin is the harbinger of spring.

I had learned from my eighth grade English class to look up new words I encountered, a habit I am now very grateful for. So I looked up harbinger. Here is my simplified paraphrasing of its definition.

Definition   A *harbinger* is one that foreshadows what is to come.

Usually it refers to a person. But I am applying it in my title of this article to a thing — Paul's salutation.

I think it was in my study of Romans, years ago, that I first noticed the connection between special phrases in the salutation[117] and thematic treatment of topics in the book.

Over the years as I have continued to study more and more of Paul's epistles as core books I have been very aware of Paul's salutations. A careful reading of his salutations puts you well on the way to focusing on important thematic ideas in his books.

Paul's Salutations

In our world, salutations in letters are very brief and contain only a few words or two like Dear Mom, Dear Sirs, To Whom It May Concern, etc. Not so with epistles in Paul's time. And I am thankful for the very wordy difference.

Definition   A *salutation* is the opening line of a letter which describes to whom the letter is addressed.

Definition   A *Pauline Salutation* is the opening paragraph in any of Paul's letters which follows the form of from /to with some greeting words thrown in and some qualifying phrases tucked here and there.

---

117. Alford specifically identifies the doctrinal inserts in Paul's salutations and calls them fore-announcements.

Definition   A *Pauline salutation extension* refers to the immediate paragraph which follows the salutation and which often links the salutation to the body of the letter as well as leads into the body itself as part of the body of the epistle. It functions to extend the thematic intent of the salutation.

Paul's salutations are intriguing. Comparative study of them identifies several functions that Paul accomplishes in his salutations.

Function 1.   He claim's apostolic authority;

Function 2.   He qualifies, in a terse explanatory way, his ministry;

Function 3.   He foreshadows (a good motivating technique) some major concept(s) he will deal with in the epistle;

Function 4.   He sponsors mentorees;

Function 5.   He identifies the recipient(s) — usually with a unique name or phrase if a church;

Function 6.   He sometimes gives his own personal state;

Function 7.   Greets, usually with some form of a blessing.

Not all of these occur in every salutation. But all of them do occur in some salutation. A recognition of these functions can alert us to read the rest of the epistle with a focus.

Paul's Salutations Displayed

Glance quickly through each of Paul's salutations. I will highlight some important features. I will then identify the functions accomplished by each and will identify the foreshadowing phrases. Finally I will try to correlate between the foreshadowing phrases and the overall theme of each book.

Romans 1:1-7

1 Paul, a servant of Jesus Christ, called to be an apostle, separated unto the gospel of God, 2 Which he had promised before by his prophets in the holy scriptures, 3 Concerning his Son Jesus Christ our Lord, which was made of the seed of David according to the flesh; 4 And declared to be the Son of God with power, according to the spirit of holiness, by the resurrection from the dead: 5 By whom we have received grace and apostleship, for obedience to the faith among all nations, for his name. 6 Among whom you are also the called of Jesus Christ: 7 To all that are in Rome, beloved of God, called to be saints: Grace to you and peace from God our Father, and the Lord Jesus Christ.

1 Corinthians

1 Paul, called as an apostle of Jesus Christ as God willed it, and Sosthenes, our brother, 2 To the church of God which is at Corinth, to those who are especially set apart in union with Christ Jesus, to live holy lives, with all who in every place call on the name of Jesus Christ our Lord, and theirs too. 3 Grace to you and peace from God our Father and the Lord Jesus Christ.

2 Corinthians

1 Paul, an apostle of Jesus Christ by the will of God, and Timothy our brother, To the church of God which is at Corinth, with all the saints who are in all Greece. 2 Grace to you and peace from God our Father and the Lord Jesus Christ.

Galatians

1 Paul, an apostle, not of men, neither by man, but by Jesus Christ, and God the Father, who raised him from the dead; 2 And all the believers which are with me, unto the churches of Galatia: 3 Grace be to you and peace from God the Father, and [from] our Lord Jesus Christ, 4 Who gave himself for our sins, that he might deliver us from this present evil world, according to the will of God and our Father:

5 To whom be glory for ever and ever. Amen.

Ephesians

1 Paul, an apostle of Jesus Christ by the will of God, to the saints which are at Ephesus, and to the faithful in Christ Jesus: 2 Grace be to you, and peace, from God our Father, and from the Lord Jesus Christ.

Philippians

1 Paul and Timothy, the servants of Jesus Christ, to all the saints in Christ Jesus which are at Philippi, with the bishops and deacons. 2 Grace be unto you, and peace, from God our Father, and from the Lord Jesus Christ.

Colossians

1 Paul, an apostle of Jesus Christ by the will of God, and Timotheus our brother, 2 To the saints and faithful brethren in Christ which are at Colosse: Grace be unto you, and peace, from God our Father and the Lord Jesus Christ.

1 Thessalonians

1 Paul, and Silvanus, and Timotheus, unto the church of the Thessalonians which is in God the Father and in the Lord Jesus Christ: Grace be unto you, and peace, from God our Father, and the Lord Jesus Christ.

2 Thessalonians

1 Paul, and Silvanus, and Timotheus, unto the church of the Thessalonians in God our Father and the Lord Jesus Christ: 2 Grace unto you, and peace, from God our Father and the Lord Jesus Christ.

1 Timothy

1 Paul, an apostle of Jesus Christ by the commandment of God our Savior, and the Lord Jesus Christ, which is our hope; 2 Unto Timothy, my own son in the faith: Grace, mercy, and peace, from God our Father and Jesus Christ our Lord.

2 Timothy

1 Paul, an apostle of Jesus Christ by God's design, to proclaim the promised life which is in Christ Jesus, 2 To Timothy, my dearly beloved son. May you have Grace, mercy, and peace, from God the Father and Christ Jesus our Lord.

Titus

1:1 I, Paul, am ministering as a servant of God and an apostle of Jesus Christ to help mature God's own chosen followers. I want them to know the truth that leads to godliness. 2 I want them to have a faith and a knowledge grounded in an expectation of eternal life. God, who can not lie, promised this eternal life before the beginning of time.   3 At His appointed time, He revealed His truth about this. God our Savior entrusted me with this task and commanded me to preach it. 4 I write to you, Titus, one who is like my very own son because of our common faith.

Philemon

1 Paul, a prisoner of Jesus Christ, and Timothy our brother, to Philemon our dearly beloved, and fellow laborer. 2 Hello also to our beloved Apphia, and Archippus our fellow soldier, and to the church in your house. 3 Grace to you, and peace, from God our Father and the Lord Jesus Christ.

Table 33.1   Functions Identified in Paul's Salutations

Book	Fn 1	Fn2	Fn3	Fn4	Fn5	Fn 6	Fn7
Rom	√	√	√		√		√
1 Co	√		√	√	√		√
2 Co	√		√	√	√		√
Gal	√		√		√		√
Eph	√				√		√
Php		√		√	√		√
Col	√			√	√		√
1 Th				√	√		√
2 Th				√	√		√
1 Ti	√		√	√	√		√
2 Ti	√		√	√	√		√
Tit	√	√	√	√	√		√
Phm		√		√	√	√	√

Table 33.2   Foreshadowing Phrases

Book	Phrases
Rom	1. ...gospel of God, ... 2. promised before by his prophets in the holy scriptures, 3. Concerning his Son Jesus Christ our Lord, ... the seed of David according to the flesh; 4. declared to be the Son of God with power, according to the 5. spirit of holiness, by the resurrection from the dead: 6. ...obedience to the faith among all nations, for his name. 7. ...called of Jesus Christ: ...called to be saints:
1 Co	1. set apart in union with Christ Jesus, to live holy lives,
2 Co	1. saints who are in all Greece
Gal	1. apostle, not of men, neither by man, but by Jesus Christ, and God the Father, 2. who raised him from the dead 3. Who gave himself for our sins, 4. that he might deliver us from this present evil world, according to the will of God and our Father:
Eph, Php, Col, 1,2 Th, Phm	none; extension yes
1 Ti	which is our hope
2 Ti	to proclaim the promised life which is in Christ Jesus
Tit	1. to help mature God's own chosen followers. 2. I want them to know the truth that leads to godliness. 3. I want them to have a faith and a knowledge grounded in an expectation of eternal life. 4. God, who can not lie, promised this eternal life before the beginning of time. 5. At His appointed time, He revealed His truth about this. 6. God our Savior

When you do detailed study of each of the books and are aware of these foreshadowing elements you will see them reflected in the theme of the book as a whole, in various parts of the structure of the book, and the emphasis of small contextual units as well as even larger contextual units.

Conclusion

I want to suggest 4 ways that an awareness of Paul's salutations and his use of them can help us as we read and study his epistles.

1.   We always read better when looking for things. In our study of effective readers[118] we uncovered the basic principle that when you read looking for something you read much more alertly and discover much more than if you are reading just generally looking for things.

[118.]   See my booklet, *Reading on the Run.*

2. In his salutations, Paul stresses some important things to him. If they are important to Paul we want to know why.

3. It should make us aware of the basic principle of intentional selection. The Spirit of God superintended the writing of the inspired word and has not given us all that could be given but has selected that which we need. So we should recognize the importance of words. They are there not by happenstance but for reasons. This should also make us more conscious of our own words. We should use words that count.

4. Paul's use of phrases to describe God is important. He uses phrases to describe God in terms of God's revealing Himself to Paul to meet certain needs Paul faced. When we experience God, we should use language that describes God in terms of those experiences.[119] As leaders our language describing God will influence our followers. We should use our titles and phrases for God proactively so as to affect our followers.

Paul's salutations foreshadow what he will deal with in his epistles. We should read them with extra care, knowing that they will help unfold truth in the epistles.

[119.] The archetype of this in the Bible is Daniel. His use of names and phrases to describe God captures who God was for him.

Power Gates — Experiences That Renew and Enable Leaders

Introduction

One of the great macro lessons seen in Moses' life, and which runs throughout all leadership eras is stated as,

Presence Lesson   The essential ingredient of leadership is the powerful presence of God in the leader's life and ministry.

This macro lesson applies to all leadership, whether power gifted or not.[120]

Our studies of leaders' lives has pointed out that all leaders at one time or another come to a point in their ministry in which they know they must have the power of God.[121] As we have studied the power experiences comparatively we have been able to identify two major categories of power needs. One of the needs focus around *life power*, that is, the enabling power of God to live the Christian life — modeling a victorious life which is essential for certain ministries. A second need focuses around gifted power — the ability to minister, usually publicly, with great power. The experiences which reflect God's meeting these needs are then labeled as power gates, that is, the opening of the person to the power from God to meet their need.

The passage through a power gate usually requires a paradigm shift. Before the shift, there is the need for power. The person knows it is there but can not break through to get it. The experience with God opens the person to the perspective that allows the receiving of that power. That is a paradigm shift.[122]

[120.] The three clusters of spiritual gifts include word gifts, power gifts, and love gifts. The power gifts are a category of spiritual gifts which authenticate the reality of God by demonstrating God's intervention in today's world. These include: tongues, interpretation of tongues, discernings of spirits, kinds of healings, kinds of power (miracles), prophecy, faith, word of wisdom, word of knowledge. They demonstrate power. but what we are talking about here is more than power gifts. It involves demonstrating God's power in ministry no matter what the gifting. Love gifts need to be validated by God's powerful presence and working. Word gifts need to be validated by God's powerful presence and working.

[121.] Such books as Edman's *They Found the Secret* or Choi's *Powerlines* are dealing with leaders and their appropriation of power.

Entering Into Power—Life Power

Life power refers to the enabling grace of God in a life to enable a leader to walk above the controlling authority of sin in a life and to demonstrate in an ever increasing way the fruit of the spirit.

Comparative studies of these experiences revealed a pattern.

Life Power Pattern
+ Need + Surrender + Appropriation by Faith ± a validating experience.

The symbol + means that it was always there. The symbol ± means it may or may not be there. Those seeking this power always had a need. The shift always required some sort of surrender to God which opened the possibility of the need being met. After the surrender there was the realization that the power is available already; it must simply be appropriated by faith. Sometimes after this moment of accepting by faith thee was some sort of validation by God in some unusual way. Often this did not occur.

Entering Into Power—Gifted Power

About half of the leaders in Edman's book, **They Found the Secret**, went through the life power pattern as described above. But the other half went through a different pattern, the *Gifted Power Pattern*.

Going through the gifted *power gate* involves a seeking for power in ministry. Public rhetoricians, like D.L. Moody Charles Finney and for example, usually needed this kind of paradigm shift.

Gifted Power Pattern

+ Need ± Surrender + **Unusual Validating Experience + appropriating faith**.

All going through this paradigm shift evidenced a strong need for the power. Sometimes, but not always, this involved a surrender to God for that power. Almost always the breakthrough for the paradigm shift came with some unusual validating experience. It was the experience, not a cognitive understanding of it, that made the difference in the paradigm shift. And then afterwards there was the step of faith to believe that God had empowered and that the experience was the authentication of God's validation. The leader then learned to use faith repeatedly to see God's power in ministry.

The Ideal Power Leader

The Gospel of John presents Jesus as the ideal leader with regard to power. Jesus demonstrated gifted power both in Word Gifts, Power Gifts and Love Gifts. And his teaching on abiding was foundational for those wanting to have life power.

[122.] The *life power*, paradigm Shift is one of most important paradigm shifts taught in the Gospel of John. It is taught three times in John 4:14, 7:37-39, 15. John uses right brain techniques to present *life power*. He prefers to teach in terms of pictures: 1. Artesian well. John 4 What Jesus is to you will satisfy your inner self. 2. Life giving spring. 3. John 7:37-39 what you have will overflow to others. Productive Vine. John 15, its source a shared life with Christ — fruitful.

Conclusion

Going through a power gate does not ensure that a leader will operate in power the rest of his/her life. It simply opens one up to God's power working. There must be the continual appropriation by faith.

Recognize that you will need power. And you will most probably come to a crisis point in your leadership where you must have power — either life power or gifted power.[123]

I have just one word of exhortation for you. Do not be satisfied with a powerless life or a powerless ministry. Seek God as Moses did for His Powerful Presence.

> Exodus 33:15 15 And Moses said unto God, If your powerful presence does not go with me then I am out of here as a leader.

And so must it be for all of us who are leaders.

See **Glossary,** *ultimate contribution; public rhetorician, saint.* See **Articles,** *Paradigms and Paradigm Shifts — Biblical Examples; Focused Life.*

[123.] One symptom of which power gate you will need hinges on your *ultimate contribution* categories. Folks with a *public rhetorician ultimate contribution* will usually be driven to a *gifted power gate.* Those with a *saint ultimate contribution* will usually be driven toward a *life power gate.*

Article 35

Principles of Truth

Introduction

Leaders who finish well are described by six characteristics.[124] Two of these claim that,

> **They maintain a learning posture and can learn from various kinds of sources—life especially.**

> **Truth is lived out in their lives so that convictions and promises of God are seen to be real.**

How does a leader get truth from the scriptures—one of the sources for learning? How does a leader get truth, form convictions, and arrive at promises from God?

Further, this leadership commentary has described a Bible centered leader.

A *Bible Centered leader* refers to a leader whose leadership is being informed by the Bible and who personally has been shaped by Biblical values, has grasped the intent of Scriptural books and their content in such a way as to apply them to current situations and who uses the Bible in ministry so as to impact followers.

How does one get informed by the Bible on leadership? How does a leader get values which shape him/her?

This article suggests perspectives that help answer these questions. It details my own framework—the perspectives that have guided me as I comment on the Scriptures, suggest observations, guidelines, values, principles of truth, macro lessons, etc.

Principles

Observations of truth provide one useful result of leadership studies. These truths help us understand other leadership situations and predict what ought to be. They also help us in the selection and training of leaders since they give guidelines that have successfully

---

124. Six characteristics of a good finish include the following. Leaders ho finish well have: (1) a vibrant personal relationship with God; (2) a learning posture; (3) Christ-likeness in character; (4) lived by Biblical convictions; (5) left behind ultimate contributions; (6) and fulfilled a sense of destiny.

been applied in past leadership situations. These truths are usually seen first as specific statements concerning one leader in his/ her situation. They are then generalized to cover other leaders and like situations. The question of how generally they can be applied to others is a genuine one. The certainty continuum and screening questions provide cautions about this.

Definition   *Principles* refer to generalized statements of truth which reflect observations drawn from specific instances of leadership acts or other leadership sources.

God's processing of leaders includes shaping toward spiritual formation, ministerial formation, and/or strategic formation. Analyzing formational shaping, serves as an important stimulus for deriving principles.

A few examples will help clarify. Analysis of God's use of the integrity check, word check, and obedience check to develop spiritual formation in numerous young leader's lives led to the following three principles.

> **Integrity is foundational for leadership; it must be instilled early in a leader's character.**

> **Obedience is first learned by a leader and then taught to others.**

> **Leadership gifts primarily involve word gifts which initially emerge through word checks**

Analysis of Samuel's final public leadership act in 1 Sa 12 (see especially vs 23) led to the following truth.

> **When God calls a leader to a leadership situation he calls him/ her to pray for followers in that situation.**

The Certainty Continuum and Related Definitions

Attempts to derive statements of truth from leadership studies meet with varied success. Some people seem to intuitively have a sense of generalizing from a specific situation a statement which apparently fits other situations. Others are not so good at this skill. This part of leadership theory is in is infancy stage. In the future we hope to delineate more structured approaches for deriving statements and for validating them. But for now we need to recognize that these statements often can not be proved as truth (in the sense that physical science can prove truth) hence we, as researchers, need to be careful of what we say is truth. Below is given the certainty continuum and the major generalization concerning the derivation of *truth* statements. These are an attempt to make us as researchers cautious about applying our findings.

Principles of truth are attempts to generalize specific truths for wider applicability and will vary in their usefulness with others and the authoritative degree to which they can be asserted for others.

Description   The *certainty continuum* is a horizontal line moving from suggestions on one extreme to requirements on the other extreme which attempts to provide a grid for locating a given statement of truth in terms of its potential use with others and the degree of authority with which it can be asserted.

The basic ideas are that:

1. Principles are observations along a continuum.

2. We can teach and use with increasing authority those principles further to the right on the continuum.

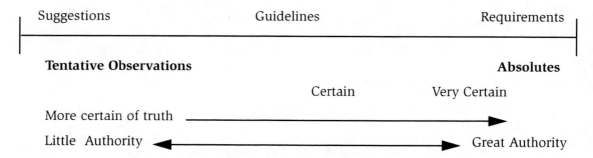

Figure 35.1   The Certainty Continuum

I am identifying principles as a broad category of statements of truth which were true at some instant of history and may have relevance for others at other times.

There is little difference between *Suggestions* and *Guidelines* on the continuum. In fact, there is probably overlap between the two. Some *Guidelines* approach *Requirements*. But there is a major difference from going from *Suggestions* to *Requirements*—the difference being *Suggestions* are optional but *Requirements* are not. They must be adhered to.

Definition   *Suggestions* refers to truth observed in some situations and which may be helpful to others but they are optional and can be used or not with no loss of conscience.

Definition   *Guidelines* are truths that are replicated in most leadership situations and should only be rejected for good reasons though there will be no loss of conscience.

Definition   *Absolutes* refer to replicated truth in leadership situations across cultures without restrictions. Failure to follow or use will normally result in some stirrings of conscience.

Absolutes are principles which evince God's authoritative backing. All leaders everywhere should heed them.

Suggestions are the most tentative. They are not enjoined upon people. They may be very helpful though.

Remember that a *Suggestion* or *Guideline* may move to the right or left if more evidence is found in the Bible to support such a move. If a *suggestion* or *guideline* identified in one place in the Scriptures is found to be abrogated, modified or somehow restricted at a later time in the progressive flow of revelation then it will move most likely to the left. However, if later revelation gives evidence of its more widespread usage or identifies it more certainly for everyone then it will move to the right.

Six Assumptions Underlying Derivation Of Principles

Principles are derived from Biblical leadership situations as well as from life situations. Several assumptions underlie my approach to deriving principles of truth. The following six assumptions underlie my approach to getting truth.

1. Truth Assumption: All truth has its source in God.

I need not fear the study of secular material (social science materials, leadership theory, present day situations, etc.).   If there is any truth in it I can be certain it is of God. For there is no truth apart from God. I don't have to limit truth to the Bible. The Bible itself shows how God has revealed truth by many different means. These means were certainly not just limited to ancient written revelation. The problem then lies in how to discern if something is truth.

2. Source Assumption: All of life can be a source of truth for those who are discerning.

The central thrust of Proverbs 1:20-33 and in fact the whole book of Proverbs is that God reveals wisdom in life situations. The book of Proverbs is more than just content for us to use; it is a modeling of how that content was derived over time and in a given society. We can trust God to reveal wisdom in the life situations we study (whether from the Bible or today). Truth that evolved in Israeli history came to take on at least guideline status and much of it became absolutes.

3. Applicability Assumption: Just because a statement of truth was true for a specific given situation does not mean the statement has applicability for other leaders at other times. Wider application must be determined via comparative means.

A statement of truth is an assertion of fact drawn from a specific situation. The dynamics of the situation may well condition the statement. That is, the truth itself may apply only in situations which contain the same dynamics. The fact that the truth did happen means it is at least worthy of study for potential wider use. Because of the consistency of God's character we know that the truth can not violate His nature. But its happening is not sufficient justification for its use anywhere at anytime by any leader.

4. Dogmatic Assumption: We must exercise caution in asserting all truth statements as if they were absolutes.

Fewer truths will be seen as absolutes if screened with applicability criteria. The use of applicability criteria, especially that of comparative study, will force one to identify a higher level function behind a given principle. Thus a statement of truth at some lower level when compared with other situations and similar statements of truth might lead to a higher order generic statement of truth. These higher level statements of truth, though more general in nature, preserve the function intended rather than the form of the truth. Such statements will allow more freedom of application. Statements which do not carry wide applicability or have attached to them dynamics of situations which can not be fully assessed will most likely have to be asserted with less dogmatism.

5. Dependence Assumption. We are forced more than ever to depend upon the Holy Spirit's present ministry to confirm truth we are deriving.

Because of the sources (life as well as Biblical) from which we are drawing truth, we will need more dependence upon the ministry of the Holy Spirit. That is, we will be forced to situationally rely on and become more sensitive to the Holy Spirit's leading and voice. We will need to recognize giftedness in the body and learn to trust those who have spiritual gifts which expose, clarify, and confirm truth (discernings of spirits, word of knowledge, word of wisdom, teaching, exhortation, etc.).

6. Trust Assumption. Because we are following Biblical admonitions (Heb 13:7,8; 1 Co10:6,11, Ro 15:4) in our attempts to derive truth we can expect God to enable us to see much truth.

God does not command us to do things that are impossible. God's commands contain within in them the promise of enablement. Because there are great needs for more and better leadership and because we need leadership truth to develop that leadership and because God has told us to study leaders to learn from their lives, we can expect God to lead us to truth that will greatly affect our lives. By faith we can trust Him to do this.

Conclusion

For each of the **Key Leadership Insight** sections for individual books I have listed statements called observations, principles, values, lessons. Each of these will need to be assessed on the certainty continuum to determine their level of applicability.

See *integrity check, word check, and obedience check, spiritual formation, ministerial formation, strategic formation,* **Glossary.**

Redemptive Drama, The Biblical Framework

Introduction

In each of the overviews on the various individual books in the leadership commentary series I have a section called **Where It Fits**. In that section, I try to deal with the application of my first general hermeneutical principle,[125]

Language Principle 1 Book and Books

In The Spirit, Prayerfully Study The Book As A Whole In Terms Of Its Relationship To Other Books In The Bible (i.e. the Bible as a whole) TO INCLUDE:

a. its place in the progress of redemption (both as to the progress of revelation, what God has said, and also the notion of what God has done in redemptive history)

b. its overall contribution to the whole of Bible literature (i.e. *its purposes — why is it in the Bible?*) and

c. its abiding contribution to present time.

I seek to find **Where It Fits** using two basic overall frameworks:

1. *The Unfolding Drama of Redemption* — that is, telling the story of what God has said and done in the Bible.[126]

2. *The Leadership Framework*. Since this is a leadership commentary series, I want to trace the contribution of a book to leadership. The leadership era it fits in helps inform us as to how to interpret its leadership findings.

This article is concerned with the first of these two frameworks: *The Unfolding Drama of Redemption*. I have previously dealt with the second framework in several articles.[127]

[125.] See Appendix G in *Having A Ministry That Lasts* for the whole hermeneutical system I use.

[126.] I am deeply indebted to a teaching mentor of mine, James M. (Buck) hatch who introduced me to this framework in his course, Progress of Redemption, given at Columbia Bible College. I have used his teaching and adapted it in my own study of each book in the Bible in terms of the Bible story as a whole. I have also written in depth on this in my handbook, *The Bible and Leadership Values.* This article is a condensed version of that larger explanation.

I will first introduce the overall framework with a diagram. Then I will give a brief synopsis for each chapter of the redemptive drama. Finally, I will list the Bible books in terms of the chapters of the redemptive drama.

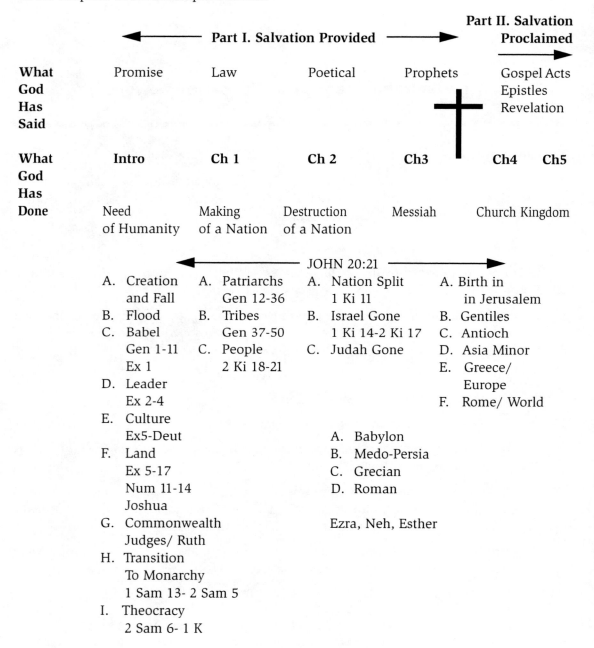

Figure 36.1 Overall Framework — Redemptive Drama Pictured

---

127. See **Articles**, *Six Biblical Leadership Eras — Overviewed; Macro Lesson Defined; Macro Lessons — List of 41 Across Six Leadership Eras.*

The **Time-Line of the Redemptive Story** contains six sections,

> Introduction,
> Chapter 1. The Making of A Nation,
> Chapter 2. The Destruction of A Nation,
> Chapter 3. Messiah,
> Chapter 4. The Church, and
> Chapter 5. The Kingdom.

This story is briefly explained in a Running Capsule of the Redemptive Story. The story traces **what God does** and **what He says** throughout the Bible. And it shows that there is a progressive revelation of God throughout the whole drama. The Bible is unified around this salvation history. Once this is recognized then the notion of intentional selection becomes important. Each book in the Bible is there for a purpose and contributes something to this salvation story.

It is this framework which provides the macro context for studying each book of the Bible. Where is the book in the progress of redemption time-line? What does it contribute to it? Why is it there? What would we miss if it were left out? Understanding each book in terms of its own purpose is a preliminary first step that must be done before we can interpret it for leadership findings.

The Running Capsule for the Redemptive Story

I will first give an overview and then give more detail from each part of the redemptive drama.

Overall

At the center of the Biblical revelation is the concept of a God who has intervened in human history. He created the human race. He has revealed himself to that race. That race rebelled against His desires. In its fallen state it continually rebels against His wishes and desires and for the potential that it could accomplish.

So He started again and selected specifically a people through whom He could reveal Himself to the world. God moves unswervingly toward His purpose which is to redeem people and relate to them. He moves toward His purposes whether or not the people He has chosen follow them or not. They can willingly be a part in which they enjoy the blessings of God or they can be by-passed and He will find other ways to accomplish His purposes. He patiently works with them to include them in His purposes. But when all is said and done He moves on with or without them.

All the time He is increasingly revealing more of Himself and His purposes to His people. They come to know Him as a mighty God, all powerful and controlling, yet allowing human beings their choices. He is a holy God, that is, a being of perfection. He reveals His purposes as that of having a Holy people following Him. People who are becoming Holy as He is holy. They learn that to fall short of His demands or standards is to sin against Him and is deserving of retribution if justice is to be satisfied.

Part I of the redemption drama, **SALVATION PROVIDED**, is His selection of a people, which will prove foundational to accomplishing His purposes. Out of that people will come one who is central in the decrees of God. Not an afterthought but mysteriously beyond our thinking, known to God. Look at Revelation 13:8, the Lamb slain before the foundation of the world. In terms of what we know of God today, we see this Part I as revealing to us, God the Father, that is, the God who is source of all that we are and to whom we relate, infinite, eternal, powerful, a spirit.

God protects that line through which He will come over a period of many years and in times of failure on their part to know Him and obey Him as they should.

His incarnation into the world begins Part II of the Redemptive Drama, **SALVATION PROCLAIMED**. Galatians 4:4, in God's time. That incarnate God, manifest in the flesh, to communicate directly with the human race, to be a part of it, to share in its joys and sorrows, finally pays the supreme price of rejection, by a world who wanted to call its own shots, the death of the Cross, perfection paying the perfect price to satisfy God's Holy just demands. The great dilemma was solved, how God could be absolutely just and yet lovingly receive to Himself, those for whom justice demanded the harsh penalty of death. That time in which Jesus lived and walked and taught and did so many things to reveal God to us is the time, as we now know it of God the Son, God revealed to a human race as one of that race. Having accomplished the first portion of His work, the Cross, He ascended to heaven and will yet come again. Having ascended, He sent the Holy Spirit into the world, the intimation of what is to come, the Spirit who indwells those people He has chosen.

In the meantime while we wait we are involved in Part II **Salvation Proclaimed**, which shows that this message was more than just for the Jews but for a whole world. And that is what we are about today, the proclamation of that reconciling message, that God has provided a way in which sinful human beings can be rightly related to Him and progress to live a satisfying and fruitful life, in harmony with His purposes. And as they live this purposeful life, demonstrating the power and presence of God in their time on earth, they know that God is going to make all things right someday — there is a justice coming; the Lord Jesus, now a risen Savior, a life-giving Spirit will return to claim His own. There will be a time of His reigning on earth and then there will be eternity. And we who have been called out, as a people to His name, will reign with Him for all eternity. In terms of what we know today, this is the Age of God, the Spirit.

Introduction

Genesis tells us of many beginnings. It tells of the beginning of the creation, the human race, of sin in the world, of the spread of the race, of judgment on the race and a new beginning for the race. It does not satisfy all our questions. We would ask more and want more. But it does give us the backdrop for the salvation story. Humanity is in need. It can not get along with itself. It has alienated itself from God. Left to itself it will be destructive at best. There is a need. And the salvation story which begins in Genesis chapter 12 will give God's response to meet that need.

Chapter 1. The Making of a Nation

God's basic plan is to choose a people and to reveal Himself and His plans for reconciling the world to Himself through that nation. Chapter 1 tells of the story of God's building of the nation.

If I were to pick out the most important events in the making of a nation, Chapter 1 of the redemptive drama I would say the following would certainly be a part of it.

1. The call of Abraham — the Abrahamic Promise
2. The renewal of the covenant with Isaac
3. The renewal of the covenant with Jacob
4. The deliverance of Jacob and sons through Joseph
5. The call of Moses
6. The power encounters in Egypt and the Exodus
7. The Red Sea deliverance
8. The Spies in the Land/corporate failure of a faith check
9. The Giving of the 10 Commandments/covenant
10. Moses' failure — striking the rock
11. Moses' outstanding leadership in the desert years with a rebellious followership and his transition of Joshua into leadership
12. Crossing of Jordan
13. Circumcision at Gilgal
14. Joshua meets the Captain of the Hosts
15. Capture of Jericho
16. Failure at Ai
17. Success at Ai
18. Gibeonite deception
19. Capture of Land (lack of total obedience)
20. Repetitive Failure — moving from dependence to independence. The Cycle of the Judges (need for centralized influence)
21. Samuel's unifying influence
22. Saul's anointing and failure
23. David's anointing and success
24. David's failure and discipline
25. David's preparation for building the temple

Lets examine some of the Bible books which present these events.

From Genesis

From the introduction we know that humanity is not in good shape and is in need of intervention by God. And God has a plan thought out in eternity past.

God chooses one man, Abraham, and Promises (*The First Great Revelation — The Promise*) to make of him a great nation and to give them land and to bless the world through his offspring. (Gen 12:1-3, 7; 15:4,18, et al) Now God plans to use the nation He will bring forth to be a channel of redemption and revelation of Himself. So He begins to build a nation. For a nation you need people (including numbers) a coherent culture, a land, and a leader.

God begins to work on these things — the people first (the land has people on it who will be judged eventually when they are too evil to be redeemed). From this one man, who exemplifies faith in God's promise, comes a son, Isaac. Isaac has two sons, one of whom,

Jacob, becomes the successor of the family line through which God will work — the 12 heads of the tribes: Reuben, Simeon, Levi, Judah, Zebulun, Issachar, Dan, Gad, Asher, Naphtali, Joseph, Benjamin.

Joseph, a son of Jacob's old age and his favorite, is sold into slavery by his jealous brothers (Acts 7:9 Because the patriarchs were jealous of Joseph they sold him as a slave into Egypt. But God was with him and rescued him from all his troubles. He gave Joseph wisdom and enabled him to gain the goodwill of Pharaoh king of Egypt; so he made him ruler over Egypt and all his palace.) Joseph, a person of proven integrity, rises to power through a series of providential appointments in which he shows wisdom from God upon several occasions. God gives some dreams to Pharaoh, the ruler of Egypt, which predict some good years followed by famine years. Joseph gives a wise plan to Pharaoh on how to prepare for it. He is put in charge and is right on target to protect his own family when the famine hits. The family comes to Egypt and rides through the famine years. It stays and expands in the land. Joseph , never losing sight of God's promise, exacts a promise from his brothers and fellow Israelites that they will take him back into the land when God takes them back. That is how Genesis ends.

From Exodus

Exodus opens many years later. There are many Israelite descendants, so many in fact, that the Egyptian King is fearful of them so he subjugates them. They are slaves and being ill-treated. Persecution takes the form of enforced labor and attempts to cut down the population (executing the boy babies).

God, having fulfilled the first part of his plan, getting a people, now works on the second part — getting a leader. Moses, an Israelite baby is preserved providentially and taken into the palace and educated as an Egyptian royal class person. As he reaches adulthood he recognizes that his people by blood relationship are in great bondage. So he wants to free them. His first attempt to help them is a disaster. He kills an Egyptian and has to flee Egypt. He goes to Midian, settles down, marries a Midianite woman, and has a family. After forty years, God selects him via a miraculous revelation, to go back to Egypt to lead God's people out of Egypt and into the promised land. Moses goes back and after 10 major confrontations with the Egyptian ruler (in which God-given power is seen — Moses certainly has spiritual authority) the people are freed to leave. But on the way the Egyptian ruler has second thoughts and pursues with his military. The military should overtake the Israelites who will be trapped by the Red Sea. God miraculously intervenes and they escape across the Red Sea on dry ground. The sea moves back as the military forces start to cross and they are wiped out. This is the heart of *the Exodus*.

From Exodus and Leviticus

God next begins to build the people culturally into what He will need. He gives them the LAW, the second great revelation and reveals more of Himself, His standards, and His purposes. The tabernacle which He gives the plans for reveals more of who God is in terms of access and revelation. The rest of EXODUS is given to that, revealing who God is as is the whole of LEVITICUS. It is especially in Leviticus that the holiness of God is developed — an understanding of sin and its implications; what atonement is (that is, being made right with God by making up for wrong against Him).

From Numbers

After disobedience and a lack of faith prevent the people from going in to the land (see NUMBERS) they wander for 40 years in the Sinai desert until the older rebellious people die off. During the desert years they learn to trust in God's provision. God reveals Himself primarily through his leader Moses. Near the end of the 40 years they are again ready to go into the land. God has a people, a culture, a leader, Moses, and a leader to take his place, Joshua. Moses prepares them for that push into the land by giving them a series of addresses (DEUTERONOMY — second law). These messages, his final words to them, reflect warnings drawn from their desert experience, remind them of standards of obedience which reflects what they have learned of God, and gives encouragement in the form of expectations as they enter the land. He closes his final words to them with songs of warning and blessing that portend the future. And thus we are ready for the third part of God's plan to build Himself a people — getting them into the land.

From Joshua

Joshua transitions into leadership with some sterling miraculous interventions by God which give him the spiritual authority he will need to follow Moses (a hard act to follow) as leader. Joshua seizes Jericho, after following a supernaturally revealed plan for its capture. He proceeds after an unexpected failure, which teaches an important corporate lesson on obedience, to the people, to split the land in two militarily and then begins to mop up in the north and south. The land is allotted. Each tribe has a portion, just as Moses had planned. They decentralize and begin to settle into their spots — with much trouble. After having been so long in a centralized authoritarian mode, they enjoy being decentralized and having autonomy. But this decentralization eventually leads to spiritual deterioration. This brings us up into the times of the judges.

From Judges

For a long period of time, longer than we in the United States have been a nation, the twelve tribes live scattered. There is frequent civil war in specific locales and much fighting with various surrounding nations and peoples who were not totally destroyed when the land was taken.

In short there is an oft repeated cycle: the people deteriorate spiritually getting far from God, God brings judgment upon them, they finally recognize that their problem is relationship with God — they repent and cry out for God's help. He sends along leaders, very charismatic who usually lead a volunteer army to defeat their enemies. There are at least 13 of these including: Othniel, Ehud, Shamgar, Deborah (Barak), Gideon, Abimelech, Tola, Jair, Jephthah, Ibzan, Elon, Abdon, and Samson. Some of these are more well known than others. Gideon and Samson for example. These are evil times and few there are who follow God.

In a section of the Judges (Judges 2:7) the writer sums it up well, "After Joshua had dismissed the Israelites, they went to take possession of the land, each to his own inheritance. The people served the Lord through out the lifetime of Joshua and of the elders who outlived him and who had seen all the great things the Lord had done for Israel." And then again in the closing portion a repeated phrase haunts us — Judges 21:25, "In those days Israel had no king; everyone did as he saw fit." These are the pre-kingdom years. Corporately the people are negatively prepared for the kingdom which will come.

From Ruth

There is a spark of life during those dreadful times. Ruth introduces us to that life by showing that there were some people of integrity who honored the Lord. This little romantic book shows how God provides and also allows us to see how the line through which the redeemer will later arise progresses.

The Judges and Ruth are pre-kingdom times. They prepared the Israelites to want a centralized structure after so much independence and autonomy. The Israelites were dependent upon voluntary armies raised up in times of crisis. Many times, other of the tribes than the one threatened, were not interested in their local squabbles and would not fight for them. Thus the entire commonwealth of tribes comes to the place where it needs, wants, and will accept a kingdom. Again God steps in and provides a transition leader — Samuel.

From 1 Samuel

The first thirteen chapters show how Samuel was providentially raised up as a leader. His ministry as judge was not just a momentary deliverance but a continual one. He visited the different tribes and judged them — that is, established law and justice for them. Samuel paves the way for a centralized kingdom. Crises around the people spur the need; Samuel's own sons are not able to replace him. The people demand a king — showing their need for one but also showing that they basically did not trust the unseen King. God gives them one king, Saul, who outwardly is what they would expect. But he fails repeatedly to follow God. His kingdom is spiritually bankrupt. God replaces him with David, whom God describes as *a man after my own heart.* The last part of 1 Samuel describes Saul's fall and David's early pre-kingdom years, in which David is gaining military expertise as a guerrilla warfare leader with a para-military band.

From 2 Samuel and 1 Chronicles and the Psalms

2 Samuel and 1 Chronicles give David's story — one written earlier to it and one written later. David is a long time in getting the kingdom as Saul's descendants try to hold on to the kingdom. After seven years of civil war, David is ruling a smaller part of Israel, the kingdom is united. God gives a covenant to David concerning his descendants. The poetical literature, particularly the Psalms, emerge more solidly from this era. David is an artistic person who spends time alone with God in worship. Many of the Psalms come out of those times alone with God, many spurred on by crises in David's kingdom. The kingdom is established under David and expands. In mid-life David has a major sin which tarnishes his lifetime. He has one of his military leaders killed in order that he might take his wife for himself. It and failure to manage his family well lead to a rebellion by one of his sons Absalom. David is deposed briefly but comes back winning a strategic battle. He is reinstated. Most of the rest of his kingdom is downhill. David's son, Solomon, after some manipulation and political intrigue succeeds David.

A number of the Psalms are ascribed to David. They reveal something of the personal touch — what that great leader was feeling during some of the more important times of his kingdom. They particularly show his need for God and why God calls him a "man after my own heart."

From Proverbs and Ecclesiastes

Solomon has the best start of any king in all the history of Israel. There is peace in the land. The borders have expanded almost to the full extent of God's promise. There is money and resources in the kingdom as well as a good military. Times are stable. Solomon builds the temple for God — a symbol of the centralized importance of religious worship in the capital. Solomon's early years are characterized by splendor. Most likely during the early and middle part of his reign many of the Proverbs were collected. These sayings embody truth that has been learned over the years (times of the Judges, times of the kingdom) about how to live harmoniously with others. Toward the end of his reign, he slips and falls away from following God. In this latter part of his reign, he writes Ecclesiastes which sums up much that he has learned over his lifetime. Its cynical tone shows need for an intimate relationship with God that is missing.

The nation is there. There are people. They know of God and his desires for them. There is a land. But they continually fail to live up to what God wants. During the reigns of David and Solomon the kingdom reaches its zenith. And thus ends Chapter 1, the making of a nation. In it all, God is seen to weave His purpose all around a people who frequently rebel against Him. They freely choose to live as they do, whether following after God or not. But even so He manages to move unswervingly forward to His purposes.

Chapter 2. The Destruction of a Nation

The story-line of chapter 2 hinges around the following major events:

1. Solomon goes away from the Lord, great warning — had the best start of any king yet did not finish well.

2. Rehoboam (1 Kings 12) makes unwise decision to increase taxes and demands on people — kingdom splits as prophecy said. 10 tribes go with the northern kingdom, Judah with the southern.

3. The northern kingdom under Jereboam quickly departs from God. Jereboam is used as the model of an evil king to whom all evil kings are likened; He had a good start also — God would have blessed him.

4. The southern kingdom generally is bad with an occasional good Kings and partially good kings: Asa, Jehoshaphat, Joash, Amaziah, Uzziah, Jotham, Hezekiah, Josiah. But the trend was always downward. The extended length of life of the southern kingdom more than the northern kingdom is directly attributed to the spiritual life of the better kings. Spiritual leadership does make a difference.

5. During both the northern and southern kingdoms God sent prophets to try and correct them — first the oral prophets (many — but the two most noted were Elijah and Elisha) and then the prophets who wrote.

Now in order to understand this long period of history you should know several things:

1. The History books that give background information about the times.
2. The Bible Time-Line, need to know when the books were written.
3. Need to know the writing prophets: northern or southern kingdom, which crisis, direct or special.

The History Books

The history books covering the time of the destruction of a nation include 1, 2 Samuel, 1,2 Kings, and 1,2 Chronicles. The following chart helps identify the focus of each of these books as to major content.

Chart 36.1   The History Books — Major Content

1 Samuel	2 Samuel 1 Chronicles	1,2 Kings 2 Chronicles
Samuel, Saul, David	David	1,2 Kings: Solomon to Zedekiah 2 Chronicles exclusively on line of Judah

There are four categories of prophetical books. Prophetical books deal with three major crises: the Assyrian crisis which wiped out the northern kingdom; the Bablonian crisis which wiped out the southern kingdom; the return to the land after being exiled. There are also prophetical books not specifically dealing with these crises but associated with the time of them. The prophetical books dealing with these issues are:

A. Northern — Assyrian Crisis
Jonah, Amos, Hosea, Nahum, Micah

B. Southern — Babylonian Crisis
Joel, Isaiah, Micah, Zephaniah, Jeremiah, Lamentations, Habakkuk, Obadiah

C. In Exile
Ezekiel, Daniel, Esther

D. Return From Exile
Nehemiah, Ezra, Haggai, Zechariah, Malachi

In addition, to knowing the crises you must know that prophets wrote:

A. Direct to the Issue of the Crisis either Assyrian, Babylonian, or Return To The Land
Amos, Hosea, Joel, Micah, Isaiah, Jeremiah, Ezekiel, Haggai , Zechariah, Malachi

B. Special
Jonah, Nahum, Habakkuk, Obadiah, Zephaniah, Daniel.

The special prophets, though usually associated with one of the crisis times, wrote to deal with unique issues not necessarily related directly to the crisis. The following list gives the special prophets and their main thrust.

1. Jonah — a paradigm shift, pointing out God's desire for the nation to be missionary minded and reach out to surrounding nations.
2. Nahum — vindicate God, judgment on Assyria.
3. Habakkuk — faith crisis for Habakkuk, vindicate God, judgment on Babylon.
4. Obadiah — vindicate God, judgment on Edom for treatment of Judah.
5. Zephaniah — show about judgment, the Day of the Lord.
6. Daniel — give hope, show that God is indeed ruling even in the times of the exile and beyond, gives God's plan for the ages.

The Destruction of A Nation — The Return From Exile

Several Bible books are associated with the return to the land from the exile. After a period of about 70 years (during which time Daniel ministered) Cyrus made a decree which allowed some Jews (those that wanted to) to return to the land. Some went back under Zerrubabel, a political ruler like a governor. A priest, Joshua, also provided religious leadership to the first group that went back. This group of people started to rebuild the temple but became discouraged due to opposition and lack of resources. They stopped building the temple. Two prophets, after several years, 10-15, addressed the situation. These two, Haggai and Zechariah, were able to encourage the leadership and the people to finish the temple.

Another thirty or forty years goes by and then we have the events of the book of Esther, back in the land. Her book describes the attempt to eradicate the Jewish exiles — a plot which failed due to God's sovereign intervention via Esther, the queen of the land and a Jewish descendant going incognito, and her relative Mordecai.

Still another period of time passes, 20 or so years and a priest, Ezra, directs another group to return to the land. The spiritual situation has deteriorated. He brings renewal.

Another kind of leader arrives on the scene some 10-15 years later. Nehemiah, a lay leader, and one adept at organizing and moving to accomplish a task, rebuilds the wall around Jerusalem. He too has to instigate renewal.

Finally, after another period of 30 or so years we have the book of Malachi which again speaks to renewal of the people. The Old Testament closes with this final book.

A recurring emphasis occurs during the period of the return. People are motivated to accomplish a task for God. They start out, become discouraged, and stop. They must be renewed. God raises up leadership to bring renewal.

Preparation for the Coming of Messiah — The Inter-Testamental Period

I do not deal with this in detail, that is in terms of the various historical eras.[128] Some 400 + years elapse between the close of the Old Testament and the Beginning of the New

---

128. In *Leadership Perspectives*, I do deal more in a detailed way with the various historical sub-phases of this period of history. A number of books in the Catholic canon occur during this period of time.

Testament. There are significant differences in the Promised Land. The following table highlights these differences.[129]

Table 36.2   Differences in Palestine — Close of O.T., Beginning of N.T.

The End of the Old Testament	The Beginning of the New Testament
1. Palestine was part of a Persian satrapy, since Persia, an eastern nation was the greatest governmental power in the world at the time.	1. Palestine was a Roman province, since the entire world had come under the sway of the western nation of Rome.
2. The population was sparse.	2. One of the most dense parts of the Roman empire.
3. The cities of Palestine as a whole were heaps of rubbish.	3. There was general prosperity throughout Palestine.
4. The temple of Zerubbabel was a significant structure.	4. The temple of Herod the Great was a magnificent building.
5. There were no Pharisees or Sadducees, although the tendencies from which they developed were present.	5. The Pharisees and Sadducees were much in evidence and strong in power.
6. There were no synagogues in Palestine.	6. Synagogues were located everywhere in the Holy Land. There was no hamlet or village so small or destitute as to lack a synagogue.
7. There was little extra-biblical tradition among the Jews.	7. There was a great mass of tradition, among both the Jews of Palestine and those of the dispersion.
8. The Jews were guilty of much intermarriage with the surrounding nations.	8. There was almost no intermarriage between Jews and non-Jews.
9. Palestine was under the rule of a Hebrew.	9. Palestine was under the rule of an Edomite vice-king, Herod the Great.
10. The Hebrew governor was regarded by the Jews as their spiritual leader.	10. The scribes and priest were regarded by the Jews as their spiritual leaders.

In addition to differences, there were some similarities between end of O.T. times and beginning of N.T. times.

1. **Freedom from idolatry**. God had used the Babylonian Captivity to free His people from their oft-repeated tendency to idolatry.

2. **Israel in two great divisions**, the Jews of the Homeland (Isolation) and the Jews of the Dispersion (who were scattered throughout the world). In the time of Malachi a relatively small proportion of God's chosen people was located in Palestine, while by far the larger part was still in exile. Although Palestine was much more thickly populated in the time of Christ than in the time of Malachi, the same general situation prevailed as to the two-fold division of Israel into Palestinian Jews and Jews of the Diaspora (Dispersion), with a far greater number in exile than in the land of Canaan.

---

129. These notes are adapted from material studied with Frank Sells at Columbia Bible College in his Old Testament survey course.

3. **Externalism and dead orthodoxy.** A comparison of Malachi (the last prophetical book of the Old Testament) and Nehemiah (the last historical book of the Old Testament) with the Gospels indicates that the outward conformity of the Pharisees to the law which they inwardly revolted from, was but an advanced step of the hypocritical conformity which had marked many Israelites at the end of Old Testament days.

It was during the inter-testamental period that these changes occurred. Daniel had foretold of the various empires that would emerge after Babylon: the Medo-Persian, the Grecian, and the Roman. Each of these were used by God to prepare the way for the coming of Messiah, the next chapter in the redemptive drama.

Galatians 4:4 states that Messiah came at the "fullness of time." That is, the time was ready. Some have suggested a fivefold preparation for Christ's Coming.

1. Religious Preparation — both negative and positive
2. Political Preparation — world at peace
3. Cultural Preparation — lack of meaning; cultural vehicle through which to spread the Gospel
4. The Social Preparation — great needs; life under bondage
5. The Moral Preparation

Chapter 3. Messiah

At the right moment in time — Jesus was born. His miraculous birth attested to his uniqueness.

He was the fulfillment of the Old Testament as to many of its prophecies, types, symbols. He was the seed of the woman who dealt a fatal blow to the seed of the serpent (Genesis 3:15); he was the tabernacle who lived among us (Exodus 25-40); he was the arch type of the brazen serpent, lifted up that people might look, see and be healed (Numbers 21); he was the arch types of the Levitical offerings , the perfect sacrifice (Leviticus 1-5); he was that prophet like unto Moses (Deuteronomy 18); he was the ultimate fulfillment of the Davidic covenant (2 Samuel 7); he was the Messianic Sufferer (Psalm 22); he was the one who was anointed to preach good news to the poor, to proclaim freedom for the captives, and release from darkness those who are prisoners, to proclaim the year of the Lord's favor (Isaiah 61:1ff) and the Suffering Servant (Isaiah 53); he was the righteous branch from David's line (Jeremiah 23); he was the one shepherd, the servant David, the prince of Ezekiel (Ezekiel 37); he was the one greater than Jonah, the sign after three days he arose (Jonah 2); he was the proper leader coming out of obscure Bethlehem (Micah 5:2); and we could go on.

Matthew showed he was the Messiah King, rejected. Mark showed him to be vested with divine power, a person of action and authority. Luke showed him to be the perfect representative of the human race: one of courage, ability, social interests, sympathy, broad acceptance. And John showed him to be Immanuel, God with us, revealing God to us and acting to demonstrate grace and truth, the heartbeat of the divine ministry philosophy.

The bottom line of the story line is given in a quote taken from John, "He was in the world, and though the world was made through him, the world did not recognize him. He came unto his own, but his own did not receive him. Yet to all who received him, to those who believed in his name, he gave the right to become children of God, children born not of natural descent, nor of human source but born of God. The Word became flesh and made his dwelling among us. We have seen his glory, the glory of the One and Only, who came from the Father, full of grace and truth." (John 1:10-14).

The story of this chapter of the redemptive drama ends abruptly. But there is a post-script. Each of the Gospel stories and the Acts tell us of Jesus Christ's resurrection. After His death He arose and was seen for a period of about 40 days upon various occasions. During those days He gave the marching orders for the movement He had begun. The great commissions repeated five times, Matthew 28:19,20, Luke 24:46,47, Mark 16:15, John 20:21, and Acts 1:8. Each of these carry the main thrust which is to go into the world and tell the Good News of salvation, that people can be reconciled to God. Each also carries some special connotation. It is these marching orders which set the stage for Chapter 4, The Church, in the redemptive story.

Chapter 4. The Church

The essence of the story line of chapter 4, is contained in the book of Acts. Its central thematic message is the essence of the story line.

Theme: **The Growth Of The Church**

- which spreads from Jerusalem to Judea to Samaria and the utter-most parts of the earth,
- is seen to be of God,
- takes place as Spirit directed people present a salvation centered in Jesus Christ, and
- occurs among all peoples, Jews and Gentiles.

This basic phenomenon reoccurs as the Gospel spreads across cultural barriers throughout the world. Though the message of the book of Acts covers only up through the first two thirds of the first century its basic essence reoccurs throughout the church age until the present time in which we live.

About half of the book of Acts tells of the formation of the church in Jerusalem and its early expansion to Jews, Samaritans, and finally to Gentiles. The latter half of the book traces the breakout of the Gospel to Gentiles in Asia and Europe. The structure of the book highlighted by the linguistic discourse markers (the Word of the Lord grew) carries the notion of a God-given church expanding.

Structure: There are seven divisions in Acts each concluding with a summary verse. The summary verses: 2:47b, 6:7, 9:31, 12:24, 16:5, 19:20, 28:30,31

I.	(ch 1-2:47)	The Birth of the Church in Jerusalem
II.	(ch 3-6:7)	The Infancy of the Church in Jerusalem
III.	(ch 6:8-9:31)	The Spread of the Church into Judea, Galilee, Samaria
IV.	(ch 9:32-12:24)	The Church Doors Open to the Gentiles
V.	(ch 13-16:5)	The Church Spreads to Asia Minor

| VI. | (ch 16:6-19:20) | The Church Gains a Foothold in Europe |
| VII. | (ch 19:21-28) | The Travels of the Church's First Missionary To Rome (The Church on Trial in its Representative Paul) |

As to details there are many important pivotal events in the Acts, many of which have similarly reoccurred in the expansion of the Gospel around the world and throughout church history. Acts begins with Jesus' post resurrection ministry to the disciples and his Ascension to heaven. Then the disciples are gathered at Jerusalem praying when the Pentecost event, the giving of the Holy Spirit to the church, as promised in Luke's version of the Great Commission, happens and Peter gives a great public sermon which launches the church.

Early church life is described. Peter and John imbued with power heal a lame man at the temple gate and are put in prison. They are threatened and released. An incident with Ananias and Sapphira shows the power and presence of the Holy Spirit.

> Stephen an early church servant has a strong witness and is martyred for it. General persecution on the church breaks out. The believers are scattered and preach the gospel where ever they go. Phillip, another early church servant leads an Ethiopian palace administrator to Christ and has ministry in Samaria.

> Saul, the persecutor of Christians, is saved on the road to Damascus. Peter demonstrates Godly power in several miraculous events. Peter is divinely chosen to preach the Gospel to a Gentile, Cornelius. Herod kills James and imprisons Peter. Peter is miraculously delivered.

> The story line now switches to follow the missionary efforts of Barnabas and Paul (formerly Saul) to Cyprus and Asian minor. It then goes on to follow Paul's efforts which go further into Asia minor and Greece. Paul makes a return visit to Jerusalem where he is accused by the Jewish opposition in Jerusalem. Eventually after several delays and hearings he is ordered to Rome. The book ends with the exciting journey to Rome, including a shipwreck.

The books of the New Testament were written to various groups during the church chapter. Many were written by Paul. These generally were letters to the various churches which had resulted from his missionary efforts. Each was contextually specific — written at a certain time, written at a certain stage of Paul's own development as a leader, and dealing with a specific situation — either an individual in a church or to a corporate group, some church at a location or in a general region.

Other New Testament books were not written by Paul. The book of Hebrews, author uncertain, John's three letters, Jude's one letter and Peter's two letters all are of a general nature. With the exception of possibly 2nd and 3rd John, these letters were written to believer's in general in scattered regions — probably Asia minor.

All of these, Paul's letters, and the general books, deal with the church. They give us insights into church problems, church situations at that time, and the essence of what the church is and how Christians ought to live. These New Testament books are filled with leadership information. Each of them represents a major leadership act of a leader seeking to influence followers of Christ. Many of them have actual details that reflect leadership values, leadership problem solving, and leadership issues. All of them have important modeling data.

We would have an unfinished story if we were left only with *just these* New Testament books. We would have a task. And men and women would be out and about the world attempting to fulfill that task. But where is it leading. What about those Old Testament prophecies yet to be fulfilled about *that day*. Our story is incomplete. We need to know how this redemptive drama is going to end. And so the Revelation.

Chapter 5. The Kingdom

The final book of the Bible is aptly named. The Revelation (unveiling, revealing, making clear) of Jesus Christ (the unveiling of Jesus Christ) brings closure to the redemptive drama. This final book in the Bible has among others these purposes:

1. to reveal future purposes of Jesus Christ and graphically show the power He will unleash in accomplishing His purposes, which include bringing about justice and bringing in His reign,

2. to show those purposes and power to be in harmony with His divine attributes, and

3. to bring a fitting climax to the redemptive story developed throughout Scripture.

The theme statement of the book of Revelation highlights the fitting climax of the redemptive drama.

Theme: **God's Ultimate Purposes For His Redemptive Program**
*   center in the Person of His Son,
*   involve His churches,
*   will take place in a context of persecution and struggle — as described cryptically by many visions,
*   will focus on the triumph of Jesus and his judgment of all things in harmony with his divine attributes, and
*   will be realized in final victory for His people and ultimate justice accomplished in the world.

God's intent from the first of Genesis on has been to bless His people with His eternal presence. Ezekiel closes his book with that thought in mind. Numerous of the prophets point to a future day in which things would be made right and God would dwell with His people. The plan has had many twists and turns but through it all God has sovereignly moved on to His purpose.

Some have followed hard after God and were included in His purposes. Others refused to follow God. They were cast aside. God moved on.

In the New Testament God prepares a way where He can reveal Himself in justice and love and reconcile all people unto Himself. The Cross climaxes all of God's preparation to bless the world. The message of the Cross is seen to be for all. The church goes out into all the world. It has its problems. But always it seeks to be part of God's future purposes looking forward to Christ's return. Were there no Revelation, the Redemptive Story would be incomplete. The Revelation brings to a fitting climax all of God's working to bless the world. There is an ultimate purpose in history! Justice is meted out! And then a final blessing — God's eternal presence with His people.

Suggested Chronological Writing of New Testament Books

When we study a given book of the bible we should know where it occurs in the redemptive drama. We should be familiar with what God has revealed to that point in time and what God has done redemptively up to that time. Table 36.3 below lists each book of the Bible in terms of the Chapter in the redemptive story in which it falls. I have attempted to list each book in chronological order though there is not scholarly consensus on when some of these books were written.

Table 36.3 Bible Books Related To Chapters of the Redemptive Drama

The Bible Books: Chapter 1. The Making of a Nation

Exodus	Joshua	2 Samuel	Ecclesiastes
Leviticus	Judges	1 Chronicles	Song of Songs
Numbers	Ruth	Psalms	
Deuteronomy	1 Samuel	Proverbs	

The Bible Books: Chapter 2. The Destruction of a Nation

1,2 Kings	Hosea	Zephaniah	Daniel	Nehemiah
2 Chronicles	Micah	Jeremiah	Haggai	Malachi
Jonah	Isaiah	Lamentations	Zechariah	
Joel	Nahum	Obadiah	Esther	
Amos	Habakkuk	Ezekiel	Ezra	

The Bible Books: Chapter 3. Messiah

Matthew   Mark   Luke   John

The Bible Books: Chapter 4. The Church

James	2 Corinthians	Colossians	Titus	2 John
Acts	Galatians	Philemon	2 Timothy	3 John
1 Thessalonians	Romans	1 Peter	Hebrews	
2 Thessalonians	Ephesians	2 Peter	Jude	
1 Corinthians	Philippians	1 Timothy	1 John	

The Bible BOOK Chapter 5. Kingdom

Revelation

Regional Churches And Plurality of Leaders

Introduction

The New Testament gives lots of room for various forms of leadership structures in churches. A plurality of leaders was one form of leadership. Consider the following verses which show a plurality of leaders.

Titus 1

5 The reason I left you in Crete was that you might straighten out what was left unfinished concerning church leadership. I directed you to appoint church **leaders** in every town.

Acts 20

17 And from Miletus he sent to Ephesus, and called the **elders** of the church.

1 Timothy 3

1 This is a reliable saying, "If anyone aspires to leadership oversight, that one desires a good work." ...

8 Similarly a lesser church leader should have good character, ...

11 Similarly, women leaders[130] should have good character,...

1 Timothy 5

17 Church **leaders** that are exercising good leadership should be evaluated as worthy of double pay—especially the ones who are working hard teaching the word. ...

20 Those **leaders** that are sinning rebuke before all, that others also may fear.

---

[130]. I have not dealt with the issue of female leadership in this article except to note that they exist in this passage in Timothy. Priscilla, listed in this verse, was most likely a Bible teacher. Phoebe, listed in Ro 16:1 was serving as a leader also. For detail on this see **Article,** *Gender and Leadership*. See also *Leadership Topic 6* in 1 Ti.

Philippians

1 Paul and Timothy, the servants of Jesus Christ, to all the saints in Christ Jesus which are at Philippi, with the **bishops** and **deacons**.

Plurality is well established. But the extent of leadership exercised by plurality is not so clear: plurality in a house church? plurality in a local church? plurality in a regional church? plurality worldwide? Nor is the relationship between a group of leaders serving as a plurality specified. How do they relate to one another?

But note also the notion of a strong leader, though unnamed here, even in a situation with plurality of leadership.

Philippians

4: 3 And I intreat thee also, true **yokefellow**, help those women which labored with me in the gospel, with Clement also, and [with] other my fellow labourers, whose names [are] in the book of life

The New Testament also allows for various structures of the groups these leaders influenced. Note the following verses which seem to indicate very small groups of believers meeting in homes — that is, house churches.

Philemon

2 Hello also to our beloved Apphia, and Archippus our fellow soldier, and to the church in your house.

Romans 16

3 Greet Priscilla and Aquila my helpers in Christ Jesus…5 Likewise greet the church that is in their house.

10 Salute Apelles approved in Christ. Salute them which are of Aristobulus' household (indicating a group of believers, most likely).

11 Salute Herodion my kinsman. Greet them that be of the household of Narcissus, which are in the Lord household (again indicating a group of believers, most likely).

14 Salute Asyncritus, Phlegon, Hermas, Patrobas, Hermes, and the brethren which are with them (again indicating a group of believers, most likely).

15 Salute Philologus, and Julia, Nereus, and his sister, and Olympas, and all the saints which are with them (certainly indicating a small group of believers).

The New Testament also recognized larger groups of believers who met, probably in a city wide grouping.

Philippians

1 Paul and Timothy, the servants of Jesus Christ, to all the saints in Christ Jesus which are at Philippi, with the bishops and deacons.

Further, there were groups, probably associated with a city wide base which were in a region (probably made up of house churches and local churches scattered about).

2nd Corinthians

1 Paul, an apostle of Jesus Christ by the will of God, and Timothy our brother, To the church of God which is at Corinth, with all the saints who are in all Greece.

Galatians

1 Paul, an apostle, not of men, neither by man, but by Jesus Christ, and God the Father, who raised him from the dead; 2 And all the believers which are with me, unto the churches of Galatia:

What are we to make of these notions, plurality of leadership and various size groups over which leadership was exercised? My position is, we should be clear as the Bible on them: nothing less, nothing more, and nothing else. That will allow lots of freedom for different forms of leaderships and structures. Certain things happened historically. Tradition has played a strong role in how we look at leadership today. But Biblically, we most likely have lots more freedom than is seen today.

Various Size Groupings: Small to Large

Probably it will help to define various size groupings of believers as seen in the New Testament.

Definition	A *house church* was a small group of believers which met in someone's home with undetermined regularity and uncertainty as to leadership.
Example	The church that met in Philemon's house (Phm 2). The groups that met in the various homes in Rome (Romans 16:3,10,11,14,15).
Example	The host, person in the household in which the group met, probably exercised some kind of leadership (Priscilla and Aquila; Aristobulus; Narcissus; Asyncritus, Phlegon, Hermas, Patrobas, Hermes; Philologus, Julia, Nereus, and Olympas — all in Rome). Archippus probably led the church that met in Philemon's house.
Definition	A *local church* was a group of believers which gathered together usually on Sunday to sing, share truth from God, and partake in the Lord's supper.[131] There was appointed leadership consisting of elders and lesser leaders, deacons.[132]

[131.] See 1 Co 11 for regularity and verse 20 especially for Lord's Supper. See 1 Co 14 as a whole to show that the body participated in sharing revelatory truth from God. See 1 Co 16:2 which indicates regularity. See 1 Co 14:23 which shows the notion of a local church gathering. Col 3:16 which gives indication of a gathering and what they did. See 1 Ti 5:17 showing dual functions the leaders did — teaching and ruling. Note Php 4:2 for example of a ruling elder-solving problems.

[132.] See **Article**, *Pauline Leadership Terms in the New Testament*. Also note 1 Ti 3 and Tit 1 where apostolic leaders like Timothy and Titus appointed leaders. See also Acts 14:21-23 where Barnabas and Paul apostolically appoint leaders in the fledgling churches begun on their first missionary journey.

Example	Phillipi, Ephesus
Example	Php 4:2 yokefellow. Rom 16:1 Phoebe
Example	The lesser leaders, which we call deacons, probably did service type of tasks in the local church (Acts 6, 1 Tim 5). This was a responsibility in which to grow and prove faithfulness. Such faithfulness could lead to becoming an elder, a recognized higher leadership level in a local church.
Comment	A given local church would probably have a plurality of leadership including multiple elders and multiple deacons. See Phillipi and Ephesus where the leaders are spoken of in the plural. (Php 1:1; 1 Ti 3:1-13; Acts 20)
Comment	Elders did two basic functions: 1. looked out for the spiritual welfare of the believers by teaching the word that is, truth from God to help the believers grow (oral tradition first and then later as the canon grew taught it); and by praying for the people, 2. led the local church — set its direction and helped it function as a group. They probably baptized folk and led the Lord's supper.
Definition	*Regional churches* consisted of a group of house churches or local churches in a given larger geographical situation
Example	Churches of Galatia — Paul addresses them as a group (Gal 1:2). Churches in Greece — Paul addressed them as a group (2 Co 1:1); Colosse — definitely a local church and most likely a regional since Laodicea believers and Philemon's house church read the circular letter sent to Colosse. Crete — believers were located in the various towns. Individual towns were to have a leader(s).
Example	Leadership in regional churches is unclear. However, the Ephesian letter describing gifted leaders such as apostles, prophets, evangelists, pastors, teachers probably referred to regional leaders who traveled about ministering to more than one local church or house church in a region.[133] Paul has been describing the church universal in chapters 1-3. It appears in Eph 4:12-17 that he is applying this leadership to the broader size of structure rather than just a local church.
Definition	The *worldwide church*, sometimes called the universal church is composed of all the believers everywhere (and probably of all time) who make up the body of Christ.

Having defined the notion of plurality of leadership and also allowing for a strong leader over a group and the various sizes of groups we can probably give some observations which speak to the freedom we have in leadership today.

[133.] John validates the notion of these traveling ministers (see 3, 5-9, 12 for veiled references to traveling ministers). Paul raises money for several of them (among which is Stephanus and Timothy).

Conclusion

Here are observations that are drawn from the cursory treatment I have given about plurality and structures of churches.[134]

1. The New Testament house churches, local churches, and regional churches certainly allowed for a plurality of leaders. And this plurality could operate with or without some stronger leader to guide it (one among many concept).

2. There could be a strong leader who dominated the leadership in a house church, local church, or regional church. Traditionally the term bishop came into being historically to describe a strong regional leader to whom all local churches related.

3. Leaders were appointed by apostolic types: Paul, Timothy, Titus. This function should happen today as well.

4. As to selection criteria for leadership, probably more important than *how many* leaders there are either in a house church or local church or regional church is *what kind* of leaders. At least this is true for house churches or local churches. The selection criteria focusing on character is paramount. For regional churches, the character issues would be a pre-requisite. In addition, the gifting would be important: apostleship, prophet, evangelist, pastor, teacher.

5. Eph 4:12-17 probably refers to regional leaders. A given local church may or may not have had the whole spectrum of leaders (apostles, prophets, evangelists, teachers, pastors)

6. Lesser leadership roles (deacons) provides experience for growth into more responsible leadership roles (elders/bishops).

7. Elders/bishops could be remunerated for their ministry. Paul, the exemplary apostolic leader for the church era, had freedom to accept remuneration or not. He would not if accepting it might thwart his ministry effort.

8. Spiritual authority, not positional authority, seems to be the major criterion on leadership at the various levels: house church, local church, regional church.

Let me restate some of the above observations in terms of leadership guidelines or values:

Leadership Principles/ Values Suggested by this concept:

a. Character is crucial to leadership and must be the basis on which leaders are selected.

b. A Spirit-controlled conscience should be the norm for a leader.

c. Varying levels of church leadership and differing roles (probably based on giftedness) should be expected in local churches. The varying levels should be part of an overall leadership selection process.

[134.] See also the *Leadership Topic 6, Leadership Guidelines* in 1 Ti, where I give observations flowing from Paul's advice to Timothy in the Ephesus situation.

d. A plurality of leadership can be used in a local church.

e. Plurality of leadership does not mean a lack of strong leadership. Plurality is not identified with consensus.

f. A foundational emphasis underlying leadership selection is the identification of integrity, character, and traits of exemplary being and behavior in a culture. Leadership in a local church should be above criticism (as to character) by the surrounding culture.

g. Lower levels of leadership should be allowed for a time of testing of younger leaders.

I close where I began. There is much freedom concerning leadership. While our traditional forms most likely fall into applications of this freedom, we as leaders need to be aware that there is probably much more freedom for how we view leadership today, than is the case in most of our leadership situations.

Shunning — Paul's Advice on This

Introduction

If you have seen any modern day movies, like *The Witness*, about the Amish folks that live in Pennsylvania or Iowa or elsewhere, you have been introduced to the practice of shunning.

Definition   *Shunning* is the practice of habitually and deliberately avoiding social interaction of any kind with someone.

It carries the connotation of abhorrence of something — the reason for the shunning. Paul used this notion, not the actual label, as a form of apostolic discipline.

Paul faced several situations involving either orthopraxic heresy or orthodoxic heresy[135] in several churches which required some discipline. What was his approach? Shunning! How did he discipline? By commanding that the believers shun the ones needing discipline. Did it work? Lets consider several situations in chronological order.

At Thessalonica — Early in Paul's Ministry

Paul wrote two letters to the young church at Thessalonica. He was a relatively young Christian worker at the time. In the first letter he was dealing with an orthodoxic heresy, a false view that the second coming had already happened. He treats the problem by teaching the truth about the 2nd coming. He actually gives no advice about what to do about those that have taught this. He gives only the slightest hint,

> 1 Th 5:14 Now we exhort you, brethren, *warn them that are unruly*, comfort the feebleminded, support the weak, be patient toward all.

It is not clear however, that the unruly are the ones causing the problem.

Paul is much clearer in the second letter to the Thessalonians. Here he is dealing with a behavioral problem.

> 2 Th 3:6 Now we *command* you, fellow believers, in the name of our Lord Jesus

---

135. Heresy refers to deviation from a standard, whether in belief (orthodoxy) or practice (orthopraxy). e.g. See 1Ti where both are present in the Ephesian church (as prophesied in Ac 20:30).

Christ, that you *withdraw* yourselves from every fellow believer that *walks disorderly*, that is, does not obey the oral teaching which I gave you. 7 For you yourselves know how you ought to follow our model: for we did not ourselves *behave disorderly* among you; 8 Neither did we eat any man's bread for free; but worked long and hard that we might not be a burden to any of you: 9 We behaved in this fashion, not because we didn't have the right to demand such help, but to make ourselves a living example — a model you could follow. 10 For the time we were with you, this we *commanded* you, that if any would not work, neither should that one eat. 11 For we hear that there are some who refuse to work but instead waste their time doing nothing productive — in fact, just the opposite, they gossip all the time. 12 For such folks, by the authority of our Lord Jesus Christ we command and exhort, that they mind their own business and do some productive work, earn their own living, not sponging off of others. 13 Don't get discouraged about your daily work. Stay with it. 14 And if any person refuses to obey what I am commanding in this epistle, note that person, and *have no company with him or her*. This may shame him/her into action. 15 Yet don't look on that person as an enemy. Reason with that one as a fellow believer.[136]

The problem Paul addresses in the above context is believers in a church community who are refusing to work at some job or duty in society. In fact, they are not only refusing to work but are spending their time meddling in others affairs and gossiping about them. Hence they are a problem for the church — financially draining and having a bad testimony by divisively gossiping about folks — probably fellow believers.

The words, *walks disorderly* or *behave disorderly* mean to avoid working at some productive job earning money.[137] And So Paul, like a military commander, in an apostolic manner, directly confronts the problem head on.[138] He *commands* — a word used of a military commander giving an order to those who must obey it. He *exhorts* — the word describing the spiritual gift of exhortation and meaning to apply something. Here is what he says, "Get to work. And if some won't obey my command, then refuse to have anything to do with them (*have no company with him or her*)."

So here is the solution Paul gives to the problem. "Teach the truth and model it, that is, work productively. And don't be a burden on the church. Warn those who won't do this. Then if they continue to refuse to work productively, avoid them. Stop solving their financial problems in a co-dependent way. Shame them into obeying." Will this really work? More on this later.

[136.] In my opinion, Peterson captures the force of this context the best of any modern English translation.

[137.] The closest English words we have to describe this kind of behavior is malingering or dawdling. Malingering is feigning sickness to avoid work. Dawdling is aimlessly being idle. Neither captures exactly the Greek words (underlying the phrase walk disorderly).

[138.] This is an illustration of two Pauline leadership styles: Apostolic and Confrontive. Both of these styles are highly directive. Crisis situations usually demand highly directive leadership styles. The *apostolic leadership style* is a method of influence in which the leader assumes the role of delegated authority over those for whom he/she is responsible, receives revelation from God concerning decisions, and commands obedience based on role of delegated authority and revelation concerning God's will. The *confrontation leadership style* is an approach to problem solving which brings the problem out in the open with all parties concerned, which analyzes the problem in light of revelational truth, and which brings force to bear upon the parties to accept recommended solutions. See **Article**, *Pauline Leadership Styles*.

At Ephesus — Toward the End of Paul's Ministry

Toward the end of Paul's ministry he again uses the shunning idea as a disciplinary tool. In 1 Ti 6:3-5 Paul gives a running conclusion to what he has been teaching in the whole epistle and uses it as a lead in to a final admonition concerning money and its use.

> 1 Ti 6:3 Let me describe the person who teaches otherwise to the things I have been writing in this epistle. Such a one doesn't agree with my wholesome words, which are the words of our Lord Jesus Christ and to my teaching which leads to godliness. 4 Such a one is proud, really knows nothing and wastes time doting on questions and hurtful words. Such actions cause envy, strife, railings, evil surmisings. 5 They are perverse people with corrupt minds. They really know nothing of truth. They really want to take your money. That is really their practice of godliness. *Isolate these folks and have nothing to do with them.*

Paul has dealt with several heresies in his advice to Timothy about the church in Ephesus. There are false teachers who are causing all kinds of confusion and tending to split the church. Paul sees them as folks who are using religious teaching as a means to deceitfully fleece the hearers — get their money. From such he says, "*Isolate these folks and have nothing to do with them.*" The word used to describe shunning here is a different word from that used in the Thessalonican epistle. It is stronger — depart from them, get away from them, isolate yourselves from them. Did this disciplinary action work? More on this later.

At Crete — Toward the End of Paul's Ministry

Paul closes his epistle to Titus with strong words about shunning.

> Titus 3: 6 God provided us with this Spirit made available to us generously through the work of Jesus Christ our Savior. 7 Now then, we have been made right with God due to His gracious provision. We will become heirs. We have the hope of eternal life. 8 What I am saying to you is the Gospel truth. And I want you to stress these things, so that those who have trusted in God may be careful to live out in daily life, testimonies which reflect this *Goodnews*. These things are excellent and profitable for everyone. 9 But avoid foolish controversies and genealogies and arguments and quarrels about the law, because these are unprofitable and useless. 10 Warn a divisive person once, and then warn him a second time. After that, have nothing to do with him. 11 You may be sure that such a man is warped and sinful. He is self-condemned.

Leaders need not feel guilty over this disciplinary action. The process has allowed for a response to correct the improper teaching or behavior and its effect. If the process has not brought about change then the discipline is applied. And their should be no guilt associated with it. Remember, there may yet be a change and one must be ready to forgive and respond later.

Does it Work?

See 2 Co 2:5-11 where the shunning process worked and the person ousted from the community was forgiven. Paul's disciplinary action (which Titus was involved in) did work in Corinth. The disciplinary action was taken in 1 Cor 5:1-5 and its results seen in 2 Cor 2:5-11.[139]

Conclusion

Well, what can we say about shunning today. Can it work? In individualistic societies with lots of church options — probably not.[140] Folks, who are shunned will probably just go somewhere else and no one will even know about it.

But in group societies where community is important, yes it can work. In Thessalonica, where the believers were seen as very different from the society around them — that is, a tight community — probably yes, shunning worked. We don't have a record of the results. But if folks were shunned and had no means of income, they probably would be forced to work.

In Ephesus, again the believers were part of a community which differed from the surrounding culture. Again, probably yes, shunning worked. If folks, recognized these false teachers for what they were and refused to have anything to do with them, especially financially, it would nip the bud at the source. These teachers would be forced to move on.

In Crete — a decidedly yes. On this small island culture, the believers were a community. And Paul was trying to get them to be an effective influential community, displaying behavior which would attract others. But my guess is yes, shunning worked. Titus' strong teaching probably countered the false teaching.

It is difficult for a person enculterated in an individualistic society to appreciate what it must feel like to be excluded from the social interaction of a tight community in which being an agreeable part of the whole means everything.

Shame on us, that our church communities mean so little to us that we can leave them almost on a whim.

What can we do to make the notion of shunning as a disciplinary action more effective. One, we can actually practice it. Two, we can announce publicly to our church membership that we are shunning someone. Three, we can send letters to other churches to whom these folks try to fellowship with.

[139.] The disciplinary action is even stronger here. The Pauline leadership style of confrontation and indirect conflict are used. The *indirect conflict leadership style* is an approach to problem solving which requires discernment of spiritual motivation factors behind the problem, usually results in spiritual warfare without direct confrontation with the parties of the problem. Spiritual warfare is sensed as a necessary first step before any problem solving can take place. Not only are these Corinthians to shun this person but they are to see this person as abandoned to Satanic activity.

[140.] So that in rural America where in small village settings everybody knows everybody shunning will probably work. Or in inner city urban settings where churches replace gangs as the survival community for folks, yes, it will probably work. But in much of our urban sprawl with individualistic isolated living, probably not.

Shunning sounds so primitive. But its end results are what we are after, as church leaders. To draw people back into fellowship with correct behavior or truth a viable part of their lives. What would Paul do today in our western individualistic mega-churches?

The next time you see *The Witness*, see it with new ideas and try to appreciate how the threat of shunning was so powerful.

Six Biblical Leadership Eras

Approaching the Bible with Leadership Eyes

Introduction

In my opinion, the Bible provides one of the richest resources that Christian leaders have on leadership. The Bible is full of leadership insights, lessons, values and principles about leaders and leadership. It is filled with influential people and the results of their influence... both good and bad.

Three assumptions undergird what I will say in this article.

1. I have a strong **conviction** that the Bible can give valuable leadership insights.

2. I have made a **willful decision** to study the Bible and use it as a source of leadership insights.[141]

3. To study the Bible for leadership insights, you need **leadership eyes** to see leadership findings in the Bible. That is, there are many leadership perspectives, i.e. paradigms, that help stimulate one to see leadership findings. I have been discovering and using these in my own study.

I want to do three things in this keynote overview. I want to introduce two most helpful perspectives for studying the Bible for leadership findings: 1. Seeing Leadership Eras; 2. Recognizing Leadership Genre. I will give more space to *the Six Leadership Eras*. These two concepts will help give one *leadership eyes*. And then I want to talk about the impact of the two most important boundary times between leadership eras, Moses desert leadership and Jesus' foundational work instigating a major movement. Both of these were fundamental and foundational times of Biblical leadership. They introduced radical macro lessons that deeply impact our own leadership today.

The Six Leadership Eras

A first step toward having *leadership eyes*, for recognizing leadership findings in the Bible involves seeing the various leadership eras in the Bible. These time periods share

---

141. I have been doing this deliberately for ten years at this writing.

common leadership assumptions and expectations. These assumptions and expectations differ markedly from one leadership time period to the next. Though, of course, there are commonalties that bridge across the eras.

Definition   A *leadership era* is a period of time, usually several hundred years long,[142] in which the major focus of leadership, the influence means, basic leadership functions, and followership have much in common and which basically differ with time periods before or after it.

Table 39.1 contains the outline of the six eras I have identified.

Table 39.1   Six Leadership Eras Outlined

Era	Label / Details
I.	**Patriarchal Era** (Leadership Roots)—Family Base
II.	**Pre-Kingdom Leadership Era**—Tribal Base A. The Desert Years B. The War Years—Conquering the Land, C. The Tribal Years/ Chaotic Years/ Decentralized Years—Conquered by the Land
III.	**Kingdom Leadership Era**—Nation Based A. The United Kingdom B. The Divided Kingdom C. The Single Kingdom — Southern Kingdom Only
IV.	**Post-Kingdom Leadership Era**—Individual/ Remnant Based A. Exile — Individual Leadership Out of the Land B. Post Exilic — Leadership Back in the Land C. Interim — Between Testaments
V.	**New Testament Pre-Church Leadership**—Spiritually Based in the Land A. Pre-Messianic B. Messianic
VI.	**New Testament Church Leadership**—Decentralized Spiritually Based A. Jewish Era B. Gentile Era

The three overarching elements of leadership include: the *leadership basal elements* (leader, follower, situation which make up the **What** of leadership); *leadership influence means* (individual and corporate leadership styles which make up the **How** of leadership); and *leadership value bases* (theological and cultural values which make up the **Why** of leadership).[143] It was this taxonomy which suggested questions that helped me see for the first time the six leadership eras of the Bible. It is these categories that allow comparison of different leadership periods in the Bible. Later I will apply the taxonomy to each of the eras and give my preliminary findings.

Using these leadership characteristics I studied leadership across the Bible and inductively generated the six leadership eras as given above. Table 39.2 adds some descriptive elements of the eras.

---

142. There is one exception. Though technically, the N.T. Pre-Church Era includes the inter-testamental time, I only really focus on Jesus' ministry which lasted a short period of time. But it is so unique and so radically different from what preceded and followed it that I treat it as the essential time in this era.

143. See the **Article**, *Leadership Tree Diagram* which explains in details these three elements of leadership.

Table 39.2 Six Leadership Eras in the Bible—Definitive Characteristics

Leadership Era	Example(s) Leader(s)	Definitive Characteristics
1. Foundational (also called Patriarchal)	Abraham, Joseph	Family Leadership/ formally male dominated/ expanding into tribes and clans as families grew/ moves along kinship lines.
2. Pre-Kingdom	Moses, Joshua, Judges	Tribal Leadership/ Moving to National/ Military/ Spiritual Authority/ outside the land moving toward a centralized national leadership.
3. Kingdom	David, Hezekiah	National Leadership/ Kingdom Structure/ Civil, Military/ Spiritual/ a national leadership—Prophetic call for renewal/ inside the land/ breakup of nation.
4. Post-Kingdom	Ezekiel, Daniel, Ezra, Nehemiah	Individual leadership/ Modeling/ Spiritual Authority.
5. Pre-Church	Jesus/ Disciples	Selection/ Training/ spiritual leadership/ preparation for decentralization of Spiritual Authority/ initiation of a movement.
6. Church	Peter/ Paul/ John	decentralized leadership/ cross-cultural structures led by leaders with spiritual authority which institutionalize the movement and spread it around the world.

When we study a leader or a particular leadership issue in the Scripture, we must always do so in light of the leadership context in which it was taking place. We cannot judge past leadership by our present leadership standards. Yet, we will find that major leadership lessons learned by these leaders will usually have broad implications for our leadership.

Second Major Perspective for Getting Leadership Eyes—The Seven Leadership Genre

Further study of each of these leadership eras resulted in the identification of seven leadership genre which served as sources for leadership findings. I then worked out in detail approaches for studying each of these genre.[144] These seven leadership genre are shown in Table 39.3.

Table 39.3 Seven Leadership Genre—Sources for Leadership Findings[145]

Type	General Description/ Example	Approach
1. Biographic[a]	Information about leaders; this is the single largest genre giving leadership information in the Bible/ **Joseph**	Use biographical analysis based on leadership emergence theory concepts.
2. Direct Leadership Contexts[b]	Blocks of Scripture which are giving information directly applicable to leaders/ leadership; relatively few of these in Scripture/ **1 Peter 5:1-4**	Use standard exegetical techniques.

---

144. See Article, *Leadership Genre—Seven Types*. See also For **Further Study Bibliography, Leadership Perspectives—How To Study the Bible for Leadership Findings**. Altadena: Barnabas Publishers.

3. Leadership Acts[c]	Mostly narrative vignettes describing a leader influencing followers, usually in some crisis situation; quite a few of these in the Bible/ Acts 15 Jerusalem Council	Use three-fold leadership tree diagram as basic source for suggesting what areas of leadership to look for.
4. Parabolic Passages[d]	Parables focusing on leadership perspectives: e.g. stewardship parables, futuristic parables; quite a few of these in Matthew and Luke./ **Luke 19 The Pounds**	Use standard parable exegetical techniques but then use leadership perspectives to draw out applicational findings; especially recognize the leadership intent of Jesus in giving these. Most such parables were given with a view to training disciples.
5. Books as a Whole	Each book in the Bible[e]; end result of this is a list of leadership observations or lessons or implications for leadership/ Deuteronomy	Consider each of the Bible books in terms of the leadership era in which they occur and for what they contribute to leadership findings; will have to use whatever other leadership genre source occurs in a given book; also use overall synthesis thinking.
6. Indirect Passages	Passages in the Scripture dealing with Biblical values applicable to all; more so to leaders who must model Biblical values/ **Proverbs; Sermon on the Mount**	Use standard exegetical procedures for the type of Scripture containing the applicable Biblical ethical findings or values.
7. Macro Lessons[f]	Generalized high level leadership observations seen in an era and which have potential for leadership absolutes/ **Presence Macro**	Use synthesis techniques utilizing various leadership perspectives to stimulate observations.

a. See the **Article**, *Biographical Study in the Bible—How To Do.*

b. I have identified many of the direct leadership texts and have exegetically analyzed the more important of these.

c. Many leadership acts have been identified and more than 20 have been analyzed. There is much work to do on analyzing leadership acts.

d. I have studied every parable, exegetically, in Matthew, Mark and Luke for its central truth and applicable leadership lessons.

e. I have done this for each book in the Bible over the past 10 years. My findings are included in **The Bible and Leadership Values**. Though I have made a good start, there is much more to be done here. I am intending other Handbooks which include all of the top 25 Bible books on leadership.

f. This area needs the most research. Several PhD research projects are now focused on this.

The Criteria For Evaluating An Era

What Are the Distinguishing Characteristics We Are Looking For? I have used the following categories:

1. Major Focus—

Here we are looking at the overall purposes of leadership for the period in question. What was God doing or attempting to do through the leader? Sense of destiny? Leadership mandate?

[145.] See the **Article**, *Leadership Genre—Seven Types.*

2. **Influence means—**

   Here we are describing any of the power means available and used by the leaders in their leadership. We can use any of Wrong's categories or any of the leadership style categories I define. Note particularly in the Old Testament the use of force and manipulation as power means.

3. **Basic leadership functions—**

   We list here the various achievement responsibilities expected of the leaders: from God's standpoint, from the leader's own perception of leadership, from the followers. Usually they can all be categorized under the three major leadership functions of task, relational, and inspirational functions. But here we are after the specific functions.

4. **Followers—**

   Here we are after sphere of influence. Who are the followers? What are their relationship to leaders? Which of the 10 Commandments of followership are valid for these followers? What other things are helpful in describing followers?

5. **Local Leadership—**

   In the surrounding culture: Biblical leaders will be very much like the leaders in the cultures around them. Leadership styles will flow out of this cultural press. Here we are trying to identify leadership roles in the cultures in contact with our Biblical leaders.

6. **Other:**

   Miscellaneous catch all; such things as centralization or decentralization or hierarchical systems of leadership; joint (civil, political, military, religious) or separate roles.

Thought Questions—

In addition to the above categories, I try to synthesize the questions that I would like answered about leaders and leadership if I could get those answers. With these thought questions I am considering such things as the essence of a leader (being or doing), leadership itself, leadership selection and training, authority (centralized or decentralized), etc.

My preliminary findings for these categories for each leadership era follows.

1st Leadership Era: Patriarchal Leadership

1. **Major Focus—**Pass on the promise and heritage of the Most High God to the family; priestly role (regularity) — intercede, sacrifice, and worship the Most High God;

2. **Influence means—**apostolic style, father-initiator, father-guardian, full range of Wrong's typology: force, manipulation, authority (coercive, inducive, positional — fatherly head, competence, personal), spiritual authority

3. **Five basic leadership functions—**(1) Godly/ priestly functions:- demonstrate absolute loyalty to God; - demonstrate reality of the unseen God; - pass on heritage of what is known (revelatory) of God and His ways and desires, very little revelation, animistic; - pass on sense of destiny; — God's prophetic promises; (2) Primarily performing the inspirational function—largely through modeling; the relational function consisted primarily of keeping the family together and obedience to the patriarch. Inspirational

function -Creating hope in God -Creating sense of God's intervention in life; (3) Mediate Blessing of God: - contagious blessing; - heritage blessing; (4) Military head — protection of family; (5) Civil — judge/ justice

4. **Followers**—Family members: (1) Age/masculine-oriented; (2) Almost all of 10 Followership Laws in force; (3) Oldest to receive blessing and birthright; (4) The one receiving blessing and birthright passes it on to next generation

5. **Local Leadership**—in the culture around the Patriarchs: - tribal heads; - City States / Regional heads (called kings);
    - local priests (practitioners/ animistic); - local military

6. **Other**— Highly Decentralized; each given family responsible to God

Thought Questions—1. How did other families relate to God (Melchezidek's, Labin's, etc.)? 2. What were expectations of Patriarchs as leaders? by followers? by God? by surrounding culture? 3. What was the foundational aspect of character? What was integrity to the Patriarchs? 4. What was the birthright? What was the blessing? 5. If modeling was the primary training methodology, what were the most important positive leadership qualities modeled by Abraham? by Isaac? by Jacob? by Joseph? by Job? 6. Using a modified form of the six characteristics of finishing well, how did the Patriarchs finish? Abraham? Isaac? Jacob? Joseph? Job?

2nd Leadership Era: Pre-Kingdom Leadership

1. **Major Focus**—Uniting of a people, preparing them to follow God, preparing them to invade the promised land, settling them in the land. The Desert leadership is one of discipline, a heavy time of revelation, and supernatural events backing leadership. The Challenge Era is one of stretching of faith to overcome the many obstacles involved in capturing the land. The Judges Era has the major challenge of how to unite disparate peoples, survive attacks, and degeneration of relationship to God. In each there is Charismatic Leadership: You lead because of spiritual authority, personal authority or competence not because of nepotism or birth; a formal priestly role is secondary — there is an inheritance with this role — and this leadership is weak, probably because of that.

2. **Influence means**—apostolic style, father-initiator, father-guardian, full range of Wrong's typology: force, manipulation, authority (coercive, inducive, positional — fatherly head, competence, personal), spiritual authority

3. **7 basic leadership functions** seen include: (1) Centralize Authority/ Develop Authority Structures:- military, political, religious;- tribal/ trans-tribal (elders); (2) Primarily performing the inspirational function: -Creating hope in God; -Creating sense of God's intervention in life. (3) Revelatory (Desert)/Inscribe and pass on the basic revelation of God as given in the law/how to live separated lives; (4) Military head — protection/ mobilize an on-call army distributed over the tribes; (5) Civil — judge/ justice/ set up legal system for interpreting and applying the law; (6) Fulfill Promise of Taking the Land; settling it; (7) Call to renewal; recrudescence; see God work anew.

4. **Followers**—12 large tribes:(1) Age/ masculine-oriented leadership; (2) Almost all of 10 Followership Laws in force; centralization out of balance; leadership more nepotistic than functional; reciprocal commands a legalistic thing carried by enforcement of law.

5. **Local Leadership**—in the surrounding culture:- tribal heads; - City State / Regional heads (called kings); - local priests (practitioners/ animistic); - local military

6. **Other**—Highly centralized during desert and capturing of land; highly decentralized during Judges era/ continuity of leadership a major problem except for the first transition from Moses to Joshua

Thought Questions:

1. How were leaders selected and developed? 2. What did they do at the different levels? 3. What is missing from the Judges Era that was the driving force of the Warfare Era? 4. What has happened to the Abrahamic mandate? Which of the eras, if any, are concerned with that mandate? 5. How does this era compare with the Patriarchal, spiritually?

3rd Leadership Era: Kingdom Leadership

1. **Major Focus** —The Kingdom united the dispersed tribal groups into a more cohesive nation which could provide government and military protection. The Davidic covenant was part of an on-going means to bring about Abraham's promise and to manifest the concept of God's rule on earth as well as provide resources to bring others into relationship with God. It never lived up to its ideals.

2. **Influence means**—the full range of Wrong's typology: **force, manipulation, authority** (coercive, inducive, positional) — fatherly head; competence, personal, spiritual authority.

3. **6 basic leadership functions** seen include: (1) Centralize Authority/ Develop Authority Structures:- military, political, religious; - tribal/ trans-tribal (elders); (2) Revelatory (Particularly in the Divided Kingdom and the Single Kingdom)/ Much of the corrective revelation done by the prophets was oral. But there was also the Prophetic revelation which was inscribed. Often these writings were a call to repentance, renewal, and a return to kingdom ideals; (3) Military head — protection/ have a standing army that could defend against the attacks that were coming more frequently from the expanding empires or ambitious kings. They would also mobilize an on-call army distributed over the tribes to go along with the standing army in big crises. (4) Civil—judge/justice/set up legal system for interpreting and applying the law; (5) Call to renewal; recrudescence; see God work anew (prophetic function); (6) Persevere as a people of God; maintain a base from which God could work. Major Problems: communication and control; followership scattered over large area; -large empires on the rise.

4. **Followers**—a. United Kingdom-12 large tribes, also the many surrounding small kingdoms that were conquered b. Divided Kingdom — Northern-10 1/2 Large Tribes c. Southern — About 1 1/2 tribes — mostly Judah; Leadership (1) Age/ masculine oriented; (2) Almost all of 10 Followership Laws in force; centralization out of balance; leadership more nepotistic than functional;

5. **Local Leadership**—in the surrounding cultures: - tribal heads; - kings of territories with a number of cities; usually one dominated and was walled; - local priests (practitioners/ animistic); - military.

6. **Other**— Large Empires are vying for world dominion or at least for large influence: Assyria, Egypt, Babylon

Thought Questions: 1. Why were the prophets raised up? 2. According to Deuteronomy what was the place of the law for the Kings? Was it followed? 3. Was the central religious function (the three yearly treks) carried out? 4. Why was the nepotistic approach to leadership selection used? Was it successful? 5. How does this era compare spiritually with the Pre-Kingdom era?

4th Leadership Era: Post-Kingdom Leadership

1. **Major Focus**—The nation no longer exists. It has been disciplined by God. Leadership during this time must do several things: analyze what happened and why; bring hope during this time; demonstrate the importance of godliness under oppressive conditions; demonstrate the importance of God's sovereignty; point to the future in which God is going to work.

2. **Influence means**—largely by modeling, spiritual authority, toward latter time in the time of the return, Jewish leaders again take up roles: political, religious, quasi-military for the Jewish people.

3. **Basic leadership functions** seen include: The inspirational function is dominant. The need for community in little pockets brings out the need for the relational function of leadership. The rise of the synagogues — small communities upholding their Jewish origins and religion bring about the need for scribes, and those who interpret the written scriptures.

4. **Followers**—Pockets of scattered Jewish people

5. **Local Leadership**—in the surrounding cultures: - tribal heads; - City States / Regional heads (called kings); - local priests (practitioners/ animistic); - local military; - emperors/ kings/ heads of powerful international groups formed by conquering vast territories and kingdoms/ various administrative leaders under these

6. **Other**: ?

Thought Questions: 1. Why did Jewish leaders prosper during these oppressive days? 2. What kinds of leadership did they participate in? 3. What has happened to the Abrahamic promise? How did the Jewish people feel about it in these days? 4.How were religious leaders selected (e.g. for the synagogues)?

5th Leadership Era: Pre-Church Leadership

1. **Major Focus**—Galatians 4:4. This is the acme of charismatic leadership. Jesus models servant leadership and ideal spiritual authority — all aspects of it. The end result of this leadership is revelation, redemption, and a movement to universalize the redemption to all humankind.

2. **Influence Means**—the entire range of Pauline leadership styles are demonstrated. The whole range of Wrong's Typology is seen.

3. **Leadership Functions:**

(1) Provide the redemptive base reconciling God and humankind and its major ramifications, the revelation and enabling power for human beings to realize their idealized human potential.

(2) Provide a leadership mandate that will utilize all three major leadership functions in its fulfillment. Task, relational, and inspirational functions are essential to the accomplishment of the mandate. (3) Create a movement that will institutionalize the leadership functions for on-going effective leadership. (4) Provide a call for renewal to Israel. (5) Present the Kingdom of God in concept and power. (6) Provide a revelatory base, model, and standards for future revelation.

4. **Followers**—In the land there were remnants of the tribes, mixed ethnic groups (like Samaritans), religious leadership like the Pharisees, Saducees, and the political leaders of the Roman empire along with garrisons of Roman Military to give authority as well as the Jewish Religious leaders the Sanhedrin.

5. **Local Leaders**—Sanhedrin, Saducees, Pharisees, Lawyers, Roman Military, Synagogues/ elders, Rabbis.

6. **Other**—This is a mixed era of centralized and decentralized means and authority. Jerusalem provided some means of religious centralization. There was political centralization in a number of centers. But Jesus leadership was not centralized.

Thought Questions: 1. What renewal aims did Christ specifically focus on? 2. What were the leadership selection and development processes in existence in the culture? 3. What were Jesus' leadership selection and development processes? How different? 4. How does Christ leadership compare or contrast with essential characteristics of each of the previous eras?

6th Leadership Era: Church Leadership

1. **Major Focus**—When Barnabas and Paul give their report to the elders back in Jerusalem at the Jerusalem conference described in Acts 15, there is much discussion. Finally, James summarizes the essence of the major focus of the Church leadership era, "Simon has declared how God at the first did visit the Gentiles, to take out of them a people for his name (Acts 15;14)." The central message of the book of Acts emphasizes this thrust in more detail. THE GROWTH OF THE CHURCH which spreads from Jerusalem to Judea to Samaria and the uttermost parts of the earth is seen to be of God, takes place as Spirit directed people present a salvation centered in Jesus Christ, and occurs among all peoples, Jews and Gentiles. During this leadership era, God is developing an institution that will carry His salvation to all cultures and all peoples. The development of this decentralized institution which can be fitted to any culture and people, the church, with its nature its leadership and its purposes for existing will be at the heart of this leadership era. Paul is a major architect of this leadership era. The book of 2 Corinthians is especially helpful to give us insights into early church leadership.

2. **Influence Means**—My past leadership studies have identified a number of leadership styles. In particular, I have categorized ten Pauline leadership styles. The entire range of Pauline leadership styles are demonstrated during the Church Leadership Era. The whole range of Wrong's Typology is seen including force, manipulation, authority, and persuasion power forms.

3. **Leadership Functions**—All three of the generic leadership functions are prominent: task oriented leadership, relationship oriented leadership and inspirational leadership. The major models for this era include Peter, John, and Paul with much more information given about Paul. Paul is dominantly a task-oriented leader with a powerful inspirational focus. He sees the necessity of relationship oriented leadership but that is not his strength. John is more of a relationship-oriented leader who also has a powerful inspirational thrust. Peter is dominantly a task oriented leader with inspirational thrust. As each matures they become more gentle — that is, relational leadership begins to come to the front. But always they are dominantly inspirational. God is creating new forms through which to reveal Himself to the world and followers must be inspired to participate and carry it all over the world in the face of persecution and obstacles.

4. **Followers**—The beauty of the church lies in its ability as an institutional form to fit into any culture. Since leadership in a given culture is defined in part by the followers expectations of what a leader is, we will have distinctive differences in various cultures as to leadership and followership. Each cultural situation will be different and hence have its unique demands. But there are commonalties in Biblical church leadership across cultures. This is seen especially in the values which determine why leaders operate and the standards by which they are judged. The book of 2 Corinthians helps us understand key leadership values.

5. **Local Leaders**—Various kinds of models of leadership existed in the various cultures. Paul, the main architect of local church leadership, gives us various descriptions of qualitative characteristics of leaders in his various epistles. The essential trait that flows throughout all of them is integrity. But Paul having described key character traits recognizes that these will manifest themselves differently in different cultures and situations.

6. **Other**—The church leadership era is a highly decentralized period of time. Churches are to exist in all cultures and peoples. They will be spread far and wide. Because of the decentralized nature of the church it is especially important to ask what unites it? What is common? Particularly is this important for leadership. And one of the answers is leadership values. 2 Corinthians helps us see some of the values that Paul modeled.

The Findings—The Best of Each Era

Table 39.4 summarizes some of the more important aspects of each of the leadership eras.

Table 39.4   Six Leadership Eras in the Bible—On-Going Impact Items/ Follow-Up Study

Era	On-Going Impact Items And Areas For Follow-Up Study
1. Patriarchal	Destiny leadership; Introduction of biographical study of leadership (Abraham, Isaac, Jacob, Joseph, Job); God's shaping processes introduced; intercession macro lesson introduced; character strength highlighted (Abraham, Jacob, Joseph); leadership responsibility to God instigated (accountability); leadership responsibility to followers introduced (blessing); leadership intimacy with God introduced (Abraham—friend of God, Job—trusting in deep processing). **Key Macro Lesson:** Destiny—Leaders must have a sense of destiny.
2. Pre-Kingdom	Seven Macro lessons from Moses' desert leadership (Timing; Intimacy; Intercession; Burden; Presence; Hope; Transition); Spiritual authority highlighted in Moses' and Joshua's ministries; pitfalls of centralized leadership seen; pitfalls of decentralized leadership seen; roots of inspirational leadership seen (Moses, Joshua, Caleb, Deborah, Jephthah, Samuel, David); outstanding biographical genre material. **Key Macro Lesson:** Presence—The essential ingredient of leadership is the powerful presence of God in the leader's life and ministry.
3. Kingdom	Five macros carry a warning for all future leadership (Unity; Stability; Spiritual Leadership; Recrudescence; By-Pass). Excellent biographical material both positive and negative examples (Saul, David, Asa, Josiah, Uzziah, Hezekiah, Elijah, Elisha, Jonah, Habakkuk, Ezekiel, Jeremiah and many others). **Key Macro Lesson:** Spiritual leadership can make a difference in the midst of difficult times.
4. Post-Kingdom	All five macros stress revelational perspective (Future Perfect; Perspective; Modeling; Ultimate, Perseverance). Excellent biographical genre available (Ezekiel, Daniel, Ezra, Nehemiah). **Key Macro Lesson:** Future Perfect—A primary function of all leadership is to walk by faith with a future perfect paradigm so as to inspire followers with certainty of God's accomplishment of ultimate purposes.
5. Pre-Church	Selection/ Training/ spiritual leadership/ preparation for decentralization of Spiritual Authority/ initiation of a movement. Major Biographical— Jesus' and his movement leadership. **Key Macro Lesson:** Focus—Leaders must increasingly move toward a focus in their ministry which moves toward fulfillment of their calling and their ultimate contribution to God's purposes for them.
6. Church	Decentralized leadership/ cross-cultural structures led by leaders with spiritual authority which institutionalize the movement and spread it around the world. Excellent biographical (Peter, Barnabas—a bridge leader, Paul, John); numerous leadership acts. **Key Macro Lesson:** Universal—The church structure is universal and can fit any culture. It must be propagated to all peoples.

The Foundational Transitions—Moses' And Jesus' Leadership Eras

Three figures give perspectives on Biblical leadership. Figure 39.1 illustrates the relative time involved in the six leadership eras. Figure 39.2 pinpoints distinctive features of leadership across the time-line. Figure 39.3 focuses on the two major transitions—Moses' Desert Leadership; Jesus' Movement Leadership.

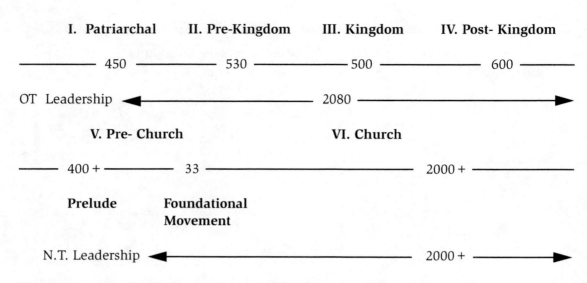

Figure 39.1   Leadership Eras—Approximate Chronological Length In Years

I. Patriarchal Leadership Roots	II. Pre-Kingdom Leadership	III. Kingdom Leadership Leadership	IV. Post-Kingdom	V. N.T. Pre-Church	VI. Church Leadership
A. Abraham	A. Desert	A. United	A. Exile	A. Pre-Messianic	A. Jewish
B. Isaac	B. Conquering The Land	B. Divided	B. Post Exile	B. Messianic	B. Gentile
C. Jacob	C. Conquered By the Land	C. Single	C. Interim		
D. Joseph					
E. Job					
Family	Revelatory Task Inspirational	Political Corrective	Modeling Renewal	Cultic Spiritual Movement	Spiritual Institutional
Blessing	(Timing)	Unity	Hope	Training	Structure
Shaping	Presence	Stability	Perspective	Focus	Universal
Timing	Intimacy	Spiritual	Modeling	Spirituality	Giftedness
Destiny	Burden	Leadership	Ultimate	Servant	Word
Character Centered	Hope	Recrudescence	Perseverance		Steward
Faith	Challenge	By-Pass			Harvest
Purity	Spiritual Authority Transition Weakness Continuity			Shepherd Movement	

Figure 39.2   Overview Time-Line of Biblical Leadership

In Figure 39.2 above, macro lesson labels occur at the bottom in the six columns. Just above the macro lesson labels are given distinctive characteristics of each of the eras. Finally, above that occurs the outline of the sub-time periods and the major time-line with the six eras.

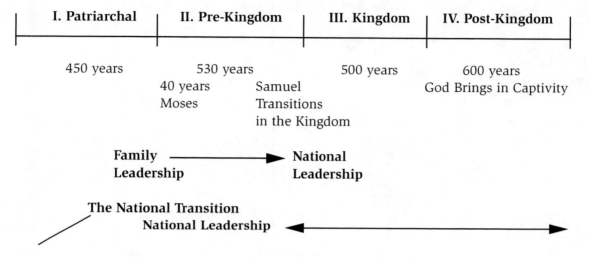

Crucial Macro Lessons: 3. Timing, 8. Intercession, 9. Presence, 10. Intimacy, 11. Burden, 12. Hope, 13. Challenge, 14. Spiritual Authority, 15. Transition.

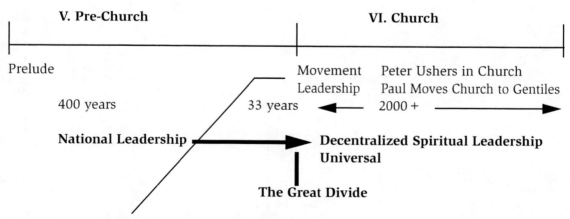

Crucial Macro Lessons: 28. Selection, 29. Training, 30. Focus, 31. Spirituality, 32. Servant, 33. Steward, 34. Harvest, 35. Shepherd, 36. Movement.

Figure 39.3 Two Major Transitions—The National Transition and The Great Divide

Note two things. These major transition times were short. God brought in major changes in a short period of time. Both transition times contain a large number of important macro lessons. For such short periods of time these are relatively large numbers of important leadership lessons.

Table 39.5 lists the transitions and key figures and the result of the transition.

Table 39.5   Transitions Along the Biblical Leadership Time-Line

Transition	Eras Involved	Key Figure/ Results
To God Directed Leadership	Begin Patriarchal Era	Abraham/ a God directed destiny involving an ethnic group and leaders from that group hearing God, getting revelation from Him, and obeying God.
Tribal to National	From the Patriarchal Era to the Pre-Kingdom Era	Moses/ A nation is established. God established concept of influential leader with spiritual authority to direct the nation; God reveals truth about Himself, life, and destiny for this nation. Major leadership guidelines (important macro lessons) flow through this transitional leadership.
Federation to Kingdom	Pre-Kingdom to Kingdom	Samuel/ A dispersed geographical/tribal society, each doing its own thing and basically not following God-given truth, is moved toward a centralized, unified national entity directed by one major leader—a king, who is to direct the nation with God's direction.
Babylonian Captivity	From Kingdom to Post-Kingdom	God/ God dismantles the kingdom structure. He disperses the followers. God by-passes the kingdom leadership altogether and begins a long preparation that will eventually emerge in spiritual leadership. In this era, individual spiritual leadership is highlighted in which God's perspective is crucial.
The Great Divide	From Post-Kingdom to Pre-Church. From a defunct national leadership to spiritual leadership which can be decentralized anywhere.	Jesus/ Jesus re-established God-directed leadership—the concept of the Kingdom of God. God by-passes the Jewish national leadership when they reject Him—i.e. His message through Jesus. Jesus at the same time of offering the kingdom also builds the foundational roots of a movement which will eventually contextualize the Kingdom of God in an institutional church form which can move into any culture on earth.
Universal Invitation	From Pre-Church to Church	Peter, Paul/ Peter ushers in the church to the Jewish followers of Jesus. Paul takes the church to the Gentiles. God's invitation of salvation and His truth for living God-directed lives become available (decentralized) to any people on the earth.

Note that that there are transition times between all the eras. Each of these are important in themselves but two stand out: Moses' Desert-Leadership; Jesus' Movement-Leadership. As is sometimes the case crucial transitions in the Bible are foundational. God focuses intently in these times and usually reveals foundational truth. Such is the case with all the transitions.

Tables 39.6 and 39.7 give the macro lessons discovered in these key transition times with suggested implications for today.

Table 39.6   Moses' Transition / Lessons / Implications

Timing —	God's timing is crucial to accomplishment of God's purposes. **Implication**(s): Leaders today, especially in their complex ministries involving multi-cultural settings, must be more sensitive to the timing of God than ever before.
Intercession —	Leaders called to a ministry are called to intercede for that ministry. **Implication**(s): Various prayer movements have gained tremendous momentum in our day testifying to the fact that God sees this as a very important aspect of leadership in our day.
Presence —	The essential ingredient of leadership is the powerful presence of God in the leader's life and ministry. **Implication**(s): Much present day leadership misses the balance of this—God both in powerful ministry and in powerful life changing impact in the leader himself/herself.
Intimacy —	Leaders develop intimacy with God which in turn overflows into all their ministry since ministry flows out of being. **Implication**(s): Doing and achievement dominate present day leadership. God through the various spirituality movements is calling leaders back to spirituality and beingness as the core of their ministries.
Burden —	Leaders feel a responsibility to God for their ministry. **Implication**(s): Accountability is missing altogether in most cultures. This is true of Christian leadership as well. Sensitivity to this needed ingredient would avoid many of the leadership gaffes that are seen.
Hope —	A primary function of all leadership is to inspire followers with hope in God and in what God is doing. **Implication**(s): This is especially true for leaders trying to reach Xers—generally without hope. But it is needed in all ministries as complex situations tend to take away hope for most Christians.
Challenge —	Leaders receive vision from God which sets before them challenges that inspire their leadership. **Implication**(s): A leader must hear from God if that leader is to influence specific groups of people toward God's purposes—the basic definition of a leader. This is deeply needed especially in the many small churches which are floundering in our day.
Spiritual — Authority	Spiritual authority is the dominant power base of a spiritual leader and comes through experiences with God, knowledge of God, godly character and gifted power. **Implication**(s): Abuse of power is one of the five major barriers facing leaders today. There are lots of leaders with all kinds of authority but few who exercise spiritual authority as a primary power base (with all its implications).
Transition —	Leaders must transition other leaders into their work in order to maintain continuity and effectiveness. **Implication**(s): Every work of God is just one generation away from failure if it does not transition emerging leaders into its decision-making influential positions.

Table 39.7   Jesus' Transition / Lessons / Implications

Selection —	The key to good leadership is the selection of good potential leaders which should be a priority of all leaders. **Implication**(s): Leadership selection is desperately needed in church and parachurch organizations. Recruitment is often haphazard at best, especially in local church situations.
Training —	Leaders should deliberately train potential leaders in their ministry by available and appropriate means. **Implication**(s): If emerging new leaders are not developed they will exit organizations and go somewhere else, depriving churches and parachurch organizations of on-going leadership. Leading with a developmental bias is the key to seeing on-going recruitment and longevity in organizational life.
Focus —	Leaders should increasingly move toward a focus in their ministry which moves toward fulfillment of their calling and their ultimate contribution to God's purposes for them. **Implication**(s): Focused leaders are few and far between. Most leaders are faddish leaders jumping on the bandwagon of other apparently successful leaders. What is needed is leaders, knowing their own focus, and following it. Focused leaders are the need of the hour.
Spirituality —	Leaders must develop interiority, spirit sensitivity, and fruitfulness in accord with their uniqueness since ministry flows out of being. **Implication**(s): As previously seen with the intimacy lesson from Moses' era, spirituality is crucial to leadership. And what is true of intimacy, one aspect of spirituality, is true as leaders develop balanced spirituality. Doing and achievement dominate present day leadership. God through the various spirituality movements is calling leaders back to spirituality and beingness as the core of their ministries.
Servant —	Leaders must maintain a dynamic tension as they lead by serving and serve by leading. **Implication**(s): Servant leadership is not naturally found in any culture. It requires a paradigm shift for any leader to move into this leadership model—which is what Jesus intended for leaders he developed. Because of accepted leadership patterns in some cultures (great power distance) this is really difficult for emerging leaders to see or accept.
Steward —	Leaders are endowed by God with natural abilities, acquired skills, spiritual gifts, opportunities, experiences, and privileges which must be developed and used for God. **Implication**(s): Accountability is greatly needed in our generation where successful leaders dominantly self-authenticate their own ministries and heed little or nothing from outside resources which could hold them accountable.
Harvest —	Leaders must seek to bring people into relationship with God. **Implication**(s): The outward aspect of the Great Commission must be carried out. God is focusing on this as He continues to raise up missionary movements from all over the world. The impetus of the missionary movement has already moved from the western world to the non-western world. We need to support this while at the same time bringing about renewal of missionary thinking in the western world.
Shepherd —	Leaders must preserve, protect, and develop God's people. **Implication**(s): God still gets most of the leadership business done at local church level. Leaders who hold to the shepherd model concepts must in fact carry local church ministries—especially as cultures become more radically opposed to Gospel values. This means that more pastoral work will be necessary if we are winning those from deteriorating cultures.
Movement —	Leaders recognize that movements are the way to penetrate society though they must be preserved via appropriate on-going institutions. **Implication**(s): New life can be instilled in parachurch organizations and churches when movement ideals are focused on. We see all around us movement leaders being raised up by God who are creating new ministries which God is blessing. This can be done more deliberately and proactively when movement dynamics are heeded.

Conclusion

The Six Leadership Eras and the seven leadership genre provide major perspectives for studying leadership in the Bible. Of particular importance are two of the leadership genre—the *macro lessons* across each leadership era and the Bible *books as a whole*. The macro lessons flowing from Moses' desert leadership and Jesus' movement foundations are particularly instructive. They apply with great force to today's leadership challenges.

See **Articles**, *Biographical Study in the Bible—How To Do; Bible Centered Leader; Leadership Act; Leadership Eras in the Bible—Six Identified; Leadership Genre—Seven Types; Macro Lessons Defined; Macro Lessons—List of 41 Across Six Leadership Eras; Principle of Truth.*

Article 40

Spiritual Authority—Six Characteristics

A Biblical leader is a person with God-given capacities and with God-given responsibility who is influencing specific groups of God's people toward God's purposes for them. To influence, a leader must have some power base. I am indebted to Dennis Wrong[146] for helping me identify a taxonomy of concepts dealing with power. Wrong has influence as the highest level on his taxonomy, power next, and authority third. Influence can be unintended or intended. In terms of leadership we are interested in intended influence. Intended influence can be subdivided into four power forms, the second level: Force, Manipulation, Authority, and Persuasion. All of these are important for Christian leaders with the final two being the most important—authority and persuasion—since spiritual authority is related to both. Authority, the third level, can further be sub-divided into coercive, inducive, legitimate, competent, personal. A leader will need to use various combinations of these power forms to influence people. However,

Effective leaders value spiritual authority as a primary power base.

This is one of seven major leadership lessons that I have identified from comparative study of effective leaders. This article defines spiritual authority and gives some guidelines about its use.

Spiritual Authority—What Is It?

Spiritual authority is the ideal power base for a leader to use with mature believers who respect God's authority in a leader. A simplified definition focusing on the notion of maturity of believers is:

Definition   *Spiritual authority* is the

- right to influence,
- conferred upon a leader by followers,
- because of their perception of spirituality
  in that leader.

An expanded definition focusing on how a leader gets and uses it is:

---

146. See Dennis H. Wrong, **Power—Its Forms, Bases, and Uses**. 1979. San Francisco, CA: Harper and Row.

Definition
Spiritual Authority is that
- characteristic of a God-anointed leader,
- developed upon an experiential power base (giftedness, character, deep experiences with God),

that enables him/her to influence followers through

- persuasion,
- force of modeling, and
- moral expertise.

Spiritual authority comes to a leader in three major ways. As leaders go through deep experiences with God they experience the sufficiency of God to meet them in those situations. They come to know God. This experiential knowledge of God and the deep experiences with God are part of the experiential acquisition of spiritual authority. A second way that spiritual authority comes is through a life which models godliness. When the Spirit of God is transforming a life into the image of Christ those characteristics of love, joy, peace, long suffering, gentleness, goodness, faith, meekness, temperance carry great weight in giving credibility that the leader is consistent inward and outward. A third way that spiritual authority comes is through gifted power. When a leader can demonstrate gifted power in ministry—that is, a clear testimony to divine intervention in the ministry via his/her gifts—there will be spiritual authority. Now while all three of these ways of getting spiritual authority should be a part of a leader, it is frequently the case that one or more of the elements dominates. From the definitions and description of how spiritual authority comes you can readily see that a leader using spiritual authority does not force his/her will on followers.

What Are Some Guidelines—To Maximize Use and Minimize Abuse

The following descriptive characteristics about spiritual authority sets some limits, describe ideals, warn against abuse and in general gives helpful guidelines for leaders who desire spiritual authority as a primary means of influence.

Six Characteristics And Limits Of Spiritual Authority

These six descriptions were derived from my own observations of leaders and from adaptations made from several writers on power such as Watchman Nee, R. Baine Harris, and Richard T. De George. Nee was a Chinese Christian leader. The other two are secular authorities on power and authority in leadership.

Table 40.1   Six Characteristics of Spiritual Authority

Characteristic	Statement
1. Ultimate Source	Spiritual authority has its ultimate source in Christ. It is representative religious authority. It is His authority and presence in us which legitimates our authority. Accountability to this final authority is essential.
2. Power Base	Spiritual authority rests upon an experiential power base. A leader's personal experiences with God and the accumulated wisdom and development that comes through them lie at the heart of the reason why followers allow influence in their lives. It is a resource which is at once on-going and yet related to the past. Its genuineness as to the reality of experience with God is confirmed in the believer by the presence and ministry of the Holy Spirit who authenticates that experiential power base.
3. Power Forms	Spiritual authority influences by virtue of persuasion. Word gifts are dominant in this persuasion. Influence is by virtue of legitimate authority. Positional leadership carries with it recognition of qualities of leadership which are at least initially recognized by followers. Such authority must be buttressed by other authority forms such as competent authority, and personal authority.
4. Ultimate Good	The aim of influence using spiritual authority is the ultimate good of the followers. This follows the basic Pauline leadership principle seen in 2Co 10:8.
5. Evaluation	Spiritual authority is best judged longitudinally over time in terms of development of maturity in believers. Use of coercive and manipulative forms of authority will usually reproduce like elements in followers. Spiritual authority will produce mature followers who will make responsible moral choices because they have learned to do so.
6. Non-Defensive	A leader using spiritual authority recognizes submission to God who is the ultimate authority. Authority is representative. God is therefore the responsible agent for defending spiritual authority. A person moving in spiritual authority does not have to insist on obedience. Obedience is the moral responsibility of the follower. Disobedience, that is, rebellion to spiritual authority, means that a follower is not subject to God Himself. He/she will answer to God for that. The leader can rest upon God's vindication if it is necessary.

Remember,

Effective leaders value spiritual authority as a primary power base.[147]

See power forms (various definitions), **Glossary**. See **Articles**, *Influence, Power, and Authority Forms; Leadership Lessons—Seven Major Identified.*

[147.] They also know that it will take varied forms of power including coercive, inducive, positional, personal, competence and others to influence immature believers toward maturity. But the ideal is always there to use spiritual authority with mature believers.

Spiritual Gift Clusters

Introduction

All Christians have at least one spiritual gift.

Definition

A *spiritual gift* is a *God-given* unique capacity imparted to each believer for the purpose of releasing a Holy Spirit empowered ministry via that believer.

While this is true for the body in general, leaders usually are multi-gifted. Over their time of ministry experience, at any one given time, they will be repeatedly exercising a combination of gifts. The set of gifts that a leader is demonstrating at any given time is important. It has a special label

Definition

A *gift-mix* is a label that refers to the set of spiritual gifts being used by a leader at any given time in his/her ministry.

Just as most leaders are multi-gifted and have a gift-mix, so too churches as a whole and Christian organizations as a whole corporately reflect gift-mixes. One way to assess this corporate gift-mix is to use a three fold category of giftings. These categories originated out of a study of Paul's affirmation to churches (corporate groups) for their impact on their surrounding communities. These affirmations occurred in an almost formula-like way in many of his salutations in his epistles. His full affirmation formula included faith, love, and hope. With some churches he would give partial affirmation. And with one church, with which he was extremely displeased he gave no affirmation at all. A study of these affirmations led to the identification of the functions implied in them: faith—the ability to believe in the unseen God (the function of the POWER gifts) , love—the manifestation of the reality of the unseen God in the lives of those who know Him (the function of the LOVE gifts), hope—the expectation of what He is doing; that is, the clarification of who He is, what He desires and what He is doing (the function of the WORD gifts).

The identification of clusters of gifts that did those functions followed as did the actual naming of them as **WORD, POWER,** and **LOVE** clusters. This identification of clusters led to the correlation between Word gifts and leadership. *All leaders we had studied always had at least one word gift in their gift-mix; many had more than one.* This idea is a powerful implication for the selection and development of leaders.

The notion of spiritual gift clusters provides a special perspective, in fact a tool, that can aid strategic planning for a corporate group.

Three Corporate Functions Of Gifts: Word, Power, Love

These three crucial corporate functions were called power gifts, word gifts and love gifts and are described and illustrated as follows.

Description	*Power gifts* demonstrate the authenticity, credibility, power and reality of the unseen God.
Examples	miracles, kinds of healings, word of knowledge
Description	*Love gifts* are manifestations attributed to God through practical ways that can be recognized by a world around us which needs love. They demonstrate the reality of relating to this God.
Example	mercy, helps, pastoring
Description	*Word gifts* clarify the nature of this unseen God and what He expects from His followers. People using these gifts both communicate about God and for God.
Example	exhortation, teaching, prophecy

Pictorial View of the Three Corporate Functions: Word, Power, Love

Below in Figure 41.1, given in pictorial form,[148] are the three clusters, along with the individual gifts that aid these functions. Notice some gifts operate in more than one cluster.

Figure 41.1   Power, Love And Word Gifts Pictured

---

148. This is technically called a Venn diagram. All of the gifts listed in a circle belong to that circle. Where there is overlap, it means that the gifts in the overlap belong to both circles involved in the overlap (or all three circles as the case may be).

Power gifts =	faith, word of knowledge, discernings of spirits, miracles, tongues, interpretation of tongues, healing, word of wisdom, prophecy. These all help demonstrate the reality of the unseen God.
Love gifts =	governments, giving, mercy, helps, pastoring, evangelism, healing, word of wisdom, word of knowledge. These all demonstrate the beauty of that unseen God's work in lives in such a way as to attract others to want this same kind of relationship.
Word gifts =	exhortation, teaching, apostleship, ruling, prophecy, faith, pastor, evangelism, word of wisdom, word of knowledge. These all help us understand about this God including His nature, His purposes and how we can relate to Him and be a part of His purposes.

Figure 41.1   Power, Love And Word Gifts Legend

The Notion of Balance

Balance describes a proper relationship between manifestations of love, word, and power clusters operating in a given context so that God's witness in that situation can be adequate. Balance does not mean equality or equal amounts of gifts. Balance means having the appropriate mix of word, power, and love gifts for God to accomplish His purposes through the group to the people of its geographic area.

In the three profiles shown below an oval labeled with A means a **Word cluster.** An oval with B means a **love cluster.** An oval with C means a **power cluster.**

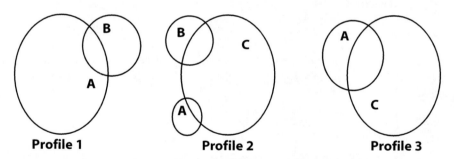

Profile 1   Profile 2   Profile 3

Figure 41.2   Three Example of Corporate Mixes of Word, Power, Love

Profile 1 represents a church with a strong word ministry—since there is absolutely no power it means dominantly teaching and exhortation gifts. This would be a typical Bible Church. It has some compassion ministry but it is clear that it is dominantly a classroom type of church. The love cluster is about half within and half without the church. This means that there are probably a number of helps and governments gifts operating in the church doing service ministries and a number of mercy, helps types reaching out of the church. This church could use some power gifts in order to break through and reach new people for Christ. Its leadership gifts are probably pastoral and teaching. There could be some evangelism. No apostolic or prophetic types would probably be welcome here.

Profile 2 is church which has strong power gifts. Since it has power gifts there will be some word ministry through the prophetical, word of knowledge, word of wisdom gifts. It has very little word gifts which means that for the most part there will be little teaching and any exhortation would be in terms of the power gifts. It also has some love gifts working both in and out of the church — more outside than in. But its minimum word gifts means probably no Sunday School ministries so it probably doesn't need as many helps and governments inside the church. The question is how to get word gifts in here. There will probably be a big back door in this church. The leadership gifts in this church are probably apostolic, maybe evangelistic, maybe prophetic. There is probably a need for pastoral ministry and certainly a need for a teaching/ discipleship ministry.

Profile 3 is a church dominated with power gifts but one which has some ministry in the word. This means the leadership gifts in the church are probably apostolic and prophetical with possibly some teaching and a little pastoring. What is probably missing is an evangelistic thrust—no love gifts working. This church probably is having a hard time getting people to do ministry jobs in the church.

If I were to ask you how would you assess balance in each of the three profiles? What would you say? You could say it is unfair to ask. Balance determines whether or not the cluster fits the situation. You would need to know the contextual situations. For example, if Profile A was in the highlands of Papua New Guinea it would extremely out of balance—for power gifts are needed to get a hearing. But if it were in an early start-up church plant in a bedroom community of middle to upper middle class business types it would be appropriate. Profile 3 might be appropriate for early ministry in an inner-city location since power is needed to get breakthroughs. But later on this church will not keep its members till it develops a teaching/ discipleship thrust which need word gifts.

Conclusion

Spiritual gift clusters provide a tool for assessing development in a church. A church should know its people in terms of their gifts. Strategic planning will need this kind of assessment.

See giftedness set, spiritual gifts, various gift definitions, **Glossary**. See **Article**, Developing Giftedness.

Spiritual Gifts, Giftedness, and Development

Introduction

All Christians have at least one spiritual gift.

Definition
: A *spiritual gift* is a *God-given* unique capacity imparted to each believer for the purpose of releasing a Holy Spirit empowered ministry via that believer.

While this is true for the body in general, leaders usually are multi-gifted. Over their time of ministry experience, at any one given time, they will repeatedly exercise a combination of gifts. The set of gifts that a leader is demonstrating at any given time is important. It has a special label

Definition
: A *gift-mix* is a label that refers to the set of spiritual gifts being used by a leader at any given time in his/her ministry.

My research on leaders and giftedness and my Biblical studies on *The Stewardship Leadership Model* resulted in the concept of the giftedness set.

Definition
: The *giftedness set* describes natural abilities, acquired skills, and spiritual gifts which a leader has as resources to use in ministry. Sometimes shortened to giftedness.

Ministry flows out of beingness. Beingness describes the inner life of a person and refers to intimacy with God, character, personality, giftedness, destiny, values drawn from experience, gender influenced perspectives. The axiom, ministry flows out of being means that one's ministry should be a vital outflow from these inner beingness factors. Giftedness is a strong factor in beingness.

Out of my study also emerged the following observation,

> **When Christ Calls Leaders To Christian Ministry He Intends To Develop Them To Their Full Potential. Each Of Us In Leadership Is Responsible To Continue Developing In Accordance With God's Processing All Our Lives.**

This article deals with the notion of the giftedness set and suggests that a leader can develop himself/herself over a lifetime—a strong value flowing from the Stewardship model.[149]

Giftedness Set

God endows a leader with natural abilities and later spiritual gifts. Along the way leaders pick up acquired skills. Comparative studies[150] resulted in a time-line which describes how the process develops over time. Figure 42.1 shows this.

I. Sovereign Foundations	II. Growth Ministry	III. Focused Ministry	IV. Convergent Ministry
	Transition into Ministry		
Natural Abilities	Occasional Late Blooming Natural Ability		
Acquired Skills	Acquired Skills	Occasional Important Acquired Skill	
	Occasional Spiritual	Gift Needed for Effective Ministry	
	Early Dominant IndicationsSpiritual SpiritualGifts GiftsEmerge	Gift-Mix Firmed Up Giftedness Set Firmed Up	Giftedness Set Developed and Used With Great Effectiveness

Figure 42.1   Giftedness Development Over Time

As the giftedness set begins to emerge, a leader soon finds that one component of the set dominates the others. The other two components supplement or synergize with the dominant element.

Definition   The dominate component of a giftedness set—either natural abilities, acquired skills, or spiritual gifts is called the *focal element*.

About 50% of leaders studied in the research have spiritual gifts as focal. Another 35%

[149.] Stewardship values which relate to giftedness include: 1. Leaders ought to build upon abilities, skills, and gifts to maximize potential and use for God. 2. Leaders should recognize that they will be uniquely gifted both as to gifts and the degree to which the gift can be used effectively. 3. Leaders should know that they will receive rewards for their productivity and for zealously using abilities, skills, gifts, and opportunities for God. See **Article**, *Jesus—Five Leadership Models: Shepherd, Harvest, Steward, Servant, Intercessor.*

[150.] For almost 10 years,1985-1995, I studied leaders with a focus on giftedness analysis. The heart of this article flows out of that research. See **For Further Study Bibliography**, Clinton and Clinton, **Unlocking Your Giftedness—What Leaders Need To Know To Develop Themselves and Others.**

have natural abilities as focal. About 15% have acquired skills as focal. This is important self-knowledge for a leader who wants to develop and wants ministry to flow out of being-ness.

It is toward the notion of giftedness set developed and used effectively that I am talking when I say that Christ intends to develop a leader to full potential.

Development—What Does It Mean

A leader can not develop natural abilities. These are givens, innate with their person-hood. Though a leader may discover some latent natural ability later in life due to circumstances of ministry. Can a leader develop a spiritual gift? The answer is not certain from Biblical evidence. But certainly a leader can develop acquired skills and can develop synergizing issues related to spiritual gifts.

Definition   *Development* of a leader means an increase in efficiency and effectiveness in ministry due to addition of skills or other issues which enhance the leader's use of natural abilities, acquired skills, or spiritual gifts in ministry.

My research studies show that leaders develop their giftedness due to programmatic means (designed training), happenstance (day-to-day learning in the normal course of life's activities and processes), and by deliberate development (disciplined self-initiated learning).

Deliberate development takes place through formal or informal apprenticeships or other mentoring relationships, personal growth projects, and/or some identified plan of growth. Deliberate development ought to be the norm for a leader who has a developmental bias.

Studies into each of the leadership gifts[151] (Apostleship, Pastoral, Evangelism, Teacher, Prophecy, Exhortation) from a developmental perspective have resulted in numerous suggestions for development for each of the gifts.[152]

Conclusion

Leaders can develop over a lifetime. It happens. But with an awareness of how development can happen, a leader can much more efficiently develop, when self-knowledge and self-initiative are taken.

[151.] These are the primary gifts in the Word Cluster. All leaders have at least one of these words gifts and usually are multi-gifted. See **Article**, *Spiritual Gift Clusters*.

[152.] See **For Further Study Bibliography**, Clinton and Clinton, **Unlocking Your Giftedness**, ch 10, pages 251-280, where suggestions for developing spiritual gifts of the Word Cluster are given. It is beyond the scope of this article to give these suggestions since the suggestions run to 30 pages by themselves.

Article 43

Starting Point Plus Process Model[153]

The book of Philemon suggested some principles under the label social issue. In that book, the whole social institution of slavery was being undermined by Christian values. The two principles about social change that were listed include:

a. One means for overcoming a social evil is to undermine it at value level. Many Christian values speak to social issues.

b. Major social change will take a long time to implement. One of the reasons for this is the way God works to bring about change in a culture. The starting point plus process model seeks to identify God's methodology for changing cultures and cultural practices.

The Starting Point Plus Process model, outlines 4 major assertions suggesting how God brings about change in cultures and cultural practices. The basic motif is that *God begins where people are and progressively reveals Himself and applicable truth to move them toward supracultural ideals.*

Four Major Assertions

1. Assuming a valid faith-allegiance response,[154] God allows for a range of understanding of Himself and His Will for people, for He starts where people are rather than demanding that they immediately conform to His ideals.

2. This range of understanding of God can assume a variety of potential starting points anywhere from sub-ideal toward ideal perception of God and His ways.

3. God then initiates a process which involves a revelational progression from a sub-ideal starting point toward the ideal.

4. This process of beginning with a range of sub-ideal starting points of perception and behavior and moving by revelational progression from the sub-ideal toward the ideal can be applied to any doctrine of Scripture and any Scriptural treatment of behavioral patterns.

---

153. This model is adapted from C.H. Kraft's *Christianity and Culture.*

154. By a faith-allegiance response is meant a valid decision to place God as top priority in a life—a trusting response for God's salvation and work in a life.

Marriage Example

Unacceptable Starting Points Concerning Marriage Behavior	Sub-ideal But Acceptable Starting Points Concerning Marriage Behavior	Toward Ideal Concerning Marriage Behavior

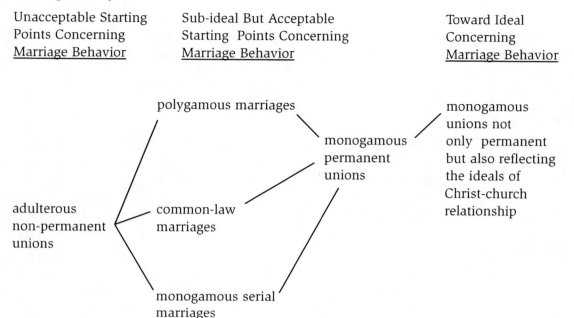

Figure 43.1   Starting Point Plus Process Model-Marriage

As can be seen above, God works in a cultural situation to move toward the ideal on the right. Assuming that a group within a culture has come to Christ and are giving allegiance to Him above all else, God will begin to work. But assume they are at the far left. God will reject the starting point and immediately move that group toward a sub-ideal position. God will move them over time further right toward the sub-ideal and eventually toward the ideal. This is actually the Biblical record of how God worked on marriage in the Old and New Testament. God does not expect immediate attainment toward an ideal but movement toward it. It took hundreds of years to move toward the ideal of monogamous unions not only permanent but reflecting the ideals of Christ-church relationship.

Slavery—A Typical Example

This same *starting point plus process model* can be applied to many kinds of issues and doctrines in which a given culture or society fall short of Biblical ideals. For example, consider the slavery issue. This is a sub-ideal position with regard to the view of a human being made in God's image. So God begins by accepting the viewpoint of slavery but works to improve the conditions under which it takes place. Then He works to eliminate it in its varied forms (actual slavery; pseudo-slavery like Mexican immigrant workers illegally in the United States, child slaves sold into sexual prostitution in Asia, etc.). Then He works to eliminate ethnic prejudice, a subtle form of corporate slavery. And so on, until He obtains the ideal of interdependency between various ethnic groups with respect for all individuals and groups as made in the image of God.

Women in Leadership—Another Example

Or consider gender and leadership. I believe that *the starting point plus process model* is seen at work again as God moves from sub-ideal positions on females in some cultures where they are only slightly better than chattel all the way across to the ideal where men and women are equal in standing before God and others (at least due to gender alone) and where men or women are leaders depending on calling and gifting.

Conclusion

We must not expect immediate perfection on some truth in the Scriptures by groups new to this truth, especially when it has taken years to bring the church to this position. And what is true with corporate groups like churches and parachurches is true of individuals. We should expect to reject positions that are less than sub-ideal. But we should be willing to patiently work to move people from sub-ideal to ideal.

Acknowledgment

This model was first identified by one of my colleagues, Dr. Charles H. Kraft in his book on ethnotheology, entitled *Christianity in Culture*. The above description of his model is my adapted version taken from my doctoral dissertation.

See **Article**, *Gender and Leadership*

Time Line—Paul

A major leadership genre is the biographical source. Below is given 12 steps to use for studying this source. Notice steps two and three in Table 44.1 below.

Table 44.1   Twelve Steps For Doing Biographical Study

Step	General Guideline
1	Identify All The Passages That Refer To The Leader.
2	Seek To Order The Vignettes Or Other Type Passages In A Time Sequence.
3	Construct A Time-Line If You Can. At Least Tentatively Identify The Major Development Phases In The Leader's Life.
4	Look For Shaping Events And Activities (technically called process items, or critical incidents).
5	Identify Pivotal Points From The Major Process Items Or Critical Incidents.
6	Seek To Determine Any Lessons You Can From A Study Of These Process Items Or Pivotal Points.
7	Identify Any Response Patterns Or Any Unique Patterns As You Analyze The Life Across A Time-Line.
8	Study Any Individual Leadership Acts In The Life.
9	Use The Three Overall Leadership Categories To Help Suggest Leadership Issues To Look For (leadership basal elements, leadership influence means, leadership value bases).
10	Use The List Of Major Functions (task functions, relationship functions, and inspirational functions) to Help Suggest Insights. Which were done, which not.
11	Observe Any New Testament Passages Or Commentary On The Leader. Especially Be On The Lookout For Bent Of Life Evaluation.
12	Use The Presentation Format For Findings On Bible Leaders To Help You Organize Your Results.

This article briefly describes steps two and three. A time-line is the end result of applying steps 2 & 3. Time-lines provide an integrating framework upon which to measure development in the life, to organize findings, and to pinpoint when shaping activities occur in a life.

Important Definitions for Time-Lines

Definition	The *time-line* is the linear display along a horizontal axis which is broken up into development phases.
Definition	A *unique time-line* refers to a time-line describing a given leader's lifetime which will have unique development phases bearing labels expressing that uniqueness.
Definition	A *development phase* is a marked off length on a time-line representing a significant portion of time in a leader's life history in which notable development takes place. Example Below has 4 development phases indicated by Roman Letters I, II, III, IV.
Definition	A *sub-phase* is a marked off length on a time-line within a development phase which points out intermediate times of development during the development phase. In the Example below Development phase III. has 3 sub-phases indicated by A, B, and C.

All leaders can describe a time-line that is unique to them. A unique time-line is broken up into divisions called development phases which terminate with boundary events. Development phases can themselves be subdivided into smaller units called sub-phases which have smaller boundary terminations.

Below is given the Apostle Paul's time-line with several findings about his life displayed. Paul's life, ministry, and development. I have also numerous other findings about Paul's life, ministry and development located on his time-line. Such things as; pivotal points, mentoring, development of life purpose, development of major role, isolation processing, other process items such as—paradigm shift, leadership committal, double confirmation, divine contact, conflict, crises, ministry conflict, word, obedience, integrity check. Time-lines are very useful to give perspective and force one to see across a whole lifetime of development.

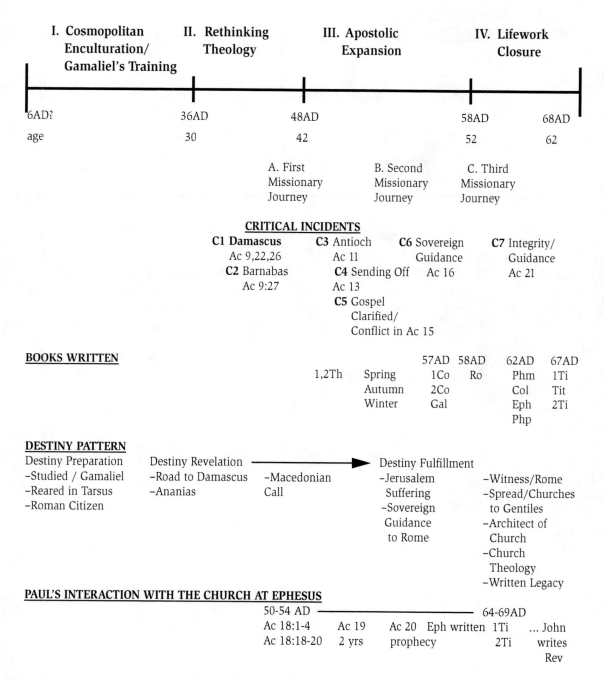

Figure 44.1   The Apostle Paul's Time-Line

For **Further study**: See paper, *Getting Perspective by Using Your Time-Line* listed in the **For Further Study Bibliography**. See also **Article,** *7 Leadership Genre*; **See Section Time Lines of Biblical Leaders.**

Timothy—A Beloved Son in the Faith

Effective leaders view relationships in ministry as both a means and an end.

This is one of seven major lessons that I have derived from comparative study of effective leaders. Probably in no leader in the Bible, other than Jesus, is this seen any plainer, than in the life and ministry of Paul the Apostle. Paul was a strong task oriented leader. But he knew the value of relationships. In his epistles he lists almost 80 people by name whom he had personal relationships with. Paul believed that he ought to personally relate to those around him in ministry. It was good in itself. It was good to accomplish ministry too. Paul indicates this notion of a strong relationship when he uses the phrases: *my own son in the faith, my beloved son, as a son with the father, son, dearly beloved son, my son, own son after the common faith, my son.* For three—Timothy, Titus, and Onesimus—it meant strong intimate relationships. Table 45.1 lists the instances and uses of these strong, special, intimate relationships by Paul.

Table 45.1   Paul and Intimate Relationships

Reference	Phrase	Who	Use
1Co 4:17	who is my beloved son	Timothy	Sponsoring Timothy to the Corinthians so they will receive him with respect as Paul's representative.
Php 2:22	as a son with the father	Timothy	Sponsoring Timothy to the Philippians so they will receive him with respect as Paul's representative.
1Ti 1:2	[my] own son in the faith	Timothy	Greeting of encouragement to Timothy personally.
1Ti 1:18	son	Timothy	Exhortation to Timothy to boldly act as a leader in a tough situation remembering the prophecies and operating with a clean conscience.
2Ti 1:2	[my] dearly beloved son	Timothy	Greeting of encouragement. The most intimate of all the phrases.
2Ti 2:1	my son	Timothy	An exhortation to go on, drawing on the enabling grace found in union with Christ

| Tit 1:4 | [mine] own son after the common faith | Titus | A word of encouragement; a word sponsoring Titus before the Cretian believers. |
| Phm 1:10 | my son | Onesimus | Sponsoring of Onesimus to Philemon. Shows how strongly Paul believed in him. |

Let me suggest an exercise for you. Go back and read each of the references listed in Table 45.1. Read the surrounding context as well. And imagine you are Timothy hearing those words or Titus or Onesimus. How would you feel to hear such words? Paul knew the motivational importance of affirmation. And a personal strong intimate relationship expressed openly to the person not only affirms but motivates them.

Table 45.1 shows that Timothy was Paul's closest associate. He was a beloved and true son in the faith. Leaders need to pass on their heritage. They need to leave behind ultimate contributions. One sure way of doing this is to have relationships with those to whom they minister and with whom they minister. Values are passed on. Ministry methodology, though adapted, lives on. Vision is caught and lives on.

Effective leaders view relationship as both a means and an end in ministry.

Paul did. Who are your true sons and daughters? Who will carry on your values, ministry philosophy, and vision?

Titus and Ministry Tasks

Introduction

Titus is one of three mentorees very close to Paul.[155] He was a Gentile Greek, probably from Syrian Antioch.[156] Paul probably led him to Christ (see Acts 11:26 and implications of Titus 1:4). Paul was very close to Titus. Note the sobriquets Paul uses with Titus;

Table 46.1 Paul's Descriptive Phrases Identifying Titus

Descriptive Phrase	Location
His true son in the faith	Titus 1:4
His spiritual brother	2 Co 2:13
His partner and fellow helper	2 Co 8:23
A positive role model	2 Co 8:23

In fact, a glance at all of the times Titus is mentioned will prove instructive.

Table 46.2 Titus Mentioned in Scripture—15 Times

Location	Implications/ Other Comments
2Co 2:13	Paul is close to Titus. Considers him a spiritual brother. Titus has been sent on a mission (crisis in Paul's leadership) to the Corinthians and Paul awaits his answer, anxiously.
2 Co 7:6	Titus has returned with news about the Corinthian crisis. It is good news. And a great comfort to Paul. The first epistle to the Corinthians had borne fruit.
2 Co 7:13	Titus was refreshed with joy in his ministry at Corinth. It could have been a disaster. But God worked mightily.
2 Co 7:14	Paul had gone out on a limb to proclaim that the Corinthians would respond positively. Now it proved true and Titus experienced what Paul said.

[155.] Paul uses the endearing term son, when referring in the latter days of his ministry to Timothy, Titus, and Philemon.

[156.] See Wilmington's **Complete Guide to Bible Knowledge — New Testament People,** p 153.

2 Co 8:6	Paul had sent Titus not only to deal with problems in the church but to raise money. Here he is talking about how the Philippians gave mightily and how he hopes that Titus can see the same kind of giving spirit with the Corinthians.
2 Co 8:16	Titus recognized the importance of this money raising task and the need to confront the Corinthians on it. He accepted this responsibility. He went not only because Paul wanted him to but because he, himself, wanted to. He knew how important this ministry task was.
2 Co 8:23	Paul gives a word to sponsor Titus. Here he calls him a partner and fellow helper — that is, a trusted colleague in the ministry. This is an illustration of Paul's sponsoring mentoring.
2 Co 12:18 (twice)	Paul is defending his authority in contrast to the so called pseudo-apostles. Here he defends his financial integrity and motives in ministering. And he claims that Titus' values in life and ministry is consistent with his own views.
2 Co 13:14	Some manuscripts have "The second [epistle] to the Corinthians was written from Philippi, [a city] of Macedonia, by Titus and Lucas." At the least Titus was certainly there, note all the remarks about him during the epistle.
Gal 2:1	Titus accompanied Barnabas and Paul to Jerusalem when Paul was defending his view of the Gospel — grace alone. Titus was a product, a demonstration of Paul's ministry. He was on display as to what God could do with a Gentile convert..
Gal 2:3	Circumcision was not a part of the equation either. Paul's view was vindicated. Titus was also made known to the leaders of the movement of the Way. This networking function would be important later as he picked up Paul's mantle among the Gentiles.
2 Ti 4:10	Here is this last epistle we see that Titus has gone to Dalmatia — most likely a final ministry task.
Tit 1:4	Here we see the closeness of Titus and Paul — my own dear son after the common faith.
Tit 3:15	Some manuscripts read, "It was written to Titus, ordained the first bishop of the church of the Cretans, from Nicopolis of Macedonia".

Summary

Titus is mentioned 15 times in Paul's epistles. We find out more about him as to ministry in the 2nd Corinthian letter and the personal letter to him at Crete. While we do not have enough information to do a biographical sketch of his life we do know at least four things about him:

1. He was used by Paul as an Apostolic trouble shooter. His ministry was dominantly apostolic.

2. A number of ministry tasks were given Titus. In fact, were a primary mean of developing him — particularly releasing him to further responsibility.

3. He was a cross cultural worker. Probably from Antioch in Syria, he traveled with Paul on missionary journeys. His ministry in Corinth and Crete and Dalmatia were all cross-cultural ministries.

4. He knew the Word of God — particularly Paul's teaching. Paul's instructions to him at Crete could not have been complied with if he didn't know the word.

Titus was a trusted colleague. He developed into a leader who could pick up Paul's mantle.

This article will talk about one of Paul's methods for developing his fellow workers. If you look at Paul and his relationships to his team of fellow workers you will see that Paul had a developmental mentality toward them. He was constantly wanting them to develop as leaders and participate with him in ministry. One of his favorite means of developing a leader was to give him an important mission and send him away to do it. Notice how many of his fellow workers were frequently out on ministry errands for Paul. This kind of assignment is categorized under a broader development methodology — called ministry tasks.[157]

Titus illustrates well the notion of a ministry task and how a leader, like Paul, used it to develop Titus.

Ministry Task Defined and Described

Introduction

Emerging leaders early on in their informal training are often given small tasks by mentors, masters, supervisors, pastors or other leaders who are associated with them. The tasks can be small and informal or formal. These tasks are often indicators of loyalty, submission, use of gifts, initiative, and further usefulness. God honors the principle of Luke 16:10, "The one that is faithful in that which is least is faithful also in much; and the one that is unfaithful in little will be unfaithful in much." An important thing to keep in mind about ministry tasks is that the *ultimate assignment is from God* whether or not the ministry task is self-initiated or assigned by another. *Ultimate accountability* is to God. One of the signs of maturity in an emerging leader is the recognition of this fact and the desire to please the Lord in a ministry task.

Definition

A *ministry task* is an assignment from God which primarily tests a person's faithfulness and obedience but often also allows use of ministry gifts in the context of a task which has closure, accountability, and evaluation.

Example

Barnabas' trip to Antioch in Acts 11 was an apostolic ministry task which was definable and had closure, as well as accountability, and evaluation.

Example

Paul's year or so at Antioch with Barnabas as mentor was a ministry task which was a springboard to the missionary task of Acts 13 with Barnabas.

[157.] Ministry task is one of 51 shaping activities (called process items) which have been observed in our study of how God develops leaders across their lifetimes. We have studied more than 1500 leaders. Ministry tasks, as defined and described in this article occur frequently among leaders, as they develop.

Titus and Ministry Tasks

Titus had five ministry tasks including three with the Corinthian church, one in Crete and one in Dalmatia. The ministry tasks at Corinth were primarily confrontational ministry tasks. In all of them he was essentially testing Paul's spiritual authority.

His major task, at least from the standpoint of information available, was a broad comprehensive apostolic task at Crete.

Nothing is known about the final ministry task at Dalmatia, though some have speculated that it was an evangelistic task.

Ministry Tasks Explained Further

This shaping activity in a leader's life focuses on two developmental tasks:

1. character formation and
2. identification of leadership potential.

It tests character in the nature of doing some specific ministry assignment. This item tests for and develops the qualities of availability, faithfulness and dependability. It also points out leadership potential. This ministry task process item not only occurs in this transitional period when a leader is moving into leadership but also throughout the early stages of full time ministry.

Example Of Ministry Tasks — Titus

Introduction

Titus was apparently given several ministry tasks. We can identify five in the scriptures and draw lessons from three of them. The tasks are listed below. Dr. Edmond Hiebert (1954:146,147) identifies the first three. I assume his time analysis of Titus' ministry with Paul.

Table 46.3   Titus' Ministry Tasks

Task	Where	Main Intent	Comments
1	Corinth	Initiate giving for Jerusalem project.	Titus completed this task. The Corinthian Church was initially enthused about giving. Titus was evidently a person of tact and persuasive ability.
2	Corinth	Titus was sent there to ascertain accountability; He was to take disciplinary measures depending on how they were responding.	Titus completed this task with heartfelt involvement. Discipline was applied. Apparently the problem of divisions was solved, somewhat. Paul does not deal with any of those major problems in 2 Corinthians where the issue is spiritual authority.
3	Corinth	1. Complete Jerusalem project. 2. Test loyalty to Pauline authority. 3. Follow-up on discipline.	Results here are unknown.

| 4 | Crete | Apostolic Leadership involving:
1. Appointment of leaders
2. Grounding in teaching
3. Modeling a Christian lifestyle.
4. Establishing mission giving. | Here the thrust is on appointing leadership which will model a Christian lifestyle in the Cretan context. The exact outcome is not known but tradition indicates it was successful. See Titus 3:15 footnote in which Titus is implied as having an important role in Crete. It is clear from the letter that Titus is released to operate in full apostolic ministry in Crete. |
| 5 | Dalmatia | Evangelistic | Unknown; but most likely pioneer work. |

MINISTRY TASK CONTINUUM

Introduction

Small ministry tasks can be early indicators of leadership potential. In earlier development phases the thrust of these small ministry tasks is INNER-LIFE GROWTH FACTORS. When ministry tasks are given in later development phases they will usually be under MINISTRY FACTORS. The primary thrust of the ministry task when given in earlier development phases will be toward the development of the person given the task. Those given in later development phases will have a thrust toward accomplishment of the task. The continuum given below indicates these thrusts. Ministry tasks are transition items. They test (like integrity, obedience, and word checks) and hence belong in the Inner-Life Growth Phase. They also give ministry experience and develop ministry skills (like many of the other ministry process items) which puts them also in the early part of growth ministry processing.

THE MINISTRY TASK CONTINUUM — Luke 16:10 in Action

LITTLE   MUCH

Primarily for   **Primarily For**
Person Doing Task   **Doing Task**

During the development of a leader, that leader will have ministry tasks to the left of the continuum. Most of those task will be working on the character of the leader, though some ministry accomplishment will result. But the main emphasis is on the work in the leader not that through the leader. As the leader develops further assignments will be more to the right on the ministry task — they will still build into the leader but there will be more emphasis on the achievement of the task. And then as a leader fully develops, assignments will be primarily for doing the tasks. The below continuum identifies Titus and his ministry tasks along the continuum.

Example Using Titus' Ministry Tasks

LITTLE   MUCH

Primarily for   **Primarily For**
Person Doing Task   **Doing Task**

		X	X	X	X
		Task 1	Task 2	Task 3	Task 4
		Corinth	Corinth	Corinth	Crete

We do not see any early ministry tasks given Titus. The responsibilities involved with the tasks at Corinth and Crete are given to a leader who is well on his way to be developed. But each task insured that Paul could release Titus for more responsible tasks.

A final note of importance concerns recognition of accountability. The ultimate source of the assignment of a ministry task is God. On the human side the task may appear routine, natural, or not very significant. But ultimate accountability for the task is to God through human authority. To be able to sense that a given task is really an assignment from God can bring great fervor regarding accomplishing the task and a sense of contributing towards God's purposes. Paul was the human originator of these tasks. Yet, Titus was responsible for them — to Paul yes, but ultimately to God.

Some Final Thoughts On Ministry Tasks

A ministry task should be differentiated from ministry experience in general. A ministry task is specifically a test. Perceived as a special assignment from God, a ministry task usually pertains to a specified ministry experience that can be completed and evaluated for the purpose of testing the leader's availability, faithfulness and skills.

God's pattern seems to be to assign small ministry tasks. Usually the first ones are self-initiated in response to integrity, word, or obedience checks. Other tasks follow upon right responses until tasks of great responsibility can be given to the leader with confidence. Titus exemplifies this pattern.

Ministry tasks are used in at least the five following ways:

1. Assess an emerging leader's faithfulness.
2. Assess an emerging leader's readiness to obey.
3. Facilitate emergence of gifts.
4. Actual accomplishment of task.
5. Allows closure with regard to developmental issues.

The steps involved in a ministry task, more apropos on the left hand side of the continuum, include:

1. recognition of the task,
2. obedient response,
3. accomplishment of task,
4. closure assessment,
5. expansion.

The immediate cause for a ministry task can be self or another person. Where self-initiated the prompting is usually in response to sensitivity to the Holy Spirit. The ultimate cause is God who is superintending the development process.

The ministry task is a valuable tool for more experienced leaders in assessing potential leaders. This processing should be deliberately used and closure assessment given as a means for leadership selection. One should guard against the assigning of ministry tasks for selfish reasons. Its primary focus should be for development of the potential leader.

Titus was developed in many ways as he traveled with Paul. Ministry tasks were an important way that Paul did this. Ministry tasks allowed for release of ministry. Each had its mandate but there was lots of freedom for Titus to carry them out. The ministry task is a tool to transition a leader.

See **Glossary**, *ministry tasks*. See **Articles**, *Timothy, Beloved Son*; *Titus — Ministry Tasks; Titus — An Apostolic Worker; Apostolic Functions*; *Paul — and His Companions; Paul — Developer.* See also Edmond Hiebert **Introduction to the Pauline Epistles**.

Titus—An Apostolic Worker

Introduction

Titus is one of three mentorees very close to Paul.[158] He was a Gentile Greek, probably from Syrian Antioch.[159] Paul probably led him to Christ (see Acts 11:26 and implications of Titus 1:4). Titus is mentioned some 15 times in Scripture. Table 47.1 reflects these references.

He is the recipient of a book, the book of Titus which informs his apostolic ministry. It is from the Galatian reference, the Corinthian references and the book of Titus that we can imply some information about Titus.

Table 47.1   Titus Mentioned in Scripture — 15 Times

Location	Implications/ Other Comments
2Co 2:13	Paul is close to Titus. Considers him a spiritual brother. Titus has been sent on a mission (crisis in Paul's leadership) to the Corinthians and Paul awaits his answer, anxiously.
2 Co 7:6	Titus has returned with news about the Corinthian crisis. It is good news. And a great comfort to Paul. The first epistle to the Corinthians had borne fruit.
2 Co 7:13	Titus was refreshed with joy in his ministry at Corinth. It could have been a disaster. But God worked mightily.
2 Co 7:14	Paul had gone out on a limb to proclaim that the Corinthians would respond positively. Now it proved true and Titus experienced what Paul said.
2 Co 8:6	Paul had sent Titus not only to deal with problems in the church but to raise money. Here he is talking about how the Philippians gave mightily and how he hopes that Titus can see the same kind of giving spirit with the Corinthians.
2 Co 8:16	Titus recognized the importance of this money raising task and the need to confront the Corinthians on it. He accepted this responsibility. He went not only because Paul wanted him to but because he, himself, wanted to. He knew how important this ministry task was.

---

158. Paul uses the endearing term son, when referring in the latter days of his ministry to Timothy, Titus, and Philemon.

159. See Wilmington's **Complete Guide to Bible Knowledge — New Testament People,** p 153.

2 Co 8:23	Paul gives a word to sponsor Titus. Here he calls him a partner and fellow helper — that is, a trusted colleague in the ministry. This is an illustration of Paul's sponsoring mentoring.
2 Co 12:18 (twice)	Paul is defending his authority in contrast to the so called pseudo-apostles. Here he defends his financial integrity and motives in ministering. And he claims that Titus' values in life and ministry is consistent with his own views.
2 Co 13:14	Some manuscripts have "The second [epistle] to the Corinthians was written from Philippi, [a city] of Macedonia, by Titus and Lucas." At the least Titus was certainly there, note all the remarks about him during the epistle.
Gal 2:1	Titus accompanied Barnabas and Paul to Jerusalem when Paul was defending his view of the Gospel — grace alone. Titus was a product, a demonstration of Paul's ministry. He was on display as to what God could do with a Gentile convert.
Gal 2:3	Circumcision was not a part of the equation either. Paul's view was vindicated. Titus was also made known to the leaders of the movement of the Way. This networking function would be important later as he picked up Paul's mantle among the Gentiles.
2 Ti 4:10	Here is this last epistle we see that Titus has gone to Dalmatia — most likely a final ministry task.
Tit 1:4	Here we see the closeness of Titus and Paul — my own dear son after the common faith.
Tit 3:15	Some manuscripts read, "It was written to Titus, ordained the first bishop of the church of the Cretans, from Nicopolis of Macedonia".

There is not enough information to do more than a brief bio sketch of Titus. Figure 47.1, which follows shortly gives an educated guess at Titus' time-line.

Important Definitions for Time-Lines

The following definitions help you interpret the time-line.

Definition   The *time-line* is the linear display along a horizontal axis which is broken up into development phases.

Definition   A *unique time-line* refers to a time-line describing a given leader's lifetime which will have unique development phases bearing labels expressing that uniqueness.

Definition   A *development phase* is a marked off length on a time-line representing a significant portion of time in a leader's life history in which notable development takes place.

Titus has 3 development phases indicated.

Definition   A *sub-phase* is a marked off length on a time-line within a development phase which points out intermediate times of development during the development phase.

Titus has tentative sub-phases, 2 per development phase.

Definition   A *boundary* is a time period which encompasses a transition from one development phase to another.

Two boundaries are indicated on Titus' time-line as well as eight milestones, in time-line jargon, called critical incidents.

Titus' Time-Line

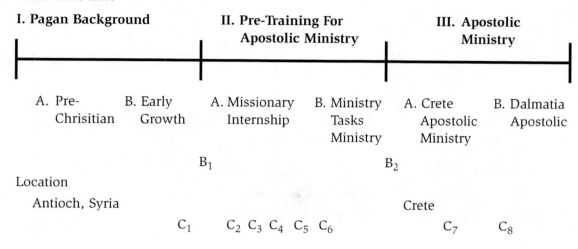

Figure 47.1   Tentative Time-Line for Titus

Legend

B_1 Titus Boundary 1 = transition from secular life to traveling ministry with Paul and team

B_2 Titus Boundary 2 = transition from missionary training to Apostolic leader

C_1 Titus saved; possibly through Paul's ministry (see Acts 11:26 and implications of Titus 1:4).

C_2 Titus goes with Paul to Galatia. This was a critical contextualization issue (see Galatians 2:1,3). Later Titus would have to do contextualization work with the believers on Crete.

C_3 Titus is on Paul's missionary team; though not mentioned in the book of Acts it is clear from the numerous references in the Corinthian letters that Titus was with Paul and sent out on various trips with special ministry task and then would return back to Paul.

C_4 Ministry Task 1.[160] Titus initiates giving for Jerusalem project in Corinthian church.

C_5 Ministry Task 2. Titus was sent there to ascertain accountability; He was to take disciplinary measures depending on how they were responding.

C_6 Ministry Task 3. Titus is resent to Corinth to 1. complete the Jerusalem project, 2. test loyalty to Pauline authority, and 3. follow-up on discipline. The results of this are not known. However, the inclusion of 2 Corinthians in the canon is probably indicative of a successful completion of this task.

C_7 Titus transitions into apostolic Leadership with his major ministry task at Crete. It involved: 1. the appointment of leaders, 2. the grounding in teaching of the believers in this regional church, 3. the modeling of a Christian lifestyle and the 4. establishing of mission giving. Here the thrust is on appointing leadership which will model a Christian lifestyle in the Cretan context. The exact outcome is not known but tradition indicates it was successful. See Titus 3:15 footnote in which Titus is implied as having an important role in Crete. It is clear from the letter that Titus is released to operate in full apostolic ministry in Crete.

C_8 Titus goes to Dalmatia, most likely sent there by Paul. Conjecture is that this was an evangelistic mission.

---

160. A *ministry task* is an assignment from God which primarily tests a person's faithfulness and obedience but often also allows use of ministry gifts in the context of a task which has closure, accountability, and evaluation. It is one of 51 shaping activities, called process items, describing how God develops a leader.

Titus' Apostolic Gifting

Because of the demands of Paul in the Titus epistle and because of the type of apostolic ministry[161] Titus was involved in we can surmise what his gift-mix probably looked like.

Figure 47.2 Venn Diagram — Titus Apostolic Gift-Mix

Titus and Apostolic Functions

In two previous articles[162] I have developed a tentative listing of apostolic functions. Below in Table 47.2 are listed apostolic functions. Note the ones Titus was involved in.

Table 47.2   Apostolic Functions—Titus

Function	Apostolic Thrust	Seen In Titus' Ministry
1. Start New Ministries	pioneer new work	No
2. Appoint Leaders	leadership selection	Yes
3. Establish Works	leadership development; edification ministry with believers	Yes
4. Intercede for Works, both new and old	release spiritual power in situations	No
5. Combat Heresy[a] (both orthodoxy and orthopraxy)	correct and stabilize a deteriorating situation	Yes
6. Resource New Ministries and Old Ones	resource apostolic ministries; give help to needy church situations	Yes

---

161. See **Article**, *Apostolic Giftedness — Multiple Gifted Leaders*, where three kinds of apostolic ministries are defined: Phase I. Ground Breaking Apostolic Work (like Paul and Barnabas in Thessalonica), Phase II. Edification Work (like Titus in Crete), and Phase III. Corrective Work (like Timothy in Ephesus).

162. See **Articles**, *Apostolic Functions; Apostolic Giftedness — Multiple Gifted Leaders*.

7. Test New Ministries for Validity	authenticate God's work	No
8. Contextualize the Gospel to Cross-cultural Situations	apply truth to complex cultural situations	Yes. A significant ministry task for Titus. Cretan cultural has many values degrading from Christian testimony

a. Heresy refers to deviation from a standard, whether in belief (orthodoxy) or practice (orthopraxy). e.g. See 1Ti where both are present in the Ephesian church (as prophesied in Ac 20:30).

Conclusion

Titus was a valued co-worker for Paul.

Titus was developed in many ways as he traveled with Paul. Ministry tasks were an important way that Paul did this. Ministry tasks allowed for release of ministry. Each had its mandate but there was lots of freedom for Titus to carry them out. The ministry task is a tool to transition a leader.

Titus' ministry in Crete was complicated in that he had to introduce values into a Cretan culture which had many counter values. His was a primitive situation in which new believers had a relatively small church base to work from. He too had to do leadership selection — to get leaders of integrity to help him model the needed changes. It is clear that in the letter to Titus that Paul is transitioning[163] Titus into apostolic ministry. He is releasing Titus, passing on the mantle, for apostolic ministry.

Here is to me a surprising observation on Titus' apostolic ministry in Crete. Paul never stressed his use of power gifts.[164] However, Paul did admonish him to use the gifts he had with power — dominantly teaching, exhortation.

Apostolic ministries will vary due to local cultural situations and gifting of the apostolic leaders as well as the type of apostolic ministry being done, Phase 1, or 2, or 3.

Several final observations about this Gentile missionary — probably the first to go out in obedience to the Great Commission.

1. He was used by Paul as an Apostolic trouble shooter. His ministry was dominantly apostolic.
2. A number of ministry tasks[165] were given Titus. In fact, were a primary means of developing him — particularly releasing him to further responsibility.
3. He was a cross cultural worker. Probably from Antioch in Syria, he traveled with Paul on missionary journeys. His ministry in Corinth and Crete and Dalmatia were all cross-cultural ministries.
4. He knew the Word of God — particularly Paul's teaching. Paul's instructions to him at Crete could not have been complied with if he didn't know the word.

Titus was a trusted colleague. He developed into a leader who could pick up Paul's mantle. And I think he did.

---

163. See **Articles**, *Leadership Transition Concepts; Leadership Transitions — Timothy and Titus; Leadership Transition — Jesus and Disciples.*
164. Frequently, in the present apostolic movement it is the power gifts that are stressed.
165. See **Article**, *Titus and Ministry Tasks,* which shows how Paul used ministry tasks as a major way of developing Titus.

Article 48

Union Life — Intimacy With God

Introduction

One of the most famous union life verses appears in Col 1:27.

> 27 To whom God would make known what is the riches of the glory of this mystery among the Gentiles—**Christ in you**, the hope of glory. Col 1:27

Note the phrase **Christ in you**. Paul uses this concept of being **in Christual[166]** many times in his epistles. It is the essential phrase describing union life. What is union life?

Definition   *Union life* is a phrase which refers both to the fact of the spiritual reality of a believer joined in spirit with the resurrected Spirit of Christ and the process of that union being lived out with Holy Spirit power so that the person is not dominated by sin in his/her life.

In essence, it is the life of a believer who is living above the controlling authority of sin in a life, not a perfect life, but also not controlled by sinful habits, tendencies, sinful addictions, the sinful self. It is a believer walking sensitively to the Holy Spirit's leading and moving inexorably to being conformed to the image of Christ. That is the life of Christ in and through the believer—in fact, it is not to strong to say Christ in the believer as that person. Christ in me as me.

Today, with our modern emphasis on dysfunctionality, 1000s are bound by a past which will not allow them to live freely. Without wanting to negate the complexities of these foundational shaping events and people in our pasts I do want to say that there is provision for victory in Christ. That is what union life is all about. Union life is certainly part of the answer to that need and maybe perhaps the answer.

Throughout Christian history people serious about their Christianity have longed for a more zealous life-style expression of it. They have longed to have a deeper walk with God. They have sought to appropriate that walk with God. Union life has been the experience of many a saint who has sought this deeper walk. Different names have been used to

---

[166.] Paul uses the phrase *in Christ* 74 times, *in Jesus* six times and *in him* eight times referring to aspects of union life.

describe this mystical union and its effect in life. Such terms as the exchanged life, replaced life, deeper life, victorious life, normal Christian life and life on the highest plain can be found in the literature. Various methodologies have been tried to attain that "more committed" expression. Numerous movements have sprung up. The phrases listed above convey rather esoterically what these various believers have discovered.

Paul comprehensively explains this kind of life in Ro 1-8. He models it in Php. He also shows its power in his own life in 2Co. John treats the concept in metaphorical fashion—living water, vine and branches. The Bible also deals with the concept using the term, New Covenant. This article will give an overview of this important concept.[167] I as a believer living in Union Life can know this beautiful union—Christ in me as me. It is entered into simply by faith by knowing and appropriating what Christ has already done at the cross.

Bible Passages Dealing With the Union Life Concept

Union life is promised in the O.T. God reveals the New Covenant in the O.T. and then points to its realization in the book of Heb. Essentially the New Covenant, a promise made to corporate Israel becomes individualized in its N.T. application shown in Heb.

> 31 Behold, the days come, says the LORD, that I will make a new covenant with the house of Israel, and with the house of Judah. 32 Not according to the covenant that I made with their fathers in the day [that] I took them by the hand to bring them out of the land of Egypt; which my covenant they brake, although I was an husband unto them, says the LORD. 33 But this [shall be] the covenant that I will make with the house of Israel; After those days, says the LORD, **I will put my law in their inward parts, and write it in their hearts**; and will be their God, and they shall be my people. 34 And they shall teach no more every man his neighbor, and every man his brother, saying, Know the LORD: for they shall all know me, from the least of them unto the greatest of them, says the LORD: for I will forgive their iniquity, and I will remember their sin no more. Jer 31:31-34.

Heb applies union life to the N.T. church as part of what Christ has done.[168]

> 8 For finding fault with them, he says, Behold, the days come, says the Lord, when I will make a new covenant with the house of Israel and with the house of Judah: 9 Not according to the covenant that I made with their fathers in the day when I took them by the hand to lead them out of the land of Egypt; because they continued not in my covenant, and I regarded them not, says the Lord. 10 For this [is] the covenant that I will make with the house of Israel after those days, says the Lord; I will put my laws into their mind, and write them in their hearts: and I will be to them a God, and they shall be to me a people: 11 And they shall not teach every man

---

167. Theologically we are dealing with the notion of sanctification when we talk about union life.

168. Thematically, Heb is teaching that *God's Redemptive Revelation in Christ* is superior to any other, is final, and therefore demands a continued faithful allegiance. Part of its superiority is the realization of New Covenant through Christ.

his neighbor, and every man his brother, saying, Know the Lord: for all shall know me, from the least to the greatest. Heb 8-10

Paul describes union life by the phrase in Christ, in Jesus, the supply of the Spirit of Jesus or joined unto the Lord. Some of his most famous union life verses include the following:

15 But when it pleased God, who separated me from my mother's womb, and called me by his grace, 16 To **reveal his Son in me**, that I might preach him among the heathen. Gal 1:16

20 I am crucified with Christ: nevertheless I live; yet not I, but Christ **lives in me**: and the life which I now live in the flesh I live by the faith of the Son of God, who loved me, and gave himself for me. Gal 2:20

26 [Even] the mystery[169] which hath been hid from ages and from generations, but now is made manifest to his saints. 27 To whom God would make known what is the riches of the glory of this mystery among the Gentiles—**Christ in you**, the hope of glory. 28 Whom we preach, warning every person, and teaching every person in all wisdom; that we may present every person grown up and mature in Christ Jesus: 29 Whereunto I also labor, striving according to his working, which works in me mightily. Col 1:27

17 But he that is joined unto the Lord is one spirit. 1Co 6:17

Peter describes the foundation for union life in breath taking language.

Whereby are given unto us exceeding great and precious promises—that by these you might be **partakers of the divine nature,** having escaped the corruption that is in the world through lust. 2Pe 1:4

Most believers can read these verses and still not know anything about union life. What does it look like? Paul models it for us in all of his epistles. But it is most clearly seen in Php.

What Does Union Life Look Like? See Philippians.

Whereas Paul teaches conceptually about union life in the book of Ro, he demonstrates it in the book of Php. Table 1 describes seven characteristics of union life as modeled by Paul in Php.

---

[169]. A mystery, in Pauline language, means something not previously revealed by God but now revealed by God and opened up so people can see its truth. Union life is such a concept.

Table 48.1   Seven Characteristics of Union Life Modeled By Paul in Philippians

Characteristic	Vs	Explanation
Christ-centered	1:20-22	Paul's daily life involved a centeredness in Christ and a desire to have this Christ impact his everyday testimony.
Inner Resources	1:19; 3:9,10; 4:13.	Paul knew that the Spirit of Christ indwelled and that Spirit was his source of power. It was the same kind of power as that which raised Jesus from the dead—resurrection power.
Joy	1:4, 25, 26; 2:2, 17, 18, 2:29; 4:1.	Joy in the midst of hard, shaping life experiences, should be the hallmark of a believer in union with Christ. Joy is a fruit of the Spirit that distinguished a believer from an unbeliever, particularly in distressing circumstances. Joy is referred to throughout Php. Paul uses five different words for joy.
Relationships	2:1-3; 4:2 and general tone throughout	A believer in union with Christ recognizes also that he/she is related to every other believer in the body. Such a recognition longs for unity with them—like mindedness, good relationships.
Sovereign Mindset	1:12; 2:17; 4:11,12.	Sovereign mindset refers to an attitude demonstrated by the Apostle Paul in which he tended to see God's working in the events and activities that shaped his life, whether or not they were positive and good or negative and bad. He tended to see God's purposes in these shaping activities and to make the best of them. A person in union life sees God's activities through life's experiences (Ro 8:28-30) as shaping toward the image of Christ.
Destiny/ Growth To Maturity	3:10-14; 15-16.	Paul has a driving goal to move toward maturity in Christ. (see also Ac 20:24 and 2Ti 4:7,8). A believer in union life presses on toward growth an maturity.
Peace	4:6,7.	Paul speaks of the God of peace and the peace of God. A believer can know this fruit of the Spirit, this aspect of victory in the life, in the midst of pressing life circumstances. In fact, it like joy, is a hallmark of a believer in union life.

Explanation—The Left Brained Approach —Logical Presentation Given in Ro 1-8.

Until a believer fully enters into the notion that Christ has indeed paid the full penalty for all his/ her sins, those committed in the past, those being commuted in the present (known or unknown), and those to be committed in the future, it is very unlikely that that believer will enter into and experience *Victory* in the Christian life. The Ro 3:21-31 passage (dealing with justification—that is, God's means of justifying a sinner deserving of punishment by the sacrificial death of Christ for him/her—technically called the vicarious atonement) is the foundation for believing truth about *Victory in Christian living*. Some will by faith accept this truth without any preamble and enter into it, forever being freed from guilt. Others will perhaps need deliverance from some past dysfunctional hold as a preamble to seeing guilt forever gone.[170] In any case, a guilt free past is a pre-requisite or co-requisite to moving on to *Victory*.

---

170. Inner healing in which God miraculously provides knowledge about something enslaving from the past and breaks that hold or the Catholic approach of mediated authority (confession, penance, absolving) are two approaches I have seen effective in breaking past holds. For others, the Good News of the Gospel alone is sufficient. The passage in 1 Corinthians 6:9-11 shows experientially that such holds can be broken.

The Christian life from beginning to end, Ro 1:16-18, is by faith. We accept what Christ did for us on the **Cross** to pay for our sins and make us guilt-free before a just God. We must also accept by faith what He has provided for *Victory in our lives*—that it is true that we can live increasingly knowing that sin does not control our lives. We do not claim perfection but we can live knowing we do not have to be dominated by some controlling sin in our lives. And we can experience this so as to encourage us as we move toward Christ-likeness in our lives.

The second look at the work on the **Cross** provides us with the revelation from God, the factual basis, which we accept by faith just like we did forgiveness of sins. We **KNOW** (Ro 6:6,7) it to be true, that we were mystically included with Christ in his death so as to break the controlling authority of sin in our lives and to be raised with him to know a resurrected life, free from this controlling authority of sin. It is a done deed.

We habitually **COUNT** (Ro 6:11) on it both implicitly and explicitly, moment by moment, as we sensitively follow the Spirit's leading. We know we can count on it. We give ourselves to this kind of life. It is by **FAITH** that we totally **SURRENDER** ourselves to this process, longing and wanting it in our lives.

And we know that it will take **SPIRIT FREEDOM**. But just in case we think it is us doing it we come face to face with the reality of the power of sin in our lives. And we are driven by deep need to want the **SPIRIT FREEDOM** and to know without it we are helpless and hopeless to experience that Victory in our lives (Rom 7).

And **SPIRIT FREEDOM** is there—again we know guilt free exposure before God and we recognize that without it we are helpless and hopeless to experience that *Victory* in our lives. And **SPIRIT FREEDOM** can be. We are assured within of our **Adoption** into the family—heirs with Christ. We will grow up to be like Christ. The Spirit stands ready always to point out our need and take care of giving us *Victory* in that need. It is a process over time for the total full perfection to be. But it will happen. It is an inevitable process moving forward to completion. We will become Christ-like. It is so certain that the whole process is **spoken of in the past** (prophetic past idiom). We were saved, we are being perfected, we will be totally perfected. Or another way of saying it: we were saved from sins, we are being saved from sin's control, we will be freed forever from its presence. We were saved. We are being saved. We will be yet totally saved (Rom 8).

Summarizing, Paul teaches logically that a believer's sins were taken care of at the **Cross**. Such a believer can be freed of guilt for those sins. But not only were sins dealt with at the **Cross** but also the controlling authority of sin in a life, the sin principle, was dealt with. A believer can accept this provision of enabling power to live above the controlling authority of sin in a life simply by faith. And a believer can continue to count on this enabling power. It is the Holy Spirit who will sensitively lead that believer to experience the power of the inward Christ life over sin. Such a believer, walking sensitively with the Holy Spirit will increasingly know more of this enabling power over time. Such a believer, in this life, will inexorably move toward experiencing this Christ life. It is an on-growing, ever increasing, process of growth.

Conclusion

Throughout this leadership commentary I have used the notion of,

Ministry flows out of being.

I have described being as comprised of at least the following: intimacy with God, character, personality, giftedness, destiny, values drawn from experience, gender influenced perspectives. Now I want to take it one step further. Ministry flows out of what being? I want to suggest that in addition to these characteristics ultimately I am talking about being involving the *union life being*—a person's beingness is complete when that person realizes intimacy as union with Christ.

Have you discovered this mystery, Christ in you as you—union life?

See **Articles,** *Sovereign Mindset, Abiding—Seven Symptoms.*

Word Disciplines and Bible Centered Leadership

Introduction

Paul, in the book of Titus, made some powerful demands upon Titus concerning ministry in Crete. It was clear that Titus had to know God's Word (part of that was in process; involved knowing Paul's oral teaching).

Note the demands on Titus.

Titus 2:

1   Your teaching must be solid, through and through. 2 Teach the older men to be temperate, worthy of respect, self-controlled, and solid in what they believe. They should demonstrate love and endurance.

3 Likewise, teach the older women to be reverent in the way they live.

... No one should be able to malign the word of God because of their daily behavior.

6 Similarly, encourage the young men to be self-controlled. 7...Teach with integrity. Show that what you teach is important.   8 What you say should be irrefutable. Those who oppose you will have no grounds to condemn you. In fact, they will be embarrassed, because they can not deny what you have said and done.

9 Teach slaves ...

15 These, then, are the things you should teach. Encourage and rebuke authoritatively.   Don't let anyone put you down.

Titus had to teach all age groups. He had to teach cross-gender. He had to teach with power. His teaching had to be irrefutable. It is clear that Titus needed to be a Bible Centered Leader.[171]

[171.] See **Article**, *Bible Centered Leader*, for more details on this.

Definition   A *Bible Centered leader* refers to a leader whose leadership is signifi-
                      cantly informed from the Bible and who personally has been shaped
                      by Biblical values, has grasped the intent of Scriptural books and their
                      content in such a way as to apply them to current situations and who
                      uses the Bible in ministry so as to impact followers.

There are two central components and two complementary concepts in this definition.

1. Essential Component: A leader whose leadership is being informed by the Bible,

2. Necessary Credibility Component: A leader who personally has been shaped by
   Biblical values,

3. Necessary Contextual Component: A leader who has grasped the intent of Scriptural
   books and their content in such a way as to apply them to current situations and

4. Essential Component: A leader who uses the Bible in ministry so as to
   impact followers.

In my classes dealing with leadership studies in the Bible I have a series of Bible tests
to help folks assess their Bible knowledge. The longest of these is rather detailed — a 300
question test that takes 6-8 hours. Its purpose is to let students know their strengths and
weaknesses in the Bible. It also helps them identify their core material.[172] I want them to
know the information in the Bible. But understand this. *Knowing the facts of the Bible does
not guarantee that a leader will be a Bible Centered Leader.* But **not knowing the facts of
the Bible will guarantee that you are not a Bible Centered Leader.**

So I stress that emerging leaders need to establish habits of life long mastery of their
core material. The following are some word disciplines that I have identified that can make
the difference in a leader moving toward becoming a Bible Centered Leader.

Word Disciplines Needed

Our studies of leaders today reveals that a number of them became Bible Centered
Leaders because they had good word disciplines in their lives. Here are some word disciplines that can prove useful.

[172.] All leaders are *word gifted*. Word gifted folks have special material in the Bible which God has used in their
lives and which they in turn use in their ministry. We call this material, core material. Leaders should continually be mastering and using their core material over their lifetimes. Their core material will also be
expanding as they develop over their lifetimes. See **Glossary**.*word gifted, core material.*

Table 49.1   Some Word Disciplines

Discipline	Purpose	Where to Go for Help[a]
Devotional Habits	Learn to hear from God so as to move the heart and will; forms basis for impacting others with the Word	See *Having A Ministry That Lasts,* ch 4, p 83-93. See also *Fellowship With God.*
Analytical Habits-— Synthesis of Large Portions of Scripture	See the overall perspective on what God is doing using a book of the Bible. Helps one to recognize dynamical equivalence between Bible and modern day application.	See the *Bible and Leadership Values* for the application of this to each book in the Bible. See Appendix G in *Having A Ministry That Lasts.* The first three hermeneutical principles deals with this kind of study.
Analytical Habits — detailed exegetical skills with small units of Scripture,	Enables one to identify observations, guidelines, principles and values from Bible material. Such material has the potential to be transferable to today's situations.	See Appendix G in *Having A Ministry That Lasts.* The last four hermeneutical principles deals with this kind of study.
Analytical Habits — word study skills	Allows one to do thorough, good Bible study. Gives credence to exegetical work.	See *Interpreting the Scriptures: Word Studies.*
Analytical Habits — special hermeneutics	Gives skills to interpret unusual language in Scriptures. Gives evidence of thorough knowledge of word and credence to study as well as pointing out emphatic issues from Bible.	See Appendix G in *Having A Ministry That Lasts* for special language principles which outlines the special language forms you should be able to study. See also *Interpreting the Scriptures: Figures and Idioms; Parables — Puzzles With a Purpose; Hebrew Poetry.*
Perseverance — On Going Study of Core Material (principle of base + advance)	The Base + advance principle provides a guiding value toward being a person of excellence.	See *Having A Ministry That Lasts,* chapters 4 and 5, note especially p 128-132 and 135 for Base + Advance concept.
Impact Communication	It is not the knowledge of the Bible which makes one an effective Bible Centered Leader, it is the use of the Bible to impact lives.	See *Having A Ministry That Lasts,* chapter 7 communicating with impact.

a. All of the items listed in this column are my own publications available through Barnabas Publications, my own publishing arm.

The Equipping Formula

Few leaders master the Word without a proactive, deliberate approach which plans to do so. So then, I suggest that life long habitual study of the Bible is done best if a leader has some framework for approaching the study of the Bible. All of the above word disciplines fit well into the equipping formula, a framework for guiding one into life long study. Notice, it is made up of 4 components. Two of them are obligatory (+) and need to be in place all the time. Two are optional (±) and need to be in place when required by your ministry situation.

Mastering the Word
for Gifted Power =

+	regular devotional input
+	progress on mastering your core set (material)
±	familiarity reading in all of Word
±	situational study

Definition   *Regular devotional input* means a disciplined quiet time in which you use the Word to feed your own soul and your intimacy with God and His ways.

Definition   A *Core Set* is a collection of very important Bible books, usually from 5-20, which are or have/been extremely meaningful to you in your own life and for which you feel a burden from God to use with great power over and over in your ministry in the years to come. (Core materials include core passages, core Psalms, core parables, core topics, core bios, core values)

Definition   *Familiarity reading* means a regular reading program through the whole Bible or various portions of it to keep up familiarity with the Word.

Definition   *Situational study* is the study of a concentrated portion of the Word for some personal reason, or for direct use in a ministry setting.

You need to plan around the Equipping Formula always heeding obligatory and also using optional when needed. The base plus advance will guide you as you continue to master your core material. It will force you to work on your impact communication as well since on-going mastery involves developing communication events delivering results of your study to others.

Conclusion

Desire to be a Bible Centered Leader is not enough. You will need a major commitment of the will toward becoming a disciplined student. of the Word. Remember the challenges to Titus? Why not make them your own.

Titus 2:

1   Your teaching must be solid, through and through.

7...Teach with integrity.   Show that what you teach is important. 8 What you say should be irrefutable. Those who oppose you will have no grounds to condemn you. In fact, they will be embarrassed, because they can not deny what you have said and done.

15 These, then, are the things you should teach. Encourage and rebuke authoritatively.   Don't let anyone put you down.

Titus

Apostolic Leadership

Appendices

CLINTON'S
BIBLICAL LEADERSHIP
COMMENTARY SERIES

Glossary—Leadership Definitions

The following leadership related definitions are referred to in the Titus commentary. Some Glossary concepts may occur in the Titus articles which are not included here. See **Clinton's Encyclopedia of Biblical Leadership Insights** which contains the full glossary.

Item	Definition
Bible Centered leader	a leader (1) whose leadership is being informed by the Bible and (2) who personally has been shaped by Biblical values, (3) who has grasped the intent of Scriptural books and their content in such a way as to apply them to current situations and (4) who uses the Bible in ministry so as to impact followers.
Capture	a technical term used when talking about figures of speech being interpreted. A figure or idiom is said to be captured when one can display the intended emphatic meaning of it in non-figurative simple words. e.g. not ashamed of the Gospel = captured: completely confident of the Gospel.
Centrality	In short, a Christ centered life. One of nine spirituality components. It focuses on one's personal relationship with and experience of Christ. It assesses personal experience with the person and work of Christ.
Community	In short, recognizing the interdependence of God's people. One of nine spirituality components. This component blends exteriority, interiority and Spirit sensitivity so that the checks and balances of Christian community both constrain and stretch the growing believer toward development and use of giftedness for others.
Contemporary Models	see Mentor models

Contextualization   the process of taking something meaningful in one context and making it relevant to a new context context and more specifically the transfer of Biblical and revealed truth from one culture's understanding of it to some other specific culture's understanding of it. e.g. the Christian movement which began in a Jewish context had to be reinterpreted by Paul to a non-Jewish context, the Gentiles.

Corporate Testimony   refers to the reputation that Christians as a whole, as a religious movement have in the surrounding culture. Paul hits this hard in Titus and other epistles--part of that was probably because of his trial and the accusations against Christianity (Luke tries to counter the bad reputation of Christianity in Acts--one of the major purposes in Acts).

Deep Processing   refers to a collection of process items which intensely work on deepening the maturity of a leader. The set includes the following process items: conflict, ministry conflict, crisis, life crisis, leadership backlash and isolation.

Development   In short, continuing to grow throughout life. One of nine spirituality components. This integrative spirituality component suggests that there should be ongoing progress in every spirituality component through life. It refers to evaluation, affirmation, and feedback which helps assess progress in any component and ultimately toward conformity to Christ.

Divine Appointment   a Pauline leadership value seen in 2Co. *Leaders ought to be sure that God appointed them to ministry situations.*

Exhortation   one of the 19 spiritual gifts. It is a spiritual gift belonging to the word cluster. The *gift of Exhortation* is the capacity to urge people to action in terms of applying Biblical truths, or to encourage people generally with Biblical truths, or to comfort people through the application of Biblical truth to their needs. **Its central thrust is To Apply Biblical Truth.**

Exteriority   In short, living out the inner life. One of nine spirituality components. This component suggests overflow of interiority into life-- the horizontal aspects of spirituality--its effects on our relationships with believers and unbelievers in the world in which we interact.

Focused Life (lives)   A *focused life* is a life dedicated to exclusively carrying out God's unique purposes through it, by identifying the focal issues, that is, the major role, life purpose, unique methodology, or ultimate contribution, which allows an increasing prioritizing of life's activities around the focal issues, and results in a satisfying life of being and doing.

Foreshadowing	refers to Paul's technique of inserting qualifying clauses and phrases into his salutation which hint at subjects or topics or themes that he will later develop in his epistle.
Fruitfulness,	In short, being and doing what God intends. One of nine spirituality components. Inner (character--fruit of Spirit) and Outer (external fruit—results of giftedness and achievement for the Kingdom) measure of God's purposes for the believer and fulfillment as a human being.
Gifted Power	refers to the empowerment of the Holy Spirit when using giftedness; 1Pe 4:11 gives the basic admonition for this to the use of word gifts. It is naturally extended to other areas of giftedness.
Goodwin's Expectation Principle	Bennie Goodwin in a small booklet on leadership published by InterVarsity Press identified a social dynamic principle which is helpful in developing leaders. In my own words, *Emerging leaders tend to live up to the genuine expectations of leaders they respect.* The challenge embodied in the expectation must not be too much or the young leader will not be able to accomplish it and will be inoculated against further challenges. The challenge must not be too little or it will not attract. It must be a genuine expectation. Paul uses this with Timothy several times (see fn 1Ti 6:11; 2Ti 1:5).
Hapax Legomena	a word occurring only one time in the original text of the Bible. Its meaning must be determined from the surrounding context or from other documents other than the Bible which were extant at the time of the writing of the Bible book containing the word.
Interiority	In short, development of the inner life. One of nine spirituality components. This component looks at the development of the inner life--vertical aspects of spirituality with God--the devotional life and disciplines of silence, solitude, fasting, and prayer help.
Leadership Functions	*Leadership functions* is a technical term which refers to the three major categories of formal leadership responsibility: task behavior (defining structure and goals), relationship behavior (providing the emotional support and ambiance), and inspirational behavior (providing motivational effort).
Leadership Position	a general term to refer to a formal, titled, recognized leadership resposibility in a New Testament Church (like deacon, elder, pastor, bishop, etc.) A leadership transition concept.
Leadership Roles	a leadership transition concept. refers to any major role an emerging leader has which is released to that leader by a more senior leader. It is a step forward in assuming the total role of the leader that is senior.

Leadership Style	the individual tendency of a leader to influence followers in a highly directive manner, directive manner, non-directive manner, or highly non-directive manner. It is that consistent behavior pattern that underlies specific overt behavior acts of influence pervading the majority of leadership functions in which that leader exerts influence. The style is the means that the leader uses in influencing followers toward purposes. I identify 10 Pauline leadership styles. See Clinton **Coming To Conclusions on Leadership Styles.**
Leadership Tasks	a term used to describe the leadership transition of an emerging leader, especially the accepting of responsibility for ministry tasks and ministry assignments
Leadership Transition	*Leadership transition* is the process whereby existing leaders prepare and release emerging leaders into the responsibility and practice of leadership positions, functions, roles, and tasks.
List Idiom	an idiomatic use of a list of items. The initial item on the list is the main assertion and other items illustrate or clarify the primary item.
Love Gifts	a category of spiritual gifts which are used to demonstrate the effects of God's transformation of lives and His care for people. Love gifts demonstrate the beauty of the unseen God's work in lives in such a way as to attract others to want this same kind of relationship. These include: pastoring, evangelism, gifts of healings, governments, helps, giving, mercy, (word of knowledge, word of wisdom sometimes).
Macro-Lesson	is a high level generalization of a leadership observation (suggestion, guideline, requirement), stated as a lesson, which repeatedly occurs throughout different leadership eras, and thus has potential as a leadership absolute. Macro lessons even at their weakest provide at least strong guidelines describing leadership insights. At their strongest they are requirements, that is absolutes, that leaders should follow. Leaders ignore them to their detriment. Example: *Prayer Lesson: If God has called you to a ministry then He has called you to pray for that ministry.*
Mentor Sponsor	one of nine mentor roles. A mentor sponsor is one who helps promote the ministry (career) of another by using his/her resources, credibility, position, etc. to further the development and acceptance of the mentoree.
Mentor Teacher	one of nine mentor roles. A mentor teacher is one who imparts knowledge and understanding of a particular subject at a time when a mentoree needs it.

Metaphor	a figure of speech which involves an implied comparison in which two unlike items (a real item and a picture item) are equated to point out one point of resemblance. e.g. *The Lord is my shepherd.* These can be simple (all elements present) or complex (verbal metaphor, some element may be missing and has to be supplied). 2Ti 1:6 *stir up the gift* is complex, a verbal metaphor. Gift is compared to a flame which has gotten low. Timothy is urged to develop and use with power that gift.
Metonymy	a figure of speech in which one word is substituted for another word to which it is related. This is to emphasize both the word and call attention to the relationship between the two words. e.g. Philemon *6 communicate your faith* to *communicate what you believe and on which you have strong convictions.*
Ministry Challenge	One of 51 shaping activities identified in leadership emergence theory. It is a faith challenge usually occurring in mid-career to a leader, which stretches the leader beyond his/her normal leadership skills and experience.
Ministry Task	one of 51 process items that God uses to shape a leader. A ministry task is an assignment from God which primarily tests a person's faithfulness and obedience but often also allows use of ministry gifts in the context of a task which has closure, accountability, and evaluation. e.g. Barnabas trip to Antioch; Titus had 5 ministry tasks.
Orthodoxic	refers to the correct understanding or stating of Christian truth or revelatory information from God.
Orthopraxic	refers to the correct practice or application of Christian truth in everyday life.
Power Gates	refers to a paradigm shift in which a leader meets with God in some kind of experience which opens up the possibility of living the Christian life in power or ministering in gifted power.
Power Gifts	a category of spiritual gifts which authenticate the reality of God by demonstrating God's intervention in today's world. These include: tongues, interpretation of tongues, discernings of spirits, kinds of healings, kinds of power (miracles), prophecy, faith, word of wisdom, word of knowledge.
Progressive–Release	a leadership transition concept which refers to an approach to leadership transition which gradually gives responsibility to an emerging leader so that the leader increasingly takes responsibility. Usually involves an order of ministry tasks, leadership tasks, leadership roles; responsibility for one of the three major leadership functions (task, relational, inspirational), the role of the leader doing the transition).

Prophecy	one of the 19 spiritual gifts. It is in the *Word Cluster* and *power cluster*. A person operating with the *gift of prophecy* has the capacity to deliver truth (in a public way) either of a predictive nature or as a situational word from God in order to correct by exhorting, edifying or consoling believers and to convince non-believers of God's truth. **Its central thrust is To Provide Correction Or Perspective On A Situation.**
Salutation	the name for the opening paragraph of Paul's epistles written to specific people or generally to churches usually following a form of 1. From Paul 2. to recipient, 3. greeting or blessing.
Sense of Destiny	an inner conviction arising from an experience or a series of experiences in which there is a growing sense of awareness that God has His hand on a leader in a special way for special purposes. See destiny pattern.
Shunning	the practice of ousting a person who is heretical (orthodoxic or orthopraxic) from the benefits of Christian community and avoiding the person and the person's teaching or lifestyle.
Spirit Sensitivity	in short, obeying the Holy Spirit Daily. One of nine spirituality components. This component touches the realm of the Spirit; It reflects experience which recognizes the Holy Spirit in daily life. It essentially assesses the believer's sensitivity to Spirit life. It is an integrative component which relates centrality, interiority, and exteriority to life.
Teaching	one of the 19 spiritual gifts. It belongs to the Word Cluster. A person who has the *gift of teaching* is one who has the ability to instruct, explain, or expose Biblical truth in such a way as to cause believers to understand the Biblical truth. **Its central thrust is To Clarify Truth.**
Timing Macro Lesson	One of 39 macro lessons identified in the Bible. It states, God's timing is crucial to the accomplishment of God's purposes.
Uniqueness	in short, developing along gifted lines. One of nine spirituality components.This spirituality component recognizes that each spirituality model will be tailored by the Spirit to fit a believer. While there are some common factors there is much that will differ. Each new believer's giftedness, personality, gender, and spiritual history will be part of his or her spirituality model. No two spirituality models are the same.

Usus Loquendi refers to the local use of a given word. Words usually have more than one meaning, local uses. But in a given context they will be used, usually with one of their possible meanings, though sometimes 2 or so may be blended.

Word Gifts a category of spiritual gifts used to clarify and explain about God. These help us understand about God including His nature, His purposes and how we can relate to Him and be a part of His purposes. These include: teaching, exhortation, pastoring, evangelism, apostleship, prophecy, ruling, and sometimes word of wisdom, word of knowledge, and faith (a word of). All leaders have at least one of these and often several of these.

Bibliography — For Further Study

Alford, Henry
   1871   The Greek Testament in Four Volumes, Vol III. 5th Edition. London: Deighton, Bell, and Co.

(Bratcher, Robert G. et al)
   n.d.   Good News Bible—Today's English Version. New York: American Bible Society.

Bruce, A. B.
   1929   The Training of the Twelve. 3rd Edition. Garden City, N.Y: Doubleday, Doran & Co.

Butt, Howard
   1973   The Velvet Covered Brick: Christian Leadership in An age of Rebellion. New York: Harper and Row.

Choy, Leona Frances
   1990   Powerlines—What Great Evangelicals Believed About the Holy Spirit, 1850-1930. Camp Hill, PA.: Christian Publications.

Clinton, Dr. J. Robert
   1977   Disputed Practices. Redone in 1994. Altadena, Ca: Barnabas Publishers.
   1977   Interpreting The Scriptures: Figures and Idioms. Altadena, Ca: Barnabas Publishers.
   1983   Interpreting The Scriptures: Hebrew Poetry. Altadena, Ca: Barnabas Publishers.
   1986   A Short History of Leadership Theory. Altadena,Ca: Barnabas Publishers.
   1986   Coming to Conclusions On Leadership Styles. Altadena,Ca: Barnabas Publishers.
   1987   Reading on the Run—Continuum Reading Concepts. Altadena,Ca: Barnabas Publishers.
   1988   The Making of A Leader. Colorado Springs, Co: Navpress.
   1989   Leadership Emergence Theory. Altadena,Ca: Barnabas Publishers.
   1989   The Ultimate Contribution. Altadena,Ca: Barnabas Publishers.

1993   Getting Perspective—By Using Your Unique Time-Line. Altadena,Ca: Barnabas Publishers.

1993   Leadership Perspectives. Altadena,Ca: Barnabas Publishers.

1993   The Bible and Leadership Values. Altadena,Ca: Barnabas Publishers.

1993   Social Base Processing—The Home Environment Out of Which A Leader Works. Altadena,Ca: Barnabas Publishers.

1994   Focused Lives—Inspirational Life Changing Lessons from Eight Effective Christian Leaders Who Finished Well. Altadena,Ca: Barnabas Publishers.

1995   Gender and Leadership. Altadena,Ca: Barnabas Publishers.

1995   Strategic Concepts That Clarify A Focused Life. Altadena,Ca: Barnabas Publishers.

1995   The Life Cycle of A Leader. Altadena,Ca: Barnabas Publishers.

1998   Having Ministry That Lasts. Altadena,Ca: Barnabas Publishers.

Clinton, Dr. J. Robert and Dr. Richard W.

1991   The Mentor Handbook—Deatiled Guidelines and Helps for Christian Mentors and Mentorees. Altadena,Ca: Barnabas Publishers.

1993   Unlocking Your Giftedness—What Leaders Need To Know To Develop Themselves and Others. Altadena,Ca: Barnabas Publishers.

Davis, Stanley B.

1982   Transforming Organizations: The Key To Strategy Is Context in Organizational Dynamics, Winter, 1982.

1987   Future Perfect. New York: Addison Wesley.

Doohan, Helen

1984   Leadership in Paul. Wilmington, Del.: Michael Glazier, Inc.

Edman, V. Raymond

1960   They Found the Secret. Grand Rapids: Zondervan.

Gerlach, L.P. and Hine, V.H.

1970   People, Power, Change: Movements of Social Transformation. New York: Bobbs-Merrill Co.

Graham, Billy

1997   Just As I Am. San Francisco: Zondervan.

Hall, Clarence

1933   Samuel Logan Brengle—Portrait of a Prophet. Atlanta: Salvation Army.

Harville, Sue

1976   Reciprocal Living. Coral Gables: West Indies Mission.

1977   Walking in Love. Coral Gables: West Indies Mission.

Hersey, Palul and Ken blanchard
  1977   Management of Organizational Behavior—Utilizing Human Resources. Englewood
             Cliffs, N.J.: Prentice-Hall, 1977.

Hiebert, D. Edmond
  1954   An Introduction to the Pauline Epistles. Chicago: Moody Press.

Kinnear, A.
  1973   Against the Tide. Eastbourne, England: Victory Press.

Kraft, Charles H.
  1979   Christianity and Culture. Maryknoll, N.Y.: Orbis Books.

Leupold, H. C.
  1959   Exposition of the Psalms. Grand Rapids: Baker Book House.

Morgan, G. Campbell
  1903, 1936 The Crises of the Christ. Old Tappan, N.J.: Fleming H. Revel Co.
  1990   Handbook for Bible Teachers and Preachers. 5th Printing. Original 4 Volume Series,
             1912. Grand Rapids, Michigan: Baker Book House.

Peterson, Eugene H.
  1993   The Message—The New Testlament in Contemporary Language. Colorado Springs,
             Co: Navpress.

Skinner, Betty Lee
  1974   Daws—The Story of Dawson Trottman, Founder of the Navigators. Grand Rapids:
             Zondervan.

Stanley, Paul and J. Robert Clinton
  1992   Connecting—The Mentoring Relationships You Need to Succeed in Life. Colorado
             Springs, Co: Navpress.

Strong, James
  1890   The Exhaustive Concordance of the Bible (with Dictionaries of the Hebrew and
             Greek Words). Nashville: Abingdon Press.

Taylor, Ken (did original version; other Bible scholars the new version)
  1996   Holy Bible—New Living Translation. Wheaton, Il: Tyndale House Publishers, Inc.

Wilmington, Harold L.
  1990   Wilmington's Complete Guide to Bible Knowledge. Volume One—Old Testament
             People. Wheaton: Tyndavle House Publishers.

Wilmington, Harold L.
1990   Wilmington's Complete Guide to Bible Knowledge—Nld Testament People. Wheaton: Tyndavle House Publishers.

Wrong, Dennis
1979   Power—Its Forms, Bases, and Uses. San Francisco, CA: Harper and Row.

BARNABAS PUBLISHERS

BARNABAS PUBLISHER'S MINI CATALOG

Approaching the Bible With Leadership Eyes: An Authoratative Source for Leadership Findings — Dr. J. Robert Clinton

Barnabas: Encouraging Exhorter — Dr. J. Robert Clinton & Laura Raab

Boundary Processing: Looking at Critical Transitions Times in Leader's Lives — Dr. J. Robert Clinton

Connecting: The Mentoring Relationships You Need to Succeed in Life — Dr. J. Robert Clinton

The Emerging Leader — Dr. J. Robert Clinton

Fellowship With God — Dr. J. Robert Clinton

Finishing Well — Dr. J. Robert Clinton

Figures and Idioms (Interpreting the Scriptures: Figures and Idioms) — Dr. J. Robert Clinton

Focused Lives Lectures — Dr. J. Robert Clinton

Gender and Leadership — Dr. J. Robert Clinton

Having A Ministry That Lasts: By Becoming a Bible Centered Leader — Dr. J. Robert Clinton

Hebrew Poetry (Interpreting the Scriptures: Hebrew Poetry) — Dr. J. Robert Clinton

A Short **History of Leadership Theory** — Dr. J. Robert Clinton

Isolation: A Place of Transformation in the Life of a Leader — Shelley G. Trebesch

Joseph: Destined to Rule — Dr. J. Robert Clinton

The Joshua Portrait — Dr. J. Robert Clinton and Katherine Haubert

Leadership Emergence Theory: A Self Study Manual For Analyzing the Development of a Christian Leader — Dr. J. Robert Clinton

Leadership Perspectives: How To Study The Bible for Leadership Insights — Dr. J. Robert Clinton

Coming to Some Conclusions on **Leadership Styles** — Dr. J. Robert Clinton

Leadership Training Models — Dr. J. Robert Clinton

The Bible and **Leadership Values:** A Book by Book Analysis— Dr. J. Robert Clinton

The Life Cycle of a Leader: Looking at God's Shaping of A LeaderTowards An Eph. 2:10 Life — Dr. J. Robert Clinton

Listen Up Leaders! — Dr. J. Robert Clinton

The Mantle of the Mentor — Dr. J. Robert Clinton

Mentoring Can Help—Five Leadership Crises You Will Face in the Pastorate For Which You Have Not Been Trained — Dr. J. Robert Clinton

Mentoring: Developing Leaders... Without Adding More Programs — Dr. J. Robert Clinton

The Mentor Handbook: Detailed Guidelines and Helps for Christian Mentors and Mentorees — Dr. J. Robert Clinton

Moses Desert Leadership—7 Macro Lessons

Parables—Puzzles With A Purpose (Interpreting the Scriptures: Puzzles With A Purpose) — Dr. J. Robert Clinton

Paradigm Shift: God's Way of Opening New Vistas To Leaders — Dr. J. Robert Clinton

A Personal Ministry Philosophy: One Key to Effective Leadership — Dr. J. Robert Clinton

Reading on the Run: Continuum Reading Concepts — Dr. J. Robert Clinton

Samuel: Last of the Judges & First of the Prophets–A Model For Transitional Times — Bill Bjoraker

Selecting and Developing Those Emerging Leaders — Dr. Richard W. Clinton

Social Base Processing: The Home Base Environment Out of Which A Leader Works — Dr. J. Robert Clinton

Starting Well: Building A Strong Foundation for a Life Time of Ministry — Dr. J. Robert Clinton

Strategic Concepts: That Clarify A Focused Life – A Self Study Guide — Dr. J. Robert Clinton

The Making of a Leader: Recognizing the Lessons & Stages of Leadership Development — Dr. J. Robert Clinton

Time Line —Small Paper (What it is & How to Construct it) — Dr. J. Robert Clinton

Time Line: Getting Perspective—By Using Your Time-Line, Large Paper — Dr. J. Robert Clinton

Ultimate Contribution — Dr. J. Robert Clinton

Unlocking Your Giftedness: What Leaders Need to Know to Develop Themselves & Others — Dr. J. Robert Clinton

A **Vanishing Breed:** Thoughts About A Bible Centered Leader & A Life Long Bible Mastery Paradigm — Dr. J. Robert Clinton

The Way To Look At Leadership (How To Look at Leadership) — Dr. J. Robert Clinton

Webster-Smith, Irene: An Irish Woman Who Impacted Japan (A Focused Life Study) — Dr. J. Robert Clinton

Word Studies (Interpreting the Scriptures: Word Studies) — Dr. J. Robert Clinton

(Book Titles are in Bold and Paper Titles are in Italics with Sub-Titles and Pre-Titles in Roman)

BARNABAS   PUBLISHERS

Unique Leadership Material that will help you answer the question:
"What legacy will you as a leader leave behind?"

"The difference between leaders and followers is perspective. The difference
between leaders and effective leaders is better perspective."
Barnabas Publishers has the materials that will help you find that
better perspective and a closer relationship with God.

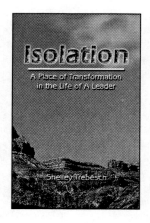

BARNABAS   PUBLISHERS

Post Office Box 6006 • Altadena, CA 91003-6006
Fax Phone (626)-794-3098 • Phone (626)-584-5393